# ARGUMENT now

## A BRIEF RHETORIC

Jonathan Alexander
University of Cincinnati

Margaret M. Barber
Colorado State University, Pueblo

New York San Francisco Boston
London Toronto Sydney Tokyo Singapore Madrid
Mexico City Munich Paris Cape Town Hong Kong Montreal

Senior Acquisitions Editor: Lynn M. Huddon
Marketing Manager: Wendy Albert
Senior Supplements Editor: Donna Campion
Media Supplements Editor: Jenna Egan
Managing Editor: Valerie Zaborski
Project Coordination, Text Design, and Electronic Page Makeup: Stratford Publishing Services. Inc.
Cover Design Manager: John Callahan
Cover Designer: Kay Petronio
Cover Illustration/Photo: PictureQuest
Photo Researcher: Stratford Publishing Services. Inc.
Manufacturing Buyer: Dennis J. Para
Printer and Binder: R.R. Donnelley & Sons—Harrisonburg
Cover Printer: Coral Graphic Services

For permission to use copyrighted material, grateful acknowledgment is made to the copyright holders on pp. 383–384, which are hereby made part of this copyright page.

Library of Congress Cataloging-in-Publication Data
Alexander, Jonathan.
Argument now : a brief rhetoric / Jonathan Alexander, Margaret M. Barber.
p. cm.
Includes bibliographical references and index.
Summary: "A college-level text focusing on academic writing, particularly agrumentative writing, as well as thinking about and debating issues. Emphasis is on writing with computers and includes discussion of forms such as hypertextual writing on the World Wide Web"—Provided by publisher.
ISBN 0-321-11360-8
1. English language—Rhetoric—Data processing. 2. English language—Computer-assisted instruction. 3. Academic writing—Data processing. 4. Persuasion (Rhetoric) I. Barber, Margaret M. II. Title.
PE1431.A53 2005
808'.042'0285—dc22
2004025002



Please visit our website at http://www.ablongman.com

ISBN 0-321-11360-8

2 3 4 5 6 7 8 9 10—DOH—07 06 05

# Contents

*Preface* xi

PART one **Writing Orientations** 1

**Introduction** 2

**Chapter 1**
**Writing Processes: A Review** 6

Approaching the Writing Situation: Purpose and Audience 7

Thinking about Purpose 7

Thinking about Audience 9

Capturing Your Ideas: Prewriting Strategies 11

Prewriting about Reading 12

Writing in a Journal 13

Freewriting 13

Listing 16

Finding a Focus 18

Organizing a Writing Project 20

Choosing a Form or Genre 20

Clarifying Your Thesis 21
Developing an Outline 21
Writing the First Draft 23
Starting the Rough Draft . . . At Last! 25
Effective Introductions 25
Effective Theses 26
Effective Conclusions 27
A Student Writer in Action: A Rough Draft 29
More than Type, Click, Print: Rewriting and Revising 34
Revising for Unity, Coherence, and Style 35
Rewrite—radically! 35
Revise for unity. 36
Revise for coherence. 36
Revise for style. 37
Getting Help: Peer Review 38
Tracking Changes 41
Finishing Touches: Editing and Proofreading 42
Spell-Checkers and Grammar Checkers 43
A Writer in Action: Galen Geer's Revised Draft 45
Useful Links 50
Additional Writing Activities 51

**Chapter 2**
**Something to Talk About: Understanding Academic Writing** **52**
What Makes Writing "Academic"? 53
Academic Writing: Audience and Purpose 53
Academic Writing and the Public 54
Some Key Characteristics of Academic Writing 54
■ *Writing Spotlight: Carl Sagan and Popular Academic Writing* 55
"Can We Know the Universe? Reflections on a Grain of Salt" by Carl Sagan 55
Writing for an Academic Audience: Some Conventions and Expectations 61

Academic readers read critically. 62

Informed academic readers expect outside sources and appropriate documentation. 64

Academic readers expect to see familiar genres. 68

Academic readers look for the *argument.* 69

Academic readers expect stylish and mechanically correct writing. 71

Strategies in Academic Writing 73

Comparison and Contrast 73

Definition 76

Analysis 79

■ *Writing Spotlight: Stephen Jay Gould on* Jurassic Park 80

■ *Writing Spotlight: "Join the U.S. Navy Today"* 84

Academic Writing in the Digital World: E-mail and Discussion Lists 87

Useful Links 91

Additional Writing Activities 92

PART two **Writing Situations** **93**

**Chapter 3**

**Fighting Words? Understanding Argument** **94**

Critical Reading and Argument 95

Some Elements of Argument 98

Pathos, Ethos, and Logos 98

Pathos 99

Ethos 100

Logos 105

The Basic Form of an Argument: A Claim with Stated Reasons 107

■ *Writing Spotlight: Pathos, Ethos, Logos, and Argument in a "Raccoon in a Bag"* 109

The "Raccoon in a Bag" speech by David Crockett 110

Kinds of Arguments 113

Inductive Arguments 113
Deductive Arguments and the Enthymeme 114
Cause and Effect 118
Analogies 120
Definitions 121
Examining Assumptions 122
Considering Counterarguments 126
Useful Links 129
A Writer in Action: Combining Multiple Argumentative Strategies 130
"The Children of Chaos" by Douglas Rushkoff 130
Additional Writing Activities 140

**Chapter 4**
**New Worlds, New Ways: Contemporary Argument 142**
The Limits of Aristotle's Approach 143
Toulmin's Model 146
Claim 149
Warrant 149
Backing 149
Grounds or Data 150
Reservations 150
Qualifier 150
Using Toulmin's Model Electronically 151
Rogerian Argument 152
■ *Writing Spotlight: Rogerian Argument in Action* 154
"Towards Reconciliation: Common Ground in the Education Curriculum" by Robert Leston 154
Evaluating an Argument 158
Avoiding Logical Fallacies 161
Useful Links 167
Writers in Action: Contemporary Strategies of Argument 168
"A First in the Eye of God" by Barbara Kingsolver 169
Additional Writing Activities 181

## Chapter 5
## More than Just Words Here: Visual Literacy, Visual Argument 183

Rethinking Literacy: Understanding Visual Rhetoric 184
- Visuals and Images in Texts 186
- Comics 189
- ■ *Writing Spotlight: Art Spiegelman's* Maus 191
- Pictures, Graphs, and Charts 194
- Graphic Manipulation of Text 196
- Writing Brochures and Newsletters 199
- Using Visuals in Academic Presentations 199

Visual Literacy and the Web 202

Visual Argument 204
- Visual Argument in Print 204
- ■ *Writing Spotlight: Advertisements and Argument, a Student's Essay* 206
- "64 bit, It's More Than 2 × 32 bit" by Lee Carraher 206
- Visual Argument on the Web 210

Useful Links 216

Writers in Action: Hawisher and Sullivan Talk about Women on the Web 218
- "Fleeting Images: Women Visually Writing the Web" by Gail E. Hawisher and Patricia A. Sullivan 218

Additional Writing Activities 222

## Chapter 6
## Navigating a World of Information: Conducting Research 224

Academic Research 226
- Popular Reporting versus Academic Research 226

The Research Process 227
- Stage 1. Conducting Preliminary Research and Finding a Topic 229
- Stage 2. Identifying a Research Question 233
- Stage 3. Creating a Research Proposal 237

Stage 4. Finding Information, Part One: Considering a Variety of Sources 243
Getting to Know Your Library 243
Using Library Catalogs, Online and Otherwise 245
Searching the World Wide Web 246
Conducting a Boolean Search 247
Surfing Critically 247
■ *Writing Spotlight: Reviewing a Web Site* 249
Conducting Field Research 252
Stage 4. Finding Information, Part Two: Recording Information 254
Constructing Annotated Bibliographies 254
■ *Writing Spotlight: A Student's Annotated Bibliography* 256
Taking Notes 258
Managing Your Time 265
Stage 5: Analyzing Your Information 265
A Student Writer in Action: A Research Project 267
"The Travel of Henry Timberlake to Jerusalem: A Pilgrimage That Hatched an Idea" by Hershield Keaton 268
Useful Links 282
Additional Writing Activities 283

**PART three Writing Destinations 285**

**Chapter 7**
**Putting It All Together: Combining Research and Argument 286**
Crafting Print-Based Researched Arguments: Some Basic Guidelines 287
Introducing an Argument: Considering Audience 288
Considering Research and Drafting an Outline or Project Plan 292
Drafting and Incorporating Sources 294
Composing Concluding Arguments 299
■ *Writing Spotlight: Research and Rogerian Argument* 300

"Should the Boy Scouts of America Rescind Its Policy of Discrimination Against Homosexuals?" by Scott Pedram 303
Useful Links 314
A Writer in Action: Alfie Kohn and the Issue of Competition 314
Additional Writing Activities 328

**Chapter 8**
**Putting It All Online: Research and Argument on the World Wide Web** **329**
Strategies for Crafting Researched Web Texts 330
Writing with Hypertext—Some Initial Considerations 330
Using Hypertext to Organize a Document, Part One: Source Linking 332
Using Hypertext to Organize a Document, Part Two: Text Chunking 335
Hypertext, the Web, and Argument 339
Considering Rebuttals or Counterarguments with Hypertext 344
Blogs and Argument 348
■ *Writing Spotlight: Writing and Blogging* 351
"Blogrithms: With the Internet, Everyone Becomes a Writer" by Maria Rogers 351
Some Questions and Issues to Consider about Web Authoring 354
Writing for E-Zines 357
Preparing to Submit an Article to an E-Zine 363
Useful Links 366
A Writer in Action: Mark Bernstein on Hypertext 366
Additional Writing Activities 367

Appendix: Documenting Sources
Part I: MLA Style 370
Part II: APA Style 376
Part III: Columbia Online Style 381

*Credits* 383
*Index* 385

# Preface

When we set out to write a textbook for use in our first-year composition courses, we had the most selfish intentions in mind. Namely, we wanted a book we could use in our own courses—one that would represent some of our best ideas and practices for teaching writing, all collected in one accessible, engaging, and student-friendly spot. As we worked on the text, though, we realized that many of our best ideas and practices were arising out of some fairly contemporary developments in how writers argue, debate, exchange ideas, and construct knowledge. For instance, we found ourselves excited about the possibilities seemingly inherent in using computer technologies, such as listservs and discussion boards, to help students process their thoughts and ideas. We were fascinated by the many venues for searching out and examining information readily available through any number of databases, both online and accessible through libraries and other information sources. We were stimulated by the opportunity to have students publish their writing and engage in dialogue with one another about their work on the World Wide Web. And we were challenged by the potential of visual literacies and rhetorics to expand our students' sense—and our own—of how ideas and arguments can be constructed and presented.

Given this, we wanted to write a book that would bring together both "tried and true" writing techniques and processes *and* address some of the newer ways in which debate, persuasion, and argument are emerging in the contemporary world. Put simply, we wanted a textbook to consider how argument is taking shape *now*.

Hence, *Argument Now*.

The *Now* part of our title is important, because this book begins (and ends) with the conviction that argument is changing. How people process ideas, gather evidence, weigh opinions, and disseminate insights—all are shifting due to a number of factors, from the increased use of communications technologies in information retrieval to the growing importance of considering how visuals interact with texts to communicate rhetorically in a media-saturated society. Given these factors, we have written *Argument Now* to address critical thinking, reading, and writing skills in a contemporary world marked by easy access to information, complex and divergent points of view, and emerging literacies fostered by new communications technologies. Despite such a "contemporary" orientation, we have not abandoned more traditional approaches to writing instruction. You will find, we hope, that we have designed the chapters throughout this book to take the best of what compositionists know about teaching the writing process and consider, at the same time, some more contemporary dimensions of argument and rhetoric.

For instance, chapters early in the book, grouped under the heading **Writing Orientations,** take students through a review of the writing process and then introduce them to the specifics of making claims, critically examining positions, arguing about ideas, and using different types of evidence to support or query insights and theses. We also invite students to consider the *varieties* of academic writing and forms of argument they are likely to encounter as college students and college-educated adults, from journal articles to complex Websites. We have seen very few textbooks that offer students insights into the many ways in which arguments are constructed and considered in the academy, and we have striven to compose a textbook that will excite students about the possibilities for writing and arguing effectively in a *number* of ways and with a *variety* of academically sound rhetorical tools.

After reviewing some basic writing and reading processes, we encourage students to think more specifically and critically about the many **Writing Situations** they will encounter, both in college-level courses and beyond. Chapters in this section of the book address "classical" approaches to argument in the academy as well as more contemporary ways to craft, present, and appreciate argument. So, while paying homage to Aristotelian argument and Toulmin's strategies, we also have students examine how contemporary writers, from Stephen Jay Gould to Barbara Kingsolver, use not just "data" and "evidence" to make and support their claims, but also personal experience and even references to popular culture to think critically and deeply about important subjects.

We also ask students to consider how *visuals* are used rhetorically, persuasively, and argumentatively. As students are bombarded with images—on television, in advertisements, and on the Web—it is vital that they know how to "read" such images, talk about them critically, and assess their significance, as well as the values and ideologies they often represent. We have included an entire chapter that considers such visual rhetorics in order to introduce students to how to write insightfully and meaningfully about the widespread and varied use of visuals in our culture.

The final section of the book, **Writing Destinations**, asks students to synthesize what they have learned in preceding chapters about argument, research, academic writing, and critical thinking, not only to produce complex and engaging writing projects, but also to consider how to disseminate those projects effectively, via the World Wide Web for instance. Since many students will encounter powerful persuasive appeals and arguments in textually and visually complex mediums such as the Web, it is imperative that they understand both how to read such contemporary "texts" as well as think about participating in their production. While this is *not* a textbook that leads students through a Web-composing process, we recognize that many students have basic skills in Web design; so, in composing our final chapter, we wanted to help students—and instructors—link those skills to the skills in argument and rhetoric that they developed as they worked through earlier chapters. Also, since some Web-based formats for processing, composing, and presenting a variety of arguments, ideas, and positions are relatively easy to construct, such as Weblogs, we encourage experimentation with such "digital texts." Instructors interested in exploring Web design and other Web-based formats with their students might supplement *Argument Now* with a guide to Web authoring.

To complement our "contemporary" orientation toward argument, we have carefully chosen **reading selections** that should stimulate students to think about argument and rhetoric in both provocative and productive ways. We believe that it is vital that students learn to assess critically the information that seemingly bombards them—and us—from a variety of different venues. As such, readings, prompts, and exercises throughout this book encourage students to analyze, discuss, and debate texts from several sources, including some "classic" works of argument, more contemporary readings, and even texts originally (and only) published on the World Wide Web. Our students need to learn to navigate the many ways in which information and ideas are shaped, constructed, and disseminated—hence, our use and consideration of multiple "texts" throughout this textbook. And, to provide additional relevant models for students, we feature student work in almost every chapter in "Writing Spotlight" sections, which show students analyzing argumentative texts, evaluating sources, writing research projects, and composing for the Web.

Further, exercises and writing assignments throughout the book prompt students to think—and write—about important issues and ideas by using a variety of writing processes, practicing numerous rhetorical strategies, and experimenting with several electronically enabled communications platforms, such as e-mail, listservs, discussion boards, and, of course, word processors. For instance, "Your Turn" exercises are short assignments integrated into every chapter, and they focus on specific skills or strategies discussed in the text. Many of these exercises take advantage of networked computer technology, word processing programs, the Web, and e-mail to facilitate discussion, research, composition, and revision.

AN IMPORTANT NOTE ABOUT *ARGUMENT NOW* AND TECHNOLOGY: You will probably notice that a large part of the "now" that we have kept in mind as we've written this book is the impact of communications technologies on the development of literacy and communication skills. As more and more students come into our classrooms with computer literacy skills, or with the desire to become computer literate, it is increasingly important that we help them learn how to use computer technologies—from word processors to Weblogs—to develop their critical thinking, reading, and writing skills. To facilitate such learning, we have composed *Argument Now* to provide both students and teachers with concrete, engaging, and pedagogically productive discussions and examples of how computer technologies can be used to facilitate the writing process. As such, this textbook assumes access to basic computer technologies such as word processing, e-mail, and the Web, but it does not assume that either students or teachers will know how such technologies can be used in the writing class. Indeed, one of the major goals of *Argument Now* is to demonstrate how the use of computers can greatly aid students as they develop their writerly potential. At the same time, our desire has also been to assist teachers in discovering new ways to utilize the capacity for interactivity that a networked environment permits and to implement pedagogies that value dialogic practices and encourage composing in a variety of genres, including online formats such as e-zines. Considering the rapid rate at which students are learning and using computer technologies, it only makes sense to explore—both for and with them—how computers can be used to write more effectively, more purposefully, and more powerfully.

Ultimately, *Argument Now* can only meet so many of our students' literacy needs. Faculty who have their students purchase this book will invariably tailor it to their own needs and offer their students supplementary exercises and additional materials that will improve on the work we have done here. We invite instructors to consider the Instructors' Manual for this book as a resource for additional exercises and assignments. In that manual, instructors will find brief descriptions of each chapter in the textbook that highlight our original goals in composing them. We also provide additional and alternative exercises and writing assignments, some of which take even greater advantage of computer technologies in helping students develop contemporary writing and arguing skills. Finally, we also include in the Instructors Manual, as well as on the Companion Website for this textbook (see **www.ablongman.com/alexander**), instructional materials on other forms of argument, such as personal narrations and multi-genre arguments. Such material might complement any number of approaches to contemporary rhetoric and argument.

We also hope, at least, that we have provided both faculty and students with information, exercises, and readings that will stimulate thinking about the importance of argument in its many contemporary manifestations and dimensions. Offering such stimulation—coming into an appreciation of argument as it exists and moves among us *now*—is the ultimate goal of this book.

## Acknowledgments

No book writes itself. Rather, books are coordinated efforts, pulling together the talents, thoughts, and wisdom of numerous individuals and groups. We'd like to thank those who have been particularly helpful in helping us coordinate—and finish!—this project.

Lynn Huddon, our Longman Acquisitions Editor, has been inspiring, patient, and exacting—absolutely necessary qualities in an editor working with two authors who live a thousand miles apart, as well as another thousand miles from their editor! This book would not have been the same without her guidance and keen critical eye.

Numerous faculty colleagues have fostered our thinking about teaching with computers. In particular, we need to thank Will Hochman for pushing us off the edge, as it were, and for being the first to encourage—if not force!—us to use computers in our writing classrooms, and Bill Sheidley, for his careful reading of the entire first draft, as well as continued encouragement and support. We also thank Cynthia Taylor and Ted Taylor for helping us find important resources as we worked on this book; Bea Spade, David Keplinger, and Michele Griegel McCord for helping us locate students' work for inclusion in this text; Judi Johanssen for her help with artwork; Chas Clifton, for his early interest in this project, for his creativity as a teaching collaborator, and for modeling for us practical ways to use computers to teach writing (and for keeping the MacLab in perfect working order). His Co-Director of the CSU-Pueblo Composition Program, Katherine Frank Dvorsky, and Michelle Gibson, Coordinator of Development Writing at the former University College at the University of Cincinnati, have stimulated our thinking in valuable ways. We also want to thank the many teachers in the Senior-to-Sophomore program in Pueblo School Districts 60 and 70 who have taught us much about the possibilities—and practical challenges—of working with technology.

Many other colleagues, including professional staff and administrators, offered invaluable assistance. These include Micki Markowski, Charles Barker, Sharon Pruett, and Sarah Brown, for staff and office assistance; Rhonda Gonzales, Dan Sullivan, and other faculty of the CSU-Pueblo University Library, as well as Renée Drabier, Shawn Ahlers, Dan Miller, and others in Instructional Technology Services at CSU-Pueblo; and Russell Meyer, Barbara Montgomery, John Bryan, and Janet Reed, for providing a supportive working environment that prompted us to explore more fully how to teach with technology. While working on this project, we've come to value all the more how important administrative support is in experimenting with pedagogy and technology.

Colleagues not so close to home, but readily accessible through e-mail, must also be acknowledged. In so many ways, none of this work would have been possible without the stimulating, provocative, and inspiring conversations we've had with numerous members of the computers and writing community. Attending the annual Computers and Writing Conference has pushed our thinking about technology and pedagogy in many exciting directions. In particular, we'd like to thank Janice Walker for providing information on Columbia Online Style. We also thank Gail Hawisher and Cynthia Selfe for their expert guidance and mentoring over the last several years. Their leadership in the Computers and Writing community is inspiring. Some material and ideas in Chapter 8 originally appeared in Jonathan's article, "Digital Spins: The Pedagogy and Politics of Student-Centered E-Zines," which was published in *Computers & Composition* (Volume 19, Number 4, December 2002), the ground-breaking journal that Cindy and Gail edit.

Others in unlikely places have been not only helpful, but graciously so in supporting our work, even if they were unaware of their importance to our project. Angela Cochran, pinch-hitting as lab monitor at the National College of Ireland, saved Margaret's life while she was finishing this project overseas. Jonathan thanks the many baristas at Buzz Coffee shop in Cincinnati, where he drafted, re-drafted, and revised many of these pages; their caffeinated concoctions helped keep his mind alert, even when he would rather have been taking a nap.

No list of acknowledgements would be complete without recognition of those readers and reviewers who saw this project develop from its inception to its completion. Readers carefully commented on our initial proposal, subsequent drafts, and the final "product." These helpful and generous souls include . . .

Trish Bowen, Front Range Community College; Joseph Essid, University of Richmond; Julie Freeman, Indiana University Purdue University Indianapolis; David Glaub, University of Wisconsin Parkside; Catherine Gouge, West Virginia University; Philip T. Greenfield, Mott Community College; Sibylle Gruber, Northern Arizona University; Bettina Hanlon, Ferrum College; Kimberly Harrison, Florida International University; H. Brooke Hessler, Texas Christian University; Will Hochman, Southern Connecticut State University; Joseph Janangelo, Loyola University; Billie Jones, Penn State Capital College; Ken McAllister, University of Arizona; Catherine E. Ross, University of Texas at Tyler; Nancy Ruff, Southern Illinois University Edwardsville; Jonathan Taylor, Ferris State University; Janice R. Walker, Georgia Southern University; Carl Whithaus, Old Dominion University; Marty L. Williams, Valdosta State University.

Most importantly, we need to thank our many students, including those whose work is represented in these pages, especially, Galen, Scott, Lee, Katherine, Hershield, and Dave. Without their enthusiasm and interest in writing, our lives as writing teachers would be a bit less fun and rewarding.

And finally, we thank members of family, including our spouses and partners, Mack and David, for putting up with our long hours—and time spent away from them—on this project. Our work is all the richer for their patience and understanding. We dedicate this book to Margaret's 88-year-old mother, Ruth Todd McAdow, who has set an example of personal literacy for all who know her, including her four children, who all became teachers.

—Jonathan Alexander
—Margaret M. Barber

# PART one

# Writing Orientations

INTRODUCTION

CHAPTER 1
Writing Processes: A Review

CHAPTER 2
Something to Talk About: Understanding Academic Writing

# Introduction

## Argument *Now*?

Welcome to *Argument Now*. Yes, we know—this is just a textbook, but we, the authors, are hoping it is unlike any textbook you've ever had before, particularly for a writing class. What makes *Argument Now* different? A couple of things. Read on.

Perhaps the most unique aspect of this book is that we've written it with the conviction that the best writing is done playfully—in a process that combines creativity, experimentation, invention, and imaginative intelligence. As you use this book, do not hesitate to think creatively, relax, and "play." Of course, in many ways, writing will always be hard work that requires self-discipline. It takes time and commitment to sit down in front of a computer screen or with a notepad on a beautiful day when it seems that the rest of the world is enjoying a music festival or an afternoon at the beach. But once you settle down to work, try to forget that you ever had a sense of desperation—or even panic—about getting a writing task done in time. Instead, relax and enjoy the act of creation. Once you start thinking of writing as an act of creation, even of imagination, you'll begin to discover the possibility of *play* in writing. We believe that meeting a writing challenge can be one of the most satisfying—and creative—experiences you may ever have, and you'll spot hints of our theme, playfulness, throughout the book.

What kind of writing will you encounter and be encouraged to work with in this book? Our focus will be on *academic writing*, particularly *argumentative* writing that focuses on thinking about and debating important issues, although some autobiographical writing is used at the beginning of the book to give you a chance to practice writing while drawing on your own experiences and also to help you learn new ways of approaching writing tasks and situations. Eventually, we will move on to more complex material, such as argumentative writing, persuasion, and the use of research in writing. We'll also discuss some innovative forms, such as hypertextual writing on the World Wide Web, that invite writing in a particularly creative and playful way.

At every step, we will look at how various computer technologies can assist us with a multitude of writing tasks and projects. We have several reasons for emphasizing writing with computers in this book. Writing and communicating in academic and professional life are increasingly mediated by computer technologies—which is largely why we call this book *Argument Now*. Learning those technologies—how to use them effectively, how to manipulate them, how to be creative with them—is quickly becoming vital to your survival as a literate person in the contemporary world. Beyond that, we believe that computer technologies can greatly aid you in developing various writing skills. For instance, most word processors have tools such as spell-checkers, text-summary programs, and other features that are frequently useful in working through a variety of writing tasks. Moreover, writing in a *networked* environment can allow us to share writing, confer with others, create innovative writing spaces, and even gain access to vast amounts of information on the World Wide Web, which has some superb resources for developing writing and communication skills.

Computer technologies are also fostering new ways of thinking about and using writing. E-mail allows friends and colleagues to stay in touch and share ideas—in writing. Discussion groups, blogs, and chat spaces provide forums for vigorous debate about a range of important and interesting issues—also in writing. And Web sites are often complex presentations of people, ideas, issues, and interests—all in writing. Granted, the writing in these forums is often different from the writing you will be asked to do in college, but more and more instructors—and employers—are expecting students and staff to be familiar with and use these other forms of writing. Thus, we have included in *Argument Now* a discussion of these types of compositions, and we emphasize how they can be used to assist you with a variety of academic writing tasks and situations.

## What will you find in this book?

The order of chapters in *Argument Now* reflects our belief that good writing instruction will orient you toward thinking about writing as a process of playfulness and creativity, introduce you to various writing situations you will encounter in college (and beyond), and offer you advice and strategies for taking your writing to specific "destinations," such as publishing, either in print or on the Web. Part I, "Writing Orientations," contains two chapters. The first reviews the basics of the *writing process*, with ideas throughout about how computer technologies can help you develop useful writing processes for a variety of writing situations. The second chapter introduces you to *academic* writing, the principal kind of writing you will encounter in college-level courses. Part II, "Writing Situations," offers three chapters exploring *argumentative* writing, *research* writing, and *visual literacy*. The latter is an increasingly important skill to develop given the number of media—from television to the Web—that rely on visual cues to communicate. Finally, in the remaining two chapters, grouped in Part III under the heading "Writing Destinations," we'll invite you to put into practice what you have been learning throughout this book and ask you to consider writing projects that combine *research and argument*, as well as projects that involve *writing for the Web*.

In each chapter you will find a variety of sections and features, such as separate text boxes with additional information or lists of useful links. Such features include the following:

- **Introduction:** This section sets up the basic writing focus, situation, challenge, or "destination" of each chapter.
- **Writing Spotlights:** These provide further discussion of the specific writing situations you will encounter in college, with examples from both professional and student writers.
- **Your Turn:** These short exercises are designed to prompt you to discuss or play with, usually electronically, the ideas and strategies described in each chapter.

- **Writers in Action:** These readings, appearing at the end of nearly every chapter, demonstrate effective strategies that beginning writers can use to approach various writing situations and also illustrate innovative ways of writing for a number of different purposes and audiences.
- **Useful Links:** These are online resources to help you develop your writing skills.
- **Additional Writing Activities:** These are for you to pursue on your own or as part of your instructor's course plan.
- **INTERtext** boxes link you to other parts of *Argument Now*, where you will find further discussion of topics mentioned in the chapter you are reading.
- **HYPERtext** boxes offer suggestions for online resources, particularly those on the World Wide Web, that you might want to check out for additional information about topics we discuss throughout the book.
- **ELECTRONICissues** boxes raise questions about writing in a digital world and the complications—and possibilities—involved as we move toward reading, writing, and communicating more and more with computer technologies.

Of course, a single book cannot teach you everything you need or want to know about writing. With that in mind, we have not attempted to cover all traditional approaches to composition. Instead, we offer you ideas we have learned from our many years of experience teaching students to write, frequently in networked environments. Your instructors will probably also familiarize you with methods they have favored over the years.

Ultimately, *Argument Now* is designed to help you help yourself develop, strengthen, and explore your writing skills. We invite you to challenge yourself to build on what you already know about writing and to expand your sense of the possibilities of writing in a variety of contexts—personal, professional, and academic. And, since writers benefit from carefully considered feedback, we also invite you to send us your comments about this book. You can find our e-mail and snail mail addresses on the Companion Website to this textbook at **www.ablongman.com/alexander**.

CHAPTER 1

# Writing Processes: A Review

You have already met writing challenges in your educational career, perhaps even in a work setting. You have probably written essays, poems, and a research paper or two as part of your coursework. You may even have composed a Web page, either for fun or as an assigned project. Given this experience, you probably know more about writing than you think, and all of it will help you face a variety of writing assignments and challenges during your college career.

Discovering yourself as a writer and getting your ideas into words, as well as discovering ideas in the *process* of writing, can provide an enormous sense of accomplishment. As one student exclaimed after turning in his first essay in a composition class, "I feel as if I have just given birth!" Writing, even academic writing, can be an enjoyable activity. In that spirit, we'd like to show you how to approach your writing projects with a sense of play—with a willingness to improvise and to keep trying, remembering that play, as in a championship chess match or a college basketball game, can be serious business that, when done well, results from mastery of skills and requires great effort and attention.

The purpose of this chapter is to acquaint you with some writing processes that many writers have found useful so that you never experience writer's block and so that you can face new writing challenges with justified confidence in your ability to handle them with success. Once you learn these techniques, you can adapt them to all kinds of academic writing projects, including those involving research and argument, which are the focus of this book. The following sections on the writing process offer some basic pointers for approaching almost any writing task, whether in academic or professional life, or in business, civic, or personal spheres.

## Approaching the Writing Situation: Purpose and Audience

When approaching any writing project, we should begin by thinking about its context, or the rhetorical situation in which our writing will be created and read. Whether we are writing an essay for the eyes of a teacher and classmates, a letter of application to a scholarship committee, or a training manual for employees of a business, each composition occupies a **rhetorical situation**. That is, it has a specific *purpose* and an intended *audience*. Before starting to write, then, we must ask ourselves these questions:

- What do I want to accomplish?
- To *whom* am I writing?

Answering these questions helps us explore and determine what genre we will use when writing, what level of informality or formality in style will be appropriate, and where we might publish or disseminate our writing for other readers.

### Thinking about Purpose

If we consider the first question a bit more carefully—"What do I want to accomplish?"—we find any number of other, more specific questions we could ask about a writing situation we are approaching. Consider some of the following. Are you writing for your own reasons, to express your feelings or to help yourself work out your own ideas? If so, you may write informally in a journal meant for your eyes alone. At other times, you often must write to meet a requirement: to complete an assignment made by an instructor, create a memo informing fellow employees of an important meeting, or file an accident report with the police. Such writing situations are often *directed* in that you are being asked to respond to someone else's prompting.

Writing that is chiefly explanatory or informative is, in traditional rhetorical terms, called **expository writing**. Often, however, you may use your writing to persuade someone of something. Can you imagine writing to support a political candidate or a certain position on an issue? To get your high school friends to agree to meet on Padre Island over spring break? To invite a friend to move out of the dorm and into a shared house off campus? To convince a prospective customer to buy a certain product? Such writing situations call for more **persuasive or argumentative writing**, which will be discussed at length in this book. In each case, your purpose will affect the choices you make about your composition.

## your turn

To help you start thinking more carefully about purpose, consider some of the following exercises.

1. What was the last piece of writing you did? What was your purpose in writing? Did you think about how you would accomplish your purpose with your audience before you wrote? In a few sentences, describe the audience for whom you wrote, no matter how large or small. How did your purpose and your audience influence what you said or how you said it?
2. Consider a writing task you are currently facing. It could be a book report, a summary of research findings, an essay, or the text for a Web site. *Question yourself.* Before plunging in and trying to write a full-blown essay (or letter, or poem, or whatever), take a moment to write down, in one sentence, what the purpose of your work will be. As you write and think of new purposes, expand your discussion of what your purpose will be, substituting new ideas for old ones wherever you think necessary. Watch your writing take shape before your eyes—and you will have the beginning of a working draft of your project.

## Thinking about Audience

In many ways, what you write will be affected by the *audience* to whom you are writing. You are likely to write in one way for your college instructors and in an entirely different way for your friends. Even when you write an e-mail message, you are probably aware of who will be receiving your message and what level of experience they have with your subject. Whether you are consciously altering what you say and how you say it, knowledge of your audience does—and should—influence *how* and *why* you write.

As you consider your next writing project, perhaps one for your composition course or another class, doing some initial brainstorming or note-taking about context and audience will give you an advantage as you begin to write. Jot down the answers to the following questions about your audience: Who will be reading what you are writing, in addition to yourself? Will it be one person, a close friend, or a member of your family? One of your instructors? Several members of your class? Everyone on an e-mail discussion list? A panel scoring your portfolio? A potential employer? Readers of a local newspaper? Fellow employees at work? Or an international audience on the World Wide Web? What do you know, or what can you guess, about their age, gender, religious beliefs, sexual orientation, political affiliations, economic status, or educational level?

Once you have made some attempt to characterize your audience, consider even more specific questions, such as the following:

- What do you most want your reader to get from reading what you have written?
- What level of curiosity do you think your reader already has about your subject? Will readers be receptive to your ideas(s) or information?
- Can you assume that your readers have much background knowledge on your subject?
- What do you believe they already think about it?
- How might your suppositions about the characteristics of these audiences affect the content and style of your composition?
- How might you vary your approach to appeal to audiences with different religious backgrounds, economic levels, and kinds of experience?

- How might the age or educational level of your audience affect your vocabulary or sentence length and complexity?

Your audience and the purpose of your writing, whether it be to express, explain, inform, analyze, persuade, or provide a basis for evaluation (as with an essay exam), should affect all the decisions you make as you plan your writing project.

Other writing, particularly in the digital age, such as composing an e-mail or writing in a chat room or on a discussion board, *seems* much less formal. Still, you should ask yourself questions about the writing situation: With whom am I chatting? What is the purpose of my posting? How might an e-mail message sent to a potential employer differ from one sent to, say, the World Cup Soccer Fan Society? And what about Web sites? If you have your own home page, would you list its address on a résumé or job application? Or is it personal, intended primarily for friends or family? Even with these kinds of electronic writing, which often appear in a context that seems to encourage playfulness, consideration of audience and purpose is important.

## your turn

To help you think a bit more carefully about audience, consider some of the following exercises.

1. In a paragraph, describe the primary reading audience for the writing you will do for this course. Then, in separate paragraphs, explore the characteristics of the audience for (1) a personal Web site, (2) the Web site of the International Olympic Committee, (3) the prospectus sent to clients by a brokerage house for a new stock offering, and (4) a letter to your 8-year-old niece. How might these traits affect your writing?
2. Find an editorial in a local or regional newspaper. What seems to be its purpose? Compose a brief paragraph describing the audience to which the article seems to be directed. Does the author assume a particular age range or educational level? Is the piece aimed at both sexes equally? Refer to specific passages in the editorial to support your judgments. Then rewrite the piece for one of the following publications:

**HYPERtext**

Look at the rules for several chat rooms, such as the Yahoo! Community Guidelines at **http://chat.yahoo.com/**. What do the rules tell you about expectations for participation, the "writing situation" in the communities, and the potential audiences and participants in those communities?

- The student newspaper of a local elementary school
- The newsletter of an organization of retired veterans
- The newsletter of a local high school's parent–teacher association
- A quarterly magazine for the alumni of your college or university

What assumptions did you make about your audience? How did these affect your style? Sentence length? Word choice? In a paragraph, explain why and how you altered the original editorial to suit it to the audience for whom you rewrote it.

3. If you regularly visit a discussion board or a chat room with participants you have not met face-to-face, how have you developed an idea of who your audience is? In a couple of paragraphs, write down all the clues—including names of chat rooms or discussion boards, instructions for use, names of participants, and types of discussions held—that tell you something about the audience reading what you write and the particular context of each forum. How is knowing such information *crucial* for participation in chat rooms and discussion boards? How might *not* knowing the audience and context in these forums create misunderstanding or even trouble for participants?

## Capturing Your Ideas: Prewriting Strategies

**Prewriting**, as the name suggests, is writing you do *before* composing a complete or even partial draft. Most writers prewrite. Prewriting can include taking notes, jotting down ideas, scribbling on the back of the proverbial napkin, keeping electronic files of random thoughts, or even sending oneself e-mail full of notes and ideas. Some writers create diagrams, such as clustering groups, to help them brainstorm ideas. Others make lists or write whole paragraphs at a time. You may devise new techniques yourself.

Prewriting has several goals. It can help you find a topic or record your thoughts for use in a future project. It can help you find out what you think about your chosen topic and develop ideas about it. You can use prewriting focused on a specific topic or issue to brainstorm ideas on the topic. Here are some favorite strategies for generating ideas through prewriting.

## Prewriting about Reading

For a writer, reading, thinking, and writing are inseparable. Each stimulates the other, and all should be done simultaneously. Notes taken while you read will most likely show you that process of stimulation and integration. Most of the time, you will begin to write by reading. Read to find a topic to write about, and then read some more to stimulate your thinking on the subject. Read to see how writers form sentences, develop ideas, communicate their thinking, use vocabulary new to you, and achieve a variety of rhetorical effects.

Since most writing is also a *response* to ideas or issues, most often expressed in other pieces of writing, it is an excellent idea to take notes on what you read, including the ideas you have as you respond to what you read. Frequently in your college career, your instructors will have you respond to or write about ideas that you will discover in textbooks, on the Web, in novels, or elsewhere. Taking good notes as you read is a valuable habit to acquire. Summarizing content is another form of note-taking that can help you remember what you have read long after you have returned a book to the library and forgotten about it.

Notes on reading can take many forms, such as the following:

- With pencil or pen in hand, or on an electronic notepad or computer, record your ideas *as you read.*
- Make notes in the margins of your own books and magazines, in a notebook, or on cards you keep for this purpose.

**REMEMBER**

Whether taking notes or keeping a formal reading journal, always record the name of the author, the title, the place and date of publication, and the page numbers with your notes for future reference. If you are taking notes from a Web site, record the URL (or Web address) and the author, title, and date of posting (if available). Doing so will help you keep track of the information you consult and assist you if you have to compose a reference list.

- Laptop computers are handy for note-taking because you can take them anywhere, get comfortable, and record thoughts in readable form as you go. Libraries increasingly have wireless access to the Internet.
- When you are reading material on the Web or in another electronic forum, an efficient practice is to keep a word processor window open for taking notes that can then be filed or printed out.

## Writing in a Journal

Keeping a journal that goes beyond recording responses to reading offers you a wonderful way to record a variety of ideas and insights you have on a daily basis—any one of which could be useful in helping you compose a writing project, complete an assignment, or brainstorm a topic you want to write about. Journal writing frequently serves as prewriting for other writing projects. A hardback bound notebook small enough to fit in a backpack, a spiral-bound notebook, or a loose-leaf binder all make good sites for journaling. Or keep a journal electronically. Using a separate document in your word processor, electronic notepad, or a paper notebook, keep a dated file of your daily musings in which you record ideas for possible paper or project topics and for various writing tasks, statements of purpose for your compositions, and questions about the writing situations in which you find yourself. You might label such a file "Writing Notes" or "Writing Ideas."

---

The poet David Keplinger tells us: "Keeping a journal, or just writing every day, even if it means recording a day's events, is a fundamental first step to finding out who you really are. My daily writing has changed my life."

---

## Freewriting

Another form of prewriting is **freewriting**—writing "freely" without worrying about mechanical issues such as spelling, grammar, or punctuation. Writing without inhibition often allows us to discover what we *really* think about a subject by getting us to put down anything and everything that comes to mind about the topic. When we look back at our freewriting, we are frequently surprised to see how much we knew, and we may discover unusual and original connections worth developing further. Practice freewriting to generate ideas or to explore a topic you are interested in pursuing in greater depth and detail.

How should you freewrite? As with all prewriting, there are many ways to do it, and you should experiment to find what is comfortable and productive for you. Consider the following ideas.

- First, write to record *everything* you know or think about a topic. It might be a topic suggested by the instructor, one chosen by your class, or a topic on which you are thinking of writing an essay. Write down as many ideas as you can come up with, as fast as you can. Write "off the top of your head" to capture your thoughts in words. When you think of a new direction to go on the topic, hit the return or enter key to start a new paragraph or list, and write as much as you can think of.
- Second, try "blind writing." Turn off the screen and stare at the wall or out the window. Or sit back, close your eyes, and type while your mind plays freely with your topic. Concentrate on getting your thoughts into words. Hit the slash key to mark spots where you want to make changes or corrections, but continue to make forward progress. Ignoring the words as they appear on the screen removes an opportunity for self-criticism at a point when capturing ideas and generating text should concern you more than producing a finished product.
- Third, give yourself a set amount of time. Then, once you start writing, continue until your allotted time is up. Doing so will allow you to generate text quickly, and you'll probably be surprised at how much writing you can do if you commit to writing—without stopping—for even 15 or 20 minutes. Reach into yourself for ideas, thoughts about relationships between them, and the language you need to capture them. Be *open* to connections between ideas you have never thought of before. If you think of a "wild" way of saying something, or if words come to you in ways you have not used them before, don't hesitate to write them down.

Freewriting often produces fresh ideas, turns of phrase, and inventive language that is useful in later writing. In the process, you'll generate not only text, but other *ideas*. Students are often surprised to have generated more than five hundred words of text in twenty minutes of freewriting—text often containing material worth developing later.

## your turn

Try this topic for freewriting: *technology's impact on education.* Write for fifteen minutes about your education with computers and other technologies, such as television or video. Describe two or three lessons you have learned or insights you have had about technology's impact on education and your own learning. How has writing technology changed since you learned to write? Once you have finished, look at what you have written. Did you have any surprising thoughts or write about anything you had not previously thought about?

Next, try freewriting on another topic: *your educational journey.* Look back over the process of your own education and write about what education has meant to you. You might begin by quickly making a list of questions to ask yourself, such as these: What does "education" mean to me now? What kinds of knowledge do I have? What kind is the most important to me? Did I obtain it in a formal educational setting, or elsewhere? What is the importance of education in my life? What people or events in my life contributed to my educational progress or helped shape my idea of what education would mean in my life? Were there moments that were turning points, or times when something dawned on me that I had not known before? What happened that prompted me to learn something? What are some of the educational challenges facing me and my peers today, and how am I planning to overcome them? What other questions can you think of?

Now reflect on the process of freewriting. Did reading, thinking, and writing on any of these topics make you wish you knew more about anything? Did it make you think about aspects of your life you had forgotten or ignored?

Finally, consider asking others to comment on the content of your freewriting. In a synchronous discussion or on a class e-mail list, spend ten minutes freewriting on a topic you are considering developing in an essay or project and send to the class. Then read the message that appears immediately after yours in your inbox or in the discussion and comment on it. Is the topic interesting and engaging? Is it focused enough? Too narrow in focus? Is it evident that the writer has considered possible audiences and the overall writing situation? What advice can you give that might help the writer adjust his or her topic? Send your comments to the writer; then read what your fellow student has told you and adjust your own topic in light of any advice. Compose a brief statement explaining your revised topic and post for other students to read.

## Listing

In addition to generating ideas, prewriting can also help you *develop* your ideas further. One useful strategy is **listing.** The computer can help you organize your thinking by letting you create a list of topics to be covered and then allowing you to expand the list by inserting subtopics.

To develop a sense of how this might work, try using a computer's word processor to brainstorm a list of topics or ideas on an assignment you are currently facing. Try the following steps:

- After writing out an item for your list, hit the return key twice.
- When you have listed all the topics and subtopics you can think of, insert the cursor after one topic and start writing about it. Freewrite as much as you can under each item.
- When you run out of things to say on a topic or subtopic, choose another one and do the same.
- If you find you have a lot to say on a topic and do not wish to move on to another one, do not feel obligated to break your train of thought. Just keep going.

If writing on one topic makes you think of something you can add to a topic you have already written on, insert the cursor at the appropriate spot in the previously treated topic and add your thoughts. At any point, if you wish to expand or divide your comments into paragraphs and continue on that topic, or if you want to move to another topic, go right ahead. You are using your word processor to generate an *expanding* document. There is no need to treat the topics in a linear sequence at this stage, although starting at the top of the list and moving down it, writing something on each, is a useful practice for getting started.

Let's look at an example of how this works in an essay that began when a student, Galen Geer, explored his educational journey in the freewriting exercise suggested in the "Your Turn" exercise earlier. After getting some thoughts on paper—or, in his case, onscreen—he decided to write his essay about a person who had taught him a lesson important in his life. He wasn't sure at this point which person this would be, for, as a nontraditional student with a grown son, he had been learning from other people for quite a while. He began his brainstorming by randomly listing people who had taught him in various ways:

Dad
    taught me how to hunt
    taught me what boundaries were
    loved me, in his fashion
Mother
    taught me morals
    was always there for me
Uncle Billy
    great sense of humor
    shared love of the outdoors
first-grade teacher
    taught me to read
Mrs. Root
    told me I would be a writer
    recognized my love of language
girl next door
    I discovered what love was at age 10
Jack
    scoutmaster
    taught me about the outdoors
My dog
    not a person, but better sometimes
    my hunting companion

Expanding on items in his list, he could explore his subject in more detail. When he got to Mrs. Root, he found that, in remembering her, he had a lot to say.

Ol' Lady Root

was my eighth-grade English teacher. I've thought of her more since leaving school than any other teacher I ever had. I remember how hot and humid it always was in school with no air conditioning. I felt sweaty all the time. I tried to seem tough, but what I really loved was learning about language and reading. One day in class she blew my cover, asked me what my favorite story was, and found out how much Hemingway I'd read.

told me I would be a writer

One day after I had read my paper to the class, she told me I would be a writer. She knew more than I did about myself then, apparently. She recognized my love of language. It was a long time before I thought about a writing career. Later I dropped out of school, joined the Marines, and went to Vietnam, then got a GED and went to military journalism school. I started college in California, then quit and enlisted in the Army. Got to write for division newspaper. Worked for *Soldier of Fortune*, went to Afghanistan, got burned out. Went back to school determined to get a college degree. One day I went home and visited Mrs. Root. She had kept pages of my writing all those years.

**"THE DOG ATE MY COMPUTER CORD. . . ."**

If you're using a computer, don't forget to back up your work, including your prewriting, on a disc, CD, or in a safe electronic folder. Make sure your word processing program is set to save your work every minute. In most programs look for "save" under "preferences" or in the "tools" menu to do so.

You probably noticed that this prewriting contains many incomplete sentences—and that's acceptable at this stage. Once you read Galen's complete essay a little later in this chapter, you'll also observe that several topics on his original list did not appear in the essay. Generating more ideas than you will ultimately use when you start drafting is one key to avoiding writer's block.

## Finding a Focus

After you have prewritten all you can think of, look at what you have. Consider the following questions as you peruse your prewriting:

- Where did you write the most? Where did you run out of things to say?
- Do the topics you wrote the most about have anything in common? That is, are they on closely related topics?
- What is the relationship between the items on your list? Is there a natural or obvious way to group them?

- Does your freewriting seem to support a general idea? Do one or more ideas run through what you have written? Are several of them on related subtopics? Can you see a pattern developing or a clustering of comments on one or more topics?

Choose a descriptive term for each group and insert it before each item on your list. Then rearrange your list by *cutting* and *pasting* so that what you have written on each topic is grouped together under one heading. If grouping ideas suggests new ways of relating the ideas you generated, insert and develop them accordingly.

Spend some time expanding on the topics about which you wrote the least. If your writing is in response to an assignment that asks for specific kinds of content and you see gaps in what you wrote, spend time freewriting on each of the topics where your material is thin. Do research, ask questions, think, read, and look for additional ways to expand or support your discussion in those areas. Then look for ways to elaborate further on the topics on which you found the most to say. Do not stop at this point, but probe for ideas lurking beneath the surface.

By now you should be able to identify an idea to which your comments are related. This is likely to be the developing *focus* of your piece. As an example, reread Galen's list. Each of the people on the list had influenced him, but they have more than that in common. Several of them had exerted the *same kind* of influence; they had *taught* him something. Once Galen saw this common thread, he zeroed in on one person (Mrs. Root) and elaborated on *how* and *what* she had taught him about himself. By the time he started drafting his essay, he had a clear focus on one teacher who had influenced him.

Before he began composing his rough draft, Galen analyzed his audience. He knew it would include his instructor and other students in his composition class, so he felt he was on firm ground in writing about early experiences in school. He decided to tell them what they could not already know—about the specific local context of his story in a small Oklahoma town, including his vivid memories of the hot, humid air in the school. The primary point he wanted to make was that a teacher, in the ordinary course of classroom experience, could have a profound—and positive—influence on a student's life.

# Organizing a Writing Project

Now it's time to think a bit more critically about *drafting* your essay and about the specific ways you will want to organize your project. The pointers in this section should assist you in getting that first draft well underway. Keep in mind that, at any point, you can move freely among individual "steps" in the writing process to create additional prewriting, listing, freewriting, journaling—whatever works for you if you need to generate additional ideas, consider different insights, or revise your original conceptions of your focus, your audience, or the writing situation.

## Choosing a Form or Genre

At some point you need to consider organization into *forms* or *genres* that will help others see the organization—the "flow" or progression—of your thinking. Because the **essay** is the form that much academic writing assumes, especially in the humanities, it is a primary consideration in this book. Other academic genres include research reports, conference papers, book reviews, articles, and, increasingly, electronic genres such as the Web page, which we also discuss. Often an assignment and the conventions of an academic discipline will dictate the form your writing will take. Study them carefully.

Because essays are shorter than books, they usually deal with a narrow topic and explore it briefly but thoughtfully. When writing your own essays, you should narrow your focus enough that you can explore your topic thoughtfully in the space you are given. Essays are also often argumentative in that they seek to clarify points, argue definitions, debate

**HYPERtext**

Think of an essay as a "try" at developing an idea. In fact, the word *essay* comes from the French word *essai*, or "attempt," as the early French essayist Montaigne called it. For an example of an early essay, see Montaigne's "Of Cannibals" (at **http://www.equilibrium.org/montaigne/essay04.html**), which represents his effort to understand what knowledge of another culture might teach him about his own.

issues, and present new ideas and alternative ways of thinking about a subject. Many authors use the essay to express insights and explore ideas. As a rule, in the United States, published essays embody a significant share of the intellectual life of the country. Essays, however, are not just a product of academic writers. Even famous authors of fiction, such as Stephen King, will periodically write essays, as King did in his collection of pieces on the craft of writing titled *On Writing*.

## Clarifying Your Thesis

After doing the prewriting recommended here, you probably have a good idea of the main point you want your audience to get from reading your composition. Express this as clearly and concisely as you can in one sentence. This will be a **working thesis** that should help you organize your thoughts and ideas for the project as a whole. We term it a "working" thesis because, as you compose your piece, you should feel free to revise it, perhaps focus it more precisely, or reword it for greater effectiveness.

Writing often involves a process of discovery of your own ideas. Early in the drafting process you may not have a firm thesis but, rather, may have a question you hope to answer as you explore ideas during the process of writing. In this case, you should develop a **thesis question**. The answer to this question will eventually be your **thesis**. You can still focus your thinking at the beginning by composing a sentence or two that clearly state the goal of your project.

## Developing an Outline

Place your thesis at the top of a blank page and, below it, develop an outline or sketch out an organizational plan. It may be a formal working outline, traditionally arranged with letters and numerals to designate levels of detail (e.g., I. II. A. B. 1. 2. a. b.), or it may be a simple list of topics and subtopics, perhaps taken from your freewriting or prewriting. Your word processor can probably help you format a standard outline. Fill in the topic list in as much detail as you can at this stage. The outline or plan can serve as a guide as you write, keeping you on track and headed toward your goal of giving your reader a thorough understanding of your thesis and how, or why, you have arrived at it. Include a section for each point you will make in support of your thesis. Refer to your outline often as you write, and use it to keep your thoughts organized, but don't be a slave to it. You may wish to use complete sentences rather than a list of topics. Feel free to revise it as you go along—adding topics, combining them, moving them around, and striking some out if necessary. Make a point of experimenting to find the way that using an outline works best for you.

A simple topic outline for Galen's paper might look like this:

I. School days in Blackwell, Oklahoma
   A. Mrs. Root's class
   B. Last child in my family
   C. Mrs. Root and my reading
   D. Reading my essay aloud
II. Life after Blackwell
   A. Military service
   B. Dyslexia discovered
   C. Journalism school and GED
III. Later visit to Mrs. Root

As a way of organizing his thoughts, Galen's outline provides a project plan or frame for his writing. It also allows him to see the big picture, which helps him focus on what his essay needs to accomplish as a whole. Perhaps more significantly, working on the outline prompted Galen to conceive of his essay in three distinct parts—a beginning discussing Mrs. Root, a middle probing his adult experiences with writing, and an ending returning us (and him) to Mrs. Root to talk about his experiences and thank her. In the process of outlining, Galen not only discovered a plan for his writing, but also stumbled on a creative way to organize his paper—specifically, by returning to Mrs. Root at the end of the essay, he can come "full circle," creating a nice sense of closure in his piece.

## your turn

Some writers find PowerPoint, a program that allows users to develop slide show presentations, to be a useful tool in developing outlines. In creating a slide show of your ideas and main points, you have to summarize carefully what you want to say and think through what each slide is going to contribute to the overall point you are trying to make. PowerPoint forces us to *break down* the main point we want to communicate

**INTERtext**

For more on PowerPoint presentations, check out Chapter 5, which discusses issues of visual literacy, including making brochures, using images in written projects, and making presentations that combine texts and images.

into smaller points that, taken together, will connect to make the bigger point. That process of breaking down is comparable to developing an outline.

If you have proficiency with PowerPoint (and it's a pretty easy program to learn to use), then consider how you might (1) organize Galen's outline into a PowerPoint presentation or (2) use PowerPoint to help you outline and organize a writing project on which you are currently working.

## Writing the First Draft

When you have a thesis and an organizational pattern in mind, it's time to compose your first draft, or **rough draft**. Before you start, here are some techniques that have helped many writers.

DRAFTING HINT #1: FIND A GOOD TIME AND PLACE TO WRITE. An important key to drafting well is concentration. The opportunity to work uninterrupted, long enough to get your ideas into words, is important. If you have small children or a family who do not understand your needs, you may have to write at night or in the early morning while they are asleep. Consider starting a cooperative babysitting arrangement with another student you can trust, and use it when it is time to draft an essay. If you live with roommates, you may need to escape to a library or computer lab to write if those around you will not leave you alone while you produce your first draft. A background of white noise, such as music that does not tempt you to listen carefully, can block out competing noises. So can sponge rubber earplugs. Composing the first draft of a 3,500-word research paper will take more time than a 700-word essay, of course. A large project may require several drafting sessions. It may not be easy to find opportunities for this kind of intense work, but it can be done. Experiment until you find what works for you. Once the first draft is written, you can rewrite, revise, and edit sections of your text in shorter periods of time.

---

**HOW SOME STUDENTS HAVE COPED**

One mother of school-age children made a sign to tape onto her bedroom door on weekends when she is composing a draft. It says, "Mother will talk to you at 4:00 P.M." A single father found an old typewriter at a yard sale to put next to him at his kitchen table for his young son to pound away on when Dad was writing his essays. One author of this book remembers her father's writing a master's thesis at a typewriter in a basement, with his books organized in piles on the Ping-Pong table next to him, while his children roller-skated noisily around the furnace, happy to be near him but understanding that they shouldn't talk to him while he was writing.

---

DRAFTING HINT #2: FIND THE RIGHT COMFORT LEVEL. A degree of physical comfort is often conducive to elasticity and limberness of mind, and it can help you avoid some causes of distraction, such as a growling stomach. Some writers prefer to put their feet up, lean back against pillows, and sip a favorite beverage while composing, perhaps using a laptop. Others will fall asleep doing this. Hemingway stood when he wrote. Experiment to find what works best for you, whether it's chewing gum to block out noise and keep you alert, working out-of-doors when weather allows, or sitting upright at a desk.

DRAFTING HINT #3: PUT YOURSELF UNDER PRESSURE—EARLY! "Why spend all this time prewriting and drafting?" some may ask. "I can write fast!" Writing under pressure is not for everyone, but students often insist that they do best when they try to finish an essay the night before it is due, without creating multiple drafts. We agree that the intense concentration required to write under pressure may help some writers stay focused enough to accomplish a writing task. Such last-minute writing, however, is usually not as good as the writer supposes, especially when compared to what she or he could have produced after spending time prewriting and drafting. If you want the mental kick of writing under pressure, then give yourself an early deadline for writing the first draft—

and stick to it. Then sit back and enjoy having your first draft written. Time spent away from a completed draft, followed by reflecting and rewriting, almost always leads to significant improvement.

## Starting the Rough Draft . . . at Last!

It is good practice to state your thesis in boldface type at the top of the first page of your draft. After reviewing your notes and plans, try to write as much as you can in one sitting. Look at your outline, choose one section of your project to work on, read any notes you took that are pertinent to that section—and start writing! Keep in mind that the introduction and conclusion are the first and last of your words your readers will see, so they should be clear, concise, and engaging. Do not get hung up in the introduction. If you start to get bogged down, sketch it out and move on to the body of the essay. During the process of drafting, when you think of items you wish you had said earlier, jot them down. You might even *start* with the body or main text of your project and leave the writing of the introduction until last. After seeing how the essay or writing project develops, you may have new insights about how to introduce it. After you have written through the first draft, take the notes you have made and return to the introduction, incorporating the ideas you had as you wrote. If you do this, be sure to refer to your working thesis as you proceed.

## Effective Introductions

Every essay or writing project needs an introduction to help orient the reader to the purpose of the writing. Here are some pointers for crafting effective introductions:

- Introductions should "engage" a reader—invite her or him into an essay or writing project. An introduction might begin with an anecdote, a leading question, or a provocative quotation—but don't simply quote someone without explaining where your quotation comes from! Begin with *your* writing. Be creative. A short anecdote or brief example can be effective, especially if the story illustrates an issue or idea that you will be discussing in the composition.
- Effective introductions usually contain a thesis statement that lets the reader know the main point or idea to be discussed. Let your reader

**INTERtext**

For an example of an effective introduction, check out author Douglas Rushkoff's opening paragraphs in "Children of Chaos" in Chapter 3. Note in particular the catchy—and startling—opening one-line paragraph: "Looks like this is the end." Rushkoff is clearly trying to catch our attention. The listing of items in the following paragraph, mention major crises from global warming to school shootings, is clearly designed to maintain a certain level of tension and to encourage us to read on.

know where your *focus* will be. The thesis should be easy to find, although with long projects, it may not appear until the second or third paragraph of the introduction.

• Introductions usually also provide the reader a sense of *how*, or in what order, the ideas under consideration will be explored. In other words, introductions offer readers a sense of the *organization* of the essay or project so that they will know what to expect. If you are not sure of this when you start, you may need to go back and add this passage after you have written the first draft to make sure your statement accurately reflects the organization of the piece. The more formal or academic the context, the more likely the author is to provide this guidance. Be clear and concise. An introduction may be longer than a single paragraph, but if it takes up several pages of a short essay, you need to trim it.

## Effective Theses

As you compose your draft, test all your ideas for your writing project against the thesis. Does each point you want to make support it? Do you need to change the thesis? Or do you need to bring in new material that provides better support?

It is better to state the thesis clearly somewhere in the paper than to leave the reader wondering exactly what you meant to say. Placing the thesis at the beginning gives it emphasis and ensures that readers get the point, even if they read no further. Placing it at the end of the introduction also emphasizes it and ensures that readers will have it in mind as they read the material that supports it in the rest of the essay.

If you have a surprising conclusion that you want to build up to throughout the course of the essay, you don't have to give everything away in the introduction. But you should begin by giving your reader some sense of what's going to happen over the course of the composition.

If you do not wish to reveal your thesis at the beginning of the essay, but prefer to guide the reader to a realization of what it is, you may withhold it until the end. This pattern of development has sometimes been called **climactic order.** The reader should be able to predict what the thesis will be after reading the body or main part of the composition (everything between the introduction and the conclusion), whether it's an essay, Web text, or other writing project. A dawning realization of what the writer is saying can have more impact on a reader than knowing the conclusion before seeing the evidence. You may decide to use this pattern on occasion, but use it judiciously and only when revealing your point in the introduction would detract from the impact of the presentation of your thoughts and ideas. If you are writing for the Web, remember that the reader may not read through the entire page or site before following links or digressions; if you want to be sure your thesis comes across, put it at the beginning or on your entrance page.

### your turn

To develop a sense of how different writers craft and position thesis statements, compare these Web sites: "School Vouchers: The Wrong Choice for Public Education" (at **http://www.adl.org/vouchers/vouchers_main.asp**) and "School Vouchers Issues and Arguments" (at **http://www.schoolchoices.org/roo/vouchers.htm**). As you read through the text on these sites, look for thesis statements. How far did you have to read on each site before you could guess the thesis, or position, advocated by the authors? As you go further into the sites, notice how the Web authors have organized their discussions and arguments. Is the pattern of organization is easy to grasp? Why or why not?

## Effective Conclusions

Conclusions help round out a piece of writing and give readers a sense of closure about the ideas or issues discussed in a writing project—even if those ideas need further discussion. The conclusion is your "last word," so it's important to think carefully about what you want to say. Here are some strategies for crafting effective conclusions.

• When writing the rough draft, try to write straight through to the conclusion, then take a break. When you come back, read your draft and write the conclusion that the paper "insists" be written. Think of your composition as an organic whole in which the conclusion grows naturally from the developments within the body of your work. Write what logically follows from the evidence you have provided. If your paper does not clearly demand a certain conclusion, then think again about the main point you want to leave your readers with. Look for ways to strengthen the evidence, reasons, or support you have provided for your thesis, or revise your conclusion.

• Student writers frequently compose conclusions that would make excellent introductions. After all, they have been working at crafting exactly what they want to say, and the writing in the conclusion is often crisp, clear, and concise. If you now have a clear, succinct statement introducing your topic and focus, try using your word processor's cut-and-paste functions to switch your introduction and conclusion, and consider the effect. Even if this works, you will doubtless need to adjust each one to fit its new place better. Playing with the "bookends" of your essay in this way can prompt you to think about crafting an effective introduction and/or conclusion. Then revise accordingly.

• The conclusion may summarize—but it should not simply repeat—the main idea of the essay or project. It might suggest other areas related to the main idea that readers might be interested in exploring. Conclusions often present the reader with an interesting twist on the subject or discuss implications for the future, but they should not bring up completely new subjects.

## To Sum It Up

One professional writer and professor, Bill Sheidley, offers the following advice: "I tell my students that good conclusions not only look back over the territory just traversed, but also look ahead to what can be seen from where we've arrived. In other words, they point to the next steps, or broader concerns in the material discussed in the writing project." We think this is excellent advice. Never simply *restate* your thesis; instead, think creatively about what you have accomplished in your writing project and suggest future possibilities for continuing the discussion of the ideas you have been exploring.

**INTERtext**

As an example of an effective conclusion, take a look at the last paragraph of Carl Sagan's essay, "Can We Know the Universe? Reflections on a Grain of Salt" in Chapter 2. The paragraph begins with the transitional phrase, "For myself," which signals that Sagan is going to relate the discussion in the preceding paragraphs a bit more directly to his own life and experiences. The paragraph then proceeds to summarize some main points of the essay but also places those points in a more personal context: what *does* it mean for us as people to live in an enormous, complex, and awe-inspiring universe?

## A Student Writer in Action: A Rough Draft

Here are excerpts from the rough draft written by Galen Geer, whose prewriting you have seen. A revised draft of his essay appears at the end of this chapter.

Ol' Lady Root

by Galen L. Geer

Oklahoma summers make a person sweat. Not itty, bitty drops of perspiration that trickle down your skin, but real sweat. From May to late September, Oklahoma is a land of sweating. Everyone sweats. After Labor Day, when the classrooms are again full, young people sweat in groups. In any classroom, even with the best of air conditioning, there is a lot of sweating. The boiling humidity, mental frustration and fear of being pounded into square pegs relentlessly squeezes the packed bodies until the sweat soaks shirts and straightens girls' brushed hair. Sometimes, when a teacher exposes secret dreams the sweat cools the anger.

An eighth-grade English classroom in September, 1963, was all of these things. John F. Kennedy hadn't yet been sacrificed to history and classroom air conditioning was a novelty in only the newest schools. Eight years earlier, on May 25, 1955, a tornado left half of Blackwell, Oklahoma in a radiation-free Hiroshima-like rubble. The only school building unscathed was the high school. Replacement schools had to be built. City fathers opted to build a new high school and move the junior high to the old high school. It would take years to complete, but the start of the 1962–63 school year began with the promise of every Blackwell school child in a modern classroom—except the junior high—someone had to make a sacrifice. Besides, the rooms weren't bad.

That first early September morning I found myself in the presence of "ol' lady Root" in her eighth grade English Class. The path out of high school was through her class. Each of my brothers had cleared her portals.

"You're the last one, aren't you?" she said to me, the statement framed in a question, demanding an answer.

"Yes," I said.

"Well, I guess I can retire after this year," she said. "I've had all of you."

Kids from large families are way-markers in Middle America. Teachers can mark the passage of careers by the surnames they've completed. "I remember that family," a teacher will say. "The last one came through my class just a year or two ago and who would have believed the middle one would be. . . ."

Whenever she called on me to diagram a sentence on the chalkboard my knees struggled to hold up my panic and the chalk melted to my clammy hand. Somehow I got through each ordeal. I kept my head above the raging nine-week flood of grammar and hid my enthusiasm for adjectives and verbs, compound and complex sentences. Tough guys have their image—even phony ones. Conjugating verbs wasn't cool. The first day of the second nine weeks "ol' Lady Root," ripped off my disguise. Holding the literature book in one hand she asked me what my favorite story was.

Huh? This was the first day of the second nine weeks. We weren't supposed to have read anything. How did she know? I told her it was "Soldier's Home." She asked me who had written it, and I told her Ernest Hemingway had. Then she asked me what other stories by Hemingway I had read. I needed to run. Find a place where I could hide, roll up my sleeves, tuck a pack of Lucky Strikes in the sleeve, put one behind my ear. I could be cool. "*The Old Man and the Sea, For Whom the Bell Tolls*, 'Up in Michigan,' 'Big Two-Hearted River.'" Titles rolled off my tongue. I named others and other writers.

She asked me if I had read other stories in the book, and I nodded. Then she asked me what the Hemingway story was about. She'd issued a command. I stammered, stumbled and started telling her about Hemingway's World War I tale.

Four weeks later our assignment was to write a short story. It was, for me, no problem. I wrote my story and on the appointed day brought it to class. Then ol' Lady Root threw me a curve. We'd read our stories aloud. I was terrified—trapped. My worn tennis shoes sucked at the hardwood floor. In front of popular kids, tough kids, girls who smelled sweet and girls who popped gum, I shuffled the pages. My voice cracked, then steadied. I could hear a voice—my voice—echoing off pale green plaster. My character was in the room—alive. Then, quietly someone clapped. Another joined, then another. Then my classmates were applauding. A pretty girl from another world touched my arm and smiled. I felt her touch—a catspaw breeze slipping across a farm pond. I still pretended to be a hood, but the emotional pot had been stirred. After class I asked why she said I'd be a writer. She said it was because I liked words. I used them. I loved them. She said I would struggle and it wouldn't happen overnight, but someday I would write. I asked her how she knew I'd read the stories, and she said she just knew.

What unfathomable insight had guided her to turn me away from the one-way road that dominated life in a smelter town where sulfur-poisoned air periodically drifted through bedroom windows? I still marvel how that heady combination of attention and accolades turned me away from the well-worn path to the Blackwell Zinc Smelter. In the privacy of my mind and the shadows of my room I had wanted to write but never believed it was possible—until her class. The following spring the Lucky Strikes disappeared and I won the homeroom track meet's hundred-yard dash. Winning changed more of my world. Two weeks later I made the school track team. Life had opportunities.

Hurdles came at me in singles and doubles. The first, and unknown hurdle, was dyslexia compounded by a slight nervous stutter when I was excessively tired. The dyslexia nearly doomed me. Regardless of the amount of effort I put into my studies there seemed to be a wall blocking my every turn. In the spring of 1966 I was angry, frustrated and tired. There was salvation in war. When my anger boiled over and I lashed out at the system that seemed determined to lock me out of my dreams I fled to the Marine Corps. The dyslexia dogged me. I went to Vietnam and in between tours married Patt, a college student at the University of California. After returning home I was studying for a promotion exam when she unraveled the mystery.

"You're dyslexic," she said, watching me work on math and spelling problems. Then, like a mysterious enchantress she opened doors. Identifying the problem and correcting it took less than an hour. After two years I left the drill field and was offered the military school of my choice. I knew it would be journalism school.

"You need a high school diploma or GED," I was told. My frustration seven years earlier had exploded in my fists and I'd been kicked out of high school. Now, when I was looking at the life I wanted the hurdles were there again. I found a book on the GED, studied it and applied to take the exam.

After I'd passed it orders arrived sending me to military journalism school. Fifteen weeks later I graduated and started my new career. At last I saw my articles published in military newspapers—a dream come true. I fondly remembered Mrs. Root, who had started me along the path of words.

## questions for discussion

1. Galen writes—a lot! In fact, we have omitted passages from his draft. What is the advantage of generating quantities of text? Where might some judicious cutting of the essay sharpen its focus?
2. If you were to write a letter to Galen commenting on his rough draft and giving him advice for improving it, what points would you make? Would you begin by pointing out his strengths? What are

they? Think about how you could provide the kind of feedback that you would want if you were Galen.

3. Look again at Galen's essay, and highlight the sentences that the author uses to guide the reader through his ideas and arguments. When he ends a paragraph with "Life had opportunities," for example, what do you expect to learn in the upcoming passages? Where else does he lead you to anticipate what comes next? Where could he improve on being "reader-friendly"?

## More than Type, Click, Print: Rewriting and Revising

*"A computer lets you make more mistakes faster than any invention in human history, with the possible exceptions of handguns and tequila."*
—Mitch Ratcliffe, *Technology Review*, April 1992

Congratulations! You can breathe a sigh of relief now that you have the first draft of your project in hand. It feels good to have explored your thoughts and wrestled them into sentences. At moments you may even have felt you were on a roll and begun to relish a sense of accomplishment. That's wonderful—but don't stop yet. Now it is time to turn to rewriting, revising, and making the most of what you have already done. Some writers think that revising is where the *real* writing begins because revising allows us to *play* with text—moving it around, cutting some parts, adding others. Eudora Welty, the celebrated Southern writer, would literally cut—with a pair of scissors—paragraphs from her stories and paste them in different orders, playing with the organization of her work to ensure she achieved her desired effect on her readers. Welty was not alone in using this laborious but powerful method of revision.

Fortunately, just as word processors allow us to write fast and capture our initial thoughts about what words and ideas to use, they also permit us to make changes easily. The freedom to get everything you think of quickly into text brings with it the responsibility—to yourself—of working further with that text to organize, prune, and refine it, to refocus it when needed, and to revise the style to add variety in sentence patterns and diction. The ability to read your own language in neatly presented text or on screen allows you to "re-see" your thoughts expressed in a format that you can manipulate at will. You can radically alter the order of paragraphs by cutting and pasting them in a different sequence, sans scissors, and really work your writing over to make sure that you are producing insightful and engaging text and focusing the reader's attention on the points you want to make.

*Save your drafts!* Frequently, when students revise using a word processor, they lose earlier drafts of an essay because they overwrite changes directly into the document. Although this is generally not a problem, it is sometimes interesting and useful to *see* the changes you have made over time to a piece of writing. If your instructor requires you to turn in drafts of your composition at different stages in writing it, be sure to save the series of revised drafts, ending the titles with a different number (perhaps the date on which the draft was composed). When asked for rough, revised, or multiple drafts, you will have them.

*To avoid confusion*: Develop a procedure for naming drafts that you save at different stages. If your instructor does not specify a common system for your class, use your initials and RD (for "rough draft") or REVDR (for "revised draft"), and indicate numerically where they are in the sequence. For example, Sarah Green's second revised draft of Essay II would be "SG.II.REVDR2." More than one student has turned in the wrong draft because of sloppy naming practices.

## Revising for Unity, Coherence, and Style

Some students think of revising as simply correcting spelling mistakes or figuring out where to put those annoying commas. Although ensuring mechanical correctness is an important part of the writing process, it is not really revising; it is proofreading. Although you will doubtless want to clean up glaring errors as you go, eagle-eyed proofreading can be left until you are closer to printing the final draft. Rather, when first approaching the opportunity to revise your work, consider larger issues, such as unity, coherence, and style. Let's think a bit more about each of these and its relationship to revision.

### Rewrite—radically!

Since typing on a word processor is usually faster than writing by hand, it is easy to use an old and often-practiced revision technique: simply rewriting or recomposing your essay, paper, or project from scratch. Although this may seem drastic, it's actually a good writing practice in that the draft you produce the *second* time around will generally be better than the one you originally wrote. Why? For one good reason: Writing allows us to see what we are thinking and prompts us to develop new thoughts and insights. Giving yourself the opportunity to rewrite—even radically—might help unearth some of those thoughts. Of course, you may not have time to do this with every writing assignment, but trying it with smaller bits of your writing should work just as well. Frequently, writers will identify problem areas in a piece of writing and completely rewrite, for instance, an introduction, conclusion, or individual paragraphs. The results are generally far better.

### Revise for unity.

After drafting your essay or writing project, read it carefully to see if you are sticking to your subject. Ask yourself: Is my essay focused? Do I drift from my focus? If you discover a case of "draft drift," you will need to revise to avoid leading the reader away from the topic. Think of how quickly you become annoyed with people who, in telling a story, sidetrack themselves with miscellaneous points or sidebars. Readers feel the same way. You may need to make more explicit, or clarify, the relationship of some passages to your thesis or central idea. To check for draft drift, try the following: Your word processor should make it easy to copy and paste the topic sentences—usually, though not always, the first sentence of each paragraph—into a separate file, thus creating a paragraph made up of "topic sentences." If that paragraph seems coherent, with each sentence building on the one before, chances are your essay or writing project—as a whole—is fairly focused and clear.

### Revise for coherence.

Read your writing with an eye for organization. If you are *not* maintaining your focus, ask yourself if you have organized your project effectively. Does the order or flow of the paragraphs make sense? That is, will the order of paragraphs and flow of discussion be coherent and sensible to a reader? Is the progression of ideas easy to follow? Do you use **transitions** between paragraphs, helping your reader to see the development of your thinking from one section of the essay or project to the next? Even more specifically, does your introduction actually *introduce* your topic in a creative and appealing manner? Does it signal the organization of the material that follows? Does your conclusion summarize, without repeating the vocabulary you used earlier? Does it do so in a way that leaves your reader with something to think about, such as the implications for the future of the discussion addressed in your writing? Such questions ask us to think critically about whether our work is reader-friendly. In other words, are we helping our readers think *with us*, or are we hindering their ability to understand and appreciate our insights?

## your turn

Using an essay or project you have drafted, try the exercise just described. How did it work? Did copying and pasting the opening or topic sentence of every paragraph into a separate paragraph create a fairly unified, meaningful whole? Where were the weak spots, the points that didn't flow or make much sense? How might you correct for this, if those points need attention?

Recent versions of most word processors will allow you to *summarize* your compositions. The program analyzes the entire passage and selects sentences that it thinks correspond to your main theme. If you've worked with computers and word processors before, you know that such features are hardly foolproof and should be used with caution. Still, a summarizing feature can be useful, especially if you are concerned that you might be drifting from your main focus or theme. Likewise, it's often interesting to see what the program "thinks" is your focus or theme. If it highlights something significantly different from what you intended, that you should consider (1) if you are adequately addressing your primary focus or (2) if there is a different focus or theme that you *really* want to write about.

### Revise for style.

The style, or the individuality expressed in the paper, should be appropriate to the *rhetorical situation*—the audience, context, and purpose of the work. It should be at a level of formality suited to the situation, and the diction (the language choices you make) should be appropriate for your audience and intentions. Style is important—it can render a piece of writing appealing or rhetorically ineffective. In terms of writing, we can define *style* as the impression that a writer creates through the use of words, phrases, sentence variety, organization, and even the graphic arrangement of text on the page. These elements of writing—the "ensemble" of composition, as it were—are all malleable, and their use by a writer contributes to our sense of that writer's style. Some popular style manuals in use today are *The Elements of Style*, by William Strunk and E. B. White, and *Wired Style: Principles of English Usage in the Digital Age*, by Constance Hale and Jessie Scanlon, along with many others (listed on this book's Web site).

**HYPERtext**

For online assistance with style, check out the following links:

- Strunk and White's *Elements of Style* and other reference books at **http://www.bartleby.com**
- Purdue University's Online Writing Lab (an OWL) at **http://owl.english.purdue.edu/**
- Paul Brian's "Common Errors in English Usage" at **http://www.wsu.edu/~brians/errors/index.html**
- Jack Lynch's "Guide to Grammar and Style" at **http://andromeda.rutgers.edu/~jlynch/Writing/**
- The Tutor Center, **http://www.awbc.com/tutorcenter/english.html**, available to purchasers of this book

## Getting Help: Peer Review

As noted earlier, writing is always done within a specific context or situation and usually for a specific audience. It is a good idea not only to think about the audience you are addressing as you write but also to consult members of that audience during the writing process. For example, your writing instructor will probably want to see one or more drafts of your work, and because he or she is one of the primary members (if not the only member) of the audience for whom you are writing, his or her comments will warrant your close attention. Frequently, however, you will write for a wider audience. How can you solicit feedback from a larger readership?

A writer has a number of options for getting feedback. A traditional practice has been to ask someone else—a fellow student, colleague, or knowledgeable friend—to read over your work. In class, you may form groups that remain constant throughout the term for reading and commenting on each others' drafts. Many writing teachers and editors call this **peer review** because it is done by "peers," or those with a level of knowledge akin to one's own, people familiar with your assignment and with what you are learning, who are in a position to spot problems and suggest revisions. Peer review can be useful at almost any stage during the writing process, especially after drafting and during editing.

There are many options for conducting peer review in this digital age. You can print your work out and hand hard copy to others, but to save time—and paper—consider *e-mailing your work* as an attachment to one or more fellow students so they can read and comment on it either during class or outside class time. You can also *copy and paste all or part of your draft* into the body of an e-mail message, although your original formatting may be lost. Either way, your draft can go to your entire class if your instructor has established a class discussion list. Your classmates will be able to write comments directly into your text. Using all caps within brackets [LIKE THIS] will distinguish your additions from the rest of the text. Whether via e-mail, courseware such as Blackboard or WebCT, or conferencing software on a Local Area Network, networked computers offer new ways for students to respond to one another's compositions. Look for a method appropriate for your situation.

---

### ETIQUETTE FOR PEER REVIEWERS

- Ask the author to tell you what kind of feedback would be most helpful, and then provide it.
- Begin by saying something positive about the writer's work. What two or three things about it impressed you most favorably?
- Consider carefully both the assignment and the audience the writer is addressing. Put yourself in the shoes of the intended audience.
- Offer *constructive* feedback. Be specific about what the author needs to do to improve the piece.
- Pose questions that will lead the writer to develop the content of the piece, if necessary.
- Offer negative criticism tactfully, without being insulting or hurtful.
- Save discussion of mechanics and editing until last.

---

**What should a peer reviewer look for?** As a class, you may develop your own list of questions to address during a reviewing session, in addition to any feedback specifically requested by the author. The following list suggests the kind of comments a reviewer might make, but it is by no means complete. See what you can add to it.

- Does the writer seem to have a *focus* and an *audience* clearly in mind? How can you tell?
- Is the *main* point or thesis clear? Is it supported adequately?
- Does the writing *guide* the reader through the piece, with *appropriate transitions* and sentences that help to organize the flow of thinking from one section of the essay to another? If not, where are such transitional devices needed?
- Does the writing use a *variety of sources* (if applicable) to help the writer clarify points, provide ideas for discussion, or even argue with others' views?
- Does the author use *variety in paragraph openings, organization, and length*?
- Is the style *readable*? Is it free of computer or other slang, jargon, clichés, or vocabulary that is either stilted or too formal, or too chatty or colloquial, for the writing situation?
- Is the style *clear and concise*? Is it free of extra words that clutter the text without adding to its meaning?
- Does the author consistently use *complete sentences* (rather than sentence fragments)? Is there *variety in sentence length, sentence beginnings, grammatical structure* (of simple, compound, and complex sentences) and *rhetorical patterns*?
- Does the author use *variety in choice of wording*? Is the vocabulary used correctly?
- Can you identify any stylistic habits that confuse, annoy, or delay a reader trying to get to the point?
- Has the text been carefully *proofread*? Is it free of errors in spelling, punctuation, usage, and grammar?

Once you have received feedback from a peer, colleague, friend, or teacher, you are probably ready to consider substantive changes and revisions to your initial draft. When you receive feedback on your paper or project, read it thoughtfully, looking especially for comments from two or more reviewers who agree. If you decide not to revise your work in response to repeated suggestions, you should probably be prepared to turn in a note with your project explaining why you chose to ignore those recommendations.

## Tracking Changes

Some word processors have a function called Track Changes, often found in the Tools menu (as in Microsoft Word), which will keep track of the changes you make in your draft. When selected, it will automatically allow you to see an original draft and compare it with an altered version. When a peer reviewer is working with an electronic version of your text using Track Changes, she can suggest changes for your consideration, which you may ultimately decide to accept or not. Being able to see the different texts can allow us to make more informed decisions about our writing.

**ELECTRONICissues**

Tracking changes is a technique often used by state legislatures to present suggested revisions in laws to the public for their consideration. For example, the deleted text may ~~be struck through~~ and the added text <u>underlined</u> and/or CAPITALIZED. Numbering sections allows the public to review and comment on specific items in a proposed law. If your legislature is in session, check your state's Web site and write a paragraph describing the system for tracking suggested changes in a bill to be considered in the current session.

## your turn

To practice peer reviewing, try some of the following exercises.

1. Post the introduction to an essay you are drafting to a message board, a class discussion list, or a conferencing platform and ask for specific feedback. For example, you could ask the reviewer the following questions: Does my first sentence make you want to read the second

sentence? Does the opening passage make you want to keep reading? Do I give a clear sense of what is coming next? Ask your readers to rewrite the opening sentence to make it seem more engaging than the original version, at least to that individual reader.

2. Play "Guess the Thesis": Post your essay to a message board or e-mail list after removing your thesis statement. Then see if three different readers can guess what the thesis is, on the basis of the material you provide to support it. If they disagree, go back and work at supporting your point more convincingly.
3. Send your composition without its conclusion to the class via e-mail, a message board, a synchronous conference, or on hard copy, and ask reviewers to write the conclusion they think it requires, based on the development of your ideas. If the conclusions they offer do not capture the point you want to make, rewrite portions of the composition or revise your conclusion until there is a good match between them.
4. Use a variation on the previous exercise to determine how well your essay or writing project is organized. Working with a draft on your word processor, copy and paste entire paragraphs in different order. Then ask a friend or peer to see if he or she can put the composition back into its proper order. If your peer reviewer can, then you have probably organized your piece well and made *transitions* clear enough to move the reader through the text from paragraph to paragraph. If not, consider how you *can* help your reader move more effectively through your essay. Sometimes, a peer reviewer performing this exercise with you will suggest an even *better* organizational strategy for your writing. If it works, do it—and don't forget to thank your reviewer!
5. Assume the role of a peer reviewer of Galen's rough draft earlier in this chapter. In an informal letter to Galen, comment on what he does well. Then offer constructive advice for him to consider when he revises the draft. Would you suggest any changes in focus, organization, language, or anything else?

## Finishing Touches: Editing and Proofreading

Once you have clarified your focus, paid attention to how your essay or project is organized, and consulted with your peers about your writing, you need to make sure that your work is free of mechanical or grammatical errors that will cause readers to stumble over your words or ideas. Faulty spelling, grammar, or punctuation, or just plain typographical errors, all interfere with your readers' enjoyment of your work and their ability to understand it. Reworking a text to avoid these errors and unnecessary distractions is called **editing**. We usually save this for last. Some writers ceaselessly edit their work as they write, and some experienced ones can do so successfully, but we—like many other writing teachers—caution against doing too much *early* editing, especially when you are just getting the hang of drafting. Focusing too soon on mechanical matters such as spelling and punctuation can detract from your ability to generate usable text. Although grammar and mechanics are important, do not let your attention to them block you from getting your ideas, thoughts, and insights onto your screen. There is always time later in the writing process to attend to editing. When this time comes, your computer can assist you with this task.

The first step, however, relies on you alone. It is now time to ***read what you have written.*** Read it through silently, looking for missing words and for any errors. Read it again from the bottom up, perusing each line from right to left (i.e., backward), looking for errors in spelling. Then find a place where you can be alone and read your draft aloud to yourself, sentence by sentence. Listen for missing words or awkward expressions, and correct them. Next, see if you can get a friend to read your paper aloud to you while you take notes on passages that sound stilted or don't make sense. Your teacher may allow you to pair up with someone else in class so you can read your papers to each other.

## Spell-Checkers and Grammar Checkers

Your word processor has various functions and features to assist you with editing. Spell-checkers and grammar checkers are the most commonly used. Keep in mind that when you use these, you must use them *critically*. They can help you spot typographical errors and major mechanical *faux pas*, but you should evaluate each suggestion to determine whether it applies to your particular text. A spell-checker, for example, will not catch mistakes in word usage, especially of homonyms that are pronounced alike but have different spellings and meanings. In this sentence, "Their was an error in the calculation," the spell-checker would find no problem, even though *their* is used incorrectly for *there*.

Most word processors have spell-checkers that allow you to check your spelling while you are typing. If you are a poor speller who lingers over the spelling of each word, we recommend that you write with the spell-checker turned off so you can concentrate on generating text. There's time enough later to correct spelling. Never have the spell-checker just "change all" or "correct all" mistakes. Why? Most spell-checkers do not know proper names or unusual words that you might use or coin, and you run the risk of having *all* such words changed into something else—with often amusing results, as the boxed illustration below shows. In this case a spell-checker chose a word ("thought") that was spelled correctly but was clearly not the right word for the sentence ("drought").

---

Isn't spell-check wonderful? Voilà! The computer makes everything make sense—except when it doesn't.

The City of Thornton, Colorado is probably abashed at the changes apparently wrought by spell-check on its detailed Drought Management Plan.

"While thoughts do not occur at regular, predictable intervals, they are inevitable, and in Colorado, thoughts are frequent events," says the web-published report.

Then, there is this alarming observation: "A study done by the Colorado Climate Center at Colorado State University has shown that Colorado has had five severe statewide thoughts in the past century. The most recent one ended in 1978."

This news goes a long way toward explaining the actions of the state legislature.

"Fortunately," the report concludes, "most thoughts do not affect the entire state at the same time."

–Betsy Marston, "Heard on the Street,"
*High Country News*, June 23, 2003

---

Although we recommend learning to use correct grammar and do not recommend becoming dependent on a grammar checker, if used judiciously, a grammar checker can help you spot small typing errors and let you know if you are consistently making glaring grammatical errors. If it tells you that you frequently use incomplete sentences or that your sentences often lack subject–verb agreement, take that advice as a clue that you need to study ways to avoid these errors, perhaps with the help of a handbook or your school's writing center. In all cases, you should evaluate any suggestions made by the software. Keep in mind that it does not know what you are trying to say, and its suggestions are often unusual or inappropriate. Also, grammar checkers tend to recommend a standardized style that may strip your voice of its individuality without improving it. In general, any time you use these aids, use them thoughtfully. *You* are ultimately in charge of, and responsible for, your writing.

## A Writer in Action: Galen Geer's Revised Draft

As you read Galen's revised essay, notice how he has shortened his introduction to get his readers to his thesis more quickly. The opening paragraph still sets the scene, but he has trimmed it down so that it focuses not on hot Oklahoma summers in general, but on his eighth-grade English classroom. If you could serve as a peer reviewer at this stage, what other changes would you recommend he make before he finalizes his draft?

Geer 1

Galen Geer

Dr. Margaret Barber

English Composition

31 July 2001

The Path of Words

New title picks up the idea of his educational journey.

Oklahoma summers make a person sweat. Not itty, bitty drops of perspiration that trickle down your skin, but real sweat. From May to late September, Blackwell, Oklahoma is a land of sweating, even in classrooms with the best of air conditioning. Boiling humidity, mental frustration, and fear of being pounded into square pegs relentlessly squeeze the packed bodies until the sweat soaks shirts and straightens girls' brushed hair. Sometimes, when a teacher exposes secret dreams, the sweat cools the anger.

Galen cuts out some repetitions of the word *sweat.*

My eighth-grade English classroom would expose my dreams—in ways I could not have imagined. One early

He cuts out the historical digression and omits most of his teacher's comments about his family.

September morning, I found myself in the presence of "ol' Lady Root's" eighth-grade English class, and I knew I was on the path out of Blackwell. Each of my siblings had cleared her portals.

"You're the last one, aren't you?" she said to me, the statement framed in a question, demanding an answer.

"Yes," I said.

"Well, I guess I can retire after this year," she said. "I've had all of you."

Whenever she called on me to diagram a sentence on the chalkboard, my knees struggled to hold up my panic and the chalk melted in my clammy hand. Somehow I got through each ordeal. I kept my head above the raging nine-week flood of grammar by hiding my enthusiasm for adjectives and verbs, compound and complex sentences. Tough guys have their image—even phony ones. Conjugating verbs wasn't cool. The first day of the second nine weeks "ol' Lady Root" ripped off my disguise. Holding the literature book in one hand she asked,

He substitutes dialog for indirect quotations throughout essay.

"Galen, what's your favorite story?"

Huh? This was the first day of the second nine weeks. We weren't supposed to have read anything. How did she know? "Soldier's Home," I stammered.

"Who wrote it?"

"Ernest Hemingway."

"What other Ernest Hemingway stories have you read?"

I needed to run. Find a place where I could hide, roll up my sleeves, tuck a pack of Lucky Strikes in the sleeve, put one behind my ear. I could be cool. "*The Old Man and the Sea, For Whom the Bell Tolls*, 'Up In Michigan,' 'Big Two-Hearted

Geer 3

River.'" Titles rolled off my tongue. I named others and other writers.

"Have you read all the stories in the book?" I nodded.

"What's the Hemingway story about?"

She'd issued a command. I stammered, stumbled and started telling her about Hemingway's World War I tale. When I finished she surveyed the class and said, "Galen is a good reader. The rest of you will have to keep up with him." Four weeks later our assignment was to write a short story. I wrote my story and on the appointed day brought it to class. Then ol' Lady Root threw me a curve. We'd read our stories aloud. She called names alphabetically, but when it was my turn she skipped me. I smugly watched the others sweat. After the last sucker's name had been called she said, "Now we'll hear from someone who will be a writer. Galen, please read your story."

He tightens the paragraph, cutting out several clauses.

I was terrified—trapped. My worn tennis shoes sucked at the hardwood floor. In front of popular kids, tough kids, girls who smelled sweet and girls who popped gum, I shuffled the pages. I could hear a voice—my voice—echoing off pale green plaster.

My character was in the room, alive. His music made him an outcast, and then other characters came from the walls and he risked his life for them. They found a place for him in their world. Then characters retreated to the pale painted plaster.

The room was quiet. They didn't like it. I started for my desk, the sound of my shoes mocking me. Then, quietly, someone clapped. Another joined, then another. Soon all of classmates were applauding. A pretty girl from

Breaks up long paragraph, adds dialog.

Geer 4

another world touched my arm and smiled. I felt her touch—a catspaw breeze slipping across a farm pond. I still pretended to be a hood, but the pot had been stirred.

Tightens paragraph, eliminates unneeded words.

After class I asked why Mrs. Root said I'd be a writer.

"You like words. You use them. You love them. You read them and you write them. It won't happen overnight, and you're going to struggle but you will write—you can't *not* write."

"How'd you know I read the stories?"

"I just knew," she said, then turned back to her desk. The next class was filing in. I left. I would later learn how the violence of combat changes a person and how loves lost, or torn away, also inflict change. I would find that in rare moments the scattered elements of an individual converge but the outcome remains uncertain. That day was one.

What unfathomable insight guided Mrs. Root, turning me away from the one-way road in a smelter town where sulfur-poisoned air drifted through bedroom windows? I marvel how she turned me away from the well-worn path to the Blackwell Zinc Smelter, freeing my dreams of being a writer from the privacy of my mind and the shadows of my room. The following spring the Lucky Strikes disappeared and I made the school track team. Life had opportunities.

But hurdles, in singles and doubles, slowed me. The unknown hurdle, dyslexia, was compounded by a slight nervous stutter. The dyslexia nearly doomed me. Regardless of the effort I put into my studies, there was a wall blocking me. I was angry, frustrated, and tired. When my anger boiled over I lashed out at the system that locked me out of my

Omits unneeded details about his wife.

Geer 5

dreams. There was salvation in war. Between tours I married and my wife, watching me, opened doors like a mysterious enchantress. Identifying and correcting my dyslexia took less than an hour. A few weeks later I was promoted. Two years later I was offered the military school of my choice.

"Journalism school," I said. I wrote Mrs. Root and told her what I'd done.

I needed a high school diploma or a GED. My frustration seven years earlier had exploded in my fists, and I'd been kicked out of high school. I found a book on the GED, studied it, and passed the exam. After I'd passed it, orders arrived sending me to military journalism school. Fifteen weeks later I graduated and started my new career.

A few years ago a friend who still lived in Blackwell told me Mrs. Root had died. I remembered one night when I had gone back to her. In my hand I held my certificate of graduation from journalism school and a folder filled with my published work. In the warmth of her home on a November night, Mrs. Root read my clippings.

He expands the conclusion to "bring home" his point.

"I knew you could do it," she said. Her voice was weak. Without speaking she stood and walked from the room, shuffled some papers, and returned with some notebook pages with my penciled words in her hand. I read the story, then handed it back. She carefully put it in her lap. "I'm tired," she said.

"Goodnight," I said, and went out into the night. She knew what I needed to find out, but she could only point me toward the path. The rest has always been up to me.

## questions for discussion

1. Do you think the changes Galen has made, including additions and deletions, are effective? Which ones? Are there any that you would *not* have made?
2. Galen makes fairly substantial changes to his introduction, streamlining his text so that we are introduced to Mrs. Root earlier than in the previous draft. Is this a helpful change? Why? How else might you suggest Galen alter his introductory material?
3. Galen has also made changes to his conclusion. Are they improvements? Would you have advised Galen to conclude his narrative differently? If so, how?
4. In general, one of Galen's primary revision strategies was to cut and trim his narrative. Are there spots in the original where you might have advised him to *expand* his discussion and narration, as opposed to trimming it? Why?
5. The title might seem like the least important part of a paper, and students frequently turn work in without titles. In fact, you should think carefully about what to title your piece, primarily because the title is your reader's first impression about your topic and about you as a writer. Do you think Galen improved on his original working title when he settled on "The Path of Words" for his essay?

## *Useful Links*

You'll find numerous resources available on the Web to help you get started on a variety of writing projects. Here are some of our favorites:

- The City University of New York (CUNY) library offers ideas for developing outlines: **http://www.lib.jjay.cuny.edu/research/outlining.html.**
- The following site, developed for speech communication at the University of Kansas, also has some good tips for organizing and planning thoughts and ideas with reader ease and clarity in mind: **http://www.ku.edu/cwis/units/coms2/vpa/vpa6.htm.**
- The "Computer-Assisted Writing Centre" at York University, located online at **http://www.yorku.ca/cawc/strategies/unconscious.html,** has good ideas for using the computer to brainstorm and freewrite.

## *Additional Writing Activities*

1. Take a look at an essay or writing project on which you are currently working. This might be a piece for your writing course or for another course you are taking, or for a job requirement. Consider how, after a first draft, you can revise that piece. After some reflection (and perhaps some prewriting), compose a few paragraphs in which you talk to yourself about how you are going to use some of the revision strategies you've learned to improve the piece. Then revise it according to what you have written.
2. Return to a piece you have written, perhaps one from high school or another college-level course. Write a letter or e-mail to yourself about how you would revise the piece. Point to specific strengths and weaknesses and suggest concrete strategies that you could use to revise the piece. Offer examples!
3. Using the techniques discussed in this chapter, do prewriting for a narrative about how you have come to consider possible majors, decide on a major, or pursue your own career path. What would you write about? What strategies that Galen uses would you employ in your own story? What might you do differently? Then develop a rough draft from your prewriting and share it with your classmates as part of a peer review session. Revise accordingly.

CHAPTER 2

# Something to Talk About: Understanding Academic Writing

Most of the writing you will do for college-level courses will be **academic writing**, which has its own traditions, expectations, and conventions. This chapter is designed to introduce you to academic writing and to offer tips and strategies to enhance your ability to understand academic texts and read them critically. Developing such skills will help you learn to write for a variety of academic audiences and purposes—topics that we will explore in subsequent chapters.

# What Makes Writing "Academic"?

## Academic Writing: Audience and Purpose

**Purpose** and **audience** are key elements in defining, understanding, and participating in any writing context or situation. For academic writing, these differ, sometimes substantially, from the purpose and audience of writing done in other contexts—for example, writing you would undertake for a personal reason, such as composing a diary entry or writing an e-mail to a friend.

In general, academic writing is done for many purposes, above all *to communicate ideas and discoveries, analyze or synthesize* existing work in new ways, and *invite response*. Such responses may take the form of positive or tactfully worded negative criticism and questions. The scholarly writer does not aim for a wide audience so much as to communicate the results of research and thinking to others who are in a position to offer informed response or, as in the sciences, to plan research and to test and possibly corroborate findings. Academic writing often is directed to readers associated with educational or research institutions such as colleges or universities. Hundreds of specialized academic journals publish academic writing. Increasingly, specialized online publications, mostly available by subscription, make the results of scholarly labor available to an even wider audience. Your library probably subscribes to many of these.

### your turn

Locate the titles of three journals that publish scholarly articles in your major or minor field or, if you don't have a major, on a subject that interests you. Obtain a paper copy of one, and examine the opening pages that list members of the editorial board and outline submission policies and publication standards, such as the format in which the editor(s) would like to receive manuscripts. Explore your library's subscription databases to determine which of these journals are available to you online. Can you download articles from them? Read articles from two different journals related to your major and write a one-page rhetorical analysis of the articles. To what audiences are they directed? What is the purpose of each article? What techniques do the authors use to accomplish their purposes? What stylistic features do they have in common? What is the conclusion of each? Outline the study that led the researcher to the conclusion.

In some ways, *your* immediate academic community may seem small. At first it may include only your teacher and other students in your classes. As you move into upper-division courses, however, it will expand. In fact, the larger academic community is worldwide. It crosses boundaries of departments, disciplines, and even nations. A scholar working alone in a narrow field at an American university may find her most supportive academic community in other states or in universities abroad. Members of the larger academic community often get together at conferences to read and listen to one another's work and respond in person.

## Academic Writing and the Public

Some scholars occasionally write for the general public, interpreting the knowledge in their fields for those without such expertise and thus performing a valuable service to a reading public interested in their topics. Harold Bloom is one scholar who frequently does this in the field of literary studies, and Lewis Thomas, Stephen Jay Gould, and Steven Pinker—among many others—have made advanced scientific knowledge accessible to nonspecialists. Gould has been particularly influential and effective in his ability to explain the intricacies of the biological theory of evolution to a public that is skeptical of such a provocative theory. A Harvard professor who died in 2001, Gould worked for 20 years on his last book, *The Structure of Evolutionary Theory*, to explain his understanding of evolution. A review at Amazon.com describes Gould's skill in explaining this controversial theory, noting in particular his use of "clear metaphors" and a "personable style." (We'll see an example of Gould's masterful writing a bit later in this chapter.) Another academic who wrote for popular audiences is the astronomer Carl Sagan, who was a professor at Cornell University and a widely published author. Like Gould, Sagan masterfully explained some of the more complex problems—and possibilities—of science and astronomy to the general reading public.

## Some Key Characteristics of Academic Writing

Although writers like Gould and Sagan might have focused their energies on writing for the general public, their work nonetheless demonstrates many of the hallmarks of good academic writing: inquiry, exploration, and a search for knowledge. Let's look at an example.

## WRITING SPOTLIGHT

### Carl Sagan and Popular Academic Writing

Sagan's essay, "Can We Know the Universe? Reflections on a Grain of Salt," asks a question fundamental to academic and scholarly research and inquiry: what *can* we know about our world, our universe? What makes Sagan's piece "academic," as short as it is, is the way the author lays out his discussion. Read through the piece, thinking about how Sagan sets up the initial question he wants to examine, and then how he develops possible answers throughout the piece.

---

### Can We Know The Universe? Reflections on a Grain of Salt

Carl Sagan

*Nothing is rich but the inexhaustible wealth of nature. She shows us only surfaces, but she is a million fathoms deep.*

—Ralph Waldo Emerson

Science is a way of thinking much more than it is a body of knowledge. Its goal is to find out how the world works, to seek what regularities there may be, to penetrate to the connections of things—from subnuclear particles, which may be the constituents of all matter, to living organisms, the human social community, and thence to the cosmos as a whole. Our intuition is by no means an infallible guide. Our perceptions may be distorted by training and prejudice or merely because of the limitations of our sense organs, which, of course, perceive directly but a small fraction of the phenomena of the world. Even so straightforward a question as whether in the absence of friction a pound of lead falls faster than a gram of fluff was answered incorrectly by Aristotle and almost everyone else before the time of Galileo. Science is based on experiment, on a willingness to challenge old dogma, on an openness to see the universe as it really is. Accordingly, science sometimes requires courage—at the very least the courage to question the conventional wisdom.

Beyond this the main trick of science is to *really* think of something: the shape of clouds and their occasional sharp bottom edges at the same

---

Excerpt from "Can We Know the Universe? Reflections on a Grain of Salt" by Carl Sagan from *Broca's Brain: Reflections on the Romance of Science.*

altitude everywhere in the sky; the formation of a dewdrop on a leaf; the origin of a name or a word—Shakespeare, say, or "philanthropic"; the reason for human social customs—the incest taboo, for example; how it is that a lens in sunlight can make paper burn; how a "walking stick" got to look so much like a twig; why the Moon seems to follow us as we walk; what prevents us from digging a hole down to the center of the Earth; what the definition is of "down" on a spherical Earth; how it is possible for the body to convert yesterday's lunch into today's muscle and sinew; or how far is up—does the universe go on forever, or if it does not, is there any meaning to the question of what lies on the other side? Some of these questions are pretty easy. Others, especially the last, are mysteries to which no one even today knows the answer. They are natural questions to ask. Every culture has posed such questions in one way or another. Almost always the proposed answers are in the nature of "Just So Stories," attempted explanations divorced from experiment, or even from careful comparative observations.

But the scientific cast of mind examines the world critically as if many alternative worlds might exist, as if other things might be here which are not. Then we are forced to ask why what we see is present and not something else. Why are the Sun and the Moon and the planets spheres? Why not pyramids, or cubes, or dodecahedra? Why not irregular, jumbly shapes? Why so symmetrical, worlds? If you spend any time spinning hypotheses, checking to see whether they make sense, whether they conform to what else we know, thinking of tests you can pose to substantiate or deflate your hypotheses, you will find yourself doing science. And as you come to practice this habit of thought more and more you will get better and better at it. To penetrate into the heart of the thing—even a little thing, a blade of grass, as Walt Whitman said—is to experience a kind of exhilaration that, it may be, only human beings of all the beings on this planet can feel. We are an intelligent species and the use of our intelligence quite properly gives us pleasure. In this respect the brain is like a muscle. When we think well, we feel good. Understanding is a kind of ecstasy.

But to what extent can we *really* know the universe around us? Sometimes this question is posed by people who hope the answer will be in the negative, who are fearful of a universe in which everything might one day be known. And sometimes we hear pronouncements from scientists who confidently state that everything worth knowing will soon be known—or even is already known—and who paint pictures of a Dionysian or Polynesian age in which the zest for intellectual discovery has withered, to be replaced by a kind of subdued languor, the lotus eaters drinking fermented coconut milk or some other mild hallucinogen. In addition to maligning both the Polynesians, who were intrepid explorers (and whose brief respite in paradise is now sadly ending), as well as the inducements to intellectual discovery provided by some hallucinogens, this contention turns out to be trivially mistaken.

Let us approach a much more modest question: not whether we can know the universe or the Milky Way Galaxy or a star or a world. Can we know, ultimately and in detail, a grain of salt? Consider one microgram of table salt, a speck just barely large enough for someone with keen eyesight to make out without a microscope. In that grain of salt there are about $10^{16}$ sodium and chlorine atoms. This is a 1 followed by 16 zeros, 10 million billion atoms. If we wish to know a grain of salt, we must know at least the three-dimensional positions of each of these atoms. (In fact, there is much more to be known—for example, the nature of the forces between the atoms—but we are making only a modest calculation.) Now, is this number more or less than the number of things which the brain can know?

How much *can* the brain know? There are perhaps $10^{11}$ neurons in the brain, the circuit elements and switches that are responsible in their electrical and chemical activity for the functioning of our minds. A typical brain neuron has perhaps a thousand little wires, called dendrites, which connect it with its fellows. If, as seems likely, every bit of information in the brain corresponds to one of these connections, the total number of things knowable by the brain is no more than $10^{14}$, one hundred trillion. But this number is only one percent of the number of atoms in our speck of salt.

So in this sense the universe is intractable, astonishingly immune to any human attempt at full knowledge. We cannot on this level understand a grain of salt, much less the universe.

But let us look a little more deeply at our microgram of salt. Salt happens to be a crystal in which, except for defects in the structure of the crystal lattice, the position of every sodium and chlorine atom is predetermined. If we could shrink ourselves into this crystalline world, we would see rank upon rank of atoms in an ordered array, a regularly alternating structure—sodium, chlorine, sodium, chlorine, specifying the sheet of atoms we are standing on and all the sheets above us and below us. An absolutely pure crystal of salt could have the position of every atom specified by something like 10 bits of information.* This would not strain the information-carrying capacity of the brain.

---

*Chlorine is a deadly poison gas employed on European battlefields in World War I. Sodium is a corrosive metal which burns upon contact with water. Together they make a placid and unpoisonous material, table salt. Why each of these substances has the properties it does is a subject called chemistry, which requires more than 10 bits of information to understand.

If the universe had natural laws that governed its behavior to the same degree of regularity that determines a crystal of salt, then, of course, the universe would be knowable. Even if there were many such laws, each of considerable complexity, human beings might have the capability to understand them all. Even if such knowledge exceeded the information-carrying capacity of the brain, we might store the additional information outside our bodies—in books, for example, or in computer memories—and still, in some sense, know the universe.

Human beings are, understandably, highly motivated to find regularities, natural laws. The search for rules, the only possible way to understand such a vast and complex universe, is called science. The universe forces those who live in it to understand it. Those creatures who find everyday experience a muddled jumble of events with no predictability, no regularity, are in grave peril. The universe belongs to those who, at least to some degree, have figured it out.

It is an astonishing fact that there *are* laws of nature, rules that summarize conveniently—not just qualitatively but quantitatively—how the world works. We might imagine a universe in which there are no such laws, in which the $10^{80}$ elementary particles that make up a universe like our own behave with utter and uncompromising abandon. To understand such a universe we would need a brain at least as massive as the universe. It seems unlikely that such a universe could have life and intelligence, because beings and brains require some degree of internal stability and order. But even if in a much more random universe there were such beings with an intelligence much greater than our own, there could not be much knowledge, passion or joy.

Fortunately for us, we live in a universe that has at least important parts that are knowable. Our common-sense experience and our evolutionary history have prepared us to understand something of the workaday world. When we go into other realms, however, common sense and ordinary intuition turn out to be highly unreliable guides. It is stunning that as we go close to the speed of light our mass increases indefinitely, we shrink toward zero thickness in the direction of motion, and time for us comes as near to stopping as we would like. Many people think that this is silly, and every week or two I get a letter from someone who complains to me about it. But it is a virtually certain consequence not just of experiment but also of Albert Einstein's brilliant analysis of space and time called the Special Theory of Relativity. It does not matter that these effects seem unreasonable to us. We are not in the habit of traveling close to the speed of light. The testimony of our common sense is suspect at high velocities.

Or consider an isolated molecule composed of two atoms shaped something like a dumbbell—a molecule of salt, it might be. Such a molecule rotates about an axis through the line connecting the two atoms. But in the world of quantum mechanics, the realm of the very small, not all orientations of our dumbbell molecule are possible. It might be that the molecule could be oriented in a horizontal position, say, or in a vertical position, but not at many angles in between. Some rotational positions are forbidden. Forbidden by what? By the laws of nature. The universe is built in such a way as to limit, or quantize, rotation. We do not experience this directly in everyday life; we would find it startling as well as awkward in sitting-up exercises, to find arms outstretched from the sides or pointed up to the skies permitted but many intermediate positions forbidden. We do not live in the world of the small, on the scale of $10^{-18}$ centimeters, in the realm where there are twelve zeros between the decimal place and the one. Our commonsense intuitions do not count. What does count is experiment—in this case observations from the far infrared spectra of molecules. They show molecular rotation to be quantized.

The idea that the world places restrictions on what humans might do is frustrating. Why *shouldn't* we be able to have intermediate rotational positions? Why *can't* we travel faster than the speed of light? But so far as we can tell, this is the way the universe is constructed. Such prohibitions not only press us toward a little humility; they also make the world more knowable. Every restriction corresponds to a law of nature, a regularization of the universe. The more restrictions there are on what matter and energy can do, the more knowledge human beings can attain. Whether in some sense the universe is ultimately knowable depends not only on how many natural laws there are that encompass widely divergent phenomena, but also on whether we have the openness and the intellectual capacity to understand such laws. Our formulations of the regularities of nature are surely dependent on how the brain is built, but also, and to a significant degree, on how the universe is built.

For myself, I like a universe that includes much that is unknown and, at the same time, much that is knowable. A universe in which everything is known would be static and dull, as boring as the heaven of some weak-minded theologians. A universe that is unknowable is no fit place for a thinking being. The ideal universe for us is one very much like the universe we inhabit. And I would guess that this is not really much of a coincidence.

---

If we look carefully at Sagan's essay, we can see some of the primary elements of academic writing at work. First, in the opening paragraph, Sagan clearly *identifies what he wants to talk about*—science, and what science actually can offer us in terms of knowledge. He distinguishes between, on the one hand, simply asking questions and, on the other hand, the "scientific cast of mind," which he *defines* in the third paragraph: it "examines the world critically as if many alternative worlds might exist, as if other things might be here which are not." Following this train of thought, Sagan *asks another question* in the following paragraph: "But to what extent can we *really* know the universe around us?" This question, appearing pivotally at the beginning of a paragraph, dominates the rest of the essay. It is the question that Sagan uses to *develop his ideas* for the rest of the piece. For instance, Sagan moves from discussing the Milky Way in general to analyzing what we can know about a grain of salt: "But let us look a little more deeply at our microgram of salt." Making this move allows Sagan to explore with us the complexity of even something as miniscule as a grain of salt; there's a *lot* to know, even about simple things. This movement—this deepening of the discussion—is a key characteristic of academic writing, which *explores an idea*, as opposed to simply stating the obvious.

Another example of such deepening or idea development occurs when, after considering what cannot be known, Sagan turns his—and our—attention to what *can* be known: "Fortunately for us, we live in a universe that has at least important parts that are knowable." But, as Sagan points out, part of that "knowability" involves approaching and appreciating topics, such as the theory of relativity, that might seem counterintuitive or unreasonably complex—stuff that's really, really hard to understand. Knowledge, what can be known, isn't necessarily simple. We have to learn to appreciate the complexities of our universe, and science, in Sagan's view, can help us do that.

By the end of the piece, after exploring his topic, Sagan is ready to *conclude*: "Whether in some sense the universe is ultimately knowable depends not only on how many natural laws there are that encompass widely divergent phenomena, but also on whether we have the openness and the intellectual capacity to understand such laws." You'll note that his conclusion doesn't sound *definitive*; that is, he has not provided us the keys to understanding the universe. Most academic writers won't; they're generally not that arrogant! But he does prompt us to think critically about what we *can* know—and what we cannot. That's the *point* or *thesis* of Sagan's piece, which we can find succinctly stated in the last paragraph, where Sagan encourages us to accept the wonder of a universe in which we *can* know some things and in which our curiosity leads us to think about the things we do not know. Interestingly, this reminds us of the opening paragraph, in which Sagan says that science is, more than anything else, a "way of thinking," often requiring "courage to question."

To sum up, then, much academic writing focuses on *identifying interesting questions* to talk about, *defining* what we mean by those questions, or what specifically we'll be talking about, *exploring and developing* our ideas by asking questions, and *making conclusions* or *posing theses* about our subject of inquiry. With practice, and with the examples to be discussed next, you'll develop a good ability to read and appreciate these characteristics of academic writing.

To explore academic writing in more depth, we're going to turn our attention to three topics: first, we will discuss some of the dominant **conventions and expectations** of writing in academy; second, we will explore some of the principal **writing strategies** that academics use to discuss their work and explore ideas; finally, we'll consider ways academics use **electronic forms of communication**, such as e-mail and discussion lists, to compose and play with ideas. Go to the Companion Website for links for several academic essays.

## Writing for an Academic Audience: Some Conventions and Expectations

Academics usually expect certain conventions to be followed in the production and dissemination of academic writing, and these expectations are useful to learn if you are going to write about important topics and issues in an informed manner. As with any writing situation, there are inevitably variations and exceptions, but such **writing values** are standard for much academic writing. Moreover, they are easily transferable to other writing situations in which you need to be clear, compelling, and convincing. You can use the conventions of academic writing not only for papers and projects that you will compose while you are in college, but also when you need to write more formally in your professional life or in other situations in which you want to make your points clearly and precisely—for example, writing an editorial column for a newspaper.

What, then, is valued in academic writing? Let's approach the question by considering what a *reader* of academic prose usually expects from a piece of academic writing. In general, readers in the academy read critically. Look for the use of outside sources and appropriate documentation; expect familiar, reader-friendly genres; and read for the argument—that is, for a thesis and the evidence given to support it—put forward in a piece of writing. They also appreciate writing with style, and they expect mechanical correctness. Next we'll consider each of these characteristics in more detail.

## 1. Academic readers read critically.

The reader of academic texts is prepared to have her thinking challenged and to read through a text carefully, perhaps more than once. In general, academic readers will not be easily won to a position. They will read with a skeptical eye, pick out the arguments being made, and look carefully at the reasoning and supporting evidence given as well as the quality of any experts cited as authorities. We call this **reading critically,** which doesn't mean that the reader is going to nitpick or be nasty. Rather, someone who reads critically is entering into a dialog with a piece of writing and is willing to question it without taking what it says for granted. For example, Carl Sagan's frequent use of questions throughout his short essays suggests that he knew that his readers would most likely approach his piece with some friendly skepticism; in other words, Sagan wrote out the kinds of questions that he felt his readers might have as they considered his view of science: "But to what extent can we *really* know the universe around us?" Sagan knew that such a question would come to the mind of someone reading a short piece about how we know and understand the world and universe in which we live. He knew that his readers would read *critically.*

We think of academic reading as *active*, even *interactive*—as a conversation between reader and author, much as Socrates' discussions with his students involved the give-and-take of interactive dialog. In your classrooms, a good discussion, when it really gets rolling, engages participants in listening to and responding to each other. You can see this notion of interactivity hinted at in Sagan's piece above. Note how Sagan asked questions to begin a paragraph. This is a common strategy, and it suggests that Sagan was potentially aware of questions that the reader him- or herself might have. He used such questions to propel him into further exploration and development of his ideas. He probably believed that his readers would read *critically*—that is, that they would have questions and would want him to be able to provide at least a few answers.

In synchronous written communication, as in face-to-face oral discussion, the author has the advantage of being able to get immediate feedback from the audience, but with print sources, reader and author can still, in a sense, interact. If you own the book you are reading or are reading a printout, you can make reading notes directly on the page, underlining important passages and in the margins, recording your questions, comments, and responses to the author's ideas. For instance, in the following passage from Sagan's essay "Can We Know the Universe? Reflections on a Grain of Salt," notice how we annotate (or "make notes on") this important transitional passage:

> Let us approach a much more modest question: not whether we can know the universe or the Milky Way Galaxy or a star or a world. Can we know, ultimately and in detail, a grain of salt? Consider one microgram of table salt, a speck just barely large enough for someone with keen eyesight to make out without a microscope. In that grain of salt there are about $10^{16}$ sodium and chlorine atoms. This is a 1 followed by 16 zeros, 10 million billion atoms. If we wish to know a grain of salt, we must know at least the three-dimensional positions of each of these atoms. (In fact, there is much more to be known—for example, the nature of the forces between the atoms—but we are making only a modest calculation.) Now, is this number more or less than the number of things which the brain can know?

Paragraph begins with a transitional sentence—suggesting a deepening of the discussion, turning from one idea to another . . .

Interesting example—but will this *really* tell us what we need to know about that grain of salt? Is *all* knowledge reducible to counting molecules and atoms?

Paragraph ends with a leading question, another transition . . .

How else should you read as an academic? Ultimately, whether doing peer review of your fellow students' work in a composition classroom or reading an article published by a recognized expert, you should assume a skeptical (though not hostile) attitude. Read for understanding, and then reread each piece "against the grain," jotting down your questions about matters of fact, the reasoning used, and the acceptability of any justification given for claims made by the author. It is possible to raise questions in the spirit of common intellectual pursuit while being tactful and respectful of others' thinking.

An alternative is to keep a reading log in a separate journal (either by hand or as an electronic file), in which you can expand on your observations in thoughtful responses to a writer's ideas. An **online or electronic journal,** saved to a disk you can carry with you or on a shared network, is an option that some people like for its ability to deliver the journal in readable print, and to expand as the reader inserts comments into the original notes. You can keep such a journal in a word-processed document file or even as a series of e-mail messages that you send to yourself and store in an electronic folder. A book or article becomes your own when you annotate it.

Even when you do not expect to use them for your own research, your notes furnish a record of your responses to what you read. Rereading them will help you remember the original work. Similarly, taking notes on lectures, guest speakers, and oral presentations, then organizing and typing them out afterward, will help you remember what was said.

**PEER REVIEW OF ACADEMIC WRITING**

Remember these hints about how a trained reader approaches an academic text? You can use them as a guide for peer review:

- Academic readers read critically.
- They look for the use of sources and documentation.
- They expect familiar genres.
- They read for the *argument*.
- They appreciate style.
- They expect mechanical correctness.

As you read a classmate's paper or project during a peer review session, look for these items, putting yourself in the position of the trained academic reader. This will work particularly well for essays or projects in which an academic audience is assumed.

## 2. Informed academic readers expect the use of outside sources and appropriate documentation.

Academic readers understand that knowledge is not created in a vacuum but that it comes from both careful observation and ongoing discussion with others about the world around us. In fact, most academic writing participates in conversations that have been in progress for quite some time. Sagan's piece, for example, is actually part of a larger conversation about the nature and definition of science—a conversation that has been going on for millennia. In fact, you can hear strains of the conversation in

Sagan's writing. In the opening paragraph, he refers to Aristotle and Galileo, two early men of science. Such references let us know that Sagan knows he isn't just speaking off the top of his head but is working with ideas that have been in play for a long time.

Technically, such references are called **citations**. Citations serve an important function in academic writing in that they locate a writer within the context of an ongoing conversation in a given discipline or about a given issue. Each academic writer picks up the thread of the conversation and expands or develops it in his or her unique way. Referring to others who have participated in the conversation lets us, the readers, know that the writer (1) has some familiarity with the conversation going on and (2) will expand on the discussion given what others have said in the past. Citations also show readers what has inspired a writer or what ideas and texts, specifically, a writer is working with, critiquing, or refuting in his or her work. Moreover, citations allow a reader to trace the path of the academic writer and enter the conversation him- or herself.

When writers use information from other sources, they usually *quote* and *document* their sources carefully. Indeed, academic writers usually assume that readers expect every phrase, fact, or idea drawn from a source to be scrupulously documented according to the accepted documentation style of their discipline. This is called **citing sources.** There are many **citational** or **documentational styles** such as the Modern Language Association (MLA) and the Chicago Manual of Style (CMS, also known as "Turabian") in the humanities, the American Psychological Association (APA) in nursing and the social sciences, the Council of Biology Editors (CBE) in biology, and Columbia Online Style (COS) for online sources. Such documentation is expected because academic readers want to know where the information presented to them comes from.

Citations occur both as **in-text references** or **in-text citations** and as **bibliographic entries.** In-text citations refer to the reference given in the body of the text itself, such as an author's name or a page number, whereas

**INTER**text

The Appendix to this book provides more specific information and examples on citing sources properly in both MLA, APA styles, as well as COS. Almost any writer's handbook will offer similar information.

the bibliographic entry is usually given in a list of Works Cited following the text. For instance, the following paragraph quotes the Sagan essay used earlier in this chapter and uses the Modern Language Association (MLA) in-text citational style:

> In his essay, "Can We Know the Universe? Reflections on a Grain of Salt," Carl Sagan, a noted astronomer and popular author, asks us to consider what science can—and cannot—tell us about the universe around us. Using the example of a grain of salt, Sagan shows us how complex our world is, and how difficult it is to ever fully know something. He asks, "How much *can* the brain know?" (18).

Notice how the last sentences in this paragraph use both the name of the author and a page number (in parentheses) to let us know where, specifically, the quotation comes from in Sagan's piece. The **parenthetical citation** (so called because it's in parentheses) is an example of an in-text citation. If we had not mentioned the name of the author in the previous sentence, our in-text citation would have looked like this: (Sagan 18).

The bibliographic citation gives us publication information about the essay, such as where it can be located. An example of a bibliographic entry for Sagan's essay, in MLA format, would look like this:

Sagan, Carl. "Can We Know the Universe? Reflections on a Grain of Salt." *Broca's Brain: Reflections on the Romance of Science.* New York: Ballantine Books, 1979. 15–21.

This entry, which would appear in a list called "Works Cited" at the end of an essay or text in which Sagan is cited or quoted, gives readers sufficient information to track down and find the complete article. Additional information about constructing such entries, including the use of in-text citations, can be found in the appendix to this book.

When quoting sources, keep this in mind: Ideas and unique ways of using language to express them are considered **intellectual property** that belongs to the one who published them first. That is why any idea or language you use from a source *must* be credited to its "owner." The use of someone else's words or ideas without giving credit to the author is a serious error in an academic context, tantamount to stealing. A writer responding to or using sources must be extremely careful to give proper attribution to

**ELECTRONIC** Issues

**CHEAT SITES**

In case you somehow missed this, you can download papers written by other students at what are called "cheat sites" on the Web. Some are free, and they're usually worth what you pay for them. Even essays for which one pays a stiff fee can be appallingly bad. You can find a list of sites at **http://www.newfoundations.com/Cheatsite.html.**

Using these is, of course, unethical and puts you at risk of severe consequences, including failure and possibly expulsion, if the cheating is discovered by the instructor—an expensive and humiliating lesson from which a student may never completely recover. Here's our general rule of thumb: Don't waste your time with cheat sites. Most instructors—especially any instructor savvy enough to be using this book—know how to trace the use of such sources. Moreover, it is now easier for an instructor to prove that a student plagiarized an online source than it ever has been in the past. It's likely that 10 or 12 variations of the same essay may appear on different sites, increasing the chances that the instructor will recognize language, ideas, or organizational patterns repeated in several papers.

all sources. Failing to do so is considered **plagiarism**. When done by a student, plagiarism is frequently grounds for failing an assignment, possibly the course—and even for being expelled from the institution. The key to avoiding plagiarism is to take notes carefully, always recording the source for any quotation, paraphrase, or summary one makes, as well as the page number (for print sources) from which each note was made. When using the material in your notes, you then have a handy reminder of the source that can be incorporated into the text with an in-text citation.

---

**PLAGIARISM: HOW TO AVOID IT**

Here are a few quick steps to avoiding plagiarism in your own writing:

1. Whenever you "copy" text from a source, make sure that you put all original words in quotation marks (" ") and write down *all* available information about where you found the information you are recording.

2. If you are copying material from a Web site, do not simply copy and paste material without using quotation marks *and* also recording the Web site address or URL.
3. Some writing instructors may ask you to submit copies of all outside sources. Whether this is the case or not, consider keeping photocopies or electronic copies of all sources, highlighting material that you have quoted—and making sure all quoted material appears in quotation marks in your document.
4. Whatever you do, keep track of your sources! Record important information such as authors' names, titles, page numbers, dates and places of publications, Web site addresses, and anything else you think you might need to help you find a source again, should you lose a hard copy of it.

## 3. Academic readers expect to see familiar genres.

In terms of *organization,* readers of academic writing expect an essay or other presentation, including scholarly Web sites, to be clearly laid out and organized. Organization is determined both by the purpose of the piece you are writing and the *genres* within which your audience is expecting you to work. Familiarity with these genres is crucial.

What are some of these genres? You probably know a few already. Academic writing takes many forms, ranging from long **books** and **chapters** in books to shorter **essays** (such as Sagan's piece) or **articles** published in journals or exchanged among classmates and teachers. It includes **research reports, surveys of the literature** on a given topic (usually as a preliminary step to research in that field), **book reviews**, and even **essay examinations.** Despite the explosive growth of technological capabilities for academic discussion and the new genres finding their way into academic practice such as e-zines, mastery of traditional forms, such as the academic essay or research project, is still required for participation in the academic community. You'll encounter various examples of these genres throughout the remainder of this book.

**INTER**text

For more on e-zines, or "electronic magazines," see Chapter 8.

While academic reading and working with academic texts might seem daunting, you can use what you already know about writing to help you in various academic writing situations and to become a better reader of academic texts. Granted, academic writing differs in significant ways from other writing, such as that undertaken for the purpose of recording one's own emotions, experiences, or reflections, as one would in a personal diary or a personal essay. Nonetheless, the processes and strategies used there will be valuable in an academic environment. Historians writing articles and books, for example, often organize accounts of events *chronologically*, as do scientists recounting the procedures they followed in studies or laboratory experiments. *Narrative illustrations* and *descriptive examples* incorporated into an essay or research paper can help support its thesis or help the author create an engaging introduction.

### your turn

Interview someone working in a profession you might be interested in pursuing. Ask what kind of writing they do in their work lives. Find out what standards are used to evaluate it and in what context it is read. Find some examples of such writing. Do you see a wide disparity between the professional writing in your chosen field and what you have so far been asked to do in the classroom? What are the main differences and similarities?

**INTER**text

Chapter 6, on research writing, offers advice on preparing for and conducting interviews.

## 4. Academic readers look for the *argument*.

Undergraduates practice meeting the standards and using the conventions of academic writing in essays, research projects, and newer genres such as scholarly Web sites, as well as in learning the conventions of their disciplines. Whereas experienced scholars write with the expectation of publication, undergraduates frequently write for one another or for the instructor. Academic writing is not meant to be a *private* activity. Nor can it merely express personal opinion as, for example, an editorial in a newspaper. It will usually present and defend, with evidence, a reasonable answer to an interesting question.

For this reason, academic pieces are almost always organized around **arguments**. Put simply, an argument is the main point that a writer is attempting to convey. As a reader striving to understand the writer's point, your task is to identify the argument. Sometimes this will be done for you in an **abstract**, or summary of the article that appears before the introduction when the piece is published in an academic journal. At other times, you will have to identify the sentence or paragraph in which the writer clearly states her intention in the piece. Such a paragraph can usually be found at the beginning or end of a text—at least, of one in print.

An academic writer should help facilitate the reader's job of locating the main point or argument. An experienced academic writer will usually indicate in the introduction to a book, or in the introductory paragraphs of an article or chapter, what plan of organization will be used to lay out the argument. The **conclusion** and reasons for it may be compressed into one or a few sentences, the **thesis**. The order of ideas in the thesis sentence(s) often parallels the order in which those ideas will be developed in the essay. Look back at Sagan's essay. Where does he clearly tell us what his intention, his argument, is? As we pointed out earlier, Sagan's introductory paragraphs (with their discussion of the "courage" it takes to question "conventional wisdom") prepare us for his conclusion, his real thesis, which appears in the concluding paragraphs: We live in an exciting world, a challenging universe—made all the more challenging because of what is knowable and what is *not* known. Whereas Sagan works gradually toward

**INTERtext**

For more on argument, see Chapter 3, which deals exclusively with the structure and function of arguments, particularly in academic settings. Chapter 5 contains information on arguments involving visuals (such as images, charts, and graphs), and Chapter 7 describes different strategies for combining argument and research, both in print-based texts and for publication on the World Wide Web.

his conclusion and thesis, other writers choose to begin their texts with clear thesis statements.

How can you keep track of a writer's argument? Here's one strategy. If you are reading an electronic copy of an article (or perhaps a classmate's essay), select the text of the conclusion, turn it into boldface print, and **enlarge it one size**. Then locate the reasons that the writer arrived at that conclusion and highlight or underline them. The entire argument will now stand out.

Such digital strategies have their print counterparts. There is no law that says you have to read a book of nonfiction or an article from first paragraph to last, in that order. Many expert readers begin with the concluding paragraph of an article to see where the argument made in it ultimately leads. They might ask themselves, "What evidence must I see before I will accept this conclusion?" Then they go back over the article, using subheadings and topic sentences of paragraphs as a guide to determining how the argument is designed. The reader can then concentrate on the paragraphs that develop and discuss the points that he or she questions most or has some doubts about. Skimming the entire article might be the final step for this reader.

## 5. Academic readers expect stylish and mechanically correct writing.

Keep in mind that there is no *single* version of academic style, even in the traditional genre of the academic essay. Conventions change, and they vary widely among academic fields. The occasional use of first person now allowed in scientific articles is an example. However, some stylistic conventions are fairly common, such as the following:

- Use of Internet abbreviations and so-called emoticons ("smiley faces" and the like) is considered too informal for most academic writing.
- Contractions are considered permissible in any but the most formal writing, but they should not be overused. When spelling out both words makes the style seem stilted or unnatural, using a contraction is acceptable.

- Foreign words that are not common knowledge are usually translated, if the language is not widely known (usually anything beyond elementary French, German, Spanish, or Latin) or if the passage is long.
- Clear expression is highly valued, as is conciseness that omits meaningless or trite words and phrases. At the same time, academic writers do not shy away from complex sentences and advanced vocabulary—provided the meaning is accessible to an educated, curious readership.

Finally, academic readers expect not to be distracted by incorrect spelling, grammar, punctuation, and format; any of these will detract from the writer's credibility as a scholar. Researchers and thinkers, after all, have to handle details meticulously in their work. Failure to do so in a text may raise doubts about the rest of the writer's work.

---

### GUIDELINES FOR STYLE IN ACADEMIC WRITING

How can becoming familiar with academic texts help improve *your* writing in the academy? You might consider keeping these stylistic guidelines in mind. They may be of help in your own academic writing.

- Refine your diction to avoid an overly chatty or conversational tone.
- Present your argument, your main point or thesis, in a "reader-friendly" way—that is, make sure that your reader can clearly identify, in either your introduction or conclusion, the topic you're addressing and the point you're making in your piece.
- Make sure you understand the words you use. Avoid the use of impressive-sounding words if you are not sure what they mean. Using a thesaurus can help you find varied ways of expressing the same idea, but be careful—its use can backfire if you use words from the thesaurus without being certain of their connotations and appropriateness to your context. (Your word processor should have a built-in thesaurus and dictionary.)
- Think about the difference between *abstract* and *concrete* language; it is almost always better to use concrete language unless your topic is abstract.
- Use a wide variety of sentence styles, lengths, constructions, and beginnings. Avoid opening every sentence with "I" or an introductory clause.

- Strive for variety in paragraph openings, organization, length, and emphasis. A short paragraph can underscore or highlight content, but a string of short paragraphs (or very long ones, for that matter) may become irritating to your readers.
- Check for paragraph unity, coherence, and transitions. Are your paragraphs *focused* on a single set of interrelated points? Do you *guide* your reader from one paragraph to another?

---

**BUILDING YOUR VOCABULARY**

When reading academic articles or textbooks, make a *list* of all the words that are new to you. Note the book and page number where you found them on your list. Then *look up* the word and write down its definition. *Review* the list frequently until you remember its meaning. *Test yourself* by returning to the original source and seeing if you now understand its meaning. Expect to add hundreds, even thousands, of words to your vocabulary while you are in college. Keeping a tally by the entry each time you check a definition in a print dictionary will remind you to memorize the word.

---

## Strategies in Academic Writing

Now that you are familiar with some of the conventions of academic writing, let's think about some of the *strategies* favored by academic writers. A large portion of academic writing uses strategies such as *comparison and contrast*, *definition*, *analysis*, or *argument*—or all of these. Let's look at the first three now, saving *argument* for more thorough discussion in Chapter 3.

### Comparison and Contrast

At some point in your college career, you may be asked to **compare and contrast** the theories of knowledge of two philosophers, for example, or the thinking of two theorists on another topic. Differentiating between or among concepts by defining their distinctive characteristics and examining their similarities and differences is an effective way to understand each one better. In an art course, you might be asked to compose an essay comparing the image of humans in the sculpture of Michelangelo to those found in the carvings in cathedrals of the fourteenth century; your task might be to write about their similarities and differences and what these reveal about the concept of the human, or the nature of art, in their respective times.

Looking at an example of the use of comparison and contrast will help demonstrate the usefulness—and effectiveness—of this strategy. In "'Star Wars' Despots vs. 'Star Trek' Populists," science fiction author David Brin compares and contrasts two of the most important sci-fi universes of our time—George Lucas's *Star Wars* galaxy (a long time ago and far, far away) and Gene Roddenberry's *Star Trek* galaxy (through which characters boldly go where no one has gone before). Brin uses comparison and contrast to make a point about these two "mythologies." Can you figure out what his thesis is after reading the following paragraphs, excerpted from Brin's article?

> The differences at first seem superficial. One saga has an air force motif (tiny fighters) while the other appears naval. In "Star Trek," the big ship is heroic and the cooperative effort required to maintain it is depicted as honorable. Indeed, "Star Trek" sees technology as useful and essentially friendly—if at times also dangerous. Education is a great emancipator of the humble (e.g. Starfleet Academy). Futuristic institutions are basically good-natured (the Federation), though of course one must fight outbreaks of incompetence and corruption. Professionalism is respected, lesser characters make a difference and henchmen often become brave whistle-blowers—as they do in America today.
>
> In "Star Trek," when authorities are defied, it is in order to overcome their mistakes or expose particular villains, not to portray all institutions as inherently hopeless. Good cops sometimes come when you call for help. Ironically, this image *fosters* useful criticism of authority, because it suggests that any of us can gain access to our flawed institutions, if we are determined enough—and perhaps even fix them with fierce tools of citizenship.
>
> By contrast, the oppressed "rebels" in "Star Wars" have no recourse in law or markets or science or democracy. They can only choose sides in a civil war between two wings of the same genetically superior royal family. They may not meddle or criticize. As Homeric spear-carriers, it's not their job.

> In teaching us how to distinguish good from evil, Lucas prescribes judging by looks: Villains wear Nazi helmets. They hiss and leer, or have red-glowing eyes, like in a Ralph Bakshi cartoon. On the other hand, "Star Trek" tales often warn against judging a book by its cover—a message you'll also find in the films of Steven Spielberg, whose spunky everyman characters delight in reversing expectations and asking irksome questions.
>
> Above all, "Star Trek" generally depicts heroes who are only about 10 times as brilliant, noble and heroic as a normal person, prevailing through cooperation and wit, rather than because of some inherited godlike transcendent greatness. Characters who do achieve godlike powers are subjected to ruthless scrutiny. In other words, "Trek" is a prototypically American dream, entranced by notions of human improvement and a progress that lifts all. Gene Roddenberry's vision loves heroes, but it breaks away from the elitist tradition of princes and wizards who rule by divine or mystical right.
>
> By contrast, these are the *only* heroes in the "Star Wars" universe.

**HYPERtext**

You can read the entire text of Brin's essay at *Salon*:
**http://www.salon.com/ent/movies/feature/1999/06/15/brin_main/**.

Clearly, for Brin, *Star Trek* offers us a more compellingly complex vision of the future than the storybook world of *Star Wars* (which is perhaps why Lucas's story takes place a "long time ago"). Specifically, *Star Trek*, for Brin at least, seems more "democratic"—at least more so than the *Star Wars* galaxy, in which "princes and wizards . . . rule by divine or mystical right." For Brin, this comparison and contrast serves an important purpose: it highlights key differences in two major science fiction series that have captured the imaginations of many adults and youth, and he points out how those differences reflect two divergent world views. He also uses the contrast to underscore the more attractive "democratic" features of the *Star Trek* universe, as opposed to the "elitism" of the *Star Wars* galaxy. Using comparison and contrast thus allows Brin to analyze these series and draw out an interpretation that we might not have come to if we had simply examined one "universe" or the other by itself.

## your turn

Think again about Brin's use of comparison and contrast, and compose an e-mail message to him in which you state why you agree or disagree with his interpretation. You might consider challenging his use of comparison and contrast in this particular case, especially if you disagree with him. For instance, Brin doesn't really dwell on the many similarities between *Star Wars* and *Star Trek*. What might the similarities tell us? Or you could consider *extending* his use of contrast to describe and interpret the *Star Wars* and *Star Trek* universes. Consider e-mailing your comments to Brin after you've had a chance to think about them and receive feedback from your peers.

## Definition

**Definition** of terms or concepts, especially new concepts, is often a key strategy in academic writing. It may include *etymological, historical, analytical, functional, operational*, and *descriptive* approaches to defining a key word, a significant term, or a provocative concept. You can probably think of numerous hotly contested words in our vocabulary—such as *moral, natural,* and even *legal.* What do these words mean, and how should they be used? Such words are frequently cause for much debate.

Discussing, analyzing, and defining terms can involve a number of strategies. For example, an *etymological* definition may be developed by giving the word's etymology, or an account of its origins and changing forms. A *historical* definition would include an account of how the meaning has changed over a period of time. The *Oxford English Dictionary,* the ultimate reference source for the English language (the latest edition comprises 22 huge volumes), includes examples of words quoted in historical sources to show their use contextually in different eras. *Analytical* definitions break down a concept and examine each part of it. An *operational* definition explains how something works, such as a machine or a process. A *functional* definition explains how something is used. A *descriptive* definition employing examples may be used to show the different forms a thing may take. An expanded definition may include all or some of these, as appropriate. When a word is capable of being defined many ways, the writer may *stipulate* which definition will be employed in the piece, or in the argument, to avoid confusion with other possible definitions. Another useful technique is *negation*, or stating what a thing is *not* or what a word does *not* refer to.

As an example of how complex such definitions can become, take a look at the following definitions of the word *shoe*, based on the strategies we've just described:

*Logical:* A protective covering for the foot.
*Etymological:* Word comes from Old English *scoh*.
*Historical:* Used in most societies from prehistoric times; earliest shoes were braided grass; Roman designs revealed social status; shoes and boots were considered the same until modern times; Native Americans wore moccasins; new versions include pool slippers and athletic shoes.
*Analytical:* Leather or synthetic upper with laces, Velcro, thong, or fitted enclosure to hold it to the foot; protective bottom surface made of leather, plastic, rubber, or other tough materials, may have fur lining in cold countries.
*Operational:* Protects foot by putting a tough surface between sole of foot and rough surfaces, cushioning the foot from striking pavement, insulating against poison ivy, defending against clumsy dance partners.
*Functional:* Used to protect foot from temperature extremes and dangerous surfaces, to display social status and wealth, to attract or repel potential life partners.
*Descriptive:* Sandals, boots (ski, hiking, cowboy, hunting), runners, flip-flops, stiletto heels, pumps, flats, tennis, zori, thongs, moccasins, wooden geta, raised or reinforced heels (stilettos, flats, wedgies), snowshoes, plastic, metal, wood, leather, air-cushioned, padded.
*Stipulative:* Let's stick to horseshoes here!
*Negational:* Not a sock or stocking.

As you can see, each kind of definition offers us a different way of thinking about the same thing—in this case, shoes!

How does an academic writer use definition in a longer work, such as an essay or academic Web text? You can catch a glimpse of definition at work at the end of Sagan's essay "Can We Know the Universe? Reflections on a Grain of Salt." In that piece, Sagan asks us to consider what can be known scientifically—and what cannot. In the concluding paragraph, reproduced here, the author uses a definition—in this case, of the universe itself—to help close his discussion:

> For myself, I like a universe that includes much that is unknown and, at the same time, much that is knowable. A universe in which everything is known would be static and dull, as boring as the heaven of some weak-minded theologians. A universe that is unknowable is no fit place for a thinking being. The ideal universe for us is one very much like the universe we inhabit. And I would guess that this is not really much of a coincidence.

For Sagan, the universe is defined as that which is, in part at least, not known but *knowable*—in which we, as curious, questioning beings, can exercise our intelligence on the parts that are *not* known. With such a definition, Sagan attempts to answer his earlier question: ". . . to what extent can we *really* know the universe around us?" Sagan offers us an answer by asking us to reconsider our definition of the universe—as a place ideally suited for beings, such as ourselves, who are curious, who want to experience the joys of exploration and discovery. Experiencing such joy means, however, that there must be something unknown, something to discover! Such a redefinition of the universe also helps us understand the initial definition of science that Sagan offers in the essay's first sentence: "Science is a way of thinking much more than it is a body of knowledge." Many people think that science is what is already known, the *facts* of our existence; but Sagan suggests that we need to reconsider such a definition of science, thinking of it instead as an attitude, an openness to discovery and exploration. We might think of this essay, "Can We Know the Universe? Reflections on a Grain of Salt," as one that explores the definition of science: what exactly *is* science, or scientific knowledge?

## your turn

Like *health, freedom,* or *justice, nature* is a concept that can mean different things to different people—depending on how it's defined. To explore the diverse meanings of this complex term, develop an introductory section for an essay defining the concept of *nature.* As part of your research, look at the entry for *nature* in the *Oxford English Dictionary.* Read through all the definitions, then choose one as the subject of a short paper. In your introduction, state the specific definition you're going to explore and why you were drawn to it. In subsequent paragraphs, write about the strengths and weaknesses of the definition you have chosen. For each strength and weakness, provide an example to clarify your thinking. You might also consider comparing and contrasting the definition with other, similar definitions of *nature.* For instance, you could search several online dictionaries and evaluate various definitions given. Finally, in your conclusion, assess the definition you've been writing about. Can you come up with a better one? Discuss this possibility in your paper.

**HYPER**text

"Your Dictionary" at **http://www.yourdictionary.com/** offers a wealth of information about words. Dictionaries of sign languages, including **http://www.bconnex.net/~randys/**, among many others, are also useful and fascinating studies of how people communicate in a variety of ways.

## Analysis

**Analysis**, one of the most significant hallmarks of academic writing, involves breaking a subject down into its component parts and then examining each of them, usually to make some sort of evaluative claim or decision. This technique may be used in the process of defining a concept or exploring a complex idea. Frequently, and in the best works of analysis, the writer will analyze something on the basis of his or her expertise in a field so that the writer can make comparisons and contrasts with other items or can make an evaluation based on a specialized frame of reference. In the discipline of literary study, for example, scholars and students give detailed examinations of literary works in order to learn how the original author worked, and to understand how literary texts communicate and make meaning. Of course, the methods of analysis will vary among disciplines; as you choose and become competent in your major field of study, you will learn the methods most widely used in your field.

In general, though, analysis involves looking at the many components of something and discussing how they work—or do not work—together. For instance, think of a review of a movie as a simple form of analysis. In a movie review, a writer examines various aspects of a film, such as the quality of acting, the strengths of the script, the use of special effects, and the ability of a director to pull together these components to create a compelling cinematic experience. The point of looking at each component is to examine and analyze specific strengths and weaknesses. Such an analysis also helps us understand how something complex, like a film, actually works.

## WRITING SPOTLIGHT

### Stephen Jay Gould on *Jurassic Park*

Speaking of film, let's look at an example of how an academic might approach a film. In the following short essay, Stephen Jay Gould analyzes the popular film *Jurassic Park* from his academic point of view—namely, as a biologist. Note how Gould clearly explains what he's going to do in the piece and how he provides interesting examples to support his ideas. Because this is primarily a work of *analysis*, you should note what its main purpose is: to examine a particular item (in this case, a film), look at its constituent parts, and discuss them from Gould's viewpoint as a scientist.

---

### Jurassic Park

Stephen Jay Gould

The deepest messages often lie in apparent trivialities—for example, in dialogue regarded as too insignificant to scrutinize for error or inconsistency. For me, the most revealing moment in *Jurassic Park* occurs early in the

Excerpt from "Jurassic Park" by Stephen Jay Gould in *Past Imperfect, History According to the Movies* by Mark C. Carnes.

film, as paleontologist Alan Grant, at his western field site, discourses to his assistants on the genealogical relationships of dinosaurs and birds, as illustrated by a skeleton, just unearthed, of the small dinosaur *Velociraptor*. Grant correctly points to several anatomical features that suggest a link—hollow bones and a birdlike pelvis, for example. He then ends his discourse with the supposed clincher: "Even the word *raptor* means 'bird of prey.'"

Consider the absurdity of this last pronouncement. First, Grant is flat wrong. *Raptor*, from the Latin *rapere* ("to seize," or "to take by force"), is an old English word, traced by the *Oxford English Dictionary* to the early seventeenth century and first applied to humans, not birds, in its literal meaning. (The word *rape*, now restricted to sexual assault, has the same root and originally referred to abduction by force. Titian's *The Rape of Europa* records Jupiter's seizure and transport of a woman, not whatever happened afterward.) Later zoologists borrowed *raptor* as a technical name for large carnivorous birds (just as *primates*—defined as the category for monkeys, apes, and humans—postdates usage of the same word—meaning "first," in the sense of preeminent—for church leaders).

More important, Grant's error lies in confusing a human construction—and an arbitrary one at that—with an empirical reality. The word is not the thing: the representation not the reality (though we can view only through representation—and there's the rub). The bones of *Velociraptor* speak of relationships with birds; the name that we bestowed on the creature is only our fabrication. . . .

The special effects of living dinosaurs, in particular, are spectacular and represent—in a point that should interest historians of technology—the cusp of an epochal transition between the new frontier of computer-generated images and older methods that relied on manipulation of objects (humans inside *Velociraptor* costumes, robotics based on hydraulic machinery, and, above all, the granddaddy of monster movie techniques, pioneered by Willis O'Brien in *King Kong*, stop-motion photography on small-scale models). Only three major scenes use computer animation, and even these represent a late decision, for usable techniques of adequate realism did not exist when Steven Spielberg began filming and became available only as the movie neared completion. Nonetheless, I was awestruck when I learned that actor Sam Neill (as Alan Grant) and the two children reacted to nothing on the film's set and that the stunning herd of charging *Gallimimus* dinosaurs were computer images added later!

I could list a compendium of factual errors from a professional paleontologist's viewpoint, starting with the observation that most dinosaurs depicted in *Jurassic Park* date from the later Cretaceous period. I once asked

Michael Crichton why he had placed *Tyrannosaurus*, a Cretaceous dinosaur, on the cover of the book version. He replied, with absolutely honorable candor: "Ohmigod, I never thought of that; we were just fooling around with images, and that one looked good."

Instead, I would rather concentrate on the film's two "great" errors, for these faults share two properties that motivate this book and operate on sufficiently grand scale to preclude pettiness: they pervade the movie and constitute a flawed core of its being (and of so many others in the genre). These errors belong to the juicy and informative class of faults so well characterized by the economist Pareto as expansive and informative: "Give me a fruitful error any time, full of seeds, bursting with its own corrections. You can keep your sterile truths for yourself."

1. Insufficient recognition of nature's complexity. If anyone on this planet remains unaware of *Jurassic Park*'s plot line, let me epitomize: Entrepreneur sets up theme park of living dinosaurs. He extracts dinosaur DNA from blood preserved inside mosquitoes trapped and fossilized in amber (and thus shielded from decay over a minimum of 65 million years, since the extinction of dinosaurs). His scientists amplify the DNA, put together complete sequences, inject the code into eggs, and induce embryological development. Dinosaurs of many species are thus revivified (females only, as a protection against uncontrolled breeding). The park's defenses do not work for various reasons rooted in human scheming and technical malfeasance, and mayhem of all sorts results.

The scenario is clever (it had been discussed as fantasy by several scientists before Crichton wrote his book and constitutes a marvelous and legitimate device for science fiction). However, we should understand why such revivification is impossible—for nonacknowledgment of this reason promotes one of the worst stereotypes about science and its role in our culture.

We should distinguish between two very different claims for "impossibility" often made by scientists. The first (impossible to reach the moon, impossible to split the atom) records lack of imagination and only embarrasses those prognosticators who spoke too definitely. But another species of impossibility—the true and permanent disappearance of historical records—seems ineluctable because the only conceivable data have not survived. If, for some reason, I wanted a list of every rebel crucified with Spartacus along the Appian Way (wasn't Kirk Douglas great in that scene?), I could not acquire such a record because it doesn't now exist (and probably never did). Historical items are not formed predictably under laws of nature; they are contingent configurations that, if lost, cannot be reconstituted.

Dinosaur DNA falls into the category of Spartacus's list, not into the domain of predictably reconstructible consequences of nature's laws. Someday we may (one dubious report says we already have) recover short fragments of dinosaur DNA. (One complete gene, for example, has been recovered from a 20-million-year-old magnolia leaf.) But remember that an entire organism contains thousands of different genes all necessary for revivification. DNA is a very fragile and decomposable compound; coding sequences can survive for geological ages only in the most favorable circumstances, and I see little prospect that anything close to a complete set of dinosaur genes could be preserved under any conditions. Moreover, the situation is even more hopeless—even if a complete set of genes could be reconstituted, an embryo still could not form, for development requires the proper environment in a maternal egg. Embryology cannot proceed without a complex set of maternal gene products already in place within the egg. So the scientists of Jurassic Park would not only require the complete dinosaur code but also have to know the maternal genes needed to produce proper proteins and enzymes within the egg—thus heaping impossibility upon impossibility. . . .

2. Stereotypes of science and history. Hollywood seems to know only one theme in treating the power of science—hubris, otherwise rendered (in old-style language) as "man must not go where God (or nature's laws) did not intend." The movies, throughout scores of versions, have distorted Mary Shelley's moral tale about the responsibility of creators toward their "offspring" into a story of technology transgressing the boundaries of its legitimate operation (not a word can be found in Shelley about the dangers of science or technology; nor did she or her atheistical husband discourse on what God did or did not license us to do).

Given the weight of such an overbearing tradition, the film of *Jurassic Park* inevitably took this same hackneyed course: The theme-park proprietors shouldn't have remade the dinosaurs (even though the technology to do so had been developed) because such a project violates nature's intended course—and human malefactors must therefore pay the price. In the film, mathematician Ian Malcolm plays the role of conscience for the canonical Hollywood posture. When John Hammond, the park's creator, explains his method for revivifying dinosaurs, Malcolm chides him: "The lack of humility before nature that's being displayed here staggers me." When Hammond asks whether Malcolm would oppose revivification of the California condor from preserved DNA should humans drive this great bird to extinction, Malcolm makes no objection because we would then only be reversing an unnatural act of human depredation. Why, then, object to dinosaurs, Hammond asks. Malcolm gives the pap answer: "Dinosaurs had their shot, and nature selected them for extinction." In other words, don't mess with the natural and intended order of evolutionary succession and progress (an inconsistent point, I hasten to add, because the revivified dinosaurs can beat any mammal in the park, including *Homo sapiens*). . . .

---

As you read through Gould's piece, you probably noted the clarity with which the author lays out his discussion; he tells us *exactly* what he's going to do and how he's going to analyze *Jurassic Park*. Specifically, he says that he wants to "concentrate on the film's two 'great' errors": "Insufficient recognition of nature's complexity" and "Stereotypes of science and history." Gould can undertake this analysis because he has a particular **frame of reference** from which he can think critically about the film.

What do you think about Gould's analysis? Do you agree? Even if you enjoyed the film (and one gets the sense the Gould, too, might have enjoyed *Jurassic Park* as an entertaining diversion), can you still appreciate his analysis? Bringing our individual knowledge to bear on the world around us is a hallmark of both analysis in particular and academic writing in general. How might *you* analyze a motion picture or television show on the basis of knowledge you are acquiring and developing? For instance, what might a *sociological* or *psychological* analysis of *Jurassic Park* look like?

## WRITING SPOTLIGHT

### A Student's Analysis of an Advertisement

To help us understand how analysis can be applied to a variety of rhetorical situations, take a look at the following brief essay, in which a student writer examines a U.S. Navy recruitment ad. (Check out the official United States Navy Web site to view some ads about joining the Navy: **http://www.navy.com/**) Note how this student writer, Katherine, first introduces the topic, summarizes the content of the ad, draws our attention to particular aspects of the advertisement, and then suggests a possible interpretation of the ad as a whole.

Gavin 1

Maureen Gavin

Robert Murdock

15 ENGL 101 022

Essay Three: Ad Analysis

19 November 2003

Join the U.S. Navy Today

In a recent edition of *Rolling Stone* magazine, I came across an advertisement for the U.S. Navy. This ad appeared in the May 29th, 2003 edition of the magazine. *Rolling Stone* is traditionally known as a magazine read by young people. People in high schools as well as college-age students make up the majority of readers who buy this periodical. The magazine examines stories about music, fashion, and culture that relate to a younger audience. Some articles in the edition I chose included "Campus Music Bust," "Madonna Foiled," and "Alkaline Trio Tattoo You." These articles have an obvious appeal to younger people, for they cover music on college campuses, pop music news, and the tattoo culture of young people. Older adults would not typically find these articles as points of interest.

The advertisement I chose obviously sells recruitment for the U.S. Navy. It advertises the Navy as an alternative for the usual college experience. It also gives the Web site and phone number to obtain further information and opportunities through the U.S. Navy. This ad appears clearly to the reader, but this is only on the surface.

The advertisement has many implications that may not be seen right away by the reader. The image of two helicopters dominates the photograph. The entire ad is overlaid with white grid lines. These lines give the reader the

Gavin 2

feeling of something technological, like a radar screen. This idea is extended through the use of color. Blue and green tint give the ad the look of a computer screen or radar image. This implies that the U.S. Navy offers experience in advanced technological skills. The helicopters are in motion; their blades are fuzzy, implying that they are in motion. This image is coupled perfectly with the text, which states, "Navy, accelerate your life." Just like the blades on the helicopters are moving, so will your life if you enlist. The text then gives selling points of enlisting. The advertisement asks, "How many colleges have their own landing strip?" The answer to this question would probably be none. This implies that joining the Navy is a unique, even exciting experience. Readers of the magazine would be of the age when most people enlist in the military or go to college. The ad invites readers to "See the world, earn credit for college and experience adventure you just can't find on any other campus." This statement implies that your Navy experience will be one of action and fun, and will also help you later in life since you would be earning college credit as you "see the world." This would appeal to young people since many young people want excitement, travel, and the opportunity to further their educations.

From this ad we can learn the techniques used by the American government to recruit people for the armed forces. They make enlisting something that is exciting and interesting. They are not luring young people by suggesting that they serve their country or be patriotic. They suggest instead that people can learn about technology or computers by enlisting. Most importantly, the U.S. Navy makes the reader feel like joining would be a unique experience. I notice, however, that they

Gavin 3

chose to write only about the positive side of enlisting. They did not show people dying or going through extreme training. In fact, it sounds more like a good vacation. Adventure and travel looks like a good deal, especially if you could earn credit for college while you do it. If someone unfamiliar with our culture saw this ad, they might think of the armed forces as a college or club of some kind. While I can understand why an advertiser wouldn't promote the less attractive aspects of his/her product, equating military service with education is an implication that many young people might not notice until it was too late.

After carefully explaining and examining the ad, Katherine begins to ask *critical* questions about the ad—questions that point out what's missing in the advertisement, such as a realistic portrayal of potential dangers encountered during military service, or the rigors of military training. As she points out, the advertisement makes it seem as though joining the Navy is comparable to going on a vacation. Such an association deserves critical attention, and Katherine begins to provide that in her analysis. How might you extend this analysis, asking additional critical questions?

## Academic Writing in the Digital World: E-mail and Discussion Lists

Electronic communications platforms, such as e-mail and discussion lists, have also found a place in the academic world. Many scholars use them

**HYPER**text

Yahoo! Groups offers 30,000 e-mail-based discussion groups, including numerous forums focusing on a variety of scholarly and academic pursuits: **http://groups.yahoo.com/**.

frequently to communicate with one another, share research findings, solicit critique and feedback, and disseminate their work to the larger public. For instance, it is not uncommon for colleagues in the same department, in offices along the same hallway, or even next door to each other to communicate by *e-mail.* They can have the same conversation even if one of them is at home or if they are using their computers at different times. The ease of e-mail communication has meant that scholars are collaborating as never before. For example, although the authors of this book live over a thousand miles apart, they could collaborate on such a large project by exchanging e-mail (containing notes, questions, and drafts of chapters) on a daily basis. Similar correspondence is increasingly taking place between teachers and students, with writing students sending their instructors drafts of their work for commentary and critique.

Moreover, the opportunity to converse with others on e-mail *discussion lists* is changing the way members of academic communities interact. Now members of a scholarly community can confer with many colleagues—often around the world—about a multitude of issues and ideas. You too can use these lists to become familiar with the debates currently circulating in any number of scholarly (or popular) fields. In fact, one of the primary reasons for joining a discussion list is to have the opportunity to talk about subjects that interest you with people you might never meet because of their geographic distance from you.

Perhaps more important, because discussion lists are generally grouped around certain topics or subjects, participants have the opportunity to debate points of interest, to share alternative views, and to inspire one another with their ideas and opinions. Discussion lists offer participants the chance to experience online community and group energy focused on subjects of interest. They can provide a wonderful forum through which to explore subjects for your academic papers and research projects. The Book and Writing Club at **http://groups.yahoo.com/group/thebookandwritingclub/**, for example, offers a lively exchange of ideas and thoughts about literature and writing. Or, if you want to know more about *Star Trek*, you could join a discussion list whose participants are interested in exploring a variety of aspects of this fascinating science fiction universe. Invariably, because of the number of contributors, you will discover and discuss aspects of *Star Trek* that you never would have thought about on your own. Other lists are much more academically inclined; their primary purpose is to exchange information, discuss academic issues, or debate points of argument. The List of Lists, sponsored by the Association of Internet Researchers Project, at **http://www.aoir.org/list.php**, offers a long list of such academic lists, including several focused on writing.

Instructors routinely set up e-mail discussion lists for their students to use in their courses. You may already be using one in this or another course. Instructors may invite guest experts, classes of colleagues in the same program, or classes from other institutions to participate in discussions with your class. Students writing on a class list may live many miles from one another but still have a chance to function as a community of thinkers and writers. They can focus on each other's words and thoughts, undistracted by physical presences. Getting to know each other *as writers*, we think, is an appropriate activity for a writing class. In this book, the questions for online discussion throughout each chapter suggest ways of using these lists, but you and your instructor may think of many others.

If you join a discussion list, keep in mind that you are not required to participate. You should study the archives often kept online, or "lurk"; that is, you should simply read the discussions for a week or two to learn what is customary in that forum before making a contribution. When you are ready to participate, take care not to become a list "hog" by cluttering other people's inboxes with a host of messages. Some lists have strict rules about what members can post. For example, TWAIN-L, for serious students of Mark Twain, requests that no one post a question who has not already searched all the major printed scholarly sources of information on Mark Twain.

Remember, the goal of writing on discussion lists is to communicate, and accepted styles of communication can vary widely. On some academic lists the occasional use of uncapitalized letters in names or colloquial diction is acceptable, whereas on others, strict propriety is the rule. It's just common sense that too many irregularities, misspelled words, or missing phrases distract the reader, who can usually be counted on to be reading very fast. The asynchronous nature of e-mail allows you time to give your posts quick proofreading, and doing so is a good idea. The abbreviated style often used in personal e-mail (e.g., "i am 2 late 4 U") is generally not appropriate on an academic list, or even a public one such as those sponsored by the *New York Times* for discussion of editorials and issues in the news.

### JOINING A LIST—SOME HINTS

Depending on how you set your preferences when you join a group, you can either experience the list as a "listserv", with daily e-mails or e-mail sent in digest (condensed) form, or read postings in a *message board* format. If your inbox fills up too quickly, or if you belong to several active lists, consider signing up to receive your messages in *digest form*.

### TWO IMPORTANT E-WRITING TERMS

*Synchronous* (from the Greek: *syn* = same, *chronos* = time) *conversation*: Participants contribute *simultaneously*, as with face-to-face classroom discussions or in telephone conversations, allowing the give-and-take of dialog. Possible online versions of synchronous communication include MOOs (Multiuser Object-Oriented Systems), chat rooms, and conferencing software such as DIWE InterChange.

**ELECTRONIC**issues

### PARTICIPATING ON DISCUSSIONS LISTS

As you've probably been discovering, even forums as seemingly "informal" as discussion lists are actually writing situations, with their own conventions, expectations, and preferred styles. Consider the following guidelines when participating on a list or even sending an e-mail to someone you do not know very well:

1. "Lurk" a bit first on a list; that is, before posting for the first time, see how people "talk" on the list, paying attention to content, form, and other stylistic expectations. In general, familiarize yourself with the conventions of *any* writing situation before just "jumping in."
2. Before sending a post, save it as a "draft" and then come back to it in a few hours or even the next day. Reconsider what you wrote and make sure you are being appropriate. This is particularly good advice if you have to send a professional e-mail to someone you do not know.
3. Use emoticons and other Internet abbreviations *only* if they are allowed or expected.

*Asynchronous conversation*: Participants contribute at *different* times, as when callers make a series of calls to one another's answering machines, or when a speech is delivered to an audience that must remain silent and listen to the speaker. E-mail and discussion or message boards permit asynchronous communication.

## your turn

As a group, preferably in a synchronous written discussion, develop a group of protocols for an academic discussion list. If you disagree, explain your reasoning to one another until you can reach general agreement. Print out the protocols. Then form an e-mail discussion list for your class and post a welcome message that every participant will get automatically when signing up. Have the list owner (probably the instructor) post your agreed-on protocols in the introductory message.

## *Useful Links*

Many resources online can help you understand and practice some of the conventions of academic writing. For instance, check out the following sites:

- The University of Toronto has a wonderful Writing Centre site with a special section on academic writing that includes specific material on "reading and using sources": **http://www.utoronto.ca/writing/advise.html.**
- The Longman English Pages have a special section called "Subject Areas" that offers numerous links for students who want to know more about writing in a variety of disciplines, including the humanities, social sciences, natural sciences, and business: **http://www.abacon.com/compsite/subjects/index.html.** The links included on this site take students to a number of useful resources and sites that model academic writing in specific disciplines.
- Finally, Dartmouth offers good "tips for newcomers" hoping to discover more about academic writing—very much worth a look: **http://www.dartmouth.edu/~compose/student/ac_paper/what.html.**

## *Additional Writing Activities*

1. Compose a letter to one of your former high school teachers or to someone you know who is still in high school. In it, explain as best you can what "academic writing" is. You might refer to some of the conventions, expectations, and strategies that we have discussed in this chapter, but you should also rely on your own growing body of experience with academic writing. Discuss and analyze some of the writing assignments you have encountered. Consider some of the reading you've had to do. What do these experiences suggest to you about academic reading and writing? How can you communicate what you know so that the high school student will both understand and be better prepared for the challenges of college reading and writing?
2. Find two Web sites—one that you would consider an "academic" site and another that you would consider designed for more "popular" consumption. Compare and contrast the two, pointing out how each is appropriately designed considering its intended audience. You might note, for instance, the varying degree of formality in the referencing of sources, the different use of graphics and images, and the tone of language used. How do all of these play a part in crafting texts for different purposes?
3. You have probably composed a piece, either for another course or earlier in your life, that qualifies as "academic writing." If so, take another look at this piece and write an analysis of it, pointing out where you followed or broke the conventions we have discussed in this chapter. If you were to revise the piece now, what would you change, and why?

PART two

# Writing Situations

CHAPTER 3
Fighting Words? Understanding Argument

CHAPTER 4
New Worlds, New Ways: Contemporary Argument

CHAPTER 5
More than Just Words Here: Visual Literacy, Visual Argument

CHAPTER 6
Navigating a World of Information: Conducting Research

CHAPTER 3

# Fighting Words? Understanding Argument

When you see or hear the word *argument*, do you think of yelling or fighting, of people with hair flying in disarray and angry expressions on their faces, screaming obscenities at each other? *Argument* often has such negative connotations.

You might also think of lawyers doing verbal battle in a court of law, attempting to persuade a jury or judge to convict or acquit. Theirs is without doubt a common and important use of argument. One does not need to be an attorney, however, to learn how to read and use argument effectively. In the course of everyday life, from the conversations we hear around us to the reading of academic writing, we are exposed to many arguments. To understand and work with them, we need to be able to size them up and discard those that do not meet our standards.

Indeed, much of academic reading and writing involves the creation or analysis of **argument**. To read an article presenting conclusions based on research, whether in science, history, sociology, or another field, or to comprehend an essay discussing an idea in the humanities, one needs to be able to understand the ways that arguments are constructed, presented, and evaluated. Scholars constantly use argument as a means of putting ideas on the table to invite analysis and critique. In an academic context, argument has nothing to do with fighting, snarling, or an ugly brawl. Rather, academic argument is an ongoing discussion about important issues, with scholars and writers debating a wide range of topics.

## Critical Reading and Argument

Critical readers learn to look for the arguments in almost everything of an academic nature that they read. We say "almost everything" because not all writing contains arguments. A narrative of events such as a travelogue or a diary, for example, may be simply a record of what has happened or of what one has done or seen. As soon as someone records the same events differently, however, there is food for argument, although neither account may constitute an argument by itself. Let's look at an example.

At the battlefield near Hastings in Sussex, England, where William the Conqueror's forces killed King Harold and took command of England in 1066 C.E., visitors may take a self-guided tour around the famous battlefield. As they walk, they can listen to a recorded commentary and read signs that contain diary accounts of the battle from two perspectives: that of the invading Normans and their sympathizers, and that of the native Anglo-Saxons loyal to Harold. Rather than interpreting the events according to either side's perspective, the designers of the tour let visitors compare accounts and develop their own interpretations of the events. It is a deft trick on their part to avoid arguing for one point of view or the other. Instead, the visitor becomes a historiographer who must decide whether to take either account literally, what to consider about the context from within which each writer was recording the events, and what, all things considered, probably happened at Hastings.

Reading argument in an academic context may be new to you, but encountering argument in general is not. Attempts to persuade bombard you constantly. Advertisers, political candidates, and nonprofit organizations use the media, billboards, and mail campaigns to get their messages to you: "Buy my product," "Elect me," "Give to my cause." Even with filters, unsolicited messages pop up on your computer screen or appear in your e-mail inbox with subject lines asking you to "call Suzi" or "get 4 DVDs for 25 cents each," coaxing you first to open and then read the message before you delete it. Most people cannot possibly pay attention to all the *appeals* or *urgent requests* that come their way via print media, TV, radio, and now through their computers. How does one decide which ones to read? Once read, which ones deserve a positive response, such as a purchase or a donation?

Although they surround us, persuasive appeals per se are not necessarily a bad thing. Advertisements educate as well as attempt to persuade. For instance, you may be grateful to discover a new product that meets one of your needs. You may be happy to learn more about candidates for office before choosing one to vote for, or be delighted to find a nonprofit group pledged to working for your ideals. You may want to give both of them your support.

An experienced critical reader can quickly size up these appeals by applying techniques practiced in academic reading and making quick, efficient decisions about their quality. Such a reader might ask:

- Who is attempting to persuade me? A political party? An advertiser? A group with a cause?
- Is this appeal consistent with my ideas, ideals, or beliefs?
- What do they want from me? My money? My vote?
- Why do they want it? What motivates them to ask something of me?
- What are they assuming about me? In other words, why is this particular attempt to persuade focused on *me*?
- Are they making primarily an emotional appeal, or are they appealing to my ability to reason?

As you can imagine, not all persuasive attempts are based on carefully considered or "reasonable" thinking. Sometimes, for instance, an advertiser might persuade us to buy something that we don't need or that is actually bad for us. Think of tobacco ads—clearly the appeal is designed to persuade you to buy something that physicians have deemed harmful. As an educated, critical reader in our media-saturated society, it is important to be able to assess appeals and attempts at persuasion. This ability helps one avoid being gullible or too easily swayed to act in a particular way without good reason. Even in your academic career, you will face mountains of papers (books, magazines, newspapers) and a steady stream of online communication (e-mails, Web sites, chat rooms, and instant messages), and you must determine what is worth further attention. You must be able to wade through the sea of information to find the islands firm enough to stand on. You must be able to figure out how a writer is working to convince you and decide whether the reasoning employed actually leads to the conclusion the author claims it does—that is, whether the argument is *valid*. You must also decide whether the reasons given are good enough to support the conclusion, or whether someone is trying to sway you to a position without giving you enough—or *solid* enough—evidence.

Being able to spot techniques a writer is using gives you a handle on ways to evaluate the argument and helps you differentiate between appeals that provide sufficient, representative evidence and cogent reasoning and those that do not. For instance, to be able to evaluate the quality of campaign rhetoric, letters to the editor, and sales pitches, or to sort through editorial opinion and decide whether an appeal for a vote or donation is consistent with your principles or will fulfill a purpose you think worthwhile, you as a reader must be able to see through the clouds of words and find the point being made. At the same time, you must evaluate the support and reasoning used to get to it. Understanding how to use these techniques will give you the advantage of being able to use them more effectively in academic, professional, and civic life.

In this chapter, we will concern ourselves primarily with "classical" approaches to argument, and our specific focus will be on persuasive writing that includes an appeal to the intellect, using reasoning to arrive at a conclusion; this is called **argumentation**, and it has many uses in academic and civic life. We will also consider argumentative texts that appeal to the emotions and attempt to persuade by playing on or provoking certain feelings. Although we will maintain that most *academic* arguments rely on strategies that use reasoning, we cannot overlook appeals to the "logic of the emotions," which also play their part in making arguments.

Learning to analyze persuasive writing, especially the argument it contains, is ideal preparation for learning to write persuasively yourself, using argument to achieve your goals. We will look at ways of reading persuasive texts and sizing up the arguments embedded in them. Your computer, with its networked connection to a whole digital world of information, will provide many examples. We might also see how network technology is affecting the ways we attempt to appeal to and persuade one another, including the way we argue.

## Some Elements of Argument

### Pathos, Ethos, and Logos

To start thinking critically about persuasion and argument, we need to begin at a point far removed from contemporary computer technology—the ancient world of the Greeks. The most influential writer on rhetorical practice in Western society has been Aristotle, who set forth his views on the art of spoken and written discourse over 2,300 years ago in his *Rhetoric*. Classically trained writers, who include most of those in the European-based intellectual world, have employed his techniques since that time. In order to read their work, you need to know something about Aristotle's views, both on persuasive writing in general and on the system of logic that structured their thinking and analysis of one another's ideas throughout the centuries. Here we introduce you to a few of his most fun-

**HYPERtext**

To find out more about Aristotle, visit the searchable version of W. Rhys Roberts's translation of Aristotle's famous treatise on Lee Honeycutt's site at **http://www.public.iastate.edu/~honeyl/Rhetoric/index.html**. Quotations and citations of section numbers from Aristotle's *Rhetoric* in this chapter are from this site.

damental ideas, but you can find more and even read translations from his original work on the Web. Aristotle identified three primary means of persuasion, each of which a writer may employ in varying degrees to win an audience to the desired position on an issue: *pathos, ethos*, and *logos*.

## Pathos

Aristotle called *appeals to sympathy or emotion*, whether in public speaking or writing, the use of **pathos**. You encounter arguments that rely on pathos on a daily basis. For instance, while Web surfing, have you ever had a message pop up on your screen that alerts you to a "fatal error" or "computer malfunction"? Sometimes, granted, your computer crashes, but many times, if you click on the pop-up, you'll be taken to an advertisement asking you to buy something—such as computer software to prevent crashes. The advertisers have clearly played on your computer-crashing fears to entice you to consider their sales pitch. Some advertising *spam*, or unsolicited e-mail, works in the same way:

The e-mail message doesn't actually tell you anything specific about you or your computer. It is a sales pitch, designed to work on your worst fears of computer viruses. Whereas pathos may be used to achieve positive ends—for example, to bring in donations for a fund to feed children by telling the heartrending story of a starving child or showing photographs of children with distended stomachs and soulful eyes—it can also be used for destructive ends by appealing to hatred, prejudice, or bigotry. Scare tactics are also generally uses of pathos.

A reader, listener, viewer, or Web surfer should be watchful for uses of emotional appeal and recognize them when they are being employed. An anecdote that creates emotional appeal or evokes sympathy can be an effective and appropriate way of introducing a piece written for a popular audience. In academic writing, though, persuasion by emotional appeals usually takes a back seat to appeals to reason, which we'll discuss below.

## Ethos

Another mode of persuasion is to establish the credibility, or *personal character*, of the speaker or writer. This is called establishing **ethos**. In fact, Aristotle considered character to be just about "the most effective means of persuasion" one might possess. As he said,

> Persuasion is achieved by the speaker's personal character when the speech is so spoken as to make us think him credible. We believe good men more fully and more readily than others: this is true generally whatever the question is, and absolutely true where exact certainty is impossible and opinions are divided.
>
> (ARISTOTLE, *RHETORIC*, BOOK I, 1356A)

How do writers and speakers project an ethos that makes them credible? They can tell the audience that they adhere to certain principles, or, better yet, they can have invested years in demonstrating that they do so, and they generally treat their readers or listeners with respect. They also demonstrate their knowledge of the issue by referring to other discussions pertaining to the topic and by providing evidence to support their views.

Advertisers appeal to ethos constantly by hiring celebrities to represent the products they are trying to sell. A best-selling author's endorsement of word-processing software might attract buyers for that program. A respected actor featured in an ad for life insurance, telling you that "you can trust Brothers Insurance, Inc., with your family's future," may influence buyers to purchase insurance from that company because they trust the celebrity's advice. Perhaps the actor has used the life insurance, perhaps not. It's up to the audience to decide what the testimony proves. The personal reputation of a Nobel Peace Prize winner who backs a certain political stance can play a role in public acceptance of that view. By contrast, a candidate for district attorney who has recently been arrested for driving under the influence will have difficulty projecting the ethos needed for election.

Despite Aristotle's admonition that only the contents of one's discourse should be considered in determining ethos (that is, that a speaker must stand or fall on the basis of *what* he says), in practical terms today, with media sleuths and instantaneous transmission of information about public figures available via the Internet, one who would sway an audience will find that unethical behavior will harm his/her ethos, literally with lightning speed. You can probably think of several political figures whose careers have been damaged or ended by revelations about personal behavior. Or consider the striking stories in 2001 of allegedly fraudulent accounting practices at large corporations, such as Enron; as soon as news leaked out over the Internet, investors at all levels started pulling their money out of the corporations—some within minutes, it seemed.

In terms of texts, whether printed or electronic, the image a writer presents can severely affect his or her reception by an audience, whether an instructor is looking over a student's homework or an editor a submission. A sloppy manuscript full of mechanical errors can alienate a reader, no matter how brilliant the logic it contains, partly because it may suggest that the writer believes the reader has low standards, or that the *writer* has them. In the care given to writing and presentation, the writer demonstrates respect for self and audience.

Let's look more closely at an example of both ethos and pathos. Take a look at the Web site for PETA—People for the Ethical Treatment of Animals—at **http://www.peta.org/**. This organization's site uses both ethos and pathos fairly effectively.

When we visited the site, we encountered a moving "action alert": "Kittens Crushed at Toyota Plant in Kentucky." The alert is clearly intended to be eye-catching, particularly since the text is positioned adjacent to an image of a cute little kitten. This appeal to pathos, to our emotions, made us want to read more about the mistreatment of animals.

People for Ethical Treatment of Animals PETA Ingrid Newkirk animal rights

Appeals to ethos are apparent in the site's clear design (which allows for easy navigation) and in the extensiveness of its offerings: you can search the site and browse through a number of different categories, including data and statistics about animal cruelty. You are also invited to participate in PETA's various campaigns—a sign that the organization is really willing to provide an outlet for people to express their views on the mistreatment of animals. This is not just an informational Web site; it is a call to action, and PETA wants to convey the seriousness of its mission by inviting you to participate.

At this point, you may be asking yourself a question: Are ethos and pathos sufficient to make a good argument? Granted, the PETA site uses both effectively, but can we trust all of their claims and views? If you have posed these questions to yourself, then you are really beginning to think critically. Although ethos and pathos are important, arguments do not rely on them alone. We'll consider another crucial aspect of argument, *logos*, in a moment, but first, it's your turn.

**HYPERtext**

For other rhetorical terms (beyond *pathos*, *ethos*, and *logos*), check out this online glossary, which contains many useful examples: **http://www.uky.edu/ArtsSciences/Classics/rhetoric.html.**

## your turn

Find letters to the editor, ads, or Web sites in which ethos and pathos are employed as means of persuasion. Examine the ways they are incorporated into the text and share your findings with your classmates, either in face-to-face discussions or via an electronic platform such as a listserv or discussion group.

## your turn again

Major political campaigns, usually held around important election times, also offer opportunities to consider the function of ethos and pathos in appeals, persuasion, and argument. As a class project, try collecting campaign literature, copying and taking notes on a variety of media ads published in print, on television, and on the Web. Even if an election is not imminent, you can study the Web sites of your state's governor, congressional delegates, and state legislators, asking the same questions. Or you may want to invite a speaker to your class. Your local campus probably hosts several different activist groups, such as groups promoting racial equality or gay rights. Inviting speakers from these groups, or even interviewing them, can teach you much about how activists (not just politicians!) attempt to create a sense of ethos and pathos.

During a political campaign, you can also invite one or two people running for election to be guest speakers in your class. If you can bring in opponents in the same race, have them on separate days to give each a chance to speak to you freely, without having to respond to each other. Invite them to introduce themselves so that they can bring up whatever topic they like, and then see what they mention first. While they speak to you, take notes on the ways they project ethos. Do they choose to mention their marriages, divorces,

**NOTE**

During an election campaign, especially if you live in city, candidates are more likely to accept an invitation to your class if they know they can talk to more than a few voters. Before you issue the invitation, consider inviting several classes to meet together.

grandchildren, partners, or girl- and boyfriends? Do they refer to affiliation with a church or to a long career in public service? Why do you think they volunteered information about these aspects of their lives? If they did not, what other information do they give you to convey ethos? Is the ethos projected by each of them very different, or do they seem to cultivate similar images? Discuss their use of ethos after they leave the class, or do so online afterward. See whether members of your class draw similar conclusions and discuss with one another what impressed you the most. Do you think any of the statements by the candidates backfired by creating an impression about themselves different from the one they intended to project?

Here's something specific to watch for. One way some candidates gain credibility through ethos is by treating those with opposing views respectfully, refusing to engage in ad hominem attacks. An **ad hominem** attack is an attempt to discredit one's opponent by attacking his or her character, personality, or personal life, as opposed to commenting on that individual's views. For instance, a politician might raise speculative doubts about his opponent's sexual affairs or presumed sexual impropriety as a way to lure voters away from the opponent. Such attacks generally have nothing to do with the issues being discussed during an election campaign. Such attacks on the character of the opponent, even when insinuated rather than spoken outright, are often used as diversionary tactics to avoid direct discussion of the issues. Mudslinging, however, often backfires, making the slinger look unscrupulous or unethical. Did the candidates engage in ad hominem attacks, or were they careful to avoid these? Have you seen evidence of such attacks in their political ads? If so, you might ask the candidates about them.

If you lack the time or contacts needed to invite such speakers into class, look at campaign Web sites hosted by candidates in the next (or the most recent) political election. Do the candidates provide information about themselves and attempt to use ethos effectively on their campaign Web sites? Compare and contrast sites of candidates opposing each other in the same race. What features of each site elicited your interest in or your approval of the candidate? Which ones had the opposite effect on you? Why? What did you learn about the candidate from the Web sites? What information would you like to have learned that was *not* available on the site? Are the candidates' views on public issues, such as upcoming legislation, stated clearly? How did the candidates use graphics, including photographs of themselves, their families, and their pets, to support verbal arguments made on their sites? Do you think someone else might interpret them differently? How do all of the elements of the site contribute to a candidate's ethos?

## Logos

One way a writer or speaker can show respect for members of an audience is by appealing to their ability to reason—that is, by using **logos**, or **logical argument**. In Aristotle's words, logos is "the proof, or apparent proof, provided by the words of the speech itself" (1356a). Aristotle finds the use of argument, or "rational speech," to be a feature that distinguishes human beings from other animals:

> It is absurd to hold that a man ought to be ashamed of being unable to defend himself with his limbs, but not of being unable to defend himself with speech and reason, when the use of rational speech is more distinctive of a human being than the use of his limbs.
>
> (Aristotle, *Rhetoric*, Book I., 1355b)

But argument is not simply talk. As Aristotle points out, it is "speech and reason." For instance, take another look at the PETA Web site

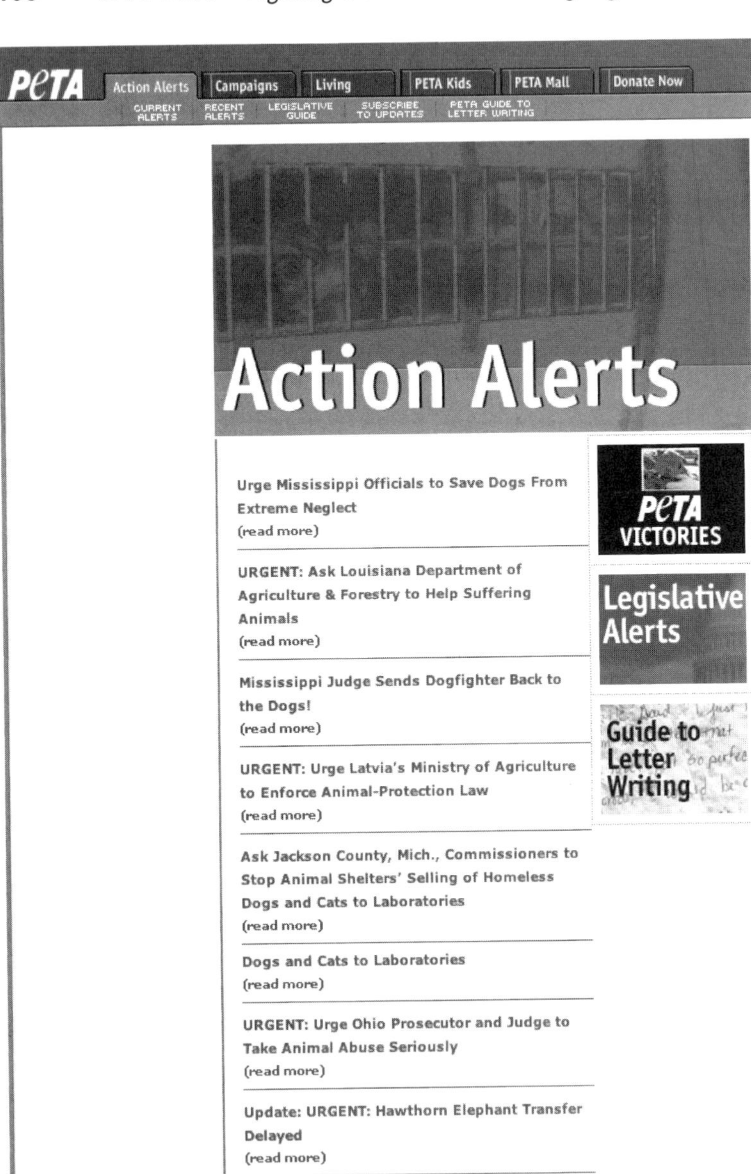
PeTA
Action Alerts
Campaigns
Living
PETA Kids
PETA Mall
Donate Now
CURRENT ALERTS
RECENT ALERTS
LEGISLATIVE GUIDE
SUBSCRIBE TO UPDATES
PETA GUIDE TO LETTER WRITING
Action Alerts
Urge Mississippi Officials to Save Dogs From Extreme Neglect
(read more)
URGENT: Ask Louisiana Department of Agriculture & Forestry to Help Suffering Animals
(read more)
Mississippi Judge Sends Dogfighter Back to the Dogs!
(read more)
URGENT: Urge Latvia's Ministry of Agriculture to Enforce Animal-Protection Law
(read more)
Ask Jackson County, Mich., Commissioners to Stop Animal Shelters' Selling of Homeless Dogs and Cats to Laboratories
(read more)
Dogs and Cats to Laboratories
(read more)
URGENT: Urge Ohio Prosecutor and Judge to Take Animal Abuse Seriously
(read more)
Update: URGENT: Hawthorn Elephant Transfer Delayed
(read more)
Urge Pennsylvania Judge to Throw the Book at Dog Beater
(read more)
PeTA VICTORIES
Legislative Alerts
Guide to Letter Writing

(**http://www.peta.org/**), particularly the section on "action alerts" (**http://www.peta.org/alert/index.asp**).

In each subsection, the Web writers attempt to provide you with facts about the mistreatment of animals and reasons why such mistreatment needs to stop. So, in addition to ethos and pathos, the writers rely on logos, on *stating reasons*, to support their claim that animals are frequently abused and that such mistreatment should end. In many ways, as we shall see throughout the remainder of this chapter, the emphasis on providing reasonable proof is the hallmark of argument.

## The Basic Form of an Argument: A Claim with Stated Reasons

In its most basic form, an academic **argument** is primarily a *claim* based on *stated reasons*. A basic argument, in its skeletal form, asserts that "something is true because something else is the case." The word *statement* in this sense is not the grammatical equivalent of a sentence. An argument may contain several statements, as does this one:

> Because I missed a week of classes to go with my family on our annual hunting trip, I lost credit for a midterm exam and an essay I didn't know about, and so I failed the course.

Here are the separate statements:

> *Statement 1:* I missed a week of classes to go with my family on our annual hunting trip.
> *Statement 2:* I lost credit for a midterm exam.
> *Statement 3:* [I lost credit for] an essay I didn't know about.
> *Statement 4:* I failed the course.

In the preceding sentence, these statements are combined into an argument; that is, one or more of them are advanced as reasons for another. The clues about the logical relationship of the statements to each other are contained in the words *because* and *so*, both of which indicate that statements 1, 2, and 3 are being advanced as reasons or causes for statement 4.

The statements in an argument may be combined into one sentence or divided into separate ones. When they are combined, the resulting sentence may be used as a **thesis sentence** for an essay advancing the argument it contains. Of course, what makes an argument an argument is that it's debatable. Consider this potential thesis:

> All cigarette smoking should be banned because smoking and secondhand cigarette smoke are physically harmful.

You might agree with the stated reason, but would you support the claim? Not all stated reasons are necessarily sufficient for adopting the proposed claim. The relationship between the two may be debatable. In this case, some have argued, the fact that cigarette smoking may be harmful doesn't necessarily mean that it is desirable—or even feasible—to adopt widespread bans on smoking. Further, not everyone agrees on how specifically harmful cigarette smoking actually is; makers of cigarettes, for instance, remain skeptical. All of this leaves room open for *argument*.

## your turn

Look at each of the following and explain why each does—or does *not*—constitute an argument as we've been describing it:

- I am hungry. It is 6:00. Are you hungry too?
- The birds stopped singing. It must be their dinnertime.
- "Ouch! You hurt me!"
- The birds are singing. It must be Wednesday.
- My friend's aunt is going to move into a nursing home because she needs full-time care, and no one in the family is able to give it.
- A hazardous-waste-burning industrial plant should not be built within 20 miles of a population center because dioxins and other pollutants it emits from its kilns could affect the health of people living any closer.
- A student in the dormitory built his own methamphetamine lab. After the police caught him, he was arrested and expelled from school.

- A student in the dormitory who builds his or her own methamphetamine lab should be arrested and expelled from school.
- Students should not use a grammar checker on word-processed documents because they will become dependent on it and be less likely to acquire knowledge of grammar themselves.
- If writers use grammar checkers to help them identify patterns of error in their work, such as sentence fragments, and then learn to avoid making these errors, their use of the grammar checker can be beneficial.

What did you come up with? Which, based on our definition of argument, qualify as arguments? Which do not, and why?

## WRITING SPOTLIGHT

### Pathos, Ethos, Logos, and Argument in a "Raccoon in a Bag"

Let's look at a more complex example of argument, actually a classic example of argument from an American historical legend. David Crockett made his "Raccoon in a Bag" speech in Washington, D.C., in March of 1830, before a committee of the House of Representatives, while he was serving as a congressman from Tennessee. At issue was a bill to build a road, an early version of an interstate highway, from Buffalo to New Orleans. The road would pass through Memphis, and the citizens of Tennessee would be taxed to help construct the road. Crockett initially seemed to favor this construction, but as he considered the welfare of his constituents, he reversed his opinion and delivered a speech opposing the construction of the road from Memphis to New Orleans; he felt that such a road would be a waste of money, because travelers could easily take a boat along the Mississippi from Memphis to New Orleans, thus making a road between those cities superfluous. (Keep in mind that, in Crockett's time, travel by river was much quicker and easier than travel by horse and buggy!)

Read the following selection and think about the arguments Crockett presents in light of what you now know about argument. Look in particular for instances of pathos, ethos, and logos, and for clear claims based on stated reasons.

### A Raccoon in a Bag

David Crockett

When I consider the few opportunities which I have had to obtain information on this important topic, I shrink at the idea of addressing so intelligent a body as this upon matters relating to it. My lips would be sealed in silence, were I not fully convinced that there has been in some instances a partial and improper legislation resorted to during the present session. I was elected from the Western District of Tennessee after declaring myself a friend to this measure; and I came here quite hot for the road—yes, the fever was upon me; but I confess I am getting quite cool on the subject of expending money for the gratification of certain gentlemen who happen to have different views from those I entertain. Let us inquire where this money comes from. It will be found that even our poor citizens have to contribute towards the supply. I have not forgotten how I first found my way to this House; I pledged myself to the good people who sent me here that I would oppose certain tariff measures, and strive to remove the duties upon salt, sugar, coffee, and other articles, which the poor as well as the rich are from necessity compelled to consume. The duties on these articles are felt to be oppressive by my fellow-citizens; and as long as I can raise my voice I will oppose the odious system which sanctions them.

Those who sustain the Government and furnish the means, have, by the illiberality of their servants, been kept in ignorance of the true cause of some of their sufferings. These servants, after the people intrust them with their confidence, too often forget the interest of their employers and are led away by some designing gentlemen, who, to gratify some wild notion, are almost willing to enslave the poorer class at least. I am one of those who are called self-taught men; by the kindness of my neighbors and some exertion of my own, I have been raised from obscurity without an education. I am therefore compelled to address the committee in the language of a farmer, which I hope will be understood. I do not mean to oppose internal improvements—my votes on that subject will show that I am an internal improvement man, though I cannot go, as the Kentuckian said, "the whole hog." I will only go as far as the situation of the country will admit—so far as not to oppress. I will not say that I will vote against the bill under all circumstances, yet at this moment I consider it a wild notion to carry the road to the extent contemplated, from Buffalo to this city, and from this to New Orleans. . . . I am astonished that certain of our Eastern friends have become so kind to us. They are quite willing to aid in distributing a portion of the national funds among us of the West. This was not so once. And if I am not deceived their present kindness is merely a bait to cover the hook which is intended to haul in the Western and Southern people; and when we are hooked over the barb we will have to yield. Their policy reminds me of a certain man in the State of Ohio, who, having caught a raccoon, placed it in a bag, and as he was on his way home he met a neighbor who was anxious to know what he had in his bag. He was told to put his hand in and feel, and in doing so he was bit through the fingers; he then asked what it was and was told that it was "only a bite." I fear that our good Eastern friends have a hook and a bite for us; and if we are once fastened, it will close the concern. We may then despair of paying the national debt; we may bid farewell to all other internal improvements; and, finally, we may bid farewell to all hopes of ever reducing duties on anything. This is honestly my opinion; and again I say I cannot consent to "go the whole hog." But I will go as far as Memphis. There let this great road strike the Mississippi where the steamboats are passing every hour in the day and night; where you can board a steamboat and in seven or eight days go to New Orleans and back; where there is no obstruction at any time of the year. I would thank any man to show this committee the use of a road which will run parallel with the Mississippi for five or six hundred miles. Will any man say that the road would be preferred to the river either for transportation or traveling? No, sir. Then, is not your project useless, and will it not prove an improper expenditure of the public funds to attempt to carry the road beyond Memphis?

---

Let's talk about the elements of argument in this speech.

Crockett begins his short speech by clearly establishing his ethos and by appealing to his listeners' sense of pathos—at the same time. In the opening paragraph, he styles himself as a humble person, even hesitant to address "so intelligent a body" as a congressional committee. He characterizes himself as one of the people, who has the people's best interests at heart. He claims that he's not arguing to further his own agenda; rather, he emphasizes, he represents the people, and therefore his audience should listen all the more carefully to what he says. Look again, for instance, at this sentence:

> I have not forgotten how I first found my way to this House; I pledged myself to the good people who sent me here that I would oppose certain tariff measures . . .

With such words, Crockett attempts to establish his ethos as an honest man, genuinely concerned with the welfare of his constituents; he doesn't want *their* money wasted. But he also uses pathos to evoke the sympathy of the committee for those he represents. He is concerned that his constituents may be taxed for purposes that will not benefit them, and he asks the committee to consider the unfairness of such a situation. He's not using logos yet: rather, in the two opening paragraphs, he focuses on emotions, using such words as *oppressive, odious*, and *suffering* to evoke an emotional response.

Toward the close of the long second paragraph, Crockett addresses the *reasons* that the proposed road, and the taxes necessary to build it, should be reconsidered. His stated reasons are simply put:

> We may then despair of paying the national debt; we may bid farewell to all other internal improvements; and, finally, we may bid farewell to all hopes of ever reducing duties [taxes] on anything.

Crockett believes that building the road—a monumental task at the time—would cost so much money that it would forestall addressing other issues, such as paying down the national debt or making other "internal improvements." Crockett is willing to negotiate a little bit, and he says that he would support the idea of a road from Buffalo to Memphis, but not from Memphis to New Orleans. Again, using logos, he backs up his position with a clearly stated reason:

> There [in Memphis] let this great road strike the Mississippi where the steamboats are passing every hour in the day and night; where you can board a steamboat and in seven or eight days go to New Orleans and back; where there is no obstruction at any time of the year.

To drive home his point, he even asks a rhetorical question:

> Will any man say that the road would be preferred to the river either for transportation or traveling?

It might be useful to keep in mind that in Crockett's time river travel was often much easier than travel by road, so the Congressman from Tennessee has a solid—and reasonable—point. And, in this way, Crockett uses a variety of argumentative techniques—pathos, ethos, and logos—to make his case.

### your turn

In a synchronous online discussion or in small groups, face-to-face, have members of your class assume the roles of Crockett's colleagues in the House of Representatives, who have just heard his speech. Respond to his argument, taking a position on whether it is sound or unsound, and develop your own arguments on whether or not to build the highway to Memphis. As an alternative, you could draft a speech in support or rebuttal of Crockett to deliver before him and his fellow representatives.

## Kinds of Arguments

Since Aristotle's time, a number of forms of argument have been developed to meet the needs of certain situations. These forms include the broad categories of *inductive* and *deductive* arguments and, more specifically, arguments based on *cause and effect*, *analogy*, and *definition*. We also need to consider more carefully the use of *assumptions* in making argumentative claims and the consideration of potential *counterarguments* as a necessary part of any argument. Let's consider these and other argumentative strategies, beginning again with Aristotle's understanding of argument and building on what you now know about the basic form and elements of argument.

### Inductive Arguments

Aristotle sums up all forms of argument as belonging to two classes: **deductive argument**, based on the *syllogism*, and **inductive argument**, based on *examples*. An *inductive argument*, which we'll focus on in this section, draws a general conclusion on the basis of particular evidence—the more, and the more representative, the better. Most arguments used in daily conversation are inductive in that you present a variety of evidence and come up with a conclusion. You probably intuitively use inductive argument or reasoning when attempting to persuade others, even in casual conversation. For example, if you are considering taking a particular course and you hear from several colleagues and classmates that the instructor of that course is challenging and a "hard grader," then you might inductively come to the conclusion that the course is difficult. You have based your claim—your conclusion—on a series of examples.

In all inductive arguments, the conclusion can follow only as a matter of *probability*, never of necessity. The more verifiable evidence presented to support the conclusion, and the more representative it is of all the evidence that could be advanced (that is, the more random the sampling of possible evidence), the *stronger* an inductive argument is judged to be. On the other hand, if insufficient evidence is presented to base the conclusion on, and if it does not represent a random sampling of all the possible evidence or if it appears to have been gathered with some kind of bias, an inductive argument is judged to be *weak*. For instance, consider the following two statements:

> Professor McManus is a more demanding teacher than Professor Zimmerman because many of my friends say that McManus requires a lot of work.
>
> Professor McManus is a more demanding teacher than Professor Zimmerman because, each term, Professor McManus requires her students to write two more essays than students write for Professor Zimmerman.

Which seems stronger to you? The first is clearly weak in that little or no real evidence is provided, whereas the second *seems* stronger because verifiable evidence is offered in support of the claim.

## Deductive Arguments and the Enthymeme

**Deductive reasoning** is based on what Aristotle called the **syllogism**. In its simplest form, a syllogism comprises one or more **premises** containing reasons and a **conclusion**. Here is Aristotle's famous example:

> *Major premise*: All men are mortal.
> *Minor premise*: Socrates is a man.
> *Conclusion*: Therefore, Socrates is mortal.

The **major premise** is a statement advanced as a reason for drawing the conclusion. It is usually a more general statement than the others. It may be a statement of principle, a belief, or something true of a large class or category of objects or ideas. In this case, use of the word *all* in the premise that "all men are mortal" refers to every member of the class, making the statement a *universal* one.

The **minor premise** (or *premises*; there may be more than one) is likewise a statement advanced as a reason for drawing the conclusion. In a valid argument, minor premises must be related in specified ways to the major premise and the conclusion. Although they can vary greatly in content, minor premises often contain evidence presented as fact or information about subgroups or individuals (e.g., "Socrates is a man").

The **conclusion** is the main point of the argument, and it follows from the major and minor premises. In a deductive argument that conforms to the rules of logic—that is, does not contain any logical fallacies or errors—the conclusion is inescapable. It follows from the premises as a matter of *necessity*. So, since all men are mortal (major premise), and since Socrates is a man (minor premise), Socrates is therefore mortal (conclusion). Case closed.

A syllogism may be stated as an **enthymeme**. As Aristotle defined it, an *enthymeme* is a summary statement (or, in logical terms, a series of statements) that includes all the important elements of the premises and conclusion and indicates the relationships among them. The enthymeme for Aristotle's syllogism given here might be: "Because all men are mortal and Socrates is a man, Socrates is mortal." Sometimes, in an enthymeme, one of the premises may be missing or unstated. In such cases, in order to evaluate the argument, you must figure out what the missing premise or assumption is. For instance, someone who makes these statements—

> Darell is a college student.
>
> He doubtless needs to catch up on sleep.

—is assuming that "all college students need to catch up on sleep." The assumption may be true, or it may not, but before judging it true or false, one has to find it. The ability to identify unstated assumptions is a vital key to being able to argue well.

An argument based on a syllogism is judged as being *sound* or *unsound*. A **sound argument** is one that meets two criteria: (1) the reasoning must be correct and (2) the premises must be true. Thus, if you are evaluating a deductive argument based on a syllogism, you must examine closely any facts set forth in the premises. If one of them can be proved wrong, then the argument is **unsound**. This is where research comes in: a reader must often do some individual investigation to determine whether all the information used to support the argument is actually true. When composing arguments, especially for an audience of critical readers in an academic context, a writer should back up anything presented as fact with all the documentation of reliable sources necessary to establish its truth with the reader.

In fact, premises in deductive arguments are often arrived at through inductive reasoning, which leads to conclusions that are, at best, only highly probable. Aristotle's assertion that "all men are mortal" was based on his observations of a limited number of men. Socrates seemed to be a man because he looked, walked, and talked like one. Someone could claim, however, that there is an outside chance that Socrates was not a man but an alien.

Further, to determine whether the reasoning in the argument is correct, you must carefully examine the relationship of elements of the premises to each other and to the conclusion; that is, one must look at the *structure* of the argument. If a deductive argument is **valid**, the conclusion necessarily follows from the premises. If the rules are not followed, the syllogism is said to be **invalid**. Also, for the syllogism to be valid, the words in the premises must be used with exactly the same meaning each time they appear; they cannot be ambiguous. An audience must agree on those definitions if it is to consider an argument to be sound.

Let's look at an example of an invalid argument. Can you tell why it is invalid?

> Some women will be happy staying at home full-time with several children.
>
> Louise is a woman.
>
> Louise will be happy staying at home full-time with several children.

Although the major premise may be correct (some women are happy staying at home full-time with several children), and although the minor premise may also be correct (Louise may indeed be a woman), the relationship between the two does not necessarily lead us to believe the conclusion: Louise may not be one of the group of "some women" who are happy staying at home and raising children. The fault here lies in not having enough information to make the claim, to posit the conclusion, based on the available premises.

Although the study of logic is beyond the scope of this book and can only be hinted at here, the thoughtful reader will be able to spot most of the common errors in deductive logic without special training. What examples of faulty logic can you find in your own experience?

As you gain practice with simple deductive arguments, you should be able to identify both the enthymeme and the syllogism on which it is based—whether you are encountering arguments in print, online, in the media, or among friends. You must then be able to identify any assumption or premise that has been omitted. If it is a principle, belief, or assumption with which you disagree, or if it appears to assume a fact in error, you may question the argument at that point. After checking the facts to determine their truth and evaluating the reasoning for correctness, you can judge the argument sound or unsound.

## your turn

Look at each syllogism and determine whether it is valid or invalid and, if valid, sound or unsound. Explain your reasons for each judgment. Then write the enthymeme for each.

All cats are blue.
This is a cat.
This is blue.

Some inexperienced drivers take unnecessary risks.
He takes unnecessary risks.
He is an inexperienced driver.

All Republicans consider themselves fiscal conservatives.
Mary considers herself a fiscal conservative.
Mary is a Republican.

All astronomers play the cello.
Stephen is not an astronomer.
Stephen does not play the cello.

No hardworking students turn in late papers.
He turned in a late paper.
He is not a hardworking student.

No one who has earned an MBA will succeed in business.
She is succeeding in business.
She has not earned an MBA.

No one who has earned an MBA will fail to succeed in business.
She has not earned an MBA.
She will fail to succeed in business

All women are immortal.
Xanthippe is a woman.
Xanthippe is immortal.

What did you discover as you worked through each syllogism? Did you see how faulty premises make invalid, even humorous arguments?

## Cause and Effect

Arguments asserting a relationship between causes and potential effects are generally inductive arguments. Let's look at an example of cause-and-effect argument that uses inductive reasoning:

> If I continue to revise my papers for my English course, then my writing will improve.

As with all inductive arguments, the conclusion follows the reasons as a matter of *probability*: your writing will improve *if* you revise. The reasons advanced here may be based on personal observations the speaker or writer has made. For instance, if you have revised your work before and earned higher marks on your written assignments, then you have a growing body of evidence to support the claim above. The argument would be stronger—that is, the probability of the conclusion's being true would be greater—if the argument included more information, such as a series of examples showing how revision led to improved and successful writing. In general, the more reasons given, the better the argument is.

For this reason, inductive arguments can be tricky. Let's look at another example. This example claims that a connection exists between a cause (a tax limitation measure) and a resulting effect (a budget crunch):

> Because of the passage of a tax limitation measure several years ago and a sluggish economy, the state of Colorado is currently facing a severe budget crunch.

While the connection between the cause and the effect may be clear, the inductive relationship between the two raises several questions. What evidence exists that tax revenues decreased, or that they did not rise at the rate needed to cover expenditures, as a result of the tax limitation measure? (Such data should be readily available in public records.) What taxes, such as those on sales or income, are in place in the state that would bring in less revenue when the economy is sluggish? More specifically, what exactly is a "sluggish economy"? What is the definition of a "budget crunch"?

When making any kind of causal claim, exercise caution. Sometimes, it is easy to confuse *causality* with *correspondence* or *correlation*. For instance, scientists have demonstrated that there seems to be a correlation between intelligence and left-handedness—which means that, all things being equal, many left-handed people are also intelligent. Correlation, or "co-relation," means that these two items (intelligence and left-handedness) are occurring at the same time. This correlation, however, does *not* imply *any* cause-and-effect relationship between left-handedness and intelligence. So, just because you are intelligent (or left-handed), that does not necessarily mean that you will also be left-handed (or, sorry to say, intelligent).

In fact, establishing causality can be difficult, and academics tend to avoid stating definitively that one thing *causes* another or that one thing is an *effect* of something else. Many academics, particular scientists and social scientists, including psychologists and sociologists, might posit a *relationship* between things—such as a correlation—and then *speculate* about the connection between the two. For example, what "causes" global warming? Scientists have been disputing the exact causes for years, suggesting that there are probably several, and they often caution us not to jump to conclusions one way or the other—not to be too quick to blame a particular culprit alone, such as emissions from cars. Most recognize that our world is complex enough that *many* potential causes need to be factored into a consideration of large-scale events.

## Analogies

An argument involving **analogy** employs a comparison between two things that are not necessarily alike. The movie character Forrest Gump gave us a memorable analogy when he told us that "Life is like a box of chocolates." Gump is not saying that life *is* a box of chocolates, but that it is *like* a box of chocolates in that when you pick a chocolate-covered candy from a box of sweets, you may not know what filling lies inside the chocolate. You may be surprised, as often happens in life. The connection, then, is between the *surprises* encountered in a box of chocolates and those encountered in daily life—surprises that you may not necessarily like.

Look back at David Crockett's speech, earlier in this chapter. In it, Crockett uses an analogy, referred to in the title of the speech: "A Raccoon in a Bag." Crockett says that the congressmen from the "East" remind him of a man who puts a raccoon in a bag and then, when he encounters another man who is curious about the contents of the bag, invites the second man to put his hand in the bag to find out what's in it! Obviously, the second man is going to get bitten; his good-natured curiosity is tricked by the first man's willingness to see him get hurt. Crockett implies that this little story is analogous to the political situation he is facing: congressmen from the East seem to be counting on the good nature of others to go along with their plan to use national funds to build the Buffalo–New Orleans road. In his speech, however, Crockett wonders if they would all get "bitten" if they did, in that the road might be a waste of money. He even uses another "pointed" analogy to make his point clear:

> And if I am not deceived their present kindness is merely a bait to cover the hook which is intended to haul in the Western and Southern people; and when we are hooked over the barb we will have to yield.

The Eastern congressmen are trying to "hook" the other congressmen into agreeing with the road construction plan; but Crockett worries that there may be a "barb" hidden in the "hook."

Such analogies are useful in making points, but you should exercise caution: Do not *overstate* the relationship between the things you are comparing. For instance, Crockett himself runs the risk of being rude when he implies that the congressmen from the East are holding a raccoon in a bag; he seems to be suggesting that they know their plan is harmful. Is that a fair assumption on Crockett's part?

## Definitions

A powerful argumentative strategy frequently used by many writers and debaters is the **definitional argument**. Defining involves creating classes or categories that help us understand the world around us. For instance, one of the most basic ways we define our humanity is by how we divide and classify our lives based on age: infancy, childhood, adolescence, adulthood, middle age, and old age. Each category comes with certain characteristics, certain attributes that supposedly *define* what it is like to be a child (playful, innocent), an adult (mature, responsible), and an older person (wise, knowledgeable). Definitions, then, are part of how we know and interpret the world.

Of course, we'll often disagree on how *exactly* to define something, usually a concept or an idea. Take *maturity*, for instance. What defines maturity? Consider the following claim:

> Angela is more mature than Bill because she is older than he is.

In this case, an evaluation is being made on the basis of a definition: Angela is mature; Bill, maybe not so mature as Angela. But note the stated reason: Angela is mature *because she is older*. Is being older sufficient reason to define someone as more "mature"? Probably not; in fact, you have probably met people who are older than you are but who are not necessarily more mature. Clearly, other criteria need to be established for determining who is—and who is not—mature.

Generally, multiple criteria are given when establishing definitional categories, and much of the debate about definitions focuses on disagreements about criteria. For instance, when we talk with students about what defines a "good essay," we try to give them a number of criteria to serve as guideposts as they work on developing their writing skills. Some criteria are easy to agree on and easy to spot in a piece of good writing; specifically, clear thesis statements, easy-to-follow organizational strategies, and correct use of grammar and mechanics all help us *define* a piece of writing as "good." Other criteria are trickier. For instance, we often say that we want students to demonstrate *creative* thinking in their essays—but what does that mean? One student's idea of creativity might strike us as dull or uninspired, or vice versa: what we think of as creative might be uninteresting to our students. Such murky criteria leave room open for debate in definitional arguments.

Definitional arguments can also be thorny because definitions change over time. For instance, consider the term *minority* in American culture. Who is defined as a minority? Many would consider African Americans a group that we could define as a minority, particularly in terms of population. But what about women? Women count for about half of the population of the United States, but many consider women a minority group as well, primarily because they have not had as much political and social influence as men. Again, the use of different criteria for the definition of the word *minority* affects what the word means and how we use it.

## Examining Assumptions

To understand arguments the audience must frequently identify one or more unstated assumptions on which the argument depends, and they must agree on the definitions used. An **assumption** is a belief or value that the arguer assumes everyone will have or hold. For instance, if we make the claim that "smoking should be banned because it is harmful to everyone's health," then we are assuming that people value their physical health.

Assumptions can, of course, be trickier and harder to identify than that example. In the argument earlier about taxes and the sluggish economy, the reader is required to make certain assumptions about changes in tax revenues and about definitions of terms ("sluggish economy") when these easily could have been supplied by the author. Even if the claim made is correct, the argument is not presented as strongly as it could be. A stronger claim might actually make reference to specific numbers, or pinpoint specifically how a decrease in tax revenues has hurt a particular part of the state economy. For instance, the claim could be made that lower tax revenues meant less funding for public schools, which, in turn, hampered the populace's ability to develop the skills necessary to attract new industries. This causal chain might be not only easier to argue but more convincing as well.

An assumption can make or break an argument. Remember: An assumption is a belief or value that the arguer assumes his audience will have or hold. Let's look at another example. DanceSafe online (**http://www.dancesafe.org/**) is the controversial Web site of an organization that attempts to educate youth about the illicit drugs they might find at raves or other large parties. According to the site's "About" section, "DanceSafe is a non-profit, harm reduction organization promoting health and safety within the rave and nightclub community." The site and its organizers have been the target of much criticism, and DanceSafe is quite controversial because it does not actively argue *against* youth taking drugs such as Ecstasy but instead, encourages youth to be aware of the effects of such drugs: "Our volunteers staff harm reduction booths at raves, nightclubs and other dance events where they provide information on drugs, safer sex, and other health and safety issues concerning the electronic dance community (like driving home safely and protecting one's hearing)." DanceSafe staff also engage in highly controversial "pill testing" for Ecstasy users. Pill testing helps to screen Ecstasy so that users can be sure they are taking only Ecstasy and not other harmful drugs.

DanceSafe organizers say they are filling a particular need among drug users:

> Our information and services are directed primarily towards non-addicted, recreational drug users. Non-addicted drug users are an under-served population within the harm reduction movement, despite the fact that they comprise the vast majority of drug users in our society. While many organizations exist that provide services to drug-dependent individuals, few groups address the needs of the majority of non-addicted, recreational users. We hope to fill this gap. When needed, we will always refer people to appropriate treatment programs.
>
> (**http://www.dancesafe.org/documents/about/index.php**)

What do you think? In many ways, DanceSafe's argument rests on at least three specific assumptions: first, that "recreational drug users" are not addicted; second, that "just say no" campaigns against drugs do not work; and third, that providing information to youth is sufficient to convince them to take care of their health. Perhaps most important, the argument seems to assume that one can be a "non-addicted, recreational user" and not suffer any serious side effects from drug use, provided, of course, that the drugs have been screened properly. The argument assumes a sharp distinction between recreational use and addictive use.

What happens to DanceSafe's argument if you do *not* accept these assumptions? Well, you might agree that there are many "non-addicted, recreational" drug users, but you might *not* agree that nonaddictive drug use is acceptable. In fact, you might consider *all* illicit drug use to be potentially harmful or addictive. If so, DanceSafe's argument would probably strike you as unconvincing because you would question why recreational drug users are using drugs in the first place. Put another way, if you think that *any* drug use is harmful, then you would want to address the drug use itself as the primary issue.

## your turn

Here's an assignment for a synchronous discussion (either electronic or face-to-face) that will challenge your understanding of how we bring our assumptions with us into a wide variety of situations and offer you a chance to practice argumentation skills. Try the exercise, either as part of a course or on your own with classmates or friends, and see what you come up with.

---

### The Lifeboat

Once upon a time, a large passenger liner was traveling across the North Atlantic, filled with all sorts of people. In the night, its radar guidance system went out, and it hit a large iceberg that made such a big hole in the bow that the boat began to sink fast. (OK, pretend it's the *Titanic*!). Passengers filled the lifeboats, which were set adrift in the chill night air in the expectation that someone would rescue everyone aboard. Unfortunately, except for the last two seats, the last lifeboat was filled, and dozens of people would remain on board to sink with the ship. As the ship's huge metal carcass groaned just before it split and sank, the last two passengers had to get aboard the lifeboat or face certain death.

Imagine that you are standing at the railing next to the lifeboat. Your help will be required to get anyone into the boat. You get to make the decision as to who will be the two passengers to be saved. You know a few things about the people around you. Whom will you put onto the boat? Your choices are:

• The first American pope, age 70, and recently elected. He doesn't try to save himself, but all the Catholics and many others in the group urge him to jump aboard so that he can remain as spiritual leader of millions of Christians worldwide.

• Susan, a 10-year-old girl who has spent her childhood ill with leukemia and survived a bone marrow transplant, but who at last seems to be cured. She has spent years looking forward to living a normal life and doing all the things she could not do when she was sick. Her mother pushes her forward and begs you to help her aboard, to allow her this one chance for health and happiness, even though the mother does not expect to be saved herself.

• Peter, a physician who specializes in survival skills and emergency medicine. You know that this person can help those aboard the lifeboat survive if help does not come immediately.

• Gottum Yarns, a professional storyteller who you know would entertain all those in the lifeboat and keep their spirits up to the end, even if help never comes.

• Fuzzy and Wuzzy, the last two koala bears on earth, in a secure cage, with a supply of eucalyptus leaves to keep them fed until help arrives. They are being shipped to a location where they will be used for breeding, in order to reestablish the species. (They would use just one seat on the boat.)

• Betsy, a young woman six months pregnant with twins. Her husband pushes her forward, telling her he will go down with the ship, but she must go home to care for their five other children, the oldest of whom is age 10, since they have no living grandparents or other relatives.

• Lotsa Bucks, a financier who, since the government student loan program has recently been cut back, is about to establish a fund that would enable hundreds of thousands of students to attend college who otherwise would have no hope of ever getting degrees and increasing their income levels for life.

• Sarah, a social justice activist and brilliant scientist who has been working for two decades on a cure for cancer and who just that morning announced at breakfast that she had thought of the final cure for all kinds of cancer, which she will write down and publish as soon as she returns home. You are certain she is telling the truth because she is so far the only double winner of the Nobel Prize—The Nobel Peace Prize for her activity for civil rights and also the Nobel Prize in medicine for the groundbreaking cancer research she has already done, which has led to many other life-saving discoveries.

- Michael, who has been planning a work of art that will be as great as Michelangelo's Sistine Chapel ceiling and will inspire and comfort others for the next five hundred years.

Decide quickly whom you would save. On what principle(s) do you base your decision? Send your answer to the class; then read what other people have said. It is your job to discuss your reasoning with the class and to try to convince everyone else to agree with you. If, after trying, you are unsuccessful, you may change your mind in order to agree with someone else, but you must explain why you are changing your decision. The class as a whole must agree on the final decision. Use your persuasive power to argue for the best decision, and do it quickly—the boat is sinking fast, and this class lasts only a few more minutes.

When you have finished discussing and making your decisions, reconsider your exchange. (If you've used a synchronous discussion platform such as DIWE, see if you can print out a copy of your chat so you can analyze it.) What kinds of argumentative strategies did you end up using? What assumptions were exposed as you discussed and debated who should be saved, and why? What does this exercise teach you about assumptions, argument, and the difficulty of reasoning and talking through to a conclusion?

## Considering Counterarguments

An important part of arguing is listening to alternative views and considering the opinions of those who will disagree with you. For instance, Crockett's speech is an appeal for his fellow congressmen to listen to an alternative opinion or viewpoint about the proposed road from Buffalo to New Orleans. If his opponents had not been at all interested in listening to Crockett's *counter*argument, then there would have been no discussion in the first place. They simply would have done what they wanted and built the road—case closed. Most congressional meetings, however, are *debates*: they revolve around listening to a variety of arguments and counterarguments as a way to understand and work through a problem.

Some arguments are constructed primarily as counterarguments. That is, they are designed to offer an alternative view to one that is commonly held or one that has not yet been fully examined. In the following paragraphs, student writer Isaac Thorn reconsiders the school shootings at Columbine High School and offers some counterarguments to the contention that blame for the shootings rests in part with the media. Many think that the depiction of violence on television, for instance, desensitizes youth to violence, making incidents such as the Columbine shooting more likely to happen. Isaac, however, is less convinced. In his concluding paragraphs, he critiques one editorial linking media images of violence to the school shooting and offers another view about how to respond.

Thorn 1

Isaac Thorn

A New Take on the Columbine Tragedy

For example, look at Diane Carman's editorial for the *Denver Post* titled, "Film Says It's a Gun to Die For." Ms. Carman's thesis is that "assault weapons are presented as must have fashion accessories," and therefore they are the reason the two killers used a Tec-9 automatic to dispose of most of their victims, including themselves. Making no mention of the abundance of bombs and other guns found at the scene of the crime and in the bedrooms and garages of the perpetrators of the murder, she invites us to believe that because Keanu Reeves wears a trench coat in his latest movie or because Don Johnson flossed a Bren-10 handgun in *Miami Vice*, people shot people directly because of cinematic instances such as the above. She boldly accuses *Dirty Harry* movies of making the Magnum a preferred handgun and backs it up by pointing to the increase in sales of certain models of guns featured in films or television programs. However, no mention is made of how that is the way things work in the world today.

Whatever is on TV, whether it is a feminine hygiene product, meat dehydrator, or even a handgun, it will become

Thorn 2

more popular with more exposure to the public. I found it to be rather shallow of Carman to point to our film industry as the culprit in this bizarre act of absolute pure hatred. Anything is a weapon if you hold it right, so I believe that it's of little merit to cheapshot an industry. . . . I doubt Ms. Carman or anyone thought that Arnold Schwarzenegger playing the Terminator would cause death to anyone. Now that the tragedy has occurred, though, the wolves come out and try to get the scent of blood in their noses like coke addicts do powder. Snorting up lines of useless information and often biased journalism has a price which everyone has to pay. We are all subject to rants and raves that stir up controversy where there needs to be none. I'm not saying, "Guns don't kill high school students; high school students kill high school students." I am just maintaining that we search for scapegoats like children do Easter eggs. . . . A more logical approach to an editorial on this remarkable tragedy would be to deal with the pain felt by those affected by it and not to attempt to play the problem solver when the damage is already done. Ending her article by sarcastically saying, "they know a lucrative new market when they see one," is a blatant example of the scapegoat searching we thrive on because it offers the author more attention than being responsible and ethical about this whole long and painful process that the people of Littleton community will be faced with for years to come.

Thorn 3

WORK CITED

Carman, Diane. "Film Says It's a Gun to Die For." *Denver Post Online* <www.denverpost.com/news/carman0501.html>.

Instead of looking for a scapegoat, Isaac argues for another, "more logical" approach: "to deal with the pain felt by those affected by it." What do you think? Is this more "logical"? In some ways, Isaac has a point; looking for a quick answer to a complex problem (such as why some students have brought weapons to their schools) might not be an appropriate way to address the complexity of such problems.

## *Useful Links*

There are many links on the Web to assist you with understanding arguments. Of the many we regularly introduce to our students, you might enjoy and benefit from the following:

- "Rhetoric and Composition" at **http://eserver.org/rhetoric/** offers a wonderful list of links specifically about rhetoric, including some material that will help you explore and understand classical rhetoric in particular. What can you learn from this site to complement what you've read in this chapter? How will it prepare you for future work in *writing* arguments?
- To learn about other strategies for reading and understanding persuasive appeals, check out "Hugh Rank's website for teachers and students providing some *simple* ways to analyze *complex* persuasion techniques of modern advertising and political rhetoric" at **http://webserve.govst.edu/users/ghrank/**.
- Wikipedia, the free online encyclopedia, has a good explanation of rhetoric and argument with some useful links for further exploration: **http://en.wikipedia.org/wiki/Rhetoric.**
- Do a Web search using a search engine such as Google (**http://www.google.com/**) and using search terms such as "argument," "rhetoric," or "writing arguments." Numerous college and university instructors have put up Web sites for their students to help them understand how to read and compose effective arguments. As you search, think about which sites are most useful for you—and why.

## A Writer in Action: Combining Multiple Argumentative Strategies

Many times, writers use *multiple* argumentative strategies to make their points. For instance, a writer might maintain that a change in definition could lead to different effects, or that a set of causes leads us to reconsider how we define significant concepts. Douglas Rushkoff, one of the most interesting and provocative critics of new information technologies and the cultures that use them, offers a great example of the use of multiple argumentative strategies in the introduction to his book, *Playing the Future*. This book, originally published in the mid-1990s, examines the ways in which "digital kids"—teenagers and young adults—have been using computer and Internet technologies not only to express themselves but also to reshape the way they think about the world. In the following article, the opening chapter of *Playing the Future*, Rushkoff outlines his main theses. You may not agree with all of them: Rushkoff *is* controversial at times, but his ability to provoke discussion is noteworthy. In particular, note how Rushkoff defines *youth*. Indeed, much of his argument in this article revolves around the importance Rushkoff places on youth and what youth have to tell us about the future of technology. In that sense, Rushkoff's argument focuses on *defining* youth. But he also uses a number of other strategies we've been talking about. See if you can find them.

---

### Introduction: The Children of Chaos

DOUGLAS RUSHKOFF

*"They keep changing the rules—how we're supposed to behave in each situation. They keep changing it. It's just like the world: everything keeps changing constantly."*

—*U.S. SOLDIER IN HAITI POLICE OPERATION, OCTOBER 1994*

Looks like this is the end.

Global warming, racial tension, fundamentalist outbursts, nuclear arsenals, bacterial mutation, Third World rage, urban decay, moral collapse,

---

Excerpt from "Introduction: The Children of Chaos" by Douglas Rushkoff from *Playing the Future: What We Learn From Digital Kids*.

religious zealotry, political corruption, drug addiction, bureaucratic ineptitude, ecological over-simplification, corporate insensitivity, crashing world markets, paranoid militias, AIDS, resource depletion, hopeless youth, high school shootings, and many, many other societal indicators all suggest crisis.

Is it so naïve or even childish to suggest that these may not be signs of doom at all, but only look that way? Couldn't our inability to see our way out of what feels like such a mess be more a problem of perception than of design? And if we are now ready—or simply desperate enough—to adopt a worldview based on something other than decline, decay, and death, might we have no choice but to adopt the open-mindedness of youth?

Those of us intent on securing an adaptive strategy for the coming millennium need look no further than our own children for reassuring answers to the many uncertainties associated with the collapse of the culture we have grown to know and love. Our kids are younger and less experienced than us, but they are also less in danger of becoming obsolete. They are the latest model of human being. Looking at the world of children is not looking backward at our own past—it's looking ahead. They are our evolutionary future.

Consider any family of immigrants. Who learns the language first? Who adopts the aesthetic, cultural, and spiritual values of their new country? The children, of course. Developmental psychologists have concluded that a person's ability to incorporate new language systems—to adapt—is greatest until about the onset of puberty, when it drops off dramatically. As a result, adults adjust more slowly and less completely than kids do. Were any of us immigrants in a new territory, we would be watching our children for cues on how to speak, what to wear, when to laugh, even how to perceive the actions of others.

Well, welcome to the twenty-first century. We are all immigrants in a new territory. Our world is changing so rapidly that we can hardly track the differences, much less master them. Whether it's caller ID, MTV, digital cash, or chaos math, we are bombarded every day with an increasing number of words, devices, ideas, and events we do not understand. On a larger scale, the cultural institutions on which we have grown dependent—organized religion, the medical establishment, corporations, nation states, and even the family itself—appear to have crumbled under their own weight, all within a few short decades. Without having physically migrated an inch, we have, nonetheless, traveled farther than any generation in history.

Compare the number of ideas a person is exposed to each day with the number he might have been asked to consider, say, just seventy-five years ago. Inventions like the telephone, radio, television, photocopier, fax machine, modem, cable TV, video teleconferencing, computer bulletin board, and the World Wide Web all function to increase the number of people whose thoughts we encounter. Each successive development in communications technology—whether it's a cellular phone or an E-mail account—brings a corresponding leap in the number of ideas we're forced to process.

The degree of change experienced by the last three generations rivals that of a species undergoing mutation. Children born into our electronically mediated world of computer and television monitors might best be called "screenagers." While the members of every generation experience some degree of tension with their own children, today's screenagers have been forced to adapt to such an extent that many of their behaviors are inscrutable to their elders. We feel threatened by how different they have become.

Indeed, screenagers appear to be interacting with their world in ways that are as dramatically altered from their grandfathers' experiences as the first winged creatures were from their earthbound forebears. What's more, this intensity of evolutionary change shows no signs of slowing down. Whether or not we choose to get online or use an ATM, we are living in a world where the people and territory are under constant and accelerating renovation. What we need to adapt to, more than any particular change, is the fact that we are changing so rapidly.

Today's renaissance marks a moment when human beings have achieved the ability to direct certain aspects of their own evolution through their cultural and technological innovations. In this sense, our computers and networks are not doing anything to us—we are doing something to ourselves through these new tools.

The reason this all feels so troubling is that we have very little sense of direction. We don't know where our tools are taking us, much less how they work. By pulling back a bit, though—in the manner that our children have learned to do—and viewing this process in the context of evolutionary history, we can regain our bearings. Evolution has been a process by which matter moves toward higher states of complexity and greater levels of awareness. Through the development of life-forms, matter itself appears to be groping toward greater levels of organization. Atoms form molecules, which link into chains and eventually cells. These cells have networked themselves into complex organisms, which themselves evolved into creatures, including human beings. Now, by devising mediated networks and an electronic communications infrastructure, we human beings are working to take this evolutionary process to the next stage: together, we are constructing and participating as components in a new, highly networked life-form.

The difference between our current evolutionary shift and the ones that preceded it, however, is that this one is intentional. Instead of simply waiting for it to happen on a biological level, we are enacting it as a culture. Ironically, the very devices and institutions we created to shield us from the unpredictability of nature are now in nature's service as the agents of evolutionary change.

No matter how much we may deny it, human society is very much a part of nature, and our culture is subject to the tug of evolution. Realizing this fact is half the battle. We invented most of our systems of thought and technological devices to shield us from the harsher realities of nature, but now, they appear to be forcing us to reckon with an entirely new, terrifyingly unpredictable reality: A pirated answering-machine tape can shake the foundations of the British monarchy; a camcorder tape can bring down the Los Angeles Police Department; a cable channel can erode our confidence in the U.S. court system; and an impromptu Internet conference can make kids feel better about learning from strangers than from their own teachers. If we can't come to understand the fact that our personal evolution and survival is dependent on species survival, then the battle against our own extinction is already lost. This is where the experience of a developing child can inform our cultural transition.

Because they are less entrenched in business-as-usual, young people appear much more willing to accept cultural change as a natural, even pleasurable process. From a young person's perspective, the new sorts of games, sports, television programs, fashions, and interactive media that they have embraced over the past decade all teach them coping strategies for the chaotic, highly networked culture of which we are fast becoming a part.

When I first wrote this book, in 1995, the kinds of activities and media I explored as examples of youth culture's self-education were considered "fringe," at best. Since that time, however, many of these seemingly esoteric areas of culture—the many unrelated film genres, sports, toys, and television shows—have developed into popular and interdependent mainstream activities. This is not evidence of my own predictive powers, but an indication of just how much the need for these outlets and experiences has intensified during these last few years before the millennium.

When I wrote this book, for example, the word "snowboarding" came up as a spelling error in my word processor. Today, it is an official Olympic event—even though a few of its top athletes refuse to participate (sacrificing millions of dollars in endorsements) for fear that submitting to standardized judging categories will stunt the sport's evolution.

Alternative brands, from microbreweries to independent sneaker companies, have grown from obscure, local labels into NASDAQ-listed empires, often surpassing their larger competitors and turning their young entrepreneurs into millionaires. Innovative hackers who developed useful utilities for a small network of peers have seen their inventions adopted by giant Silicon Valley firms and incorporated into bestselling programs. Obscure and cult film genres like *animé* (Japanese animation) and Hong Kong action movies have gained huge followings and mainstream distribution. *Animé* is now an accepted staple of Saturday morning kids' programming, while Jackie Chan and John Woo are among the most bankable names in Hollywood. The action heroes and camera techniques of Hong Kong martial arts pictures have even found their way into the James Bond franchise.

Many cult activities have become mainstream. A fantasy role-playing card game called Magic: The Gathering, devised by an unknown mathematician and sold exclusively by stores catering to game fanatics, is now available at the checkout line in Wal-Mart. House and ambient music, formerly distributed only in specialty DJ shops or through bootleg tape exchanges, now comprise a huge and still-growing section of Tower Records called Electronica. *Beavis and Butt-head*, a cartoon that began as a segment on MTV's late-night animated anthology, *Liquid Television*, grew, in spite of parents' fears, into an international hit and a major motion picture. It cleared the way for even more pointed and delightfully crude animated hits from inexperienced but inspired animators, such as Comedy Central's infamous *South Park*. Satirical art films of the early 90s like *Pulp Fiction* defied prevailing notions of film grammar and structure by juxtaposing the sensibilities of several movie genres at once, their humor depending largely on the audience's knowledge of recent film history. The success of these self-conscious film experiments inspired a flood of mainstream hits, like the *Scream* series, which grossed hundreds of millions of dollars by celebrating its young audience's ability to enjoy a movie made up of a pastiche of cultural references, and to watch it all with detached irony.

The reason the many subcultures described in this book have grown in popularity is because they were so effective in appealing to a youth population intent on adapting to the coming cultural shift—a shift characterized by an increasing dependence on technology and media, as well as an awareness of the many challenges and opportunities that networking and its resulting interdependency will pose. Like our children, we will be required to step back from our seemingly disjointed and conflicting experiences, and to see them instead in the context of the new, chaotic landscape on which we will be conducting human affairs.

Since I wrote this book, several phenomena have emerged that take more seriously the role of preparing young people for the future. *Teletubbies*, for example, developed by the English children's television programmer Ann Wood through years of painstaking research, was conceived to address the anxieties of growing up in a technology-dependent world. Four cute, plush, and colorful creatures—aliens, really—inhabit a futuristic flying saucer nestled into the hillside of an idyllic English country garden. Observed by a happy baby who lives in the sun—a proxy for the child viewer—the Teletubbies receive instructions from a loudspeaker that rises out of the ground, interact with roving, vacuum cleaner–like machines, and, most impressively, receive television broadcasts through antennae on their heads and then display them to one another on monitors imbedded in their stomachs.

Understandably, confused parents and educators around the world have been fearful of the impact the technophilic *Teletubbies* might have on their youngsters. Making matters worse, the characters speak in a preverbal gibberish that, though actually based on phonemes that have been shown to help toddlers develop language skills, alarms adults who feel that, as role models, the characters will promote poor speech. In reality, however, in addition to helping babies learn to speak, the program helps them come to recognize technology as a natural component of modern life. By watching the program, young viewers understand that, like the TVs in the Teletubbies' tummies, technological innovations can offer us ways to commune, to learn about each other, and to share our ideas. By accepting the seemingly alien as friendly, even loving (the Teletubbies are fond of hugging one another), our kids can find appropriate uses for our newest technological arrivals instead of being intimidated by them.

*Teletubbies* exemplifies the three main features of every evolutionary kids' activity. It promotes the humane use of communications technology, it is wildly and unexpectedly popular with children, and it is misunderstood and reviled by a majority of adults. For while young people are embracing every strategy offered to them with renewed eagerness, their parents, for the most part, are only growing more afraid of what they see as their own impending doom.

For many adults, a networked culture portends a loss of privacy and lack of order. The cultural immediacy offered by interactive media like the Internet, as well as the way the computer has insinuated itself into areas as diverse as healthcare and banking, has led the fearful to find an excuse to retreat. We are now obsessed with the "millennium bug," a simple programming error that has given survivalists a reason to build new, fortified camps in the hills of Wyoming and Colorado. Appealing to an anxious, technology-inspired fantasy of independence from the "system," the hype over the Y2K glitch has given evangelists hard evidence of the coming apocalypse and their followers justification for withdrawing from the global society their kids are hoping to build. Adult media has made a similar descent into hopelessness. The simple, almost playful paranoia of Chris Carter's *The X-Files* has been upgraded to the fetishized satanism of his spin-off, *Millennium*, in which a group of Bible-toting psychics prepare for our inevitable immersion into darkness.

The few grown-ups who sense that their kids may be on to something, on the other hand, are attempting to adopt an attitude of playfulness by buying into the youthful innovations of marketers. Adult products designed to look like toys—from Volkswagen's New Beetle to Apple's iMac—offer plastic facsimiles of open-mindedness and childlike adaptability. Unsure of how to develop these attributes in any other way, baby boomers hope to incorporate the values of youth culture into their lives by purchasing them.

Some of the very same marketers, meanwhile, are feeling threatened by the ironic stance of their young targets and the protection it affords them from traditional advertising techniques, and have developed new styles of persuasion designed to penetrate this self-conscious defensive strategy. Many of these marketers actually bought the first edition of this book. No, they were not hoping to figure out how to help young people in their quest to cope with an increasingly manipulative media space. They simply wanted to stay one step ahead of youth culture's adaptive measures. The result has been a new onslaught of advertisements that acknowledge and praise the younger generation's suspicion of marketing techniques in an effort to seduce them with new ones. TV commercials for Sprite, for example, satirize more primitive soft drink ads while begging kids to reward a more virtuous appeal to their sensibilities: "Image is nothing, thirst is everything." Likewise, the current fashion in Web design is to create sites and interfaces that lull young users into passive complacency so that they may be herded away from interactive exchanges and toward the "buy" button. The "community" areas on many music industry Web sites, for example, exist merely to gauge users' tastes and then present them with more customized advertising. The Internet's original promise as a medium for communication is fast giving way to an electronic strip mall that will trade the technology's potential as a cultural catalyst for a controlled and monitored marketplace.

Mainstream publications from *Time* to *USA Today* run covers painting a picture of today's youth as amoral, despondent, and unreachable. Attention Deficit Disorder, a rare but real affliction, is being used as a blanket explanation for a myriad of adaptive maneuvers that kids have developed to free themselves of the hypnotic spell of coercive media and advertising. Instead of looking for the root causes of these often debilitating reactions, doctors and educators convince worried parents to medicate their children with Ritalin and other psychoactive stimulants, a treatment that, when used in this inappropriate fashion, amounts to an indoctrination into a culture on the brink of collapse.

This is not a constructive approach to the profound shift we are facing at the dawn of a new millennium. For if, like immature children, we steadfastly maintain our allegiance to the obsolete institutions of the past, then we will certainly go down with the ship. On the other hand, if we can come to understand this tumultuous period of change as a natural phase in the development of new kinds of intelligence and cross-cultural intimacy, then our imaginative and creative abilities are the only limits on our capacity for adaptation. Our civilization is embarking on a kind of mass adolescence—when, in the history of mankind, have we seen so many different peoples and societies making their first tentative steps toward joining the global community? We need to learn to see these new intrusions into our lives as a teenager experiences those first flirtatious gestures from an attractive suitor. We are not being invaded—we are being courted.

As in any society in crisis, it is the children who first learn to incorporate the worst of threats into the most basic forms of play. When the plague threatened Europe with annihilation, the children sang "Ring Around the Rosie" as they ritualized the appearance of rose-colored sores, stench-camouflaging "posies," and piles of burning bodies in the streets. "Ashes, ashes," goes the simple refrain before it concludes in straightforward frankness: "We all fall down." While adults were surely horrified by their children's seeming indifference to disaster, civilization somehow survived, aided in no small part by people's ability to confront their challenges together.

What I'll attempt to show in this book is that the more frightening aspects of an entirely non-apocalyptic future are being addressed today, and quite directly, by most of the pop-cultural experiences of children and young adults. Whether it's the Teletubbies showing us how to accept our coevolution with technology or a vampire role-playing game calling for us to acknowledge the hellraising beast in each of us, these new forms have the ability to assuage our worst fears, confirm our most optimistic scientific theories, and overcome the religious and cultural absolutism that so often undermines our ability to adapt to the uncertainty of our times. The oldest of the media-empowered young people—the screenagers—have already developed into fledgling filmmakers, computer programmers, and social activists, whose worldviews are beginning to have a positive effect on our cultural values.

So please let us suspend, for the time being, our grown-up function as role models and educators of our nation's youth. Rather than focusing on how we, as adults, should shape our children's activities for their better development, let's appreciate the natural adaptive skills demonstrated by our kids and look to them for answers to some of our own problems. Kids are our advance scouts. They are, already, the thing that we must become.

That is, if in fact we choose to carry on beyond the end of our world, into theirs.

---

As you read, you probably noticed that Rushkoff builds his argument *inductively*, piling one example on top of another to slowly convince us that youth—teenagers, or "screenagers," as he calls them—have a distinct edge in both understanding and helping to shape the future. Their edge, according to Rushkoff, comes from their openness to technology, and his numerous examples of how teens use technology are meant to convince us that teens will adapt better to the future than those who are less technologically inclined. Implicit in this is also a *definitional* argument; as he puts it in his next to last paragraph, "Kids are our advance scouts [of the future]. They are, already, the thing that we must become." Part of "kids'" openness to the future relies, for Rushkoff, on the fact that they are "less entrenched in business-as-usual" and are "more willing to accept cultural change as a natural, even pleasurable process." They also *re*define change, such as increasing reliance on technology, as "play"; instead of being threatened by it, they learn to enjoy changes and transformations that others might find daunting or scary.

Besides definition and induction, Rushkoff relies on other strategies as well. For instance, he implies a cause-and-effect relationship with regard to our attitude about cultural change. If we accept and adapt to the changes occurring around us, then we'll have an easier time in the future. If we don't, then our children will leave us behind. Clearly, Rushkoff's argument depends on the acceptance of some unaddressed assumptions. Most notably, he seems to assume that technology is the wave of the future and that the next several years will be dominated by increasing reliance on technology. He might be right, but that's still a point that could be called into question.

## questions for discussion

Whether you ultimately agree with Rushkoff or not, you can see how he engages the reader, even provokes thought, with a variety of argumentative strategies. To think further about this piece and what it has to teach you about argument, consider the following discussion questions.

1. What do you think of Rushkoff's views of technology and youth? How would you characterize his vision of the future: "alarmist"? "optimistic"? "paranoid"? What elements of his writing style give you clues about that vision?
2. What elements of Aristotelian argumentation does Rushkoff use—pathos, logos, and ethos? How does Rushkoff attempt—and does he succeed or fail—to establish ethos in this introductory chapter? Has he convinced us that he can write intelligently and knowingly about youth and technology? If so, how? If not, what else could he do to improve his ethos?
3. What assumptions does Rushkoff make in this chapter? Do you accept them? For instance, does Rushkoff assume too glibly that embracing technology necessarily leads to change, or that youth inevitably hold sway over the future? What might be the limits or blind spots of such assumptions?
4. You can find out more about Douglas Rushkoff by visiting his Web site at **http://www.rushkoff.com/**. How are Rushkoff's style in this excerpt and his *online* style similar? Granted, the Web site has graphics and hyperlinks, but can you tell that the two texts were authored by the same person? How does *style* reveal authorship? What does it say about the author's attitude toward his subject? Toward his readers?
5. For another example in the use of multiple argumentative strategies, visit this *Frontline* documentary, "The Merchants of Cool: A Report on the Creators & Marketers of Popular Culture for Teenagers" (**http://www.pbs.org/wgbh/pages/frontline/shows/cool/**), which features correspondent Douglas Rushkoff discussing how marketers research trends in what passes as "cool" among youth so they can know how to market successfully to younger generations. Young people are less prone to respond to "traditional brand marketing messages," he observes, than they are to what's "cool." Marketers have to figure out just what that means at a given moment, because its meaning keeps changing.

How would you define "cool"? Are there any stable, relatively unchanging criteria for what is cool? Discuss this question and the information about the *Frontline* documentary in an electronic or face-to-face forum. Many other questions will probably arise, such as the following: What is the relationship between "coolness" and the predilection of youth to buy certain items? Is the relationship one of cause and effect—and how? In a way, we may be looking at a chicken-and-egg phenomenon: Which comes first? Do marketers actually pay attention to what youth think of as "cool" and then advise the creation and distribution of certain kinds of products? Or do they attempt to persuade youth that certain items are "cool," thus influencing and manipulating the ever-changing definition of what passes as cool? You can even question the appropriateness of the general terms used in the debate. For instance, does the conceptual category *youth* make sense, or is that just marketing shorthand to group people together in order to sell them a product? Can one draw substantive conclusions from generalizations made based on an assumption that "youth," in general, will like or be drawn to certain things?

## *Additional Writing Activities*

1. Pretend that you live in nineteenth-century New Orleans, and unlike Mr. Crockett, you very much want to see a road built from Memphis to New Orleans. You are not an Eastern congressman, so Crockett can not necessarily accuse you of hiding a raccoon in a bag. What case would you make, *contra* Crockett, in support of the road's construction? Use Crockett's speech to help you make your case. In fact, you could consider structuring your argument as a direct rebuttal to Crockett.
2. Compose a substantive e-mail message to Rushkoff himself, and comment on both the style and the content of his writing. Explain to him why you either agree or disagree with him. Draw on your own experiences and cite specific passages to help you explain your points. Share your comments with your classmates and get their feedback. (Contact information for Rushkoff is on his Web site: **http://www.rushkoff.com/**.)
3. Write a substantive letter or e-mail message to another student writer in which you convince him or her to read Rushkoff's piece,

basing your argument on how Rushkoff defines youth and whether you agree with his definition. To convince your colleague, what elements of Rushkoff's argument would you highlight? What examples would you use?

4. Taking an essay you've written for another class, either in college or in high school, write a self-reflection essay in which you examine your use of ethos, logos, or pathos. Then assess the kinds of argumentative strategies you used such as definition, cause and effect, or analogy. If you were revising the paper today, based on your developing knowledge of argumentation, how might you recast or reframe your discussion? Would a more focused argumentative strategy work for the topic you were writing about? Or would the topic call for more attention to ethos and pathos? Share your self-reflection essay with others for feedback.

# CHAPTER 4

# New Worlds, New Ways: Contemporary Argument

In the preceding chapter, we introduced you to some traditional approaches to argumentation, with a focus on classical views of argument put forward by Aristotle in particular. We spent an entire chapter on classical argumentation because Aristotle's approach to analyzing argument dominated rhetoric for two millennia; his ideas were—and have continued to be—remarkably influential. Since Aristotle's time, however, other thinkers and writers have grappled with understanding argument. Thinkers such as Stephen Toulmin and Carl Rogers, whose approaches to argument we discuss in this chapter, have given us more contemporary ways of reading, understanding, and writing arguments. These contemporary approaches are the subject of this chapter. But first, let's discuss how contemporary argument attempts to address some weaknesses or limits in the classical Aristotelian approach.

## The Limits of Aristotle's Approach

The "classic" writers you read who came from Western societies were taught Aristotelian methods in school, and they employed them rigorously in fields ranging from theology and ethics (e.g., Thomas Aquinas) to law and politics (e.g., Thomas Jefferson) and almost every other discipline that has existed in our society. In order to read and understand what they wrote, you need to be able to see what the writers are doing and the standards they are applying to the works of others. At the same time, few, if any, of those speaking and writing around you today will deliberately model their arguments on Aristotle. They may know classical rhetoric but have intellectual or philosophical reasons for resisting the use of classical forms. Why?

There are several good reasons. Trying to force all arguments into Aristotle's mold not only may prove frustrating if one is analyzing them but also may result in oversimplification of complex issues and positions. Perhaps some further explanation is in order. Aristotle's logic required that all valid deductive arguments have a *necessary* conclusion; that is, if the first two statements are true, then their combination *must* follow as necessary: all cats are blue, and if this is a cat, then this (pointing to a cat) is necessarily blue. The syllogism, however valid *logically*, is meaningless when one or more of the premises is false, as is the statement that "all cats are blue." This is especially problematic when the premise is not a general statement of fact but a statement of policy, an idea, a value that is not generally believed, or a definition about which people in the audience may disagree. For example, an ethical principle that might be used to justify a claim might be that "the personal happiness of the individual is the highest good." You, however, might think that a utilitarian principle—that the greatest good for the greatest number of people is the highest good—is a superior criterion for judging an action ethical or not.

Let's use an example familiar to citizens in many communities. In practical terms, one might know a public official who argues as follows:

Any company that brings jobs is welcome in our town.

Company XYZ will bring 100 jobs.

Therefore, Company XYZ is welcome in our town.

Someone else, however, may question that job creation alone is the criterion for deciding which industries should be welcomed. The company bringing 100 jobs to a town may also be planning to pour thousands of tons of air pollution into the air in that town. Some of these pollutants may be known to contribute to higher levels of certain diseases. Citizens in the town may already have been affected by poor air quality and may, as a result, have a higher incidence of pollution-related diseases, as well as higher health insurance rates and medical costs, than residents of towns with cleaner air.

Given this, the city official might revise the argument to read as follows:

*Major premise:* Any company that contributes to the economic well-being of the city is welcome to locate here.
*Minor premise:* Company XYZ will bring 100 jobs.
*Conclusion:* Therefore, Company XYZ is welcome to locate here.

Let's assume for a moment that the parties agree on the statement of policy in the major premise. A questioner might then examine the facts behind the minor premise and might ask questions such as these:

- What is the level of unemployment in the town?
- Will the company offer training so that local residents can acquire these jobs?
- Do these jobs pay well? Will the company agree to pay union wages?
- What is the total annual payroll?

A hard-nosed cost–benefit analysis might reveal that increased costs to the city can be expected, which would counteract the positive economic impact. For example, the county may have to pay for new roads to accommodate the traffic to and from the company's plant or may have to make more frequent repairs to roads subject to heavier traffic. It may have to bear some cost in running water and sewage lines to the plant. On the flip side, the town may receive additional tax revenues because of the presence of the operation. If so, will these be enough to pay any increased costs?

Still further analysis may raise other questions, as follows:

- Assuming the operation stays within legal air pollution limits, will the air pollution it emits adversely affect the air quality in the area surrounding the plant?

- If air quality deteriorates, will the city be as attractive to other businesses that would have considered locating there?
- Will emissions produced by the plant contain substances that have been proved to increase health risks?
- Will children and elderly people, asthmatics, and those with heart disease be negatively affected?
- Will medical costs go up for area residents?
- Will health insurance rates for the town go up because of these increased risks?
- Can the officials' assumption, in fact, be true—that the net effect of 100 jobs will be to *increase, improve*, or even (as the major premise says) *contribute to* the economic well-being of the town? Even if it cannot, should the argument be dismissed as simply fallacious?

The question is clearly more complicated than the major and minor premise would *at first* suggest. Many more interlocking and interconnected questions must be asked to understand the complexity of the situation at hand. Clearly, a more flexible method for arguing probability, rather than absolute necessity, is needed. After all, the fact that something *might* happen doesn't mean it necessarily *will* happen.

In recent years, other approaches have been developed that have proved helpful to students in addressing some of the limitations of Aristotelian argument. For instance, some feminists have objected to using Aristotle's system, noting that the syllogism doesn't leave much room for complexity or for alternatives. It pushes us to make a conclusion, to reach a decision, to judge. In this way, it runs the risk (as we have seen) of oversimplifying complex arguments. It also doesn't leave much room for negotiation and discussion. Some feminists have raised these concerns because they see traditional argument as focused on "winning" an argument, on making sure that one's opponents "lose" the "battle" of the argument. This seems a stereotypically "masculine," aggressive approach to argumentation and debate. If we are always moving, inexorably, toward reaching a conclusion or "winning" the argument, then we might not have time to consider alternatives more carefully, or to listen carefully to those making other claims and proposing counterarguments. Feminists and others often seek new approaches to argument, a mature discourse that does not seek to "win" but that recognizes the limitations of Aristotelian argument in the real world. One such effort encourages *dialogue* and *collaboration* in an effort to reach mutually agreeable and beneficial compromise as opposed to one side's "winning" over the other. We will see, with the arguments presented later in this book, how such collaborations can work.

Other criticisms point to even more basic problems with strict Aristotelian argument. For instance, the Aristotelian distinction between deductive and inductive argument may not be especially useful, since many arguments combine both approaches. Unless they become lawyers, students will rarely if ever be required to do formal deductive analysis in real life. Even law schools widely use other argumentative modes, such as Stephen Toulmin's model, discussed in the next section, to train future attorneys. Indeed, we too should consider other forms and modes of argument that allow for greater flexibility, complexity, and nuance, like that proposed by Steven Toulmin. As we'll see, Toulmin offers us a mode of understanding and analyzing arguments that takes a variety of the strategies we've been talking about into consideration. His scheme for understanding and analyzing arguments, however, also gives us some flexibility for considering alternative views, examining assumptions, and appreciating the complexities of debate in the contemporary world.

## Toulmin's Model

Stephen Toulmin was a British philosopher who resisted the formal classical model of argument and its dependence on a system of classical logic. He concluded that distinguishing between "inductive" and "deductive" modes of argument led to more confusion than clarification and that what these two modes had in common was more important than the distinctions between them. As an alternative, he suggested terminology that could be used for analyzing all arguments and that could accommodate the uncertainties present in many of them. In *The Uses of Argument* (1958) and *Introduction to Reasoning* (1979), by Toulmin, Stephen Rieke, and Richard Janik, among other works, Toulmin offered his own model, which can prove immensely helpful in analyzing all kinds of arguments.

To capture the complexity of most arguments and to expand on Aristotle's analysis of the parts of an argument, Toulmin devised the following terms to explain what he saw as the primary components of any substantial argument: *claim, qualifier, warrant, backing, data* or *grounds*, and *reservation*. The **claim** is the main point you are trying to prove, and the

**backing** and **data** or **grounds** are the information and evidence you are using to support your claim. The **warrant** is the primary assumption (the missing statement in an enthymeme, for instance) that you are making in the argument, and the **reservation** is a consideration of a counterargument or rebuttal, or the recognition of the possibility that someone might disagree with you or come to a different conclusion or claim. The **qualifier** is the recognition that you are arguing for a particular case or circumstance, not *all* cases or circumstances.

An example will help. Let's apply Toulmin's terms to elements of the following basic argument. If you make a digital copy of the paragraph below, you can "play along" with analyzing it. To do so, you should first break it down into its constituent parts, using Toulmin's terms. Then look for and graphically manipulate a claim (enlarged and boldfaced), qualifier (italicized), warrant (boldfaced), backing (italicized), data (underlined), and reservation (underlined italics).

Here's the paragraph we'll work with:

> According to a recent study by C. Arden Pope and a team of medical researchers published in the *Journal of the American Medical Association* (March, 2002), increased levels of fine particulate matter (PM < 2.5) in the air have been found to raise the incidence of death from heart disease, lung disease, and cancer among people with those diseases who breathe it. Acme Enterprises is building a new industrial facility that will increase levels of fine particulates in the surrounding air, according to its own state air-quality permit application. Possibly, people living near the plant will suffer increases in deaths from heart disease, lung disease, and cancer as a result of the plant's operation. If no one who breathes the air containing increased levels of PM < 2.5 already suffers from heart disease, lung disease, or cancer, deaths will not result.

**DEFINITION**

"PM < 2.5" is particulate matter (e.g., fine dust), smaller than 2.5 microns in diameter.

Your breakdown of the document into Toulmin's model might look like this:

**Claim:** People living near the plant will suffer increased death rates from heart disease, lung disease, and cancer.

**Qualifier:** *Possibly*, people living near the plant will suffer increases in deaths from heart disease, lung disease, and cancer as a result of the plant's operation. [italics added]

**Warrant:** Increased levels of PM < 2.5 cause increased deaths from heart disease, cardiopulmonary disease, and cancer among sick people who breathe it.

**Backing:** Recent medical research by C. Arden Pope, published in the *Journal of the American Medical Association*, demonstrates the connection between PM < 2.5 and death from the named diseases.

**Data/grounds:** Acme Enterprises is building a new industrial facility that will increase levels of fine particulates in the surrounding air, according to its own air-quality permit application.

**Reservation:** If no one who breathes the air containing increased levels of PM < 2.5 already suffers from heart disease, lung disease, or cancer, deaths will not result.

Your graphically manipulated paragraph should look like this:

*According to a recent study by C. Arden Pope and a team of medical researchers published in the* Journal of the American Medical Association *(March 2002)*, **increased levels of fine particulate matter (PM < 2.5) in the air have been found to raise the incidence of death from heart disease, lung disease, and cancer among sick people who breathe it**. Acme Enterprises is building a new industrial facility that will increase levels of fine particulates in the surrounding air, according to its own permit application. *Quite possibly*, **people living near the plant will suffer increases in deaths from heart disease, lung disease, and cancer as a result of the plant's operation**. *However, if no one who breathes the air containing increased* levels of PM < 2.5 already suffers from heart disease, lung disease, or cancer, deaths will not result.

For a better understanding of Toulmin's scheme, let's look a bit more closely at each item in it, using Crockett's argument as an example.

## Claim

According to Toulmin, all arguments have in common the fact that they put forth a conclusion or *claim*. The claim is the main point to which all other elements of the argument, including the reasoning, lead. You can think of a claim as something that someone asserts, such as a right to a piece of property (as with a mining claim) or to reimbursement of medical expenses (as when filing an insurance claim). For example, look back at David Crockett's speech in the preceding chapter. Crockett claims that *it is a bad idea ("a wild notion") to build a road all the way from Buffalo to New Orleans.*

## Warrant

The primary reason given for arriving at a claim is called the *warrant*. It is typically a general statement, or assumption, on which the rest of the argument rests. The warrant justifies use of facts, data, or even other assertions to arrive at the claim. The warrant is roughly equivalent to the major premise in classical terms (as in, we can assume that "all men are mortal"). It may be stated, assumed, or implied as a truth. Ethical principles, laws, beliefs, or even the general finding of a scientific study may be used as warrants. You can also think of a warrant in terms of a "warrant for someone's arrest"—in that a warrant *assumes* that someone has done something wrong and is now initiating the process of finding out what exactly happened, or of determining if the original assumption—the warrant—is justifiable or accurate. For example, Crockett claims that *building the road from Buffalo all the way to New Orleans* might *be a waste of money for the taxpayers.*

## Backing

If there is a chance that the audience may not agree about the truth of the warrant—and in a diverse society a wide audience probably will not—the author may provide support for it, called *backing*, to increase the likelihood that the audience will accept it. Backing may include an indication of the nature of the authority behind the warrant, such as the credentials of the scientists doing a study. Crockett backs his warrant (that a road would be a waste of money) with the observation that *traveling from Memphis to New Orleans by steamboat is relatively easy*; after all, at that time, it took only seven or eight days!

## Grounds or Data

The *grounds* or *data* may be not merely statistical data, but also any assertion of truth advanced as *support* for the claim. This may include extensive material collected or may be limited to one piece of evidence. The grounds are roughly equivalent to a minor premise in traditional deductive arguments, but they also include the evidence advanced in support of a general conclusion in traditional inductive argument. For example, Crockett alludes to other projects—paying down the debt, other "internal improvements"—that the country as a whole needs to be considering. Further, he states that his constituents elected him to oppose taxes, not increase them, and they find excessive taxes oppressive.

## Reservations

When advancing an argument, the author may decide to answer possible objections to the argument even before opponents raise them. These are called the *reservations* (also referred to as *rebuttals*). You can think of the rebuttal as your consideration of possible counter-arguments to your claim, warrant, backing, or grounds. For example, Crockett is fully willing to go part way, to consider that a road from Buffalo to Memphis might not be a bad idea, so no one can accuse him of being against "internal improvements."

## Qualifier

Because most arguments set forth claims that are *probable*, rather than necessary, the argument must include an indication of just how probable it is that the conclusion is true. These words are called *qualifiers* (e.g., words or terms such as *mostly*, *very probably*, *almost always* are *qualifiers*). As you can see, the wider variety of terms in Toulmin's model addresses the need to have a way of talking about arguments that cannot easily be reduced to syllogisms without losing any of their complexity. Crockett qualifies his opposition to taxes, for example, by pointing out that he opposes only "certain" taxes, not all of them. And he does not oppose internal improvements in general; he just will not favor them *all* (i.e., won't "go the whole hog"), including a road from Memphis to New Orleans.

## your turn

Consider the syllogistic argument that follows, and describe how Toulmin might approach it, using his terms for the major parts of a substantive argument.

*Major premise*: Any company that contributes to the economic well-being of the city is welcome to locate here.
*Minor premise*: This company will bring 100 jobs.
*Conclusion*: Therefore, the company is welcome to locate here.

What did you come up with in either case? Do you see how Toulmin's model might help to address a bit more of the complexity of an argumentative situation?

## Using Toulmin's Model Electronically

To see how you can use your computer to think through an argument using Toulmin's model, try downloading a copy of the Declaration of Independence from the Web and analyzing it using Toulmin's terminology. **Enlarge and turn to boldface the primary claim** and *place qualifiers (if there are any) in italics*, the **warrant**(s) **in boldface**, and the *backing in italics*. Underline the grounds and *place the rebuttal or reservation in underlined italics*. Remember that several arguments may be advanced in one document. Try using a different font or a different color for each group of statements that form one argument. Then delete statements that are not part of the essential structure of the argument. Arrange the elements of each argument in this order: claim, qualifier, warrant, backing, grounds, and rebuttal. Now reread the original document. Is it any clearer to you how Thomas Jefferson structured his arguments in the Declaration of Independence? Is it significant that in stating his claim in the last paragraph, he used no qualifiers whatsoever? Look for a secondary argument related to the primary one and boldface its conclusion. How is the conclusion of the secondary argument related to the primary argument?

To help yourself visualize the structure of arguments, you can also follow this procedure with editorials and other articles, particularly if you copy and paste them from your source into your word-processing program. (Reminder: Any copied and pasted documents are *not* your own, and you must cite them if you ever incorporate them into any of your own writing.)

Of course, any of the graphical manipulations you experimented with here can be used during peer review. You can exchange *your own* papers with classmates (either via a discussion board, through e-mail, as an e-mail attachment, through shared network space, or by swapping disks) and break down the argument(s) using Toulmin's categories. One quick way to test the validity of an argument is to delete all statements that are not technically part of the argument. Then analyze the argument, asking the questions suggested previously. Write a paragraph to your classmate explaining your understanding of the structure of the argument and pointing out any strong or weak points. If needed, suggest a specific way that argument might be improved during rewriting.

## Rogerian Argument

Far too often, disagreement on some kinds of issues can get bitter—bitter enough, in some cases, to lead to violence. Arguing in Aristotle's style can often take place in what resembles a battle mode. It is a style of argument that tends to encourage opponents to become entrenched in their positions, increasing their polarization rather than fostering sympathetic discussion. Some claim that this does nothing to help bring various sides together to look for solutions to mutual problems. Psychologist Carl Rogers proposed one model for nonconfrontational argumentation that works to avoid this pitfall.

First, Rogers says, the writer must not *antagonize* the audience. The first step a writer (or speaker) should take to avoid doing this is to indicate that she has listened empathetically to the point of view with which she disagrees. The writer should do nothing to put the audience on the defensive, such as using loaded or insulting language. Judgment is withheld until both sides have had a chance to listen to and attempt to understand each other. When a writer is writing to an unseen reading audience, it is important to state as accurately and respectfully as possible his understanding of the opposing position and then look for points to agree with. This, in classical terms, establishes the *ethos* of the writer as one who gives fair consideration to all viewpoints.

The key is the search for *common ground*, as well as assumptions or values on which both sides can agree. Sometimes these may be very general ("We agree that it is right to want what is best for our children"). The closer the areas of agreement are to the specific concerns of the argument, the greater the likelihood of reaching some sort of **consensus**. For instance, the writer may discuss the ways in which she is affected by the failure to find a solution to the problem; that in itself may furnish a point of common ground.

The writer must also state as fairly as possible *the position of the other side*. Quoting a spokesperson for the opposing position—allowing that view to be expressed in the words of an advocate—can be an effective technique. Conversely, presenting a one-sided view of the opposing position in biased language will likely prevent any further progress in the discussion. In other words, to characterize Gloria Steinem's views on the rights of women, quote from her voluminous writings; do not represent her views in the words of Rush Limbaugh. Let opponents speak for themselves if their wording is available. Then, after exploring the points on which both sides can agree—the "common ground" between them—the writer can offer a neutrally worded statement of the position she or he is advancing, show how it differs from the audience's, identify the situations in which she or he thinks it is valid, and point out how it is consistent with the principle or other items on which the two sides *do* agree.

The writer ends by stating a thesis, or summary of the argument, and usually, in doing so, gives up some ground on one or more points. Rather than one side's "winning" outright (which rarely happens anyway), the two sides, in a sense, negotiate a compromise. The argument ends with a statement of the thesis, or argument, as modified to take the other side's views into consideration; it does not begin with one and then proceed to build a defensive wall around it. In the conclusion, the writer may suggest several ways of **compromising** or **negotiating** on the issue and show how the reader might gain from considering one or more of them.

You can easily see an example of Rogerian argument at work—long before Rogers developed his ideas—in Crockett's piece. Crockett is fully willing to compromise, to negotiate, to give some ground in the great debate about building the road from Buffalo to New Orleans. Most notably, you can see his willingness to compromise in his concession that a road from Buffalo to Memphis might not be a bad idea.

## WRITING SPOTLIGHT

### Rogerian Argument in Action

Let's look at another brief example of Rogerian argument. In the following essay, Robert Leston considers two views about higher education—that of E. D. Hirsch, who argues that education should emphasize the common knowledge that everyone in a culture should have in order to be able to communicate and participate effectively, and that of Paulo Freire, who maintains that, when education simply provides that common knowledge, it gives students only a "partial view of reality." In Freire's view, students should not merely learn a body of common knowledge; they also should learn how to "create" knowledge and to critique what the culture has to offer. In the course of this short analysis, Leston looks at both views and attempts to negotiate a compromise—what he calls a "reconciliation" in his title—between them. You'll note that he first fully lays out Hirsch's position and tries to represent his views fairly. By doing this, he attempts to create an ethos that says he is open to considering carefully views that he might not agree with; indeed, you'll probably sense that Leston is a bit more partial to Freire's idea. Nonetheless, by the end of the essay, and in keeping with a Rogerian strategy, he tries to reconcile the two opposing views by emphasizing the common ground between them—an interest in educating students and preparing them for active participation in society. See what you think.

---

### Towards Reconciliation: Common Ground in the Education Curriculum

Robert Leston

There may be no better place to begin a look into the discussion of what should entail a responsible educational curriculum than with E. D. Hirsch, a literary critic known for his work devoted to increasing cultural literacy. Hirsch

Excerpt from "Towards Reconciliation: Common Ground in the Education Curriculum," by Robert Leston.

suggests that what is wrong with the modern educational institution is that too many students are unable to participate in what he calls the "national public discourse," defined by a "common knowledge" of information, traditions, and stories which Americans share (*Dictionary* ix). The responsibility of the schools, Hirsch's literacy campaign argues, is to help students acquire the literacy they need in order to be part of American culture.

In "Finding the Answer in Drills and Rigor," Hirsch outlines how cultural literacy can be achieved. He argues the reason American schools have not fulfilled the egalitarian aims of schooling is due to the predominance of a "progressive-education tradition, which has seriously misconceived itself as the guardian of social progress and democratic ideals" (475). Hirsch states that since progressive education measures are inadequate for teaching the literacy of the national public discourse, then those who wield power continue to do so because the newly educated will not have mastered the dominant discourse necessary to effect change (475). "Only if the poor [work] hard in school to accumulate the 'intellectual baggage' of the rich [can] they earn money and wield the levers of power" (476). To help students gain the knowledge which comes from the dominant national discourse, Hirsch advocates the "skills and drills" method many are familiar with and which has fallen out of favor with most educators during the past twenty or so years. Hirsch's call to return to "skills and drills" is based on 1980s research that points to the high academic achievement rates of the Roman Catholic schools. Following a rich and traditional curriculum, says Hirsch, "Roman Catholic schools were better at achieving equity than most public schools." As a result, "disadvantaged children prospered academically, as did their advantaged peers, and the schools narrowed the gap between races and social classes" (476). Hirsch's argument appears quite compelling from this perspective; his view is one we can imagine would be supported by many parents of young children.

One reason Hirsch is so compelling is that he recognizes that our educational system has left behind many children from the lower classes. By advocating and using standardized testing as an effective form of student measurement, Hirsch recognizes that those from relatively low socioeconomic backgrounds do not perform well in school and do not grow up to be adults who enjoy the material success of white-collar workers. The research Hirsch has available to him shows that traditional curriculums succeed in instructing students and narrowing the academic gap between students from various economic backgrounds. If the academic performance gap can be closed, then so will economic differences when those students come of age, for they will have learned to survive in a world which has rules, and by using those rules to their own advantages will learn the proper behaviors in certain contexts. If most educators were asked whether they want students from all walks of life to be successful in this world, most if not everyone, I think, would answer affirmatively. Hirsch's hope for students is one we should all share; there may be a way of rethinking and revising his strategy to make achieving our common objective more successful.

While Hirsch advocates the "skills and drills" method, it is important to remember the negative effect this method can have when gone to an extreme. Paulo Freire, author of *Pedagogy of the Oppressed*, calls the traditional teaching method the "banking concept" of teaching, a method which operates through narration in order to "fill" the minds of students. The problem with this method, according to Freire, is that the educator provides the student with a partial view of reality. The information students receive has been preselected by both conscientious and unconscientious "oppressors," and students thus learn only enough to keep the societal machine running in a way which preserves the positions of those in power (60–70). When students are simply taught the rules of the dominant discourse—what Hirsch calls "cultural literacy"—they learn to be passive recipients of the world and collectors of meaning imparted to them from teachers. Once they receive this information, they become part of the cycle again, imparting what they have inherited to others. But if, along with the information students receive, they are taught that they create meaning rather than just inheriting it, they will be able to redescribe the past in more egalitarian ways.

E. D. Hirsch's and Paulo Freire's work need not stand in opposition to one another. For Hirsch, making the student part of the system teaches her the rules of the dominant discourse, a condition which results in the student's liberation from the lower rungs of the socioeconomic ladder, but leaves the system fundamentally the same. Most educators from the liberal tradition do not define success in purely economic terms, but recognize the importance of economic stability. A life is valuable when we are able to think in ways we could not before (when we learn) and when we can become agents for change in a democratic society. To help students live valuably, then, we need to give them both the raw academic skill-sets Hirsch advocates, but help them apply that knowledge in critique of the power systems around them. If we can do this, then student success can be achieved in a spirit of both harmony and progress.

## WORKS CITED

Freire, Paulo. *Pedagogy of the Oppressed*. Trans. Myra Bergman Ramos. 30th Ann. Continuum, 2001.

Hirsch. E. D., Jr., Joseph Kett, and James Trefil. *The Dictionary of Cultural Literacy: What Every American Needs to Know*. 2nd ed. Boston: Houghton, 1993.

———. "Finding the Answers in Drills and Rigor." *New York Times* September 11, 1999. A15+. Rpt. in *Perspectives on Argument*. Nancy Wood. 3rd ed. Prentice Hall, 2001. 475–77.

---

Could you detect Leston's Rogerian strategy? A hint that he is using a Rogerian approach lies, of course, in his title: the word *reconciliation* gives it away. But also note the opening sentence of the concluding paragraph: "E. D. Hirsch's and Paulo Freire's work need not stand in opposition to one another." Such a sentence signals that the writer is ultimately more interested in establishing common ground than in simply "winning" an argument. Were you convinced? Why or why not?

Rogerian argument works best, of course, if those on both sides of the issue will agree to use it as a negotiating approach, as opposed to one side's using it while the other continues in warlike opposition. Because of its dependence on a *dialogic process*—that is, a process composed of give-and-take between both sides—it also works well in networked conversations. Because a Rogerian strategy brings together numerous positions in a debate, you can also adapt it to a number of writing situations in other courses or other areas of your life that rely on, call for, or use argumentative debates.

**INTER**text

For another example of Rogerian argument, see Scott Pedram's essay on the Boy Scouts of America in Chapter 7.

## your turn

Try some of the following exercises to practice your developing sense of how to read and understand written argument.

1. Visit the Web site of a newspaper and locate an editorial or letter to the editor. Copy and paste the editorial into a word-processing program and make an extra copy. Identify the argument, boldfacing and enlarging the conclusion, boldfacing the premises or claims, and

deleting all extra material. Then write a brief paragraph commenting on the structure of the argument in the piece. Is the conclusion stated at the beginning or the end? Is a clear thesis presented? What is the enthymeme, if one is present? Is it based on stated or unstated assumptions? What are they? Everyone in the class can use the same article, and you can compare results with one another, either face-to-face or electronically.

2. Collect several argumentative letters to an editor from a newspaper, and then divide them into those that clearly use a Rogerian approach from those that don't. What are the primary differences between the two? What kind of language do the Rogerian arguments use? Can you detect words, phrases, or sentences that suggest compromise or negotiation? What are they?

## Evaluating an Argument

After identifying the parts of an argument, it is up to you to devise appropriate questions to evaluate each of the parts and to consider their relationship with one another. Even if you have not studied the rules of formal logic or Toulmin's model in depth, you can apply common sense and do research to evaluate most arguments. We can also use Toulmin to come up with a list of questions to help us evaluate a wide variety of arguments. Each of the following questions, for instance, can be used to help you analyze and evaluate how sound—or unsound—a particular argument might be.

Here are some basic questions to ask when evaluating most arguments.

*Is the claim clearly stated and sufficiently qualified?*

Without an identifiable claim, there is no argument. Every argument must make a claim. Is it qualified adequately to avoid making too general a statement? Does the claimant use or imply the word *all* or *always* when *some* or *most of the time* would be more accurate?

*Do you accept the warrant?*

If a demonstrable truth is stated or assumed, how can you test it? Again, remember that a warrant is the assumption on which an argument rests. For instance, when you are reading through an argument, particularly an academic argument, you might assume that the writer is representing opposing views fairly and accurately. Is this a safe assumption? You might look up the original article to see if a scientific study is being represented accurately. If the warrant is a belief or principle, do you agree with it? If it is a law, is the law being cited the one that applies in this case? (This is the stuff of which legal careers are made.) If the warrant is not acceptable to you, then neither can be any argument based on it.

*What is the quality of the backing for the warrant?*

What authority is behind the warrant? What research could you do to check it? Is it a religious text, philosopher, celebrity, or other source who may represent beliefs, ethical principles, or values that you do not share? What questions can you raise about the authority behind the backing? Is it sufficiently credible to convince you to accept the warrant, or assumption, being advocated? If the backing is itself debatable, or a matter of belief, it may weaken, rather than strengthen, the argument with an audience that does not accept that view of it, or that belief. Is the study being cited reliable? Where was it published?

*What is the quality of the evidence?*

Evidence brought in support of a claim must be true. Is there any reason to suspect that the facts are not represented credibly? For example, could the writer be biased in favor of one position or other? Are you willing to take that person's word for the truth of the data? If you have any reason to question it, do research to check the facts. If the grounds are not true, then no claim they are used to support can be reliable. When they are obviously false, the argument is unsound.

What happens when the data may be interpreted in different ways? Consider this argument:

Susan said: "My grandmother in the hospital has no appetite for food right now. She must be suffering from acute chronic heart failure (CHF)."

**INTERtext**

We'll talk more about verifying research and evaluating sources of information in Chapter 6, on research writing.

A lack of appetite is one symptom of CHF, but in this case, is that what that symptom means? Other questions need to be asked: Is acute chronic heart failure the only cause of loss of appetite? Could loss of appetite be a sign of something else, such as stomach flu or a dislike of food different from what she is used to? If she is known to have chronic heart failure, does loss of appetite prove that it is "acute" rather than ordinary CHF? You can do a Web search to find the signs of CHF, but remember that even if loss of appetite *is* a sign of CHF, no conclusion could be reached on the basis of that one symptom alone. Also note that in this case, you do not have enough knowledge to determine whether the evidence given (lack of appetite) means what Susan says it does. Verification should be sought from someone with enough knowledge to make a diagnosis in the case—the grandmother's doctor.

*Are the grounds sufficient?*

If the claim is a general one based on specific evidence presented in the data or grounds, is there enough evidence to justify drawing the general conclusion? This is extremely important. Arguments in which a general conclusion is drawn on the basis of too little information are *weak*. Insufficient grounds can lead to general conclusions that are untrue. The more evidence presented in the grounds, the stronger the argument is likely to be. The evidence must have other qualities in addition to quantity, but a sufficient quantity is necessary to make a *strong* argument.

*Are grounds actually present or stated?*

It is not unusual for writers of opinion columns, letters to the editor, and even editorials to state a claim and then fail to present any grounds to support the claim. Instead, they may restate the claim in different words. In such cases, they do not really present an argument. If the grounds are absent or irrelevant, or if they merely restate the claim in different language and do not contribute a reason that the claim should be accepted, they may be said to be *begging the question.* This is a logical fallacy we'll discuss more later on.

*Is the sample randomly selected?*

This question is especially important when the general claim of an argument is based on statistics, including the results of surveys. If you are working with specialized material in a specific discipline, you will learn standards for statistical reliability within that field. When you are reading other material, it will be up to you to come up with some evaluation. If no flaws are apparent, consider a variety of questions, such as these: What is the *ethos* of the researcher presenting you information? In your estimation, could the organization or individual behind the survey be trusted to design a survey or research project without inherent bias? That is, was the evidence selected to yield the results desired by someone? Is the interpretation of the survey results credible? Academic credentials or affiliation with well-known public opinion pollsters could be important here.

*Are possible rebuttals or reservations carefully presented?*

Can you think of any reason that the claim might not follow from the grounds provided? What questions can you ask about the relationship between the claim and the data? Have opponents raised questions about specific elements of this argument that the rebuttal does not address adequately?

## Avoiding Logical Fallacies

In addition to the questions posed here, you might consider making more specific inquiries about an argument in question based on the *kind* of argument being made. For instance, some arguments make causal connections between items; others argue through similarity or analogy; and still others make claims about important definitions. If the argument made seems weak, it may be because the author's assertions are relying on **logical fallacies**, or reasoning that isn't quite reliable or that hasn't really been thought through. The word *fallacy*, in fact, is derived from the Latin word *fallere*, which means "to cheat" or "to deceive." As a writer, you will not want to insult an intelligent reader by using fallacious arguments in an attempt to win him or her over to your point of view; as a critical reader, you should be on guard against attempts to persuade you on the basis of poor reasoning. Considering the following questions will help you spot fallacies in the arguments you read—and write.

***Does the writer seem to jump to conclusions?***

There are many kinds of arguments based on insufficient data which prompt writers to jump to unsupported conclusions. Some of the following include these:

- *Hasty generalization:* Drawing a general conclusion too soon, before checking enough evidence to justify the conclusion ("I failed one math test, so therefore I must have no aptitude for math").
- *Overgeneralization:* Making a sweeping claim that might be true, but only if qualified—for example, "There are more professional sports teams made up of men than women, so men must be better athletes than women."
- *Stereotyping:* Labeling members of a group with certain characteristics that are not necessary for identification with the group—for example, "She is blonde, so she must be an airhead," or "Men are all jerks."

When you hear or read comments based on stereotyping, look for one exception to the claim. If you know of one blonde who is not an "airhead" or a man who is not a "jerk," then the generalization is untrue. If you do not know any members of a group to observe personally, you can still identify stereotyping if the label being applied to that class represents a characteristic that may occur in some members but does not seem *necessary* to define that group. Stereotyping is an example of sloppy reasoning.

***Does the argument claim a cause-and-effect relationship?***

If the argument asserts that certain causes lead to certain effects, are you convinced that that relationship actually exists? How can you test it? Does the author provide any documentation establishing that it exists? Remember that it is hard to prove cause-and-effect relationships, and you have every right to be skeptical about the connections made in such arguments. Saying something is so doesn't make it so. Furthermore, if the argument is that something will happen in the future as a result of something that has happened earlier, ask yourself if, in previous situations, such a cause has *always* had the claimed effect?

If the cause-and-effect relationship put forth in the argument seems weak or problematic, then the argument may rest on a **causal fallacy**, also known as *post hoc, ergo propter hoc* ("after the fact, therefore because of the fact"). This fallacy occurs when a writer posits in an argument that a particular effect stems from a certain cause, but in a relationship that doesn't hold up under further examination. For instance, if many intelligent people are also left-handed, one might try to assert that intelligence causes left-handedness, or that left-handedness is an indication of intelligence. But could a coincidence account for such apparent causality? For example, left-handedness and intelligence may be *correlated*, but does one actually *cause* the other? Is there really a causal relationship between the two? The cause-and-effect relationship asserted here is faulty in that *many* factors contribute to intelligence, not just being left-handed. The coincidence of left-handedness and intelligence is thus a **correlation**, not an indication of causality.

Jumping to conclusions about cause-and-effect relationships on the basis of too little evidence, or failing to consider other points that may be necessary to make a solid argument, can also result in the fallacy of **hasty generalization**. If a student argues that she writes well and therefore should always receive A grades on her papers, she is committing the fallacy of hasty generalization—that is, arriving at her conclusion on the basis of too little evidence. Good writing alone may not earn an A; other factors, such as the quality of research and the accurcy of documentation, may also play a part. As you're discovering, writing situations vary considerably, so skills used successfully in one situation may not translate into success in another. We need to consider, in this case, a *variety* of factors that lead to success in writing—not just past successes or a perceived sense of competency.

Overhasty causal arguments are sometimes referred to as succumbing to the fallacy of the **slippery slope**—that is, sliding too quickly (and hazardously) down one slope of thought instead of carefully picking your way through a terrain of ideas. For instance, if you are arguing against gay marriage, you might argue that gays shouldn't be allowed to marry because people will then want to marry their cats and dogs. Such an assertion rests on a slippery slope because you're arguing that two categorically different things (marriage between consenting adults and marriage based on bestiality) are so closely connected that one will lead to another.

***Is the argument based on an analogy?***

Is the argument based on an assumption (used as a warrant) that one thing or person is *similar* to another? If so, does the similarity prove anything about one of them, or merely illustrate, possibly in figurative terms, something that *may* be true but is not necessarily true? If you can find a critical point at which the comparison breaks down, the argument is said to be based on a **false analogy**. "The Clinton-Lewinsky affair is just like what happened with Nixon and Watergate," you may have heard someone say before drawing an elaborate comparison; in each case, a president seemed to lie about a particular situation. A writer using an analogy may find parallels between situations on some level or find it helpful in illustrating a point; in fact, a claim based on it may even be true, but the analogy itself does not prove anything. For instance, in this example, the comparison between the Clinton and Nixon scandals breaks down when we consider the purposes of the lies themselves. In one case, a president was possibly attempting to cover up a personal indiscretion; in the other case, a president was potentially covering up a plot to undermine a political rival. On closer examination, the two situations do not seem very analogous at all, and they are quite different in their severity and scope.

***Does the argument depend on a definition?***

If so, you may raise questions about the definition used. For example, in the argument "All cigarette smoking should be banned, because smoking is harmful to everyone's health," the grounds are: "Smoking is harmful." But what is *harmful*? How are we to define what *harmful* actually means? And harmful to whom? Before this argument can be advanced, both sides need to agree on that key point.

Not paying sufficient attention to the complexity of most definitional arguments can result in **begging the question**, or assuming that one's argument is transparent and thus doesn't need to be examined further. For instance, arguing that "All cigarette smoking should be banned, because smoking is harmful to everyone's health" might assume that banning smoking is the best way to proceed in convincing people to adopt healthier lifestyles. In this case, the argument is assuming that banning is, by definition, an effective means to induce health. We would say that the argument begs the question of the relationship between banning and effectiveness in health promotion.

Also, when reading or crafting your own arguments, you may want to make sure that key words are not used with different connotations in different parts of the argument. Only one meaning for each word is allowed in a given argument. For example, if one makes the argument that "contribution to economic growth of the area" is the criterion on which decisions will be based, a definition of *economic growth* should be set down and agreed upon. What constitutes economic growth? What indicators will be used, or how will it be quantified? Must a company considered to foster economic growth have certain characteristics? For instance, must it contribute to the tax base? What criteria can be agreed on that would qualify a company as a contributor to economic growth of the area? Is there an assumption that this company will have these characteristics? What evidence can be advanced to indicate that it will?

### *Does the argument stick to the point?*

**Fallacies of avoidance** consist of techniques to lead readers or listeners astray by distracting them from the reasoning or evidence in some way. For instance, **ignoring the question** is a fallacy frequently found in editorials or letters to the editor. An introductory sentence may set forth a claim, but on close examination—sometimes after wading through several hundred words of unsupported opinion—a critical reader finds that the writer never actually gives any reasons for arriving at that conclusion. A piece that purports to be argumentative in fact may contain no argument at all.

A **circular argument** accomplishes just as little by repeating the premise in the conclusion, usually in different words. "Candidate Smith will never be elected county commissioner because he doesn't have the ability to win more votes than the other candidates" is an example of a circular argument. "Theresa is going to graduate at the top of her class because she has the highest grade point average of all the students who will be finishing this year" is another. In this case as well, there is no real argument.

A conclusion that does not appear to be related to the reasons given for it is a **non sequitur**, meaning "it doesn't follow." Although technically it may be part of an argument, the argument is not coherent. To the reasonably careful reader, it will not make sense; for instance, "Children in our town's West Side neighborhood must overcome economic and social disadvantages. Therefore, state funding to their elementary school should be reduced." The relationship between the two sentences is unclear, despite the use of the word *therefore* to attempt to connect the ideas in each sentence.

To distract the audience by drawing attention away from an argument by focusing on tangential material is said to be committing the fallacy of the **red herring.** Pulling the reader's attention from the subject at hand is akin to pulling (on a string, one may assume) a "red herring"—an unexpected object—across a trail. Listen to a press conference of a national leader and note how reporters' toughest questions are often shoved aside while the interviewee strays from the subject of the question and never returns to it. For example, bringing up a controversial social issue such as gay marriage to deflect attention and questions away from economic concerns and budget crises may be a form of arguing by using a red herring.

Employing the fallacy of the **straw man** is another tactic often used deliberately to distract the audience from the real issues at hand. By exaggerating the consequences of an action or policy, or by extending a position far beyond its likely conclusion, then attacking it in the extended form, one in effect sets up a false opponent that can easily be demolished. Misrepresenting one's opponent, whether it be a person or a position, then battering the falsified version, is a technique commonly used by those who take extremist positions. Practice listening for this fallacy the next time you have a chance to listen to one of the popular radio talk shows. For instance, if a radio commentator argues that a liberal senator is against a particular tax cut because liberals are in favor of "big government" and want to fund many social programs that will bankrupt the government, then the commentator is constructing a straw man argument, and a stereotypical one as well. Not all liberals are anti–tax cuts, and many conservatives support a variety of social programs. Further, insinuating that liberals are for "big government" is not only a weak, unsupportable argument (with many ignored exceptions); it also deflects attention from the reasons why the senator is against a *particular* tax cut.

The fallacies of arguing **ad hominem** ("to the man or person") and **ad populem** ("to the people") involve appeals to prejudice, emotion, identification with an admired group or desire to dissociate oneself from a group, or closely held biases. "No patriotic American would believe," "All educated people will agree," or "Those with sex appeal will wear" are commonly used phrases that signal such fallacies.

One last fallacy is the argument **from ignorance**. It goes: "You can't prove that this isn't the case, so it must be the case." That is, if you can provide no evidence that this is not so, then it must be so. However, just because one has no evidence, or may not be willing to provide evidence, does not prove that no evidence exists that might be found. Absence of evidence is not evidence of absence.

## *Useful Links*

There are several Web sites that can assist you with understanding arguments. Of the many we regularly introduce to our students, you might enjoy and benefit from the following:

- The University of North Carolina at Chapel Hill has an excellent description of "Effective Academic Writing: The Argument" at **http://www.unc.edu/depts/wcWeb/handouts/argument.html.** What can you learn from this site to complement what you've read in this chapter? How will it prepare you for future work in *writing* arguments?

- Professor Barry Eckhouse's course, "Logic, Argument, & Persuasion" at **http://www.rhetor.com/courses/comm147fall2000.htm** describes some elements of argument in more detail and offers links for further exploration.

## Writers in Action: Contemporary Strategies of Argument

For your end-of-chapter reading, we'd like you first to revisit Douglas Rushkoff's essay, "Children of Chaos," at the end of the preceding chapter. Now that you have some familiarity with concepts and trends in contemporary argument, you can examine and appreciate Rushkoff's approach to his topic from Toulmin's and Rogers's perspectives. With Toulmin and Rogers in mind, reread "Children of Chaos" and consider the following questions for oral, written, or electronic discussion.

### questions for discussion

1. After rereading and making notes on "Children of Chaos," consider this: How might you use Toulmin's strategy to understand the argument that Rushkoff puts forward in that chapter? Try summarizing Rushkoff's position using Toulmin's strategy. Look in particular for ways of highlighting and understanding some of the warrants, or major assumptions, on which Rushkoff's thinking rests.

2. In this chapter, Rushkoff uses a number of binaries, such as youth/older people and chaos/order. After identifying several binary pairs, discuss with your classmates whether this is an effective strategy on which to build an argument. What forcefulness do binaries offer an argument? What might they miss or overlook?

3. How might Carl Rogers respond to Rushkoff's chapter? After discussing how someone adept at Rogerian argument might approach this piece, write an e-mail or letter to Rushkoff in which you offer a Rogerian critique of his argument. Consider the following questions: Does Rushkoff fairly characterize the views he is arguing against or critiquing? Does he leave any room for compromise or negotiation in his views of youth?

Another contemporary writer whose approach to argument is innovative and engaging is Barbara Kingsolver. In her essay, "A Fist in the Eye of God," Kingsolver addresses the tricky, provocative, and complex issue of the relationship between science and religion, as well as the growing use of genetic engineering, in a way that is both straightforward and subtle. At any point in the essay, Kingsolver risks alienating her potential audience by making assertions with which her readers might strongly disagree. Yet her tone throughout is measured, rational, and sensitive to alternative views. Read her piece carefully as a model of how a writer handles difficult material in a compelling way.

---

## A Fist in the Eye of God

Barbara Kingsolver

In the slender shoulders of the myrtle tree outside my kitchen window, a hummingbird built her nest. It was in April, the sexiest month, season of bud-burst and courtship displays, though I was at the sink washing breakfast dishes and missing the party, or so you might think. Then my eye caught a flicker of motion outside, and there she was, hovering uncertainly. She held in the tip of her beak a wisp of wadded spiderweb so tiny I wasn't even sure it was there, until she carefully smoodged it onto the branch. She vanished then, but in less than a minute she was back with another tiny white tuft that she stuck on top of the first. For more than an hour she returned again and again, increasingly confident of her mission, building up by infinitesimal degrees a whitish lump on the branch—and leaving me plumb in awe of the supply of spiderwebbing on the face of the land.

I stayed at my post, washing everything I could find, while my friend did her own housework out there. When the lump had grown big enough—when some genetic trigger in her small brain said, "Now, that will do"—she stopped gathering and sat down on her little tuffet, waggling her wings and tiny rounded underbelly to shape the blob into a cup that would easily have fit inside my cupped hand. Then she hovered up to inspect it from this side and that, settled and waddled with greater fervor, hovered and appraised

"A Fist in the Eye of God" is from *Small Wonder,* by Barbara Kingsolver (HarperCollins, 2002). 

some more, and dashed off again. She began now to return with fine filaments of shredded bark, which she wove into the webbing along with some dry leaflets and a slap-dab or two of lichen pressed onto the outside for curb appeal. When she had made of all this a perfect, symmetrical cup, she did the most surprising thing of all: She sat on it, stretched herself forward, extended the unbelievable length of her tongue, and licked her new nest in a long upward stroke from bottom to rim. Then she rotated herself a minute degree, leaned forward, and licked again. I watched her go all the way around, licking the entire nest in a slow rotation that took ten minutes to complete and ended precisely back at her starting point. Passed down from hummingbird great-grandmothers immemorial, a spectacular genetic map in her mind had instructed her at every step, from snipping out with her beak the first spiderweb tuft to laying down whatever salivary secretion was needed to accrete and finalize her essential creation. Then, suddenly, that was that. Her busy urgency vanished, and she settled in for the long stillness of laying and incubation.

If you had been standing with me at my kitchen sink to witness all this, you would likely have breathed softly, as I did, "My God." The spectacular perfection of that nest, that tiny tongue, that beak calibrated perfectly to the length of the tubular red flowers from which she sucks nectar and takes away pollen to commit the essential act of copulation for the plant that feeds her—every piece of this thing and all of it, my God. You might be expressing your reverence for the details of a world created in seven days, 4,004 years ago (according to some biblical calculations), by a divine being approximately human in shape. Or you might be revering the details of a world created by a billion years of natural selection acting utterly without fail on every single life-form, one life at a time. For my money the latter is the greatest show on earth, and a church service to end all. I have never understood how anyone could have the slightest trouble blending religious awe with a full comprehension of the workings of life's creation.

Charles Darwin himself was a religious man, blessed with an extraordinary patience for observing nature's details, as well as the longevity and brilliance to put it all together. In his years of studying animate life he noticed four things, which any of us could notice today if we looked hard enough. They are:

- Every organism produces more seeds or offspring than will actually survive to adulthood.
- There is variation among these seeds or offspring.
- Traits are passed down from one generation to the next.

- In each generation the survivors succeed—that is, they survive—because they possess some advantage over the ones that don't succeed, and because they survive, they will pass that advantage on to the next generation. Over time, therefore, the incidence of that trait will increase in the population.

Bingo: the greatest, simplest, most elegant logical construct ever to dawn across our curiosity about the workings of natural life. It is inarguable, and it explains everything.

Most people have no idea that this, in total, is Darwin's theory of evolution. Furthermore, parents who tell their children not to listen to such talk because "it's just a theory" are ignorant of what that word means. A theory, in science, is a coherent set of principles used to explain and predict a class of phenomena. Thus, gravitational theory explains why objects fall when you drop them, even though it, too, is "just a theory." Darwin's has proven to be the most robust unifying explanation ever devised in biological science. It's stunning that he could have been so right—scientists of Darwin's time knew absolutely nothing about genetics—but he was. After a century and a half, during which time knowledge expanded boundlessly in genetics, geology, paleontology, and all areas of natural science, his simple logical construct continues to explain and predict perfectly the existence and behavior of every earthly life form we have ever studied. As the unifying principle of natural sciences, it is no more doubted among modern biologists than gravity is questioned by physicists. Nevertheless, in a bizarre recent trend, a number of states have limited or even outright banned the teaching of evolution in high schools, and many textbooks for the whole country, in turn, have wimped out on the subject. As a consequence, an entire generation of students is arriving in college unprepared to comprehend or pursue good science. Many science teachers I know are nostalgic for at least one aspect of the Cold War days, when Sputnik riveted us to the serious business of training our kids to real science, instead of allowing it to be diluted or tossed out to assuage the insecurities of certain ideologues.

We dilute and toss at our peril. Scientific illiteracy in our population is leaving too many of us unprepared to discuss or understand much of the damage we are wreaking on our atmosphere, our habitat, and even the food that enters our mouths. Friends of mine who opted in school for English lit instead of microbiology (an option I myself could easily have taken) sometimes come to me and ask, "In two hundred words or less, can you explain to me why I should be nervous about genetic engineering?" I tell them, "Sit down, I'll make you a cup of tea, and then get ready for more than two hundred words."

A sound-bite culture can't discuss science very well. Exactly what we're losing when we reduce biodiversity, the causes and consequences of global warming—these traumas can't be adequately summarized in an evening news wrap-up. Arguments in favor of genetically engineered food, in contrast, are dangerously simple: A magazine ad for an agribusiness touts its benevolent plan to "feed the world's hungry with our vitamin-engineered rice!" To which I could add in reply my own snappy motto: "If you thought that first free hit of heroin was a good idea . . ." But before you can really decide whether or not you agree, you may need the five hundred words above and a few thousand more. If so, then sit down, have a cup of tea, and bear with me. This is important.

At the root of everything, Darwin said, is that wonder of wonders, genetic diversity. You're unlike your sister, a litter of pups is its own small Rainbow Coalition, and every grain of wheat in a field holds inside its germ a slightly separate destiny. You can't see the differences until you cast the seeds on the ground and grow them out, but sure enough, some will grow into taller plants and some shorter, some tougher, some sweeter. In a good year all or most of them will thrive and give you wheat. But in a bad year a spate of high winds may take down the tallest stalks and leave standing at harvest time only, say, the 10 percent of the crop that had a "shortness" gene. And if that wheat comprises your winter's supply of bread, plus the only seed you'll have for next year's crop, then you'll be almighty glad to have that small, short harvest. Genetic diversity, in domestic populations as well as wild ones, is nature's sole insurance policy. Environments change: Wet years are followed by droughts, lakes dry up, volcanoes rumble, ice ages dawn. It's a big, bad world out there for a little strand of DNA.

But a population will persist over time if, deep within the scattered genetics of its ranks, it is literally prepared for anything. When the windy years persist for a decade, the wheat population will be overtaken by a preponderance of shortness, but if the crop maintains its diversity, there will always be recessive aspirations for height hiding in there somewhere, waiting to have their day.

How is the diversity maintained? That old black magic called sex. Every seed has two parents. Plants throw their sex to the wind, to a hummingbird's tongue, to the knees of a bee—in April you are inhaling sex, and sneezing—and in the process, each two parents put their scrambled genes into offspring that represent whole new genetic combinations never before seen on Earth. Every new outfit will be ready for something, and together—in a large enough population—the whole crowd will be ready for anything. Individuals will die, not at random but because of some fatal misfit between what an organism has and what's required. But the population will live on, moving always in the direction of fitness (however "fitness" is at the moment defined), not because anyone has a master plan but simply because survival carries fitness forward, and death doesn't.

People have railed at this reality, left and right, since the evening when a British ambassador's wife declared to her husband, "Oh dear, let us hope Mr. Darwin isn't right, and if he is, let us hope no one finds out about it!" Fundamentalist Christians seem disturbed by a scenario in which individual will is so irrelevant. They might be surprised to learn that Stalin tried to ban the study of genetics and evolution in Soviet universities for the opposite reason, attacking the idea of natural selection—which acts only at the level of the individual—for being anti-Communist. Through it all, the little engines of evolution have kept on turning as they have done for millennia, delivering us here and passing on, untouched by politics or what anybody thinks.

Nikolai Vavilov was an astounding man of science, and probably the greatest plant explorer who has ever lived. He spoke seven languages and could recite books by Pushkin from memory. In his travels through sixty-four countries between 1916 and 1940, he saw more crop diversity than anyone had known existed, and founded the world's largest seed collection.

As he combed continents looking for primitive crop varieties, Vavilov noticed a pattern: Genetic variation was not evenly distributed. In a small region of Ethiopia he found hundreds of kinds of ancient wheat known only to that place. A single New World plateau is astonishingly rich in corn varieties, while another one is rolling in different kinds of potatoes. Vavilov mapped the distribution of what he found and theorized that the degree of diversity of a crop indicated how long it had been grown in a given region, as farmers saved their seeds through hundreds and thousands of seasons. They also saved more types of seed for different benefits thus popcorn, tortilla corn, roasting corn, and varieties of corn with particular colors and textures were all derived, over centuries, from one original strain. Within each crop type, the generations of selection would also yield a breadth of resistance to all types of pest and weather problems encountered through the years. By looking through his lens of genetics, Vavilov began to pinpoint the places in the world where human agriculture had originated. More modern genetic research has largely borne out his hypothesis that agriculture emerged independently in the places where the most diverse and ancient crop types, known as land races, are to be found: in the Near East, northern China, Mesoamerica, and Ethiopia.

The industrialized world depends entirely on crops and cultivation practices imported from what we now call the Third World (though evidently it was actually First). In an important departure from older traditions, the crops we now grow in the United States are extremely uniform genetically, due to the fact that our agriculture is controlled primarily by a few large agricultural corporations that sell relatively few varieties of seeds. Those who know the seed business are well aware that our shallow gene bank is highly vulnerable when a crop strain succumbs all at once to a new disease, all across the country (as happened with our corn in 1970), researchers must return to the more diverse original strains for help. So we still rely on the gigantic insurance policy provided by the genetic variability in the land races, which continue to be hand-sown and harvested, year in and year out, by farmers in those mostly poor places from which our crops arose.

Unbelievably, we are now engaged in a serious effort to cancel that insurance policy.

It happens like this. Let's say you are an Ethiopian farmer growing a land race of wheat—a wildly variable, husky mongrel crop that has been in your family for hundreds of years. You always lose some to wind and weather, but the rest still comes through every year. Lately, though, you've been hearing about a kind of Magic Wheat that grows six times bigger than your crop, is easier to harvest, and contains vitamins that aren't found in ordinary wheat. And amazingly enough, by special arrangement with the government, it's free.

Readers who have even the slightest acquaintance with fairy tales will already know there is trouble ahead in this story. The Magic Wheat grows well the first year, but its rapid, overly green growth attracts a startling number of pests. You see insects on this crop that never ate wheat before, in the whole of your family's history. You watch, you worry. You realize that you're going to have to spray a pesticide to get this crop through to harvest. You're not so surprised to learn that by special arrangement with the government, the same company that gave you the seed for free can sell you the pesticide you need. It's a good pesticide, they use it all the time in America, but it costs money you don't have, so you'll have to borrow against next year's crop.

The second year, you will be visited by a terrible drought, and your crop will not survive to harvest at all every stalk dies. Magic wheat from America doesn't know beans about Ethiopian drought. The end.

Actually, if the drought arrived in year two and the end came that quickly, in this real-life fairy tale you'd be very lucky, because chances are good you'd still have some of your family-line seed around. It would be much more disastrous if the drought waited until the eighth or ninth year to wipe you out, for then you'd have no wheat left at all, Magic or otherwise. Seed banks, even if they're eleven thousand years old, can't survive for more than a few years on the shelf. If they aren't grown out as crops year after year, they die—or else get ground into flour and baked and eaten—and then this product of a thousand hands and careful selection is just gone, once and for all.

This is no joke. The infamous potato famine or Southern Corn Leaf Blight catastrophe could happen again any day now, in any place where people are once again foolish enough, or poor enough to be coerced (as was the case in Ireland), to plant an entire country in a single genetic strain of a food crop.

While agricultural companies have purchased, stored, and patented certain genetic materials from old crops, they cannot engineer a crop, ever, that will have the resilience of land races under a wide variety of conditions of moisture, predation, and temperature. Genetic engineering is the antithesis of variability because it removes the wild card—that beautiful thing called sex—from the equation.

This is our new magic bullet: We can move single genes around in a genome to render a specific trait that nature can't put there, such as ultra-rapid growth or vitamin A in rice. Literally, we could put a wolf in sheep's clothing. But solving agricultural problems this way turns out to be far less broadly effective than the old-fashioned multigenic solutions derived through programs of selection and breeding. Crop predators evolve in quick and mysterious ways, while gene splicing tries one simple tack after another, approaching its goal the way Wile E. Coyote tries out each new gizmo from Acme only once, whereupon the roadrunner outwits it and Wile E. goes crestfallen back to the drawing board.

Wendell Berry, with his reliable wit, wrote that genetic manipulation in general and cloning in particular: ". . . besides being a new method of sheep-stealing, is only a pathetic attempt to make sheep predictable. But this is an affront to reality. As any shepherd would know, the scientist who thinks he has made sheep predictable has only made himself eligible to be outsmarted."

I've heard less knowledgeable people comfort themselves on the issue of genetic engineering by recalling that humans have been pushing genes around for centuries, through selective breeding of livestock and crops. I even read one howler of a quote that began, "Ever since Mendel spliced those first genes . . ." These people aren't getting it, but I don't blame them—I blame the religious fanatics who kept basic biology out of their grade-school textbooks. Mendel did not splice genes, he didn't actually control anything at all he simply watched peas to learn how their natural system of genetic recombination worked. The farmers who select their best sheep or grains to mother the next year's crop are working with the evolutionary force of selection, pushing it in the direction of their choosing. Anything produced in this way will still work within its natural evolutionary context of variability, predators, disease resistance, and so forth. But tampering with genes outside of the checks and balances you might call the rules of God's laboratory is an entirely different process. It's turning out to have unforeseen consequences, sometimes stunning ones.

To choose one example among many, genetic engineers have spliced a bacterium into a corn plant. It was arguably a good idea. The bacterium was *Bacillus thuringensis*, a germ that causes caterpillars' stomachs to explode. It doesn't harm humans, birds, or even ladybugs or bees, so it's one of the most useful pesticides we've ever discovered. Organic farmers have worked for years to expedite the path of the naturally occurring "Bt" spores from the soil, where the bacterium lives, onto their plants. You can buy this germ in a can at the nursery and shake it onto your tomato plants, where it makes caterpillars croak before sliding back into the soil it came from. Farmers have always used nature to their own ends, employing relatively slow methods circumscribed by the context of natural laws. But genetic engineering took a giant step and spliced part of the bacterium's DNA into a corn plant's DNA chain, so that as the corn grew, each of its cells would contain the bacterial function of caterpillar killing. When it produced pollen, each grain would have a secret weapon against the corn worms that like to crawl down the silks to ravage the crop. So far, so good.

But when the so-called Bt corn sheds its pollen and casts it to the wind, as corn has always done (it's pollinated by wind, not by bees), it dusts a fine layer of Bt pollen onto every tree and bush in the neighborhood of every farm that grows it—which is rapidly, for this popular crop, becoming the territory known as the United States. There it may explode the stomach of any butterfly larva in its path. The populations of monarch butterflies, those bold little pilgrims who migrate all the way to Mexico and back on wings the consistency of pastry crust, are plummeting fast. While there are many reasons for this (for example, their winter forests in Mexico are being burned), no reasonable person can argue that dusting them with a stomach explosive is going to help matters. So, too, go other butterflies more obscure, and more endangered. And if that doesn't happen to break your heart, just wait awhile, because something that pollinates your food and builds the soil underneath it may also be slated for extinction. And there's another practical problem: The massive exposure to Bt, now contained in every cell of this corn, is killing off all crop predators except those few that have mutated a resistance to this long useful pesticide. As a result, those superresistant mutants are taking over, in exactly the same way that overexposure to antibiotics is facilitating the evolution of antibiotic-resistant diseases in humans.

In this context of phenomenal environmental upsets, with even larger ones just offstage awaiting their cue, it's a bit surprising that the objections to genetic engineering we hear most about are the human health effects. It is absolutely true that new combinations of DNA can create proteins we aren't prepared to swallow notably, gene manipulations in corn unexpectedly created some antigens to which some humans are allergic. The potential human ills caused by ingestion of engineered foods remain an open category—which is scary enough in itself, and I don't mean to minimize it. But there are so many ways for gene manipulation to work from the inside to destroy our habitat and our food systems that the environmental challenges loom as something on the order of a cancer that might well make personal allergies look like a sneeze. If genetically reordered organisms escape into natural populations, they may rapidly change the genetics of an entire species in a way that could seal its doom. One such scenario is the "monster salmon" with genes for hugely rapid growth, which are currently poised for accidental release into open ocean. Another scenario, less cinematic but dangerously omnipresent, is the pollen escaping from crops, creating new weeds that we cannot hope to remove from the earth's face. Engineered genes don't play by the rules that have organized life for three billion years (or, if you prefer, 4,004). And in this case, winning means loser takes all.

Huge political question marks surround these issues: What will it mean for a handful of agribusinesses to control the world's ever-narrowing seed banks? What about the chemical dependencies they're creating for farmers in developing countries, where government deals with multinational corporations are inducing them to grow these engineered crops? What about the business of patenting and owning genes? Can there be any good in this for the flat-out concern of people trying to feed themselves? Does it seem safe, with the world now being what it is, to give up self-sustaining food systems in favor of dependency on the global marketplace? And finally, would you trust a guy in a suit who's never given away a nickel in his life, but who now tells you he's made you some free Magic Wheat? Most people know by now that corporations can do only what's best for their quarterly bottom line. And anyone who still believes governments ultimately do what's best for their people should be advised that the great crop geneticist Nikolai Vavilov died in a Soviet prison camp.

These are not questions to take lightly, as we stand here in the epicenter of corporate agribusiness and look around at the world asking, "Why on earth would they hate us?" The general ignorance of U.S. populations about who controls global agriculture reflects our trust in an assured food supply. Elsewhere, in places where people grow more food, watch less TV, and generally encounter a greater risk of hunger than we do, they mostly know what's going on. In India, farmers have persisted in burning to the ground trial crops of transgenic cotton, and they forced their government to ban Monsanto's "terminator technology," which causes plants to kill their own embryos so no viable seeds will survive for a farmer to replant in the next generation (meaning he'd have to buy new ones, of course). Much of the world has already refused to import genetically engineered foods or seeds from the United States. But because of the power and momentum of the World Trade Organization, fewer and fewer countries have the clout to resist the reconstruction of their food supply around the scariest New Deal ever.

Even standing apart from the moral and political questions—if a scientist can stand anywhere without stepping on the politics of what's about to be discovered—there are question marks enough in the science of the matter. There are consequences in it that no one knew how to anticipate. When the widely publicized Human Genome Project completed its mapping of human chromosomes, it offered an unsettling, not-so-widely-publicized conclusion: Instead of the 100,000 or more genes that had been expected, based on the number of proteins we must synthesize to be what we are, we have only about 30,000—about the same number as a mustard plant. This evidence undermined the central dogma of how genes work that is, the assumption of a clear-cut chain of processes leading from a single gene to the appearance of the trait it controls. Instead, the mechanism of gene expression appears vastly more complicated than had been assumed since Watson and Crick discovered the structure of DNA in 1953. The expression of a gene may be altered by its context, such as the presence of other genes on the chromosome near it. Yet, genetic engineering operates on assumptions based on the simpler model. Thus, single transplanted genes often behave in startling ways in an engineered organism, often proving lethal to themselves, or, sometimes, neighboring organisms. In light of newer findings, geneticists increasingly concede that gene-tinkering is to some extent shooting in the dark. Barry Commoner, senior scientist at the Center for the Biology of Natural Systems at Queens College, laments that while the public's concerns are often derided by industry scientists as irrational and uneducated, the biotechnology industry is—ironically—conveniently ignoring the latest results in the field "which show that there are strong reasons to fear the potential consequences of transferring a DNA gene between species."

Recently I heard Joan Dye Gussow, who studies and writes about the energetics, economics, and irrationalities of global food production, discussing some of these problems in a radio interview. She mentioned the alarming fact that pollen from genetically engineered corn is so rapidly contaminating all other corn that we may soon have no naturally bred corn left in the United States. "This is a fist in the eye of God," she said, adding with a sad little laugh, "and I'm not even all that religious." Whatever you believe in—whether God for you is the watchmaker who put together the intricate workings of this world in seven days or seven hundred billion days—you'd be wise to believe the part about the fist.

Religion has no place in the science classroom, where it may abridge students' opportunities to learn the methods, discoveries, and explanatory hypotheses of science. Rather, its place is in the hearts of the men and women who study and then practice scientific exploration. Ethics can't influence the outcome of an experiment, but they can serve as a useful adjunct to the questions that get asked in the first place, and to the applications thereafter. (One must wonder what chair God occupied, if any, in the Manhattan Project.) In the halls of science there is often an unspoken sense that morals and objectivity can't occupy the same place. That is balderdash—they always have cohabited. Social norms and judgments regarding gender, race, the common good, cooperation, competition, material gain, and countless other issues reside in every active human mind, so they were hovering somewhere in the vicinity of any experiment ever conducted by a human. That is precisely why science invented the double-blind experiment, in which, for example, experimental subjects don't know whether they're taking the drug or the placebo, and neither does the scientist recording their responses, so as to avoid psychological bias in the results. But it's not possible to double-blind the scientist's approach to the task in the first place, or to the way results will be used. It is probably more scientifically constructive to acknowledge our larger agenda than to pretend it doesn't exist. Where genetic engineering is concerned. I would rather have ethics than profitability driving the program.

I was trained as a biologist, and I can appreciate the challenge and the technical mastery involved in isolating, understanding, and manipulating genes. I can think of fascinating things I'd like to do as a genetic engineer. But I only have to stand still for a minute and watch the outcome of thirty million years' worth of hummingbird evolution transubstantiated before my eyes into nest and egg to get knocked down to size. I have held in my hand the germ of a plant engineered to grow, yield its crop, and then murder its own embryos, and there I glimpsed the malevolence that can lie in the heart of a profiteering enterprise. There once was a time when Thoreau wrote, "I have great faith in a seed. Convince me that you have a seed there, and I am prepared to expect wonders." By the power vested in everything living, let us keep to that faith. I'm a scientist who thinks it wise to enter the doors of creation not with a lion tamer's whip and chair, but with the reverence humankind has traditionally summoned for entering places of worship: a temple, a mosque, or a cathedral. A sacred grove, as ancient as time.

## questions for discussion

1. What do you make of Kingsolver's opening narrative, her careful observation of a hummingbird? Is this an effective way to introduce both the topic of the essay and Kingsolver's position on religion and science? Think about this: If Kingsolver is ultimately invested in asserting both the importance of science and religion (in their proper places), then how might her nearly spiritual description of her keen (nearly scientific!) observation of the hummingbird be designed to support her appreciation of *both* science and religion?

2. Thinking about the importance of audience to writing, ask yourself this question: To whom is Kingsolver writing in this piece? The essay is clearly not intended as a scientific or lab report, so, although many "academic" arguments are made, the intended audience is most likely not scientists. Perhaps, like Sagan, Kingsolver is addressing a more general, educated audience concerned with these issues or desiring to be more informed about them. What difference in her composing process do you think it made that she's not really writing to an academic audience but to a more popular audience?

3. In her essay, Kingsolver moves from considering issues of evolution to genetic engineering, all in the context of discussing the relationship between science and religion. Does she transition well from one subject to another, noting their connection and relationship? It might seem as though Kingsolver is tackling *too* much, too many topics, but is she? Is there a connection between these disparate topics? What is it?

4. Kingsolver's approach to the relationship between science and religion, we feel, is fairly Rogerian. While she forcefully asserts that

"[r]eligion has no place in the science classroom," she also maintains that she has "never understood how anyone could have the slightest trouble blending religious awe with a full comprehension of the workings of life's creation." This is a view that doesn't pit science and religion against one another, but rather asks us to consider how they might complement one another productively. What is the "common ground" or "meeting point," in her view, between science and religion? Do you accept her argument? Does she argue it convincingly? Where do you sense the argument is potentially questionable?

5. Note Kingsolver's use of *pathos* (the opening narrative), *ethos* (the references to her training in biology), and *logos* (the carefully reasoned discussion of Darwin and other scientists). Is there any aspect of the overall argument—pathos, ethos, or logos—that seems more compelling to you than the others? Why? In dealing with such a potentially controversial subject, should Kingsolver have emphasized one element of argument over another? For instance, would a stronger appeal to pathos (or ethos or logos, for that matter) have been more effective? Why or why not?

6. Kingsolver uses the phrase "scientific illiteracy" to describe how many of us are "unprepared to discuss or understand much of the damage we are wreaking on our atmosphere, our habitat, and even the food that enters our mouths." Do you agree with Kingsolver's claim that many in our population are scientific illiterates? Is this an effective definitional strategy?

## *Additional Writing Activities*

1. After choosing one of the many short essays in either this or the preceding chapter, write a critique of that essay using the evaluation questions given here. You might first answer all of the questions about the essay you've chosen, and then draft a critique by stating and discussing first what "works" in the argumentative essay, and then offer your commentary about what needs to be improved. Share your critiques with your classmates and other writers for feedback and discussion.

2. Here's a topic for an argumentative essay or project. While you or your classmates may have attended a public school at some point, from kindergarten to high school, you are probably paying (some-

times quite a bit) to attend a college or university. Should college fees, such as tuition, be provided by the state or federal government? Use Toulmin's strategy to outline an argument, suggesting either that money for such fees *should* be provided by the state or that they *should not.* You might develop outlines for *both* sides, and then work through a Rogerian approach to negotiate a compromise.

3. Imagine a dialog between Carl Rogers and Aristotle. What might the two thinkers talk about? What elements of argument might they feel they have in common, and where would they disagree about how argument should be conducted among intelligent and thoughtful people? After brainstorming a bit about such a dialog, draft an essay in which you compare and contrast what you know of Aristotelian and Rogerian argument. Conclude with a discussion of which approach you think is most useful today. Or begin with an assertion about which approach you favor, and draft an essay in support of your assertion, keeping in mind how others might disagree with you. Consider potential counterarguments carefully!
4. Compose a response to Barbara Kingsolver's essay, "A Fist in the Eye of God," in which you either argue one of her points from an alternative view or take up the issue of "scientific illiteracy" in our society. Are Americans scientific illiterates? Is this a fair assessment, or perhaps one that needs additional discussion and consideration?
5. Consider conducting your own research on genetically modified foods (an extremely controversial topic among natural foods enthusiasts, traditional versus organic farmers, the European Union versus the United States), and develop your own arguments about the issue, pro or con. Your might frame your discussion as a response to Kingsolver, siding with her or arguing against her. On what grounds would you do so? What research could you provide to support your positions?

# CHAPTER 5

# More than Just Words Here: Visual Literacy, Visual Argument

In the previous chapter we have focused on the way that *text*, which we have used in its narrow sense to refer to *written words*, can be manipulated by academics and those seeking to persuade us to do certain things, adopt certain views, or think about a situation, issue, or idea differently. Yet what we read consists of more than words. Images, pictures, and other visuals abound, and they too communicate information and prove useful in persuasive appeals.

In addition to being able to comprehend and respond to *texts*, our ability to "read" visual cues, images, and symbols complements and expands our possibilities of understanding and communicating with others. Some information, in fact, is conveyed more rapidly—and powerfully—by a visual display. A chart, for instance, can serve as a useful tool for presenting information that would be cumbersome in a purely textual format. Pictures, images, and graphics can be *informative*, not just decorative. A well-placed image also has the power to attract attention or complement a verbal text. Some Web designers will use carefully chosen images to entice you *into* a site, in much the same way that a photograph on the front page of a newspaper or magazine is intended to make you want to pick it up and read more. Like an opening paragraph that "hooks" the reader, it functions as a well-written introduction in a text-based essay. Indeed, in the digital world, especially with the use of both texts and visuals on the Web, visual literacy is increasingly becoming as important as textual literacy.

What we want to do in this chapter, then, is introduce you to the many ways in which visuals function in our society and encourage you to think critically about their use, particularly in argumentative contexts and on the Web. In other words, we want to help you develop your skills in understanding and using **visual rhetoric**—the interplay of context, purpose, and audience perception in understanding and interpreting how visuals are meaningful. Greater familiarity with visual rhetoric and visual argument will allow you to navigate the Web as a better reader and potentially help you augment your own writing projects—whether print-based or electronic—with appropriate visuals or analysis of visuals. And if you are thinking of publishing on the Web, then the ability to read visuals critically and to use them is all but crucial. Let's see how.

## Rethinking Literacy: Understanding Visual Rhetoric

To understand better how visuals communicate, let's look at the following visuals:

These signs contain verbal clues, but even before a driver is close enough to read the words, the messages come across. Almost everyone knows what a large red hexagon means, or a yellow diamond, or an upside-down triangle. If you have a driver's license, you will have been tested on your ability to read certain signs and symbols, even when they contain no verbal clues, as is true of some of these:

Indeed, a driver's inability to interpret signs could be a matter of life and death. Similarly, you would know to come to a halt if you encountered someone standing in traffic and holding her hand, palm forward, out in front of her. The fact that she is vulnerable to traffic would make you pause to avoid hitting her, but you would also respond to the *symbolism* of her action.

All of these—from the traffic signs to the woman standing in traffic—communicate visually. Our ability to understand what is meant in each case depends on our **visual literacy**. In their book *Visual Literacy: A Way to Learn—to Teach*, R. Fransecky and J. Debes define visual literacy as

> a group of vision competencies a human being can develop by seeing and at the same time having and integrating other sensory experiences. The development of these competencies is fundamental to normal human learning. When developed, they enable a visually literate person to discriminate and interpret the visual actions, objects, and/or symbols, natural or man-made, that are [encountered] in [the] environment. Through the creative use of these competencies, [we are] able to communicate with others.
>
> (Association for Educational Communications and Technology, Washington, 1972, p. 7, or see the home page of the International Visual Literacy Association at **http://www.ivla.org/organization/whatis.htm.**)

For these authors, the *visual text*—as opposed to the *verbal text*—is a fundamental form of communication, and being able to interpret symbols, signs, and "visual actions" is crucial not just to communicating with one another but also, in many ways, to our survival. As with all communication, of course, *context* and *situation* are crucial. A woman holding her hand out in the fashion we described earlier might have no significance for you if she were standing in front of her bedroom mirror. Her position in relation to her surroundings gives you clues that help you interpret what she wants to communicate. Not knowing the specific context in which to interpret actions complicates, or obscures, their possible meanings. For example, consider what the "visual action" shown here means to you:

On one hand (as it were), the "thumbs down" could be a gesture of evaluation—as in, "not good" or "not recommended." On the other hand, this could be a directional gesture—as in, put the large box *down*. To a spectator in the Roman coliseum, however, it meant "kill the fallen gladiator."

## Visuals and Images in Texts

The study of visual literacy and visual rhetoric has recently emerged as a "hot" field of academic inquiry among those who teach writing, but in many ways, the study of visual rhetoric has been around for quite some time. In several popular and critically well-received books such as *Good Looking*, art historian Barbara Maria Stafford has been arguing that the visual has been an important part of Western culture's "way of knowing" for centuries. Indeed, we could stretch that to millennia. Cave paintings 30,000 years old at Lascaux in France or Altamira in Spain had meaning to someone; the artists, priests, families, or group members knew what they meant to communicate. Today, however, we have lost our connection with the cultures in which these were created; for those paintings, we

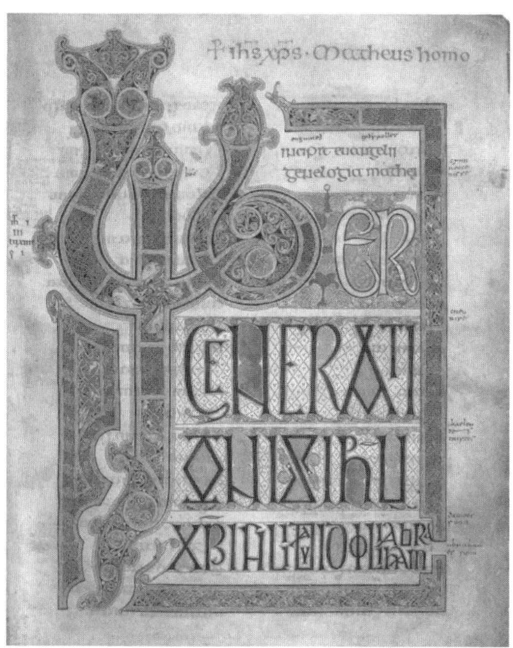

are illiterate. For somewhat more recent examples, consider illuminated manuscripts from the Middle Ages such as the Book of Kells or the Lindisfarne Gospels, and you will see that visual elements were an important component of hand-printed texts.

Even though the medieval writers used verbal text to communicate, they relied heavily on images that functioned as far more than decoration. The painstakingly made illuminations had an aesthetic purpose, to be sure, but they also shed light on the meaning of the texts. Such books, like the frescoes and stained-glass windows in European churches, tell stories that uneducated or illiterate parishioners could not read for themselves. These became important contributions to people's religious education.

**HYPER**text

To learn more about medieval illuminated manuscripts, do a quick Web search using the search term "Illuminations." Several stunning exhibits can be found online.

Many writers have understood the importance of the visual in communication. Poets who use metaphors and other imagistic language to expand or enhance the meaning of their work by suggesting images to the reader's mind's eye are aware of the power of an image. And sometimes a writer's use of the visual isn't merely metaphoric. William Blake, the English poet, created engravings in which the texts of his poems were presented with his own illustrations. As you read the following plate containing the famous poem "The Tyger," think about what the visuals add to your interpretation of it. How do they *shape* the context in which you read the text? How do you "read" the whole—text and graphics?

How does the image enhance your reading of the poem? Think in particular about the branches from the tree and how they seem to creep between the lines of the poem. What do you think Blake was trying to suggest?

F. William Ruegg and Ronald S. Broglio, from the English Department at the University of Florida, offer the following commentary on the interaction between text and visual in "The Tyger":

> In almost every plate of "The Tyger" Blake renders the stripes at the base of the tree the same color and shape as the stripes of the tyger. The stripes move from the tyger to the tree. Furthermore, the branches at the top of the plate stripe the verbal text of the poem. And finally, the cryptic "y" of "tyger" marks or stripes the word differently from the standardized spelling, "tiger." The "y" of "tyger" serves as a mark of difference. (The use of "y" also highlights other key words with "y": thy, eye, and symmetry.) By deviating from standardization, the textual figure (word and image) is marked as different from a habitual rendering of the figure. This difference is the place of fragmentation and transformation.
>
> **(http://www.lcc.gatech.edu/~broglio/eromantic/tyger.html)**

For these writers, the "deviations" highlight how the poem captures a sense of "fragmentation," a sense of chaos and danger—which also potentially suggests that things *could* be rebuilt or reconstructed at some point, holding out the hope of "transformation." The striping the writers mention, however, suggests that the text and the images are so intertwined that we can't help but wonder if transformation—that is, escape from chaos and fragmentation—is actually possible.

## Comics

Comic book artists often think of the *interplay* between text and image as creating and communicating meaning in ways that texts and images alone would not. Artbabe.com, the home page of graphic novelist Jessica Abel, at **http://ww.artbabe.com/**, is a visually stimulating page featuring some of Abel's work, as well as her discussion of her craft and a "self interview" in which she talks about being a graphic novelist. You can also preview some of Abel's work, like the following page:

12:23 A.M. WEDNESDAY
WHAT'VE YOU BEEN UP TO?
OH, JUST MAKING A FOOL OF MYSELF IN FRONT OF THE WOMAN OF MY DREAMS.
HA HA -- SO, THE USUAL?
YEAH. THE USUAL.
WELL, GLAD TO HEAR YOU HAVEN'T BEEN BREAKING CHARACTER.
"HA HA."
siiiighhhh...
LAUREN?
OH, SORRY JILL, IT'S BEN.
YEAH, THANKS.
LAUREN?
HI.
WELL, I JUST HAD A TOTAL FIASCO "DATE" WITH DARCY CARVER.
YEAH, HER.
SURE, RUB IT IN.
NO, SHE HATES ME.
NO, IT'S TOTALLY OBVIOUS.
YEAH.
LOOK, YOU WANNA GET A BEER? I NEED ONE.
YOU WANNA MEET AT LUCKY LUKE'S?
OK, SEE YA THERE IN HALF AN HOUR.
OK, BYE.
10.

Note how nothing very much is actually going on in the individual panels: a guy seems to be just sitting around talking on the phone. But observe how much information is conveyed about how he is feeling through his hand gestures and his slouch. The position of his hand changes from frame to frame, signaling shame, frustration, and even a comic acceptance of his situation. Abel has mastered the art of visual rhetoric, the ability to convey important information with a few visual cues—even for something as seemingly mundane as a date turned sour!

## WRITING SPOTLIGHT

### Art Spiegelman's *Maus*

Another brilliant comic artist is Art Spiegelman, whose famous graphic novels *Maus* and *Maus II* depict the horrors endured by his parents' family fleeing the anti-Jewish persecution of Nazis during the period shortly before World War II. Spiegelman's innovation in rendering this personal story as a graphic novel was his decision to use animals to depict people of different ethnicities. He drew the Jews as mice and the Nazis as cats. Here are the covers of the two novels. What do you see as the impact of using animals to depict the two groups?

MAUS

The images are striking and eye-catching. Comic arts expert Gene Kannenberg says the following about the uncanny use of animal imagery in *Maus*:

> Spiegelman's formal experimentation, honed in his earlier work, lies at the heart of the longer *Maus*: Jews are portrayed as mice, Nazis as cats; time runs in parallel sequences; sketch pads become panels. Yet the book's deceptively simple graphic style allowed anyone, even those readers who did not follow the comics market . . . to read and admire this ambitious work.
>
> (**http://www.sp.uconn.edu/~epk93002/fff.html**)

Certainly, Kannenberg has a point: the use of mice and cats is intriguing, potentially inviting those who do not normally read comics or graphic novels to give *Maus* a chance. But there may be other reasons as well that the two *Maus* volumes strike us as powerful. One student writer, Antonio S. Oliver, made the following suggestion:

> Quite possibly as a method to deal with his own inability to comprehend the events of the Holocaust, Spiegelman uses animal characters instead of humans. The most important two, Germans and Jews, are represented by cats and mice, respectively. Natural sworn enemies, both cat and mice lack reason and conscience. As a result, the Nazi cats find no fault in the systematic killing of Jewish mice. The image is also based on historical quotes, since Jews were called the "vermin of society" by the Nazis.
>
> (**http://www.georgetown.edu/faculty/bassr/218/projects/oliver/MausbyAO.htm**)

What do you think? Do you agree with the comments above? How might *you* have depicted the persecution of Jews and other minorities, such as gypsies and homosexuals, during the Nazi period?

## your turn

To develop a sense of the importance of visual elements and how they contribute meaningfully to an accompanying text, try comparing and contrasting pairs of written and visual texts. As an example, look at the opening section of Stanley Kubrick's classic film *2001: A Space Odyssey* and Arthur Clarke's novelization of the movie in the book of the same name. The opening sequence in the film is completely without dialogue or narration; the filmmaker communicates with us only *visually*.

In contrast, Clarke, an author, communicates with us primarily through *text*. Here is basically the same scene pictured above—but in prose:

> For a few seconds Moon-Watcher stood uncertainly above his new victim, trying to grasp the strange and wonderful fact that the dead leopard could not kill again. Now he was master of the world, and he was not quite sure what to do next.

Which is more effective? Actually, the answer to that question may ultimately be a matter of taste and preference, but note how one image might convey roughly the same information that an entire paragraph would have to explain. Moreover an image can often convey meaning more *viscerally* than just text. For instance, Clarke says Moon-Watcher feels he is "master of the world," but *seeing* him hold a bone in triumph conveys a different, yet powerful sense of what being a "master of the world" might entail. As such, while not every cliché is true, it may be the case—in some instances, at least—that a picture is worth a thousand words, more or less!

## Pictures, Graphs, and Charts

For many writers, an explanatory picture, graph, chart, or pie wheel, if properly placed and explained, can greatly enhance textual material. For those people who learn better by seeing images than by reading verbal text alone, a chart or graph can help explain a variety of subjects, issues, and topics. If used carefully, these can provide compelling *visual* demonstration of what a text means. Figure 5.1 is an example of graphics that explain the "greenhouse effect":

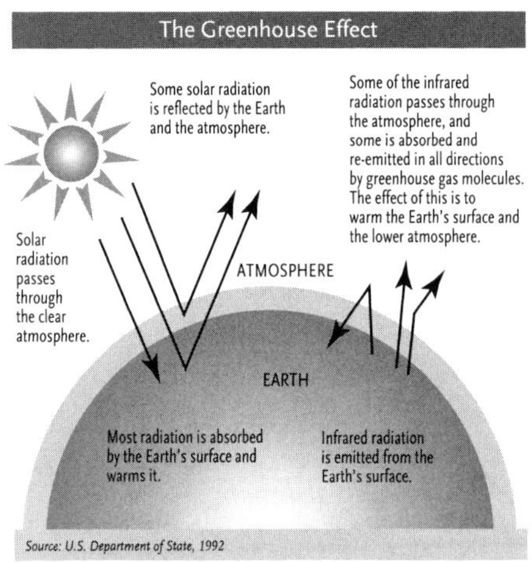


Figure 5.1

Instead of simply *describing* or *telling* a reader about the greenhouse effect and its contribution to global warming, these graphics combine text and image to offer a visual display—one that may make the concept of the greenhouse effect a bit more understandable.

Charts can do similar work. For instance, Figure 5.2 is a chart depicting "global temperature changes" for a 120- year period. On one hand, the chart seems to provide a compelling indication that global temperatures are increasing dramatically. On the other, look more closely at the actual differences in temperature depicted. You'll see that they are small, but the graph has been designed to make them *appear* much larger. Note in particular the use of jagged lines, which suggest danger. We're not suggesting that the graph is necessarily deceptive, but it should be read *critically* to determine exactly what it is telling us.

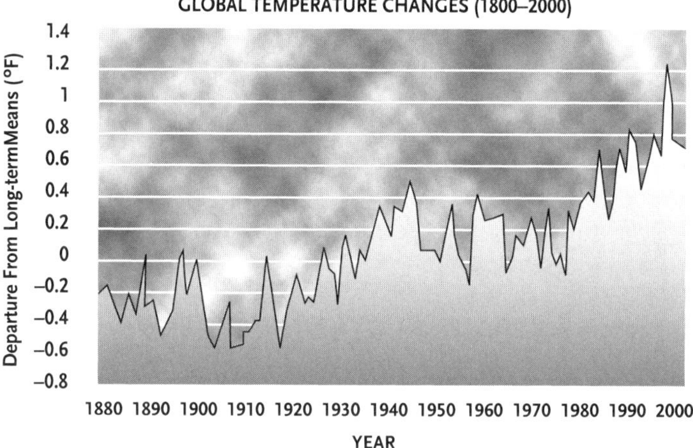


Figure 5.2

Sometimes, comparison of different graphical representations of the same event can yield surprising results and can itself be the basis for discussion and analysis. For instance, look at Figure 5.3, a map of the United States depicting the results of the 2000 presidential election. Lighter shad-

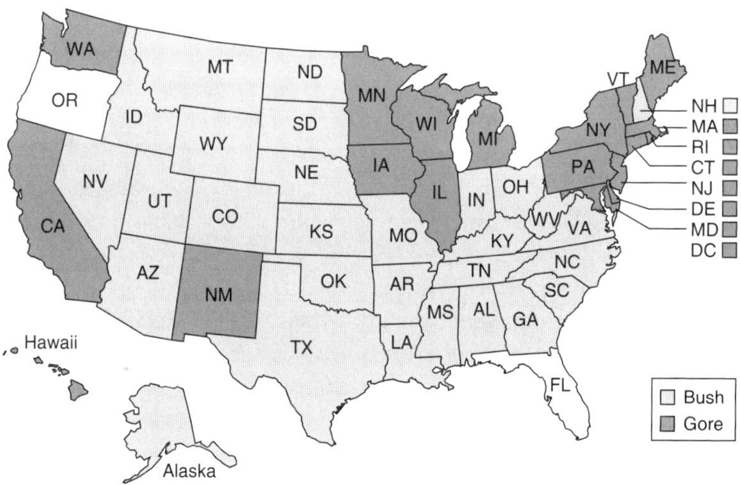


Figure 5.3

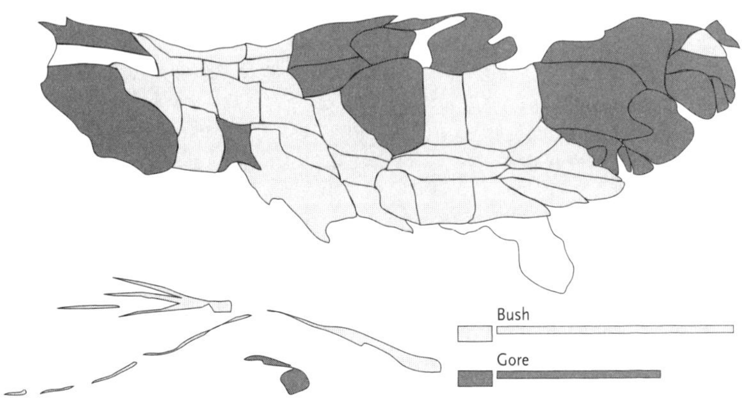


Figure 5.4

ing is used for states whose Electoral College votes were given to George W. Bush, and darker shading for those that went to Al Gore. The area with lighter shading seems to dominate, suggesting that Bush won the election by a landslide.

In Figure 5.4, however, the states have been redrawn to depict their relative populations so that states with larger populations *appear* larger than those with fewer citizens. The result is striking. There is much more of the darker shading than in Figure 5.3. In fact, the areas with lighter and darker shading seem nearly evenly matched—a fairer representation of the actual election results: it was a very close race.

If you use graphs or charts in your writing project, consider this hint: professional writers never simply insert a graphic without explaining its purpose. Frequently, novice writers will include such items and expect readers to figure out why they have been inserted. This puts an unfair expectation on readers to figure out what the author wants to say. Explaining how to read a chart is crucial, and citing the source of the image is required, just as it is for a quotation of text.

## Graphic Manipulation of Text

For your own literacy practices (your reading and writing knowledge and abilities), think of visual literacy as knowing how to read *all* of what you see, beyond the letters of the printed text themselves. Visual literacy also means knowing how to compose and lay out your text so that it is both pleasing and visually meaningful for your readers. In terms of your writing, this includes knowing how to use space, color, font styles, and graphics, and how to organize a variety of visual elements into a coherently structured whole. Some of our understanding of how visuals work with text is fairly conventional, because publishers and authors have developed practices that aid the reader of print. These include the use of paragraph breaks, quotation marks, spaces between words and sentences, and white space in margins. At the same time, word processors and the ability of the Web to combine text, image, and even sound offer us new possibilities for exploring how meaning can be made—both textually *and visually*. Let's look at some examples.

Poets more contemporary than Blake have explored the usefulness of visual rhetoric in their work and have been willing to experiment with manipulation of text. One of the best known American poets of the twentieth century, e. e. cummings, was a master of manipulating text on a page to create poetry that speaks not just with words but also with their *placement* on the page. You can tell that the poet understood the significance of the visual dimension of text by his insistence on using lowercase letters to spell his name. An example of cummings's play with the visual dimension of text is this poem:

```
r-p-o-p-h-e-s-s-a-g-r
        who
a)s w(e loo)k
upnowgath
   PPEGORHRASS
               eringint(o-
The):l
eA
        !p:
S           a
(r rIvInG .gRrEaPsPhOs)
        to
rea(be)rran(com)gi(e)ngly
,grasshopper;
```

What do you think cummings might be trying to tell us with such a visually startling strategy? Certainly, the poet's "jumping" words are meant to suggest the grasshopper's movements, but also note the use of words in parentheses. A story is being told about this grasshopper. What is it? For more on cummings, visit The Academy of American Poets online at **http://www.poets.org/poets/poets**.

You can experiment with altering the visual dimension of *your* texts by experimenting with your word processor. Do not forget to consider how **fonts**, color, text size, and other visual aspects of printed text can be used to enhance your ability to communicate. If your writing instructor allows for some flexibility in experimenting with the graphic layout of your written work, then play with unusual fonts or text size. Keep in mind, though, that such alterations should *communicate*; they should not be used just because they're "cool."

## your turn

Experiment with a short piece of writing by creatively, strategically, and *meaningfully* altering words in the text. For instance, look at the opening stanza of Emily Dickinson's poem:

Wild Nights—Wild Nights!
Were I with thee
Wild Nights should be
Our luxury!

In many ways, Dickinson was already pushing the limits of traditional printing and layout conventions with her idiosyncratic use of dashes and capitalization, both in this and many other poems. How else might we elicit a multitude of meanings in the poem by altering fonts or text sizes? For instance, note how italicizing just one word shifts the potential meaning of the poem:

Wild Nights—Wild Nights!
Were I with thee
Wild Nights *should* be
Our luxury!

You might not have thought of italicization as a *graphic* or *visual* alteration, but it is. Note how it teases out a tentative note in the poem: the speaker seems a bit more uncertain about whether wild nights will, in fact, lead to luxury. We can also play with her text a bit more exuberantly:

Wild Nights—*Wild* **Nights!**
Were I with thee
Wild Nights should be
Our luxury!

Granted, such textual alterations can appear corny, even silly, but trying out different versions of them might spark your imagination and get you thinking about some *meaningful* graphic innovations that you can play with in your own writing.

## Writing Brochures and Newsletters

Your instructor, to help you understand the use of visuals and to develop your ability to combine text and image, may have you compose a brochure or newsletter as part of a class assignment or writing project. Doing so will allow you to experiment with visuals, place them in conjunction with text, and discover how an effectively used visual can greatly enhance your written text. Even simple graphics, such as clip art, can make a statement. On the Companion Website (go to **www.ablongman.com/alexander**) to this textbook, you can find information about writing brochures and newsletters, which often incorporate visuals into text-based documents.

## Using Visuals in Academic Presentations

Writers in academic situations increasingly give presentations in media other than print. In classes or at conferences, they may project text onto a screen for the entire audience to see. Indeed, a frequent task for people in the academy—and in the world of work in general—is reporting and explaining recommendations, decisions, findings, and actions. These reports can vary in length from a short memo or letter to a multiple-page document. They may be read by several individuals or by only one specific reader.

A presentation developed with PowerPoint or other software, such as Corel Presentation, is an example of such a *multimedia* report. In fact, in addition to institutions of higher learning, many businesses have invested in data projectors and use PowerPoint, so working knowledge of this useful tool can be valuable. Using this software, you create a series of slides to present information in a visually attractive and appealing way, perhaps even using graphs, charts, and pictures to highlight certain issues or draw attention to important information. PowerPoint lets you determine the types of transitions between slides and the order in which your text appears; you can even animate your text.

An *academic* visual presentation may be based on an essay prepared in traditional format, and it may aid the writer in emphasizing her main points to an audience to whom she is presenting the paper. Some presenters print out the slides of the presentation and distribute them on a paper handout or give members of their audience a CD to use in reviewing the presentation. This can be useful since the content of the presentation usually amounts to a detailed outline of the essay or talk. Converting your written work to a PowerPoint presentation is a quick way (1) to outline your paper and (2) to check to see if the organizational strategy you have used actually makes sense and seems to flow logically and reasonably. You might want to try this with an essay or project you are working on. For an example of slides from a PowerPoint presentation, see the Companion Website, which features slides from Jonathan's presentation about the YOUth and AIDS Web Project.

When composing in PowerPoint, pay attention to organization, clarity, conciseness, and length. Be careful not to cram too many words onto a slide in such small print that it is unreadable from the back of the room. Avoid simply listing points densely on a page, but do include enough content on each slide to hold the audience's attention. Indeed, for such reports, *clear organization* is crucial. Carolyn Stoll, a writing instructor at the University of Cincinnati who has all of her writing students compose at least one multimedia presentation, gives this advice:

> All reports have an introduction, a body, and a conclusion, and informal reports are no exception. In the *introduction*, one usually explains the subject, purpose, or possible results of a given problem, action, event, or question to the reader. In the *body*, you should display a detailed account of the work reported on, including enough evidence and reasoning to allow your readers to judge if your analysis has been adequate. The *conclusion* of your report would summarize your findings and indicate their significance. The conclusion might also include

recommendations where you tell your reader what they ought to do, or what is going to be done if the decision is up to you.

## your turn

Take an essay you have written and turn it into a PowerPoint presentation. Could you convert it easily into slides? Of course, not all essays or projects can be easily converted, so don't use this as the only test for your essay's structural integrity. If you know how to make Web sites, think of how you could develop your essay into a Web site. We will discuss this possibility at greater length in Chapter 8.

### SOME GUIDELINES FOR USING VISUALS IN YOUR PROJECTS

If you're thinking about using visuals, such as charts, graphs, or pictures, in one of your writing projects, consider the following guidelines:

- Make sure that the visual makes sense. That is, don't just use a visual or image because it looks good. The visual has to contribute in some substantial way to the subject of your project.
- Take some time to *explain* the use of the visual. Don't assume that your readers will understand or read the image in exactly the same way you do. Refer to the visual in your text, commenting on it and telling the reader how *you* see and interpret it.
- Be *sparing* with your use of visuals. Too many visuals are distracting to your readers. Limiting their use will draw attention to them and allow you to make the most of them in your work.
- Color copying can be expensive. A simple black-and-white image will probably suffice for most purposes. Use color images only when color helps you make your point.
- Make sure your image is *clear*! A fuzzy image will actually *detract* from the point you are trying to make with it.

### HYPERtext

See examples of PowerPoint presentations on the Web at the Purdue Online Writing Lab (**http://owl.english.purdue.edu/workshops/pp/#presentations**). Choose a presentation to view in its entirety and evaluate it according to the criteria discussed here.

## Visual Literacy and the Web

Did you ever wonder why art books, the big coffee table books full of colorful photographs or reproductions of art, are so expensive? Images, especially in color, are expensive to print in books. You will notice that in this book there are no full-color graphic images. They are simply too expensive to include.

On the Web, however, graphics can easily be scanned and published, and readers can print them out on color printers. The only limitation is the amount of time it takes to transmit images. Still, the transmission of images is so relatively easy and inexpensive that designers of Web pages routinely incorporate them.

Despite the capacity of Web pages to manipulate text and graphics in creative and provocative ways, not everyone has greeted image-laden Web texts with open arms. Some computer experts routinely search with the image loader on their Web browsers turned off. Why? In general, Web pages load *faster* when they do not have to load images, and many feel that images seldom convey vital or significant information.

How might they be wrong? In what cases might an image on a Webtext convey information more powerfully than verbal text alone?

Let's look at an example. **Java applets** allow Web users to view "minimovies" or other kinds of information that are best expressed visually—indeed, that might *only* truly be expressed with visuals. For instance, as a lesson in perspective, staff members at National High Magnetic Field Laboratory have created a java tutorial that allows you to "View the Milky Way at 10 million light years from the Earth." You can then

**ELECTRONIC**issues

If images are used to convey concepts omitted in words on a Web page, how might an unsighted person be able to understand its meaning? What clues can Web designers provide to assist someone who cannot see the images? If you were to design a Web site, what could you do to make your page more accessible to the sight-challenged?

move through space towards the Earth in successive orders of magnitude until you reach a tall oak tree just outside the buildings of the National High Magnetic Field Laboratory in Tallahassee, Florida. After that, begin to move from the actual size of a leaf into a microscopic world that reveals leaf cell walls, the cell nucleus, chromatin, DNA and finally, into the subatomic universe of electrons and protons.

Take a look at this applet at **http://micro.magnet.fsu.edu/primer/java/scienceopticsu/powersof10/index.html** and think about how a description of the images is not as powerful as actually being able to experience them.

Many Web designers also use **Flash** software to "introduce" a Web site or as a visually stimulating supplement to existing sites written in HTML. Flash offers numerous attractions. For instance, its use allows Web designers to create a number of special effects. Some Flash sites are essentially mini-movies that play once you click "start" or games that you play much as you would video or computer games. Others have a much more hypertextual dimension in which you "click" on items—sometimes text, sometimes images—to advance a story or discover links to other information. Because of its ability to manipulate images, some Web designers are using Flash, as opposed to HTML, to code their pages. For instance, film director David Lynch's Web site at **www.davidlynch.com** advises viewers that they will need certain editions of Flash simply to view the site.

On the other hand, some who design Web sites are a bit *too* "image happy." They load their pages with spinning graphics, gyrating images, useless Flash displays, and a dazzling array of sometimes headache-inducing colors. To assist inexperienced designers, Web designers and critics of the Web as a communications tool have developed a number of *criteria* for the use of images on the Web. In your local bookstore you can easily find any number of manuals and guides offering advice on good Web design.

## your turn

In small groups, either electronically or face-to-face, discuss what you think makes for a good Web site, specifically in terms of *visual* appeal. Make a list of criteria, perhaps drawing from your experience as a Web surfer. Then, thinking about your list and choosing a few Web sites at random (perhaps some of your favorite sites), ask yourself the following questions: How does the site designer *use* images? When do they help the reader to understand the writer's meaning? When do the images or graphics *hinder* communication? When do graphics clutter the page or site? How does arrangement of elements contribute to the effect? How does the author use white space, or empty space if a background color other than white is used (which is still referred to as "white space")? How might the images be used even to *persuade*, not just inform?

# Visual Argument

## Visual Argument in Print

We have mentioned the use of visuals to complement a text or entice a viewer into a Web site. Visuals also act *rhetorically*; that is, they communicate ideas, insights, or emotions in an attempt to *persuade* us to do something—beyond just entering a snazzy Web site. Perhaps our most pervasive experience with visual rhetoric comes in the form of advertisements, which frequently combine text and image in an attempt to get us to buy products and services. Ads, including television commercials, print advertisements, and billboards, offer a nearly ubiquitous opportunity to think about how people use a combination of textual and graphic information to persuade us. For instance, think of one of your favorite commercials or print ads. How does the ad work to influence *you*?

Adbusters (online at **http://www.adbusters.org/**) is an organization that critiques the use of advertisement in our culture by using "spoof ads," which take a preexisting advertisement and "spoof" or "spin" it to tease out a contradiction in the original advertisement. For example, take a look at the spoof ads from Adbusters shown in Figures 5.6 and 5.7. What is being "spoofed" in each ad? Certainly, in the "Obsession" spoof ad, Adbusters' intention is to highlight the ways in which advertisements sell not just products but *ideas* or *values*. In the "Obsession" spoof, the spoofers insinuate that advertisements depicting beautiful people with perfectly sculpted bodies are selling not just a perfume but an image of what our bodies "should" look like. In the Adbusters ad, the spoofers seem to be suggesting that women see in the original ads unhealthy models of superthinness that they might try to emulate. Do you agree? You might want to compare this ad to some of the Calvin Klein advertisements that this ad spoofs; you can find many original Calvin Klein ads by doing a quick

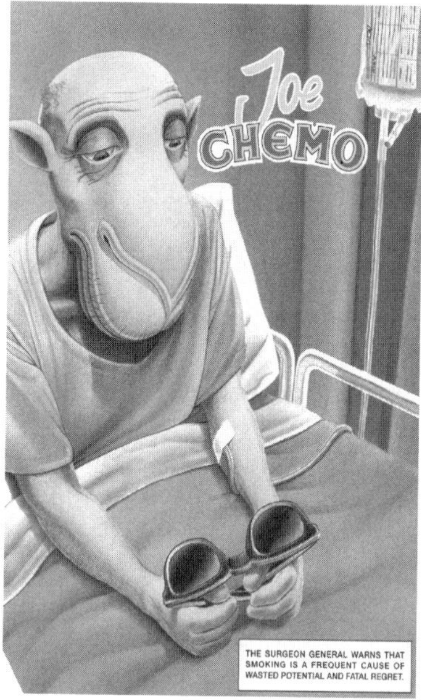


Figure 5.6

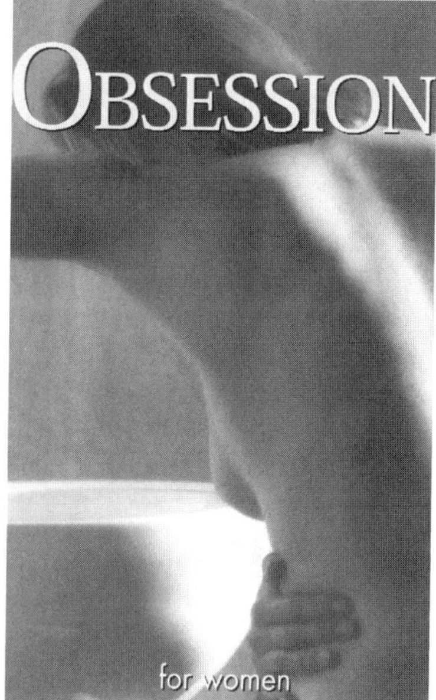


Figure 5.7

Web search or by checking out the "Unofficial Calvin Klein Ads Archive" at **http://dolphin.upenn.edu/~davidtoc/calvin.html.**

As for the "Joe Chemo" ad, what is it spoofing? You're probably familiar with the advertising character "Joe Camel," and you can clearly see the satiric spin that Adbusters is putting on this cartoon image. How might this ad work as an *argument*? Does it consider *logos, pathos*, and *ethos* equally? In general, are the ads effective? What might be their *limitations* as arguments?

Indeed, here's something to think about. Some would argue that we need to be careful in claiming that such a thing as "visual argument" actually exists. Even we are not convinced that an argument can occur without any verbal text. Images can illustrate, add pathos, and even enhance ethos, but because each image is subject to interpretation, testing agreement on what images mean requires verbal or textual statements—and so we're back to spoken or written argument. However, visuals can clearly be used to support arguments, even though they probably cannot constitute an argument by themselves. What do you think?

## your turn

If you were to create a spoof ad, what would you do? Manipulate an image taken from a magazine or an image copied from a Web source to create an ad that spoofs or puts a different spin on the original. Pay attention to your intention in spoofing the original ad: are you simply trying to mock, or are you attempting to highlight a contradiction in the ad? Be attentive to the use of graphics, to any text that appears in the ad, and to possible audience reactions.

## WRITING SPOTLIGHT

### Advertisements and Argument

The following essay was written by Lee Carraher, a student in a first-year writing course. The instructor asked her students to compose a piece in response to an advertisement, paying particular attention to what the advertisement suggested about either the people or the products depicted. In the process of thinking about the advertisements, students composed arguments analyzing and interpreting the ads they chose to write about. In this particular essay, Lee examines an advertisement (see page 207) for a computer system that offers us no real image of the actual product being sold—a computer. Instead, we see a handsome guy and a caption: "My adrenaline fix isn't what it used to be. Double the dose." Lee's analysis highlights why and how such a visual strategy is potentially effective.

Carraher 1

Lee Carraher

64 bit, It's More Than 2 × 32 bit

(actually it is 2^64 / 2^32 = 2^32 more)

The November 2003 issue of *Scientific American*, which headlined important advances in "String Theory," ran two advertisements pertaining to the rising 64-bit processor

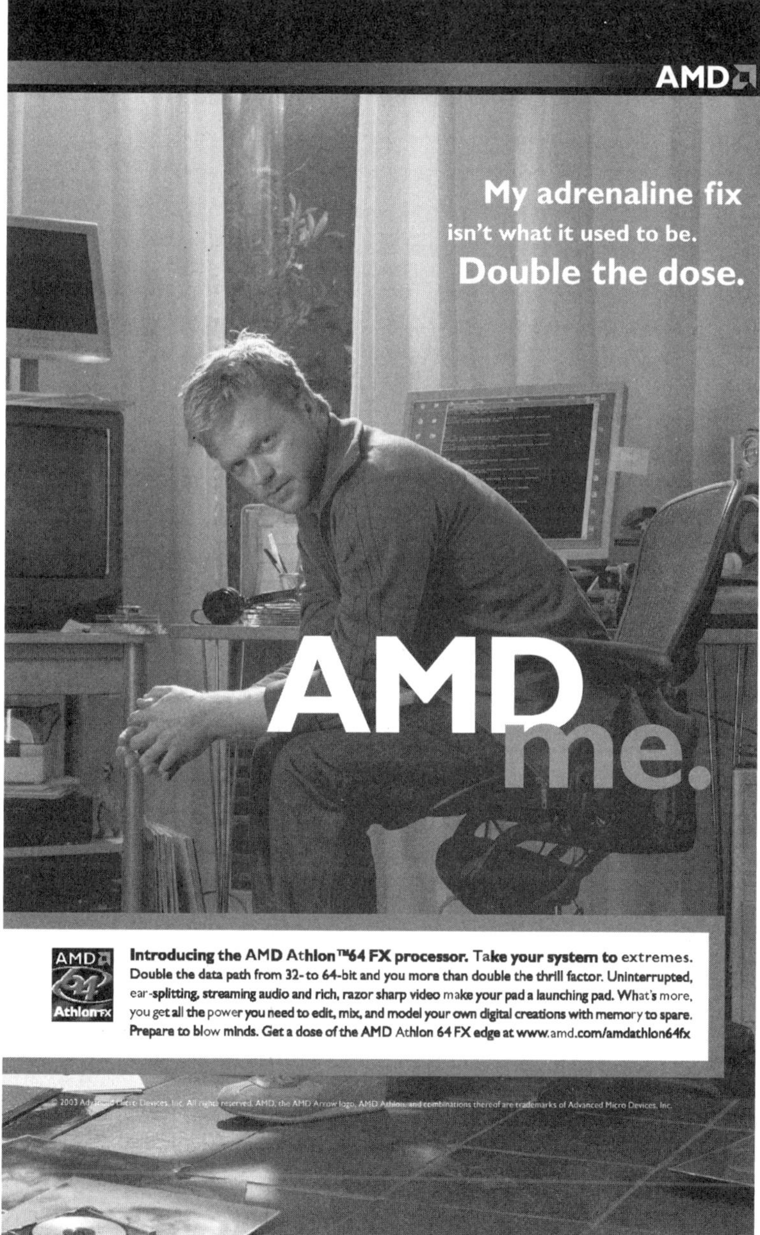
AMD
My adrenaline fix
isn't what it used to be.
Double the dose.
AMD
me.
AMD 64 Athlon FX
Introducing the AMD Athlon™64 FX processor. Take your system to extremes. Double the data path from 32- to 64-bit and you more than double the thrill factor. Uninterrupted, ear-splitting, streaming audio and rich, razor sharp video make your pad a launching pad. What's more, you get all the power you need to edit, mix, and model your own digital creations with memory to spare. Prepare to blow minds. Get a dose of the AMD Athlon 64 FX edge at www.amd.com/amdathlon64fx

standard. The IBM built, Apple G5, which advertised its superior technology and design, was pitted against the "adrenaline"-pumped AMD 64 FX. As Apple tried to sell a product with a "classic" specifications spreadsheet, AMD [Advanced Micro Devices] used popular culture to sell a product which is not even displayed in the advertisement. So why did the marketers choose to replace a discussion of the product's usefulness with other images? Further analysis of AMD's ad for a 3 oz. piece of silicon that promises "double dose of adrenaline" will help to elucidate a contemporary marketing technique.

First, we need to consider the context in which this ad appears—an issue of *Scientific American*, which is a specialty magazine appealing primarily to those with more than just a passing interest in and knowledge of science. Put another way, AMD is targeting the excitement-deprived, tech-savvy, younger- to middle-aged male go-getters that are drawn to *Scientific American*'s content. These individuals do not fear technology and instead embrace it in nearly every aspect of their lives. Attempting to be a respectable desk jockey in an often unexciting but hectic business realm may prompt many of these individuals to repress much of their wants and needs for excitement. AMD is well aware of these excitement-repressed individuals and is willing to capitalize on their wants and desires for a more exciting world to sell their product.

Analysis of how AMD targets such an audience can be done by dissecting the imagery and vocabulary used in the Athlon 64 FX ad. Upon first glance, we notice the young man, a direct reflection of AMD's target audience, hunched forward and looking confidently at the camera. His hands are clasped together. He is "on top" and in complete control of the world

Carraher 3

around him. Further analysis of the "world around him" is also telling and significant. The surrounding is a high-tech, state-of-the-art office, naturally adorned with all the latest pieces of tech gadgetry. The product itself, a minuscule silicon square, is nowhere to be found. We are only to presume it lies somewhere within his PC.

Such images are important to AMD's campaign, particularly since AMD is not selling the product itself but rather the image of success and confidence embodied in this supposedly successful individual. Above the man are the words "Adrenaline fix . . . double dose," which are superimposed in bold white letters. AMD is attempting to capture the repressed wild nature of the desk jockey or computer geek and present the company's new processor as an outlet for it. The adrenaline reference plays directly into the male insecurity of masculinity. AMD realizes the business appeal of their product, but instead of touting its *productivity*, AMD's marketers instead more specifically target the want *for dominance and excitement* in the business world.

AMD uses such an appeal to excitement to sell a processor in an attempt to shed the introverted and geeky stereotype of computer nerds and replace it with the allure of self-gratification and adrenaline-pumped action. Just as Ford Motor Company targets male toughness in their "Built Ford Tough" truck ads, AMD targets the male desire for excitement in the virtual world. AMD asserts that its product will be the vehicle through which males can achieve their goals for excitement. AMD trades images of a new product for the promise of a new image of success and excitement.

## questions for discussion

1. What do you think of Lee's claim in this particular analysis? Is his thesis clearly stated in the introduction and summarized in the conclusion? Does he develop his ideas logically in the body of the essay? Note how, in the body of the essay, Lee identifies specific aspects of the ad, focusing on the images in it. Is this effective? How might you advise him to improve on this strategy and his discussion of the ad?
2. Lee's analysis of the ad relies on a shared assumption: that "desk jockeys" and "computer nerds" want and desire a level of excitement that they don't already have. Do you accept this assumption? Lee is clearly playing with stereotypes, and he is suggesting that the ad itself plays with such stereotypes to appeal to particular users. But do you believe him when he says, of readers of *Scientific American*, "Attempting to be a respectable desk jockey in an often unexciting but hectic business realm may prompt many of these individuals to repress much of their wants and needs for excitement"? Is this a fair or even accurate portrayal of readers of *Scientific American*? If you were peer-reviewing this essay, how might you advise Lee to expand or strengthen this part of his argument?
3. How might Lee have integrated images from the advertisement into his text, so that he could have highlighted portions of the ad for discussion? Is a written description of the images in the ad sufficient to capture the potential meanings in the original advertisement? What other comments about the advertisement might you have included or highlighted in your description and discussion?

## Visual Argument on the Web

In addition to advertisements, many Web sites act as arguments, attempting to persuade others to take a particular stand or adopt a position. For instance, the "Cincinnati Boycott Against Economic Apartheid" (at **http://www.cincyboycott.org/**) seeks to inform visitors about the site owners' position. Specifically, the site discusses a Cincinnati group's decision to boycott events in downtown until the city government addresses issues of perceived racial discrimination. This particular boycott has been somewhat effective in that several major entertainers have been convinced *not* to perform in Cincinnati, in honor of the boycott. Included on the site are a number of responses—both pro and con—about the boycott, as well as an archive of news reports (from print and online sources). While the site contains *much textual* information, it has relatively few graphics.

Other sites use graphics as tools for persuasion. For instance, the YOUth & AIDS Website (at **http://oz.uc.edu/~alexanj/What.html**) opens with a simple graphic that is designed not only to encourage visitors' interest in the topic, but also to persuade them of the importance of the information contained in the site. Here is the opening page:

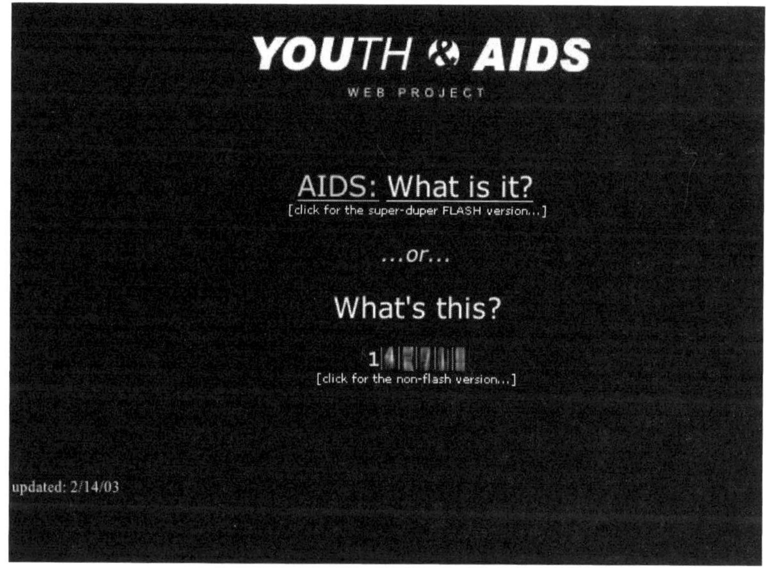


Once you click on the counter, you see the image on page 212.

This graphic display was designed by students to catch visitors' attention and to convince them that HIV and AIDS are important health risks for college-age students. The simple design is striking. One rolling counter on the first page becomes several on the next, underscoring the "increasing number of teens and young adults with AIDS." The two pages demonstrate that just a little text and a single image, judiciously used, can create a powerful, even persuasive statement. The appeal to *pathos* is clear, but there is a

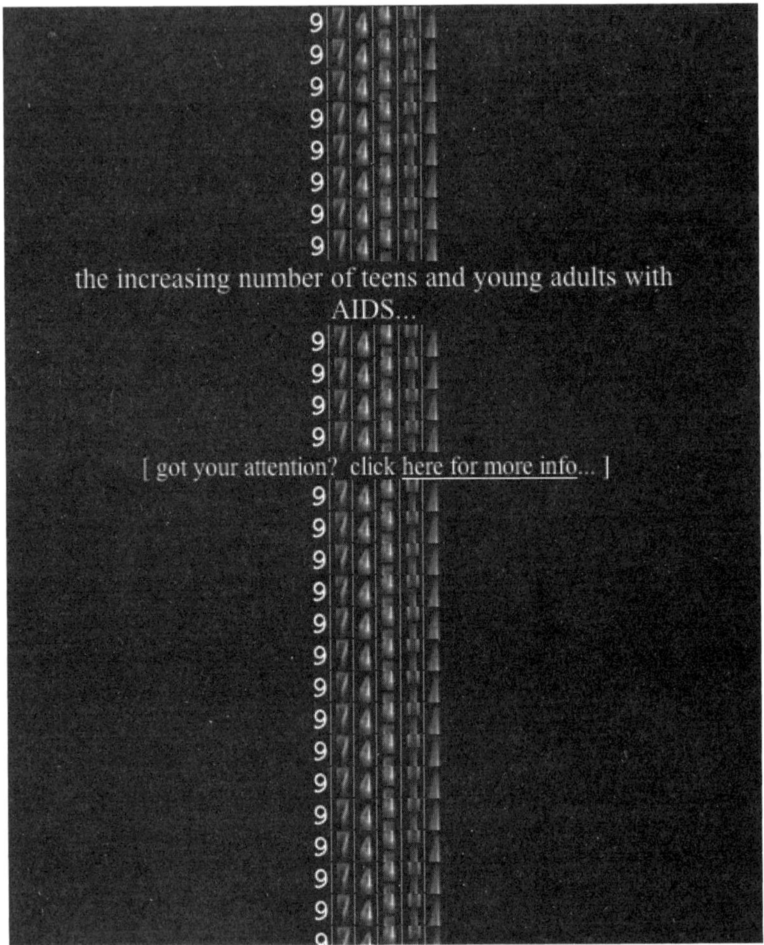


rational claim at work, too: when you click through to the next page, you receive facts and information about the devastating effect of HIV on young adult lives. One student felt that he could create a more effective opening argument for entering the site by combining both visuals and text in a Flash site. The student, Dave Myers, used simple textual messages, but he ordered and manipulated them in such a way that you can't help but follow his Flash movie from beginning to end. His screens are shown on page 214. For the full effect, click on the Flash entrance at **http://oz.uc.edu/~alexanj/What.html.**

**HYPERtext**

A key feature of the Web is its multimedia format, which allows it to combine text and images with moving pictures, sound files, and film and video clips. To search for any number of multimedia files on the Web, try one of the following search engines:

- Lycos Multimedia (**http://multimedia.lycos.com/**)
- Altavista Video (**http://www.altavista.com/sites/search/svideo**)
- StreamSearch (**http://www.streamsearch.com/radiohome.asp**)
- AudioGalaxy (**http://www.audiogalaxy.com/**)
- Internet Movie Database (**http://www.imdb.com/**)

What do you think are some of the advantages of using multimedia material on a Web site? What could be some of the disadvantages? Consider writing an opinion paper in which you argue either for or against the use of multimedia on the Web. Do *not* assume that more is necessarily better; how might it *not* be? On the other hand, how can music and other special effects add educational value to some Web sites?

What do you think of Dave's use of Flash? Note how economically he has used just a few textual messages to make his point—that AIDS is serious business. At the same time, his message is a relatively positive one: you can educate yourself and others. How might *you* have developed a Flash site differently, perhaps using pictures and images as opposed to just text?

You have probably encountered numerous Web sites that use visuals to get your attention so that you will consider buying something. You might have also experienced annoying pop-up ads that fly across your screen, begging to be read. Not all commercial sites use such annoying pop-ups, and many are quite effective in their use of visual rhetoric to advance their goals—getting you to consider making a purchase. Let's look at such a site in greater detail.

Amazon.com is one of the largest and busiest commercial sites on the Web. You may even have purchased something, such as a book or DVD, from this famous online company. Spend a moment browsing through

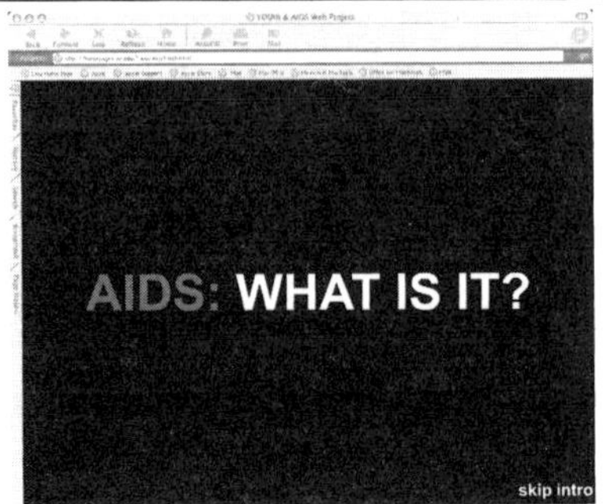
AIDS: WHAT IS IT?
skip intro

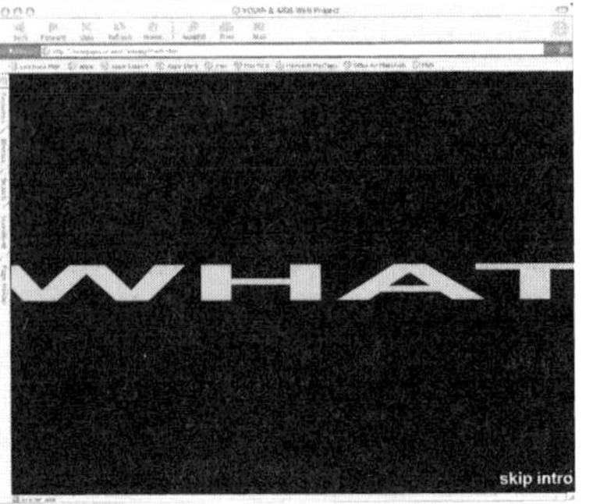
WHAT
skip intro

THE 6th LEADING
CAUSE OF
DEATH
skip intro

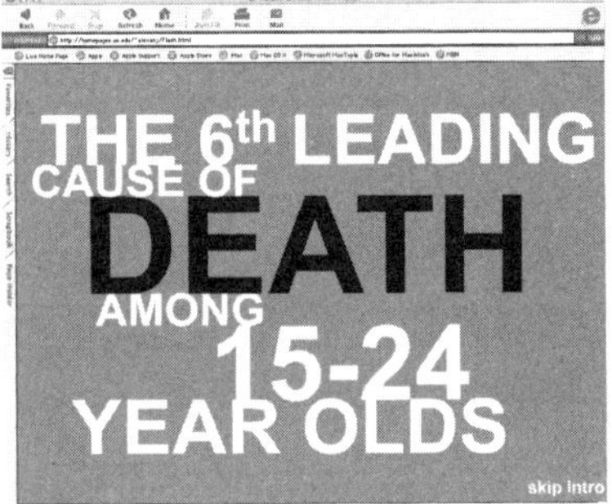
THE 6th LEADING
CAUSE OF
DEATH
AMONG
15-24
YEAR OLDS
skip intro

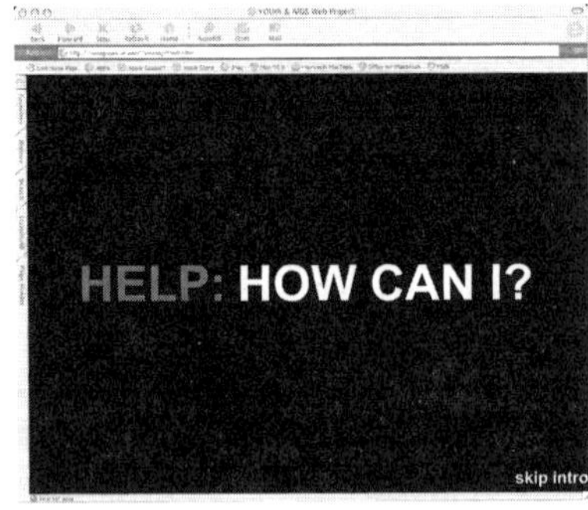
HELP: HOW CAN I?
skip intro

EDUCATE
OTHERS
skip intro

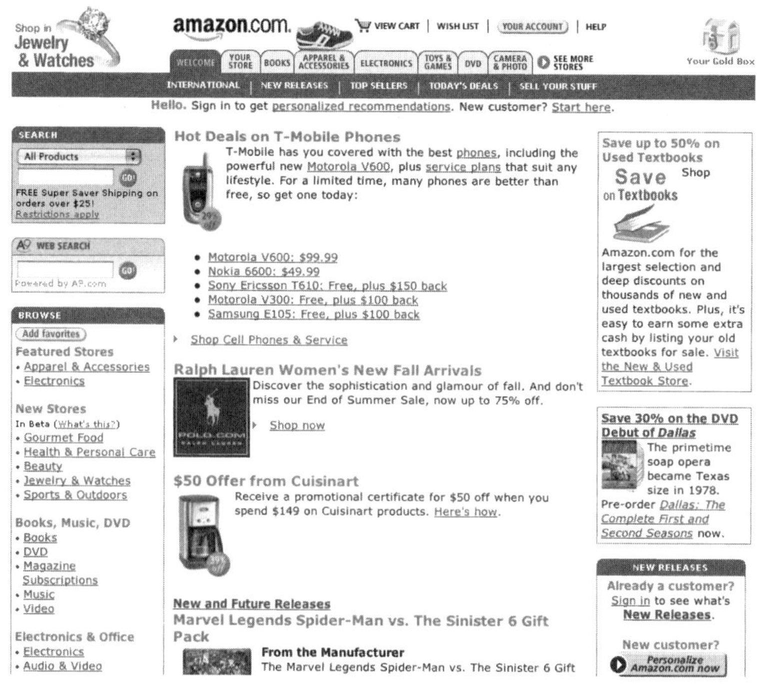


this site and think about the ways in which it acts rhetorically and argumentatively to encourage you to consider making a purchase. For example, you might notice how the site designers have attempted to make Amazon.com relatively easy to navigate so that you can quickly find the items you want to purchase. At the same time, you are constantly being told about other items that might interest you. If you click on a product, you are also presented with a list of other items, perhaps books or CDs that have been purchased by people who bought the same item you've expressed interest in by clicking to it. Pictures of products abound, tantalizing you with numerous purchasing possibilities, and you may create a wish list to which you can refer anyone shopping for gifts for you. The site also attempts to work persuasively in much more subtle ways, particularly at the textual level. For instance, note how the site invites you to sign in and "personalize" your shopping experience. Note also the number of times the word *your* is used to make it seem as though the site has been tailored to your particular interests and tastes.

Designers of other commercial sites focus their energies on particular groups of people. For instance, Disney's Web site is very "kid-friendly (see **www.disney.go.com**)." It uses Flash in an engaging, almost gamelike way. Visitors are invited to click on items and explore as though they were playing a computer game.

If your computer has a sound card and speakers, note how sound effects complement the gamelike visuals and Flash design. Clearly, the purpose of such a site is to be fun and engaging—to serve the rhetorical and persuasive purpose of inviting potential consumers inside for a closer look at Disney's products ranging from videocassettes to vacation packages.

## your turn

A Web site's ability to appeal to particular audiences is important, and many Web designers target their sites to specific readers and potential consumers. Take a look at ThinkGeek at **www.thinkgreek.com** and examine the ways in which the site has been designed to appeal to a particular group—Web-savvy geeks or self-proclaimed nerds. (Note: We use such terms with great respect, recognizing our own geekiness and nerdiness.)

Discuss with others online the effectiveness of this site in combining visuals and text to target a particular group and create a consumer base. For fun, write up a description of the type of person who might purchase stuff from ThinkGeek. What would she or he buy? Why? Post these descriptions to a discussion board for comment and discussion.

## *Useful Links*

To find out more about visual literacy, check out the following:

- An online excerpt from *Visual Literacy, Languaging, and Learning* by John L. Debes and Clarence M. Williams (at **http://www.asu.edu/lib/archives/vlhist.htm**) offers insights into the *history* of visual literacy as it has been theorized and studied. Interesting references are made to the growing importance of *film* in our culture.

- Bev Branton, a graduate student at the Ontario Institute of Education, University of Toronto, offers a marvelous set of online resources in her Visual Literacy homepage at **http://vicu.utoronto.ca/staff/branton/homep.htm.**
- For something a bit more theoretical, try an essay by Anne Wysocki and Johndan Johnson-Eilola, "Blinded by the Letter: Why Are We Using Literacy as a Metaphor for Everything Else?," available in *Passions, Pedagogies, and 21st Century Technologies*, edited by Gail E. Hawisher and Cynthia L. Selfe and published by Utah State University Press and the National Council of Teachers of English. This essay explores how the term *literacy* may not be the best term to describe the different ways of knowing (including the visual) through which we comprehend and make sense of our world.

To help you develop criteria for analyzing and evaluating Web sites, we suggest the following useful, online links.

- The Norman Nielsen Group (**http://www.asktog.com/basics/first Principles.html**) has established some *First Principles* for "the design and implementation of effective interfaces." The Group believes that "effective interfaces are visually apparent and forgiving, instilling in their users a sense of control. Users quickly see the breadth of their options, grasp how to achieve their goals, and do their work." The Group believes that computer interfaces should, in our words, be "reader-friendly," and should not interfere with a user's ability to find the information he or she wants. What do you think about their guidelines, their "first principles"? Can you add to these on the basis of your own experience?
- Clement Mok and Vic Zauderer offer "Timeless Principles of Design: Four Steps to Designing a Killer Web Site" (**http://www.newarchitect mag.com/print/documentID=23407**). Notice that three of their four principles—defining the problem, understanding the audience, and organizing information—are similar to the considerations we identified as requisite to the writing process: considering context, audience, and organization. In the digital and print worlds, many principles of writing and generating text remain consistent.

- Finally, John Lovett offers practical advice about "Design and Colour" on his site (**http://www.johnlovett.com/test.htm**). As you browse through his advice, pay attention to his discussion of how "balance" and "repetition" can aid a Web surfer.

## Writers in Action: Hawisher and Sullivan Talk about Women on the Web

In the following excerpt from their essay "Fleeting Images: Women Visually Writing the Web," Gail E. Hawisher and Patricia A. Sullivan ask, "What happens to women's online lives when the visual comes into play?" The authors attempt to answer this question by examining a number of different Web sites. In this excerpt, they discuss two commercial sites, the Victoria's Secret Web site (at **http://www.victoriassecret.com/**) and Carla Sinclair's Net Chick Clubhouse (at **http://www.flank.com/sites/netchick/**). This is a case in which the visuals serve not just to "prettify" the written text, but as the actual subject of discussion and analysis.

---

### Fleeting Images: Women Visually Writing the Web

GAIL E. HAWISHER AND PATRICIA A. SULLIVAN

#### Commercial

Commercial sites abound on the Web and when they picture women's bodies in their selling of wares these sites are open to the same kinds of feminist critique that advertisements in other venues attract. Representations of women in our society often occur as advertisements: women's bodies (and men's) used exploitatively to sell products. The World Wide Web also increasingly has its share of advertisements that depict women in much the same way as they appear in print. These are the images that the women themselves do not create and are posted to the Web not to announce their professional credentials but to sell wares to online society. These are the same images which appear daily in the popular media and, more recently, in the catalogs that have taken over snail mail. For the most part, these female bodies are objectified and bartered by others: they are not under the control of the women pictured; nor do they speak those women's words.

The Victoria's Secret website* offers an example. Here we have an image, which begins as a "thumbnail" and when clicked upon becomes a lingerie-clad woman—the new pin-up of the home catalog industry. In this representation, the woman, who gazes directly out from the screen, seems to be inviting viewers into her parlor. But this image and other similar ones at the Victoria's Secret site are not controlled by the women depicted, and instead are assembled by someone other than the woman herself. The crafters have a particular purpose in mind, ostensibly to sell the items featured, the images of the women as well as the clothes. In order to convince potential buyers to purchase this lingerie, the crafters seek to homogenize the woman's image as normal and attainable. The homogenized image is white, impeccably groomed, and perfectly formed. The Victoria's Secret webmaster seeks to be the master sculptor of the fantasy version of a desirable woman.

And as Susan Bordo has argued, "Popular culture does not apply any brakes to these fantasies of rearrangement and self-transformation. Rather, [women] are constantly told that [they] can 'choose' our own bodies" (247). The Victoria's Secret bodies do little more than foreground the current homogenized representations of "femaleness" and serve to reproduce the age old stereotypical relations among the sexes. Obviously this is not self-representation.

But there are other commercial sites offering alternative representations of women in which the women themselves very much take control. Carla Sinclair's "Net Chick Clubhouse" serves as a fascinating example. Viewers can enter her cartoon-like, colored clubhouse to find out about her and her interests, but she also provides another front door (actually there are many) which features an advertisement of her book, *Net Chick*. Samples of email about the book, along with an excerpt from the book, accompany the necessary information for ordering a copy.

Although an instance of commerce, her home page also serves as a gateway into a playful nineties' designed environment, and she adroitly mixes the commercial purpose of peddling her book (found in the office room of her house if entered from her personal address) with biographical information, toys and games (found in the rumpus room), connections to other relevant pages and so on. Reminiscent of a child's playhouse in its upbeat attitude, the Net Chick Clubhouse is hardly the typical commercial

---

*Editor's note: See **www.victoriassecret.com**

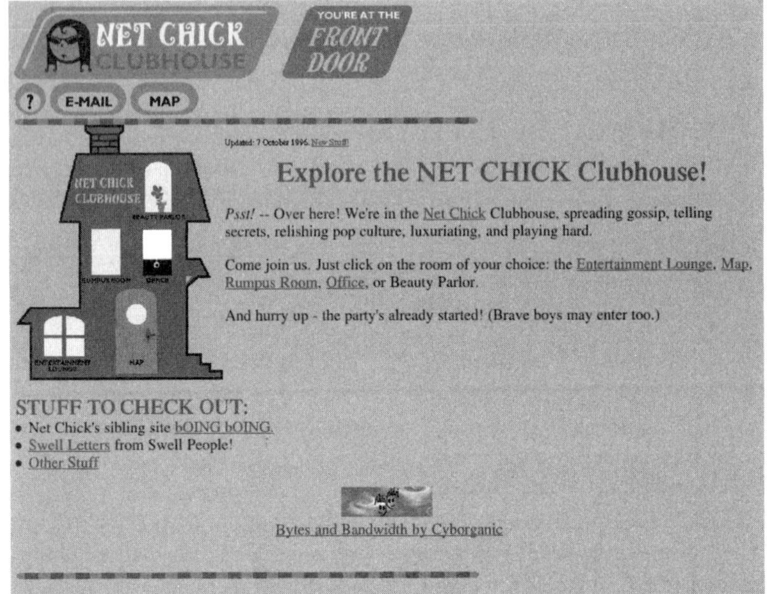


exploitation of women's bodies that the word "commercial" schools us to expect. Instead of encountering lingerie and loud pitches to buy products (as at the Victoria's Secret site), we encounter many renditions of Carla.

And who is Carla? Is she the inventor of "Magic Eight Bra," an online game in which viewers make a wish, push the cups together, concentrate, and then open them for an answer? Or, is she the image in the sultry photo that inspired Toups's choice for Babe of the Year for 1995? Or, is she the published author of a serious net book intended to educate women in the ways of the Web? The answer is "Yes" to all three questions. Her whimsical use of the bra deserves examination. . . . Because of the connections with bra-burning feminists, the bra can be seen as a symbol of rebellion. Because of its connection with constraining women's breasts, it may be seen as a token of subservience or of modesty. Because of its connection with fashion, the bra may be connected to the enhancing or reshaping of the breast—to creating allure. Because of its connection with Madonna, the bra may be seen as a provocative piece of outer wear. Regardless of the particular connection, Carla bets that her readers will respond in some way to the bra as cultural object: perhaps in Carla's mind the bra conveys some meaning to everyone she wants to reach. Ultimately, the bra is a teaser.

Carla integrates commerce into her panoply of selves—collapsing work/commerce with sexual play and children's club houses, pictures of victorian houses with the pink and blue of babies, and so on. She and others like her offer a more complex view of the commercial than does the Victoria's Secret site, though she still invites viewers to buy so that they can join in on the construction of net play. A cynical societal reading of Carla's house is that it is carefully crafted to produce sales.

### WORK CITED

Bordo, Susan. *Unbearable Weight: Feminism, Western Culture, and the Body*. Berkeley UCP, 1993

## questions for discussion

1. How do Hawisher and Sullivan use visuals as an *integral* part of their essay? Are there any visuals that you might have left out? Any that you think *should* have been included? Why?
2. Do you agree or disagree with the authors' analysis of the two Web sites discussed in the excerpt? If you *do* agree, how might you help them bolster their argument? If you *do not* agree, what evidence would you present to counter their claims?
3. Hawisher and Sullivan contend that, "as women have more control over writing their own visualizations online, we see some women representing themselves in complexly in creative, rhetorically effective ways." Identify a Web site, perhaps a personal home page, that does this, and write an essay describing how. Be specific about what you (and the authors) think of as complex in "creative, rhetorically effective ways." For purposes of contrast, identify a Web site that you think is not complex and creative in "rhetorically effective ways." Describe why you think the site does *not* meet Hawisher and Sullivan's—or your own—description.
4. At the end of their essay, Hawisher and Sullivan suggest that the "World Wide Web is doing little more than imitating the material world we all inhabit." Do you agree or disagree? What evidence from the Web could you use to support your opinion?

5. Hawisher and Sullivan look at the way women are represented, and represent themselves, on the Web, specifically in terms of visual rhetoric. How might their analysis be useful to examine other groups, such as peaceniks, antiabortion protesters, pro-choice advocates, Latinos, labor unionists, African Americans, skinheads, Asians, or fans of practically anything? Write an essay analyzing the use of the Web by other people with declared identities to represent themselves in both text and visuals.

## *Additional Writing Activities*

You can experiment with visual literacy and visual rhetoric in a number of ways. Try some of the following.

1. For one of your writing projects, choose a visual image to include as part of your text. You will want to experiment with your word processor to *insert* the image, perhaps wrapping text around it, or breaking the pages up with a carefully chosen visual. As you consider which visual(s) to add to your writing, ask yourself the following question: What images would you choose? How would they complement your writing? Do you need to offer some explanation, either in a caption or in the body of your text, to explain the use of the visual? Could you rely on your reader's own literacy practices and knowledge to "make sense" of the visual?
2. If you have the skills to do so (or are willing to learn them quickly!), create a Web page combining texts and graphics, in which the graphics are an *essential,* not just decorative, aspect of the site. For instance, you could create a photo essay about your family, friends, a favorite place, or a trip you have made. Write a commentary on your process that includes discussion of the decisions you had to make about what to represent verbally and what graphically. Why did you choose as you did? Did you use any other sites as a model for your site?
3. Turn one of your text-based essays into a Web site. What changes will you make along the way? Certainly, a Web-based format allows for greater flexibility in creating *links* between different parts of your writing. But the ease of introducing graphics and manipulating visuals, including something as simple as the color

of the *background* of your Web pages, will allow you the opportunity to consider how visuals can communicate—or detract from communication. Record in a journal the choices you make in this process, particularly your choices concerning images and graphical manipulation of text. You might even write a guide for others on how to transform printed work into Web spaces.

CHAPTER 6

# Navigating a World of Information: Conducting Research

Let's start this chapter with what may seem to be a strange question: *Do you consider yourself a researcher?* The odds are, you *are* one—and just don't know it yet. After all, you have been doing research all your life, most of it outside a formal educational setting.

How so?

Since you first discovered your hands and feet, you have been exploring—first your own body, then the small space of your crib, your toys, the room you slept or played in, then the light on the ceiling, the design in the wallpaper, and the sound of your own voice as you learned to talk. Later, you investigated what was behind cabinet doors, the sound of a spoon drumming on a metal pan, how high you could pile your blocks before they fell over. You might have done some hands-on research to find out what designs you could make with green toothpaste on the bathroom wall or dismantled a television set to see what made it work. Whatever was in your path or whatever you could reach, you examined. During your elementary school years, you inspected the world around you and developed expertise at negotiating your way around the personalities of other children in your class. You knew where the ant trails in your backyard led as well as every nook and cranny of your school's playground.

When you chose a college, you probably considered several alternatives, compared tuition costs, and talked to counselors or checked the Web to find one offering a particular course of study or other features you wanted. You probably didn't think of this as research, but it is. In fact, we could call *research* the whole process of discovering the world by exploring, asking questions, and considering how what we discover fits into the big picture of what we already know. Like writing in general, researching is a process. And we are willing to wager that you already have some insights about how it is done and how you can develop your own set of research skills.

Academic research is carried out for many reasons, the most universal being to answer a question. In presenting the results of research, a writer must show what conclusion the investigation led to and demonstrate why. Academic readers have high standards for the quality of evidence they accept as reliable. They are not interested in unsupported opinion. A researcher who has carried out an investigation conscientiously, meticulously checking all details, even seeking out and accounting for contrary evidence, will have the materials at hand to make a strong statement. As an academic reader and writer, you must know how to evaluate the reliability of evidence presented to you in support of a given conclusion, as well as how to carry out research to develop your own thinking.

## your turn

In class, in a synchronous conference, or by e-mail, tell your classmates what research you have done, both formally (e.g., in school) and on your own. Did you use the Web to find your baby's name or to compare the prices of airline tickets? Have you ever shopped for a car or searched for an apartment to rent? Checked out people on a Web site for a dating service? Explored eBay to see how much your original Barbie is worth? Looked for a job? If so, what were you looking for? Describe each step of the process you went through to find the answer. What did you conclude?

The nature of research questions and procedures will vary according to discipline, but in this chapter we will look at what they have in common. As you choose and progress in your major, you will learn the requirements of your field. Here we will look at the basics of research and at ways to use networked computers to assist in doing it. We will broadly outline the research process, and then we will look at a project done by an undergraduate student, Hershield Keaton, to demonstrate how he carried out an assignment for a traditional research paper before publishing it on the Web as a resource for interested readers.

## Academic Research

In the academic world, you will find that you are expected to read the results of others' research and do some research yourself. You will probably be asked to compose formal essays or presentations explaining what you have found and what you think about it. As with all academic writing, there are traditions, conventions, and expectations both for conducting research and for reporting on it that you will need to learn, even if you present your findings in nontraditional ways.

### Popular Reporting versus Academic Research

As a member of a popular reading audience, you are accustomed to reading work based on research. Whether you read historical novels or magazines about health, hobbies, computers, or automobiles, you are reading the results of the authors' research. Academic research, though structured more formally, is not so different in spirit from what you have done all your life to satisfy your curiosity or make important decisions. Its subjects and the forms it takes may vary from statistical research in sociology to laboratory experiments in chemistry or field investigations in entomology.

But the questions it asks—How do things work? Why are things the way they are? How could they be different?—are probably similar to questions you have asked about a variety of subjects, and in a variety of ways.

It is important to pay attention to the differences between popular reporting of research and academic research, particularly if you are to develop research skills as a college student. One difference between research presented to an academic audience and research reported to a more general one is the consistent presence, for the *academic* audience, of scrupulous **documentation**. Careful documentation lends credibility to a writer's work, especially if the writer is engaged in polemic (debate) or is introducing an argument that could cause controversy.

Researchers in an academic environment often work *collaboratively*, and they subject their work to intensive peer review. Correctness is highly valued. Generally, an academic researcher's motive is not financial reward, but to add to a body of knowledge or thinking about a subject. Colleges and universities are centers of research as well as teaching. Assignments such as term papers, essays, and other projects are designed primarily to give students experience in doing research and related activities in a variety of disciplines. Learning to do research in an academic environment, to be creative in designing a research process and to use libraries, databases, search engines, and a host of other tools, will prepare you to do research in personal and other spheres after you leave school. It's a key ingredient of lifelong learning.

## The Research Process

In this section we divide the research process into stages and then discuss ways to carry out each stage, particularly with reference to how your networked computer can assist you. Keep this in mind: as with any writing *process*, the research process is *recursive*—that is, no matter where a researcher is in the process, she or he may return from a later stage to an earlier one. Researchers may do this for a number of reasons: to find out an answer to a question that arises in the course of the research, to gather more data or find more information, or to readjust an outline or writing plan. An apt image for the research process is the Slinky, the classic toy made of a long, flexible spring of wire or plastic and wound into a spiral form, like this:

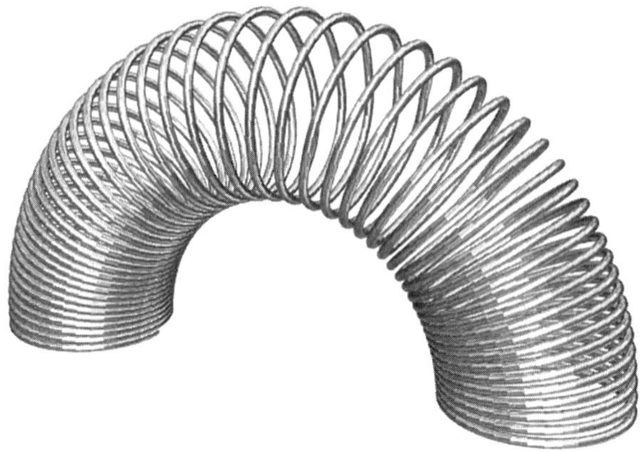

This is an image of the "ideal" recursive process, which progresses neatly, though not in a straight line, from beginning to end. However, you may feel that your process is actually more like this:

Detours along the way can be expected even in the best planned research process. They may, in fact, lead to discoveries that contribute to progress toward the end. During the course of research, many academics and writers often change their initial ideas about the topics they are studying.

Many student writers who have undertaken research with one goal in mind have found that their research convinces them to change their opinions. For instance, a student who researches the topic of gun control and begins with the belief that there should be no restrictions on the availability of guns might be swayed to reconsider her position by the time her research is completed—or vice versa. Keep the Slinky in mind as we analyze the research process.

The basic stages of the research process may be summarized as follows:

1. Conducting preliminary research
2. Identifying a research question
3. Creating a research proposal
4. Finding information and taking notes
5. Analyzing data
6. Composing a presentation of your findings
7. Publishing findings

Dividing the process into numbered steps suggests a rigid structure for a process that may, in fact, turn out to be highly recursive. With that in mind, let's look at each of the stages in more detail. In this chapter we will focus on the first five stages; we'll consider stages six and seven in Part III of this book.

## Stage 1: Conducting Preliminary Research and Finding a Topic

Your assignment will suggest the limits and the possibilities of your project. Within them, seek a topic you care about for some reason. If your assignment is to write a research paper on a controversial issue related to health, for example, then think of issues that have affected you or your family. Are you worried about not having health insurance? Is a bill before your state legislature that would create an uninsured students' medical emergency fund? Is your grandfather complaining about increased prescription drug costs? Has a coach ever encouraged you to use a supplement that has been questioned in a medical report? Does someone you know have cancer? Would you like to know what recent research developments might benefit him or her?

In the past, students generally started preliminary research in their college libraries, and it is still a good idea to see what you can find there. A search of your library's catalog will also give you an idea of local availability of sources on your topic. In this digital age, however, many students go first to the Web to see what sources of information they can find, to discover how people have approached and discussed their broad areas of interest, and to see if they can begin to focus their interests on particular topics or specific questions. To do this, surf the Web, using a search engine such as Google **(http://www.google.com)**, to find out what questions people are asking in your general topic area. (If you've never surfed the Web before, see the sections on "Searching the World Wide Web" and "Surfing Critically" later in this chapter.)

Search engines allow you to find anything that appears on a Web page about a given topic. Although they make no judgment as to its reliability or relevance to your study, they can, at this stage of your investigation, give you an idea of how much or little is "out there" on your topic. Search engines vary in the kind, quality, and quantity of information they will locate for you. Visit several, doing a search for the same topic in each, and compare the number and usefulness of the results you get. Which one gave you the most "hits"? Try narrowing your topic until you get fewer than 100. You can easily narrow a topic by using a Boolean search (discussed later) or by adding plus (+) or minus (−) signs in front of search terms to indicate that you only want, or do not want, Web pages containing those specific words. For instance, if you just search the Web with "technology" typed in to a search engine, you're likely to get around 70 million hits—pages with the word *technology* in them! Adding other search items (+technology +"colonizing Mars") will help you limit the number of relevant hits, although you will still need to narrow your search to make it manageable.

Checking a **search directory** such as Yahoo! **(http://www.yahoo.com)** or a bibliographical database (a list of documents) such as LexisNexis Academic can also give you an idea of subtopics within your general subject area. In some ways, using a database might be more helpful than simply surfing the Web because databases contain smaller sets of information. Therefore, you may find databases easier to navigate through than Web sites. Some databases include worldwide listings in many languages. The best of these are available only by subscription, usually to institutions. Some Internet service providers (known as ISPs) furnish selected databases to their customers. Check your library's home page to see the databases to which your library subscribes. Among them you may find LexisNexis Academic, FirstSearch, Academic Search™ Premier, ERIC (Educational Resources Information Center), and many others. Most libraries have Web pages with links to their subscription databases and other online resources, and most have instructions on how to use them. You may need to ask your librarian for a password to gain access to them from off campus.

As an example, here is the University of Cincinnati's Langsam Library home page:

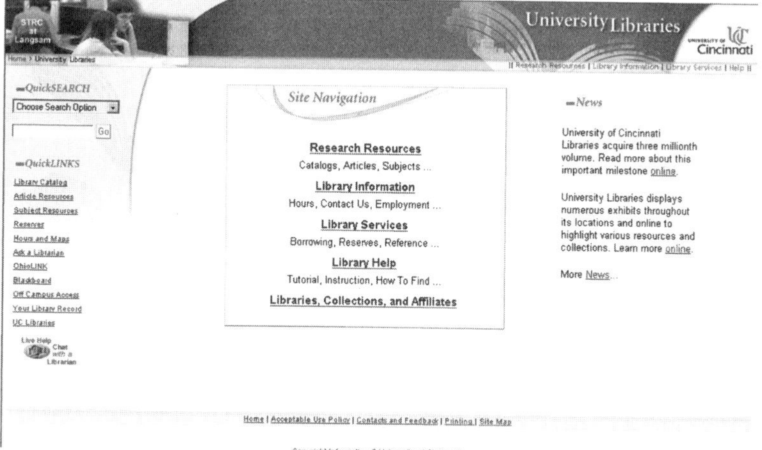


The link Article Resources will take you to this page, with instructions on how to search for information on a variety of subjects through a number of online databases and search systems:

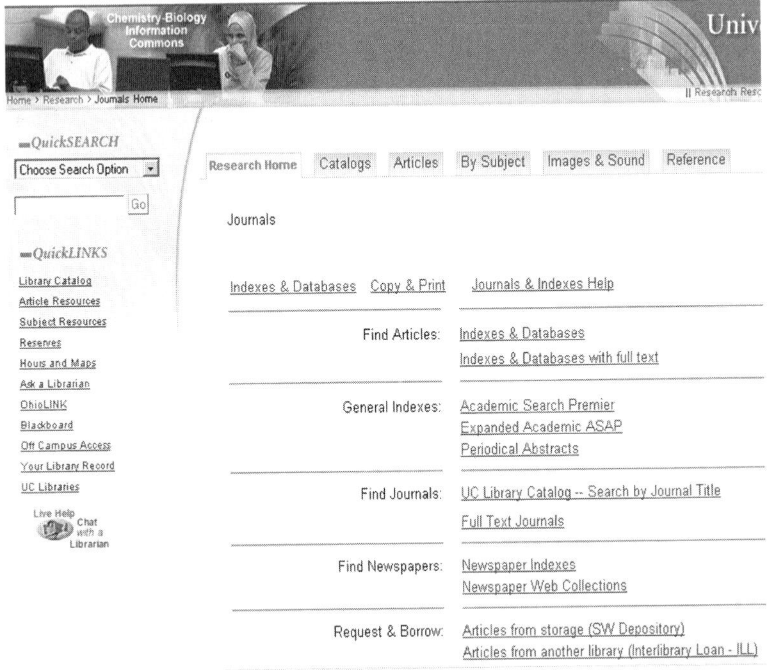


## your turn

Visit your library's home page and develop a list of the databases it has for articles on your topic. If you don't have a particular topic in mind, then try the following, just to get a sense of what kinds of information you might come up with: "colonizing Mars"; "life on Mars"; "science fiction about Mars"; "Martians."

Does your library have an online tutorial for using subscription databases? If it does, take it now. What are the characteristics of each? What databases would you use to find sources on research in business? law? health? chemistry? literature? philosophy? nutrition? politics? history?

Sometimes, students have difficulty finding topics they want to write about, and this is no small problem. If you're composing a research project, you'll want to enjoy what you're writing about, if only because you'll be spending quite a bit of time with the subject! Here are some hints for helping you find a topic if you're stuck.

- Read a good regional newspaper to get ideas on what issues are currently being debated or considered in your area. You can do the same with national newspapers. (To find newspapers online, visit Newspaperlinks.com at **http://www.newspaperlinks.com/home.cfm**, where you can choose from hundreds of newspapers from the United States and abroad.)
- Do the same with magazines you enjoy. Don't hesitate to browse a newsstand or the magazine rack of a bookstore, looking for ideas. You can often find interesting topics for further discussion in magazines such as *Time, Utne, Harper's*, or the *Atlantic Monthly*.
- Poll your classmates, family and friends for what they think are important issues and topics worthy of discussion. For instance, you could, in the course of conversation, ask someone, "What do you think is one of the most pressing issues facing our city/state/country/planet today?" Of course, you should exercise caution with such a question. You may get answers that are unreasonable to address in most college-level research projects. For example, you are unlikely to cover as complex a problem as world hunger adequately in your project—that is, unless you are writing a book!

---

**IMPORTANT:**

Do not be afraid to change your subject as you do preliminary research. You may narrow it if it turns out to be larger than you expected, or change direction altogether if there is no material available on it or if it otherwise proves unworkable.

---

## Stage 2: Identifying a Research Question

Once you have identified a broad topic area in which you would like to work, think of the questions you could pose about that topic area—questions for which you would like to discover some answers. Posing such questions and looking for answers is at the heart of research, with the

**HYPER**text

Here are some other search engines worth exploring:

**http://www.AltaVista.com**
**http://www.Excite.com**
**http://www.Go.com**
**http://www.HotBot.com**
**http://www.Lycos.com**
**http://www.NorthernLight.com**

"Web crawlers"—search engines that include several others—can be useful once your topic is sufficiently narrow. These include the following:

**http://www.metacrawler.com**
**http://www.Search.com**
**http://www.dogpile.com**
**http://www.alltheWeb.com**

With any search tool, you should become familiar with how it operates. Read any posted directions for use; they will probably save you time by helping focus your search.

emphasis here being on *search*. Some simple brainstorming will work well here.

For example, one student writer decided that she wanted to work on a project about the availability of water in her community. She was living in Colorado, and her community had been placed on "water restriction" because there was a drought at the time. Residents could use only a certain amount of water, and some uses of water—for example, to water plants—were forbidden except during very specific times of day. So, to consider this topic, she began freewriting and listing with the word *drought*:

Drought
Water
Water rights

Soon she came up with several different questions that invited research:

Who should get the water in a severe drought? Farmers? Cities? Recreational users? Industry?

Should farmers who lose crops in a drought get government subsidies?
Should water conservation be mandatory? In cities?
Should outdoor watering be allowed during a severe drought?
Should California's Imperial Valley get more water from the Colorado river?
Should it get less?
Should farmers be allowed to sell their water rights to cities?
Should interbasin water transfers be allowed?
Are new dams the answer to water shortages?
Should cloud seeding be made illegal?
What is xeriscaping?
Should xeriscaping be required in water-scarce areas?
Should planting of bluegrass be permitted in semiarid zones?
Should states be allowed to sell water to other states?
Should states be required to sell water to other states?
Should old priority laws on water use be changed in the West?

As you can see, she came up with a long list of potential questions to research. You can also see that that some of the questions pose issues or problems for debate. Remember what you have learned about argument as you think about doing research.

To work on *developing* your topic, try an approach similar to that used by this student, freewriting first with a word or two about your topic and then moving toward posing questions about that topic. Consider the questions on your list, but don't commit to any one just yet. Give yourself some time, several days if possible, to brainstorm some additional questions or possibilities. Then consider asking for feedback. Networked computers allow you to get comments on your ideas from more than one person throughout the process—and, of course, face-to-face consultation works well too. Use such feedback to help you refine a research question. Your classmates can learn from thinking about your questions, as you can benefit from considering theirs.

Here's one idea: In an electronic conference, post your topic ideas to the class. Then look at one another's topics and suggest research questions that could be asked about them. Evaluate the suggestions and propose ways of revising them. Consider these questions as you respond.

*Is the topic or question too general?*

Notice how general the following questions are. You'd need a book-length project to address any of them adaquately.

- "Is There a Cure for Cancer?"
- "What Are the Effects of Inflation on the Economy?"
- "Should Censorship Be Allowed?"
- "Religion in the Military" (not only is this too broad—it's not even a question)

*Is the topic or question too narrow?*

If there is not enough material within your reach, answering it may require primary research possible only for a trained scientist with specialized equipment and knowledge. Also, some topics just don't give you much to write about. For instance, one student writer proposed to research, for a project requiring ten typed pages, the recycling policies at her university. She found her focus to be too specific because there were few such policies. So she broadened her topic slightly to consider the following question: "How can students become more involved in recycling efforts on campus?" This question allowed her to review her campus's policies *and* to talk about strategies for getting students to recycle.

*Is the proposed question answerable?*

Not everything you might want to know can be discovered easily. A question such as "Will America Win the 'War' on Terrorism?" cannot be answered except by hindsight. You will not be able to determine if there is life on Mars, even though the topic may intrigue you. At the same time, you could examine and analyze the various methods that scientists use to determine if there *is*, in fact, life on the red planet.

*Is the project "do-able"?*

Answering the question: "Do social interactions among members of Tribe X in Country X vary according to class status?" may require months of on-site observation. You may have an excellent idea for the graduate level, but be realistic about your current limitations. Can you complete the research with the financial resources and time you have available? If not, adjust your topic accordingly.

*If your assignment is to write about a controversial issue, have you actually proposed an issue question—that is, one on which reasonable people might disagree?*

"Should steroid use by middle school athletes be permitted?" is not really controversial. "Should creatine use by high school athletes be permitted?" is more open to debate. In general, try to avoid "apple-pie" issues—those about which most people agree. "Are Fire Departments Beneficial to Society?" is an apple-pie issue because the overwhelming majority of people will agree that fire departments are beneficial to society. Almost anyone can answer this question without doing research.

*Has the question already been answered?*

To make the process more intriguing and potentially productive, choose a question to which you do not know the answer. After all, why spend time looking for something you already know? Ask your question honestly, and do not fear failure in finding an answer. Even if you do not find one, you may be led to another question you must answer before you can answer your current one. In that case, your paper can explain how you arrived at that more basic question and thus serve as an account of your intellectual journey. This is perfectly acceptable—and often exciting and worthwhile.

## Stage 3: Creating a Research Proposal

A research proposal describes your plan for carrying out a research project. Outside the classroom, variations on the research proposal are frequently used by anyone seeking funding for a project. A grant application, a prospectus for a new stock offering, a business plan submitted to a bank with a loan application—all are research proposals of sorts. They outline the project, demonstrate the ability of those undertaking it to carry it out, point out expected problems and how they will be addressed, justify the funding request, and explain the importance of the project. You can expect to be required to develop such proposals after you leave college.

For our purposes, the research proposal has two main goals. First, composing it requires you to do some preliminary investigation, think through your project, and articulate your plan for carrying it out. Even if your instructor does not require you to submit a research proposal for approval before you undertake the project, it is a good idea to make one anyway. Doing so will save you time in the long run by forcing you to organize your ideas before you waste time spinning your wheels.

Second, the research proposal gives your instructor a chance to offer you feedback on your project early in the process. Anyone doing an advanced project must submit such a proposal for approval by the experts supervising the work. Such an initial review can be invaluable. If your question is too broad or if your project cannot be done with available resources, your instructor will let you know. Your instructor also may be able to steer you to an interview or materials you would not have known about otherwise. When your proposal is approved, you have assurance that your instructor considers your project worthwhile and that you have a good chance of being successful. Even if your teacher does not require you to submit your proposal, ask him or her to look it over anyway and let you know if you are on the right track. By doing so, you may gain important and timesaving advice before you invest many hours in your project.

After selecting your question, do some prewriting and additional brainstorming for your research proposal. Write down everything you know about your subject, and then consider how you can address the *five basic parts of a research proposal*:

**Title:** The title should indicate the subject or the question the research project will attempt to answer.

**Background:** Write a statement providing the background of the project. This may include a brief summary of any preliminary research on the subject and something of the history of your interest in the topic. How did you come up with the question?

**Description:** Describe the project. Explain how you will go about looking for an answer to the question(s) you raise. In short, what is your research plan? Where will you seek information? Will you use materials in your institution's library? Will you develop a survey? Will you use interviews? If you foresee problems with your study, how will you go about solving them? If your library does not have the books you need, will you order them through InterLibrary Loan? Here is an opportunity for you to use your creativity as you come up with ideas about where to look for answers to your question. How will you publish your results?

**Significance:** What is the significance of the project? Why is it important, either to you or to others, to look for an answer to the question you raise?

**Sources:** Provide a list of the most valuable sources you used in preparing this proposal. Depending on the documentation style you will use, this will be called a list of Works Cited (MLA), References (APA), or a Bibliography (CMS).

Let's look at an example of how this might work.

Hershield Keaton's teacher, Dr. Beatrice Spade, wanted students in her class to learn all they could about the history of the Middle East and about doing research. She assigned them to write a properly documented academic paper, using a variety of sources, that demonstrated competence at employing traditional library research techniques and using the Internet for research, communication, and publication. She wanted each completed project to give evidence of the student's ability to analyze and think through ideas, organize material, and use written language purposefully—a charge no different from what is expected in most college-level classes. In addition to making an oral presentation, they were to develop a version of their project to publish on a class Web site. All students were given a common starting point: they were to read a diary written by someone who had traveled to Jerusalem in the past, and see what they might discover.

Hershield's choice of topic was limited by the assignment, but it was still up to him to decide the historical period and the nationality of the author whose travel diary he would study. He was curious about what travelers might have gone to the Middle East in the wake of Sir Francis Drake's much-publicized circumnavigation of the globe. A search on Google using "Jerusalem" and "travel" produced too many advertising sites to be helpful. The library's bibliographic databases (in this case

WorldCat), led to a man named Timberlake, but only after Hershield narrowed his search using the keywords "Jerusalem" and "travel" to sources written in English in the seventeenth and eighteenth centuries.

The project Hershield designed is ambitious, but it uses search tools available to any student who is curious about a subject. A research proposal for his project, following the format given here, might have looked like this:

Keaton 1

Hershield Keaton

Dr. Bea Spade

World History

February 2002

Henry Timberlake Explores Jerusalem: What Did He Learn?

The tentative title indicates the question he will try to answer.

**Background**

When Elizabeth I was still Queen of England and *Hamlet* was successfully playing on the stage of the Globe Theatre in London, an English merchant named Henry Timberlake set out on a two-year pilgrimage to the Middle East. Like many others before and after him, he intended to travel to Jerusalem. A merchant by trade, he and his friend John Burrel decided to combine business with religious pilgrimage and pleasure, buying spices on the way to trade upon returning home. At the time Timberlake had never written a book, nor did he ever write another one after his friend, Thomas Archer, published his diary of the two-year-long trip.

As a history major interested in current events in the Middle East, I wondered what Timberlake's diary might reveal about the Jerusalem of 1602 and about how people lived and traveled at the turn of the seventeenth century. I also wondered what its pages held about the contributions of

Keaton 2

English merchants to this age of expansion in England, such as the opening up of roads and other channels of commerce between East and West. Clearly, explorers such as Sir Francis Drake were not the only ones plying the seas for England. Merchants also traveled long distances and brought back stories of discovery and intrigue.

**Description of Study**

To study Timberlake's story, I will first need to acquire a copy of his diary, which was reprinted frequently for several decades after it was written but may now be difficult to find. Librarians at the British Museum, for whom contact information is given on the Museum's Web page, may be able to help me obtain a copy of the diary. By searching genealogical sources on the Timberlake family, I hope to learn more about Timberlake himself than his diary reveals. Then I will look in other sources from the period that might help explain allusions, references to geographical areas, and historical events to which Timberlake refers in his account. I will look for information about the history of commerce at the time of his travels and attempt to learn more about the East India Company.

I will compose a research essay explaining what I discover about Timberlake's travels. In addition, I will create a Web page on which I will make available, for others to read, the paper I have written, the full text of the diary (since it is no longer under copyright) by scanning the text and converting it to HTML where necessary, maps showing Timberlake's itinerary, a bibliography for anyone interested in pursuing the study of Timberlake, and links to other sites that will supplement the information I present.

Keaton 3

**Significance**

In addition to satisfying my curiosity about what Timberlake and explorers of his time discovered in their travels, my Web project will make the information I find available to others who are interested in the history of commerce, pilgrimage, and a part of the world we need to understand better today.

Keaton 4

WORKS CITED

Bisson, Douglas R. *The Merchant Adventurers of England.* Newark: U of Delaware P, 1993.

"Henry Timberlake." *Dictionary of National Biography*, Vol. 5. New York: MacMillan, Smith, Elder, 1908.

Klutznick, Philip M. and Ethel Klutznick. *Pilgrims and Travelers to the Holy Land.* Omaha, NE: Creighton UP, 1996.

Timberlake, Henry. *A True and Strange Discourse of the Travailes of Two English Pilgrimes.* London, 1603.

**NOTE ON COPYRIGHT**

Hershield was able to scan the text of Timberlake's diary into his Web page because it was not under copyright. If it had been published within the last few decades, he would not have been able to do so. Before publishing anything on the Web (or anywhere else, for that matter), always check to see if the material you want to publish is available for you to use as you wish. Copyright rules change, especially in this age of electronic publication. You can find current laws on the U.S. Copyright Office site at **http://www.loc.gov/copyright**.

## Stage 4. Finding Information, Part One: Considering a Variety of Sources

Data collection is what most people think of as "research," but it is actually only one stage of the entire process. Scholars begin with a **literature review**, which means that they are locating and reviewing all of the previous sources of information available on their topic or question. Gathering this knowledge is important so that they know what others have already discovered.

To accomplish this stage, you will need to use all the sources you know of, including those you locate while doing the library assignment that follows. Such sources will certainly include Internet-based materials you might find, including sources from online databases. As we will see, however, a diversity of sources will make for a better research paper, so print sources as well as any field research you might do should also definitely be considered.

*First, though, a note on evidence:* As you're looking for information, you may wonder what "counts" as information you can use, as "evidence" to help you answer your research question. Here are some clues.

**Primary sources** are those closest to the event itself, or to the subject. Someone studying the poetry of an author would use the poetry itself as a primary source. A critical article *about* the author's work would be a **secondary source**. Historical documents such as eyewitness accounts of a battle would be primary sources. A discussion of the event based on such an account would be a secondary source. For example: If you wanted to compose a research project about Julius Caesar's wars in France, then Caesar's book, *The Gallic Wars*, would be a primary source. A scholar's commentary on Caesar's account of the Gallic Wars would be a secondary source.

You should also carefully judge the relevance of your sources to your topic. If you are finding mainly sources such as articles, Web sites, or books that contain only a few sentences about your subject, then keep looking for other sources. Remember, though, that some topics might have to be addressed by looking through numerous sources and gleaning small bits of information from each of them.

### Getting to Know Your Library

Many students face a huge temptation to depend on Internet sources alone and never walk through the doors of their college libraries. Perhaps someday every source will be placed online, but that has not yet happened. You should demonstrate your ability to work with many types of sources—print, text-based, electronic, and your own field research and experience. If you do not consult a broad range of sources, you might miss just the information you need to complete your project, or to make it truly interesting for you and your readers.

Hershield started by using the library's online tools for research, which in his case led mostly to print sources that he would have been unlikely to locate without electronic databases and search engines.

How can you make sure you're considering a variety of sources? Ask librarians to help you if you get confused. (By paying tuition, you hire them to help you.) *After you have done all you can on your own*, they will probably be delighted to point you toward additional resources on your subject. You should also become acquainted with your library's Web site. Learn how to access your library's databases from on and off campus. If you need a password to reach subscription databases or journals from an off-campus site, memorize it so that you can download articles, consult sources, and find materials from a computer anywhere.

## your turn

Complete this questionnaire about your library to ensure that you are becoming familiar with its basic resources.

1. What hours and days is your library open?
2. Where is the book collection in your major topic? In what building? What floor? Are you allowed to browse there?
3. Do you need a library card? A copy card? If so, obtain both of these.
4. Visit your library's Web page. If there is a tutorial that you haven't yet taken, do so now. What did you learn from it?
5. Find the names of five free or subscription databases available to you. What electronic resources look as if they will help you the most?
6. Are computer labs or wireless services available, in case you want to take notes electronically from source material on the spot?

## Using Library Catalogs, Online and Otherwise

Look for information on your subject first in your library's catalog (which will probably be stored electronically) to find out what sources are available to you on campus. The online catalog at the University of Cincinnati is shown below.

As you can see, you can search for items by author, title, keyword, or subject. Check your library's Web site to learn the online databases to which you have free access. Subscription services, as well as some free ones, will allow you to download the "full text" of articles published in academic journals.

The *Library of Congress* (LOC) site at **http://www.loc.gov/**, will lead you to citations for every book printed in America, in addition to musical scores, photographs, special exhibitions, and much more. The online catalog includes links to several thousand other libraries worldwide, including community college libraries and libraries on several continents. By searching

UCLID UC's Online Catalog

University of Cincinnati Libraries

**Welcome to the University of Cincinnati Libraries Catalog**

**You may search for library materials using the following:**

- AUTHOR
- TITLE
- KEYWORDS in Authors, Titles, Contents, Subjects, Publishers
- SUBJECT
- MEDICAL SUBJECT
- UNIFORM TITLE/SERIES
- CALL NUMBER & NUMERIC INDEXES

Change Your Search by Location or Material Type | Full-Text Journals

- OhioLINK CENTRAL CATALOG
- Library INFORMATION
- RESERVES:COURSE NAME or INSTRUCTOR

- VIEW YOUR OWN LIBRARY RECORD
- CREATE YOUR LIBRARY PIN

- OFF CAMPUS ACCESS

- MATERIALS I would like the library to acquire

the catalogs of local libraries, patrons may be able to save waiting time by obtaining books already stored in their geographic area.

If you are looking for information specific to a country or in another language, try the *National Libraries of the World* Web site at **http://www.publiclibraries.com/world.htm**, which provides an alphabetized list of national library addresses and URLs for those with Web sites. You may be surprised at what you find. For instance, the British Library site at **http://www.bl.uk** lets you explore its collection of millions of items and even order reproductions of an array of documents in its immense collection, some for delivery online within two hours. Hershield contacted a librarian by e-mail and phone, and obtained a primary source not readily found elsewhere.

## your turn

Experiment with a variety of online information resources. Visit the Library of Congress site and explore the links. Write a few paragraphs (or post a note to a class discussion list) explaining what kinds of resources are available at that site. Then visit an exhibition in an online gallery and the Virtual Reference Shelf and write about what you find. Recent surfing on the Library of Congress page led to the online manuscripts exhibit, a photograph of President Lincoln at Gettysburg, a manuscript by Sigmund Freud, and an exhibit of baseball legend Jackie Robinson's memorabilia. Live chat with a librarian is also available through the site. What could you learn from such a chat?

### Searching the World Wide Web

As primary source material and scholarly publications become more abundant on the Web, you may find reliable sources to supplement your library research. The challenge in searching the Web is to design a search narrow enough to lead you to your information but not to vast quantities of information outside the boundaries of your project. A researcher must keep clearly in mind the questions she wants to answer and have a good idea of the kind of information that will be useful in answering them. Search engines, search directories, and specialized databases usually permit efficient negotiation of the Web. Try using those listed in the box on page 234 to find specialized information on your subject, but first become familiar with their search protocols. You can usually find these by clicking on a link called "advanced search" or "advanced searching."

Read the instructions carefully to find out if it will allow you to place quotation marks around terms (for searching for exact phrases), or use plus signs and minus signs before terms to indicate how you want to narrow the search. Using such items can greatly facilitate your searching, making the list of sources you retrieve much more manageable.

### Conducting a Boolean Search

As we have noted, a search on a research topic may yield thousands, even millions of hits using a large search engine. A **Boolean search** allows you to narrow the search by adding qualifying terms to the search to narrow results. By adding *and, or,* or *not,* in various combinations, you will narrow the search considerably. For instance, a search for "global climate change" on Yahoo! turned up 1,410,000 Web sites. "Global climate change *and* polar ice cap" turned up 9,050, still too many. "Global climate change *and* polar ice cap *and* ozone depletion *and* Mars," however, turned up only 226 pages, a number possible to scan for promising annotations (usually given under the title in the list of hits). What's a "promising" source? One that will help you answer your research question, of course!

### your turn

Choose a topic, and then check Google or Yahoo! for Web sites on it. Keep narrowing your search using Boolean operators (*and, or, not*) until you get *under* a hundred hits. Create a list of citations, using MLA or the documentation style your instructor stipulates, for the ten most informative Web sites you can find on your narrowed topic.

### Surfing Critically

Research using Internet search engines may seem deceptively easy. However, the process is complicated by the glut of material one may find and the wide variations in quality, from unreliable to scholarly.

Generally, it will be up to you to decide whether a Web site is reliable enough for your purposes. You should ask several questions of each Web site you consider using, such as:

- What is its purpose? Is it to inform? To sell something? To persuade you to take a particular position on an issue? A cursory glance at the

*Encyclopedia Britannica: Guide to Black History* (at **http://search.eb.com/blackhistory/**), for example, reveals that the site is designed to inform its readers by providing access to a large number of printed, audiovisual, and Web sources by scholars and respected sources on African American history and culture.

- What is the intended audience? Do you think that that audience expects a level of accuracy consistent with scholarly practice? The historical collections linked to the *Britannica* site, many of them affiliated with major libraries or research institutions, are chosen to appeal to an audience with high scholarly standards.
- Who is the author? Is the author affiliated with an educational institution? If you are not sure about the reputation of the author, search further on the Web to learn what you can about the person. If he or she is associated with a university, check to see whether the subject on which the author is writing is in that person's discipline. Read the person's résumé (also called *vita*), if available on the Web, to get an idea of his or her level of expertise in a given area. Behind the *Britannica* site is the long-established reputation of the *Encyclopedia Britannica* for using the research of experts.
- If no individual author is named, is the page sponsored by a group known to have expertise in the subject? The U.S. Census Bureau, for example, could be expected to provide reliable demographic data for the United States.
- Is the group politically motivated? How might a political or ideological bias be at work on the site?
- Is enough information provided on the page for you to create a citation? Is anything missing? A source that does not provide enough information to create a citation is unlikely to have credibility for scholarly purposes.
- Has the page been updated lately? If not, might the information included be out of date?
- What about the site's design? Is it amateurish? For example, does it have green print on a red background with flashing purple images scampering across the page? A flashy design might signal a greater attention to style than to content.

These are just a few of the questions you should ask as you evaluate a Web site for use in scholarly research. Can you think of others you might use? Brainstorm with your classmates.

**HYPERtext**

For guidance on evaluating a Web site for scholarly purposes, see Esther Grassian's page, "Thinking Critically about World Wide Web Resources" at **http://www.library.ucla.edu/libraries/college/help/critical/**.

Librarians have provided several services with prescreened sites on wide-ranging topics. The Librarians' Index to the Internet at **http://lii.org**, sponsored by the Library of California, will lead you to prescreened sites and links to other major search tools. Academic Info at **http://academicinfo.net/** offers links to sites reviewed for reliability, and BUBLINK at **http://bubl.ac.uk/link/about.html** is another source of sites evaluated by the Library of Networked Knowledge. If you school does not have its own library-sponsored Web page listing sites recommended for academic research, take a look at the library pages of other colleges and universities. For instance, the page of Internet Search Tools suggested by librarians at the Colorado State University–Pueblo (**http://library.colostate-pueblo.Weblinks.html#hotlinks**) is one among hundreds of these.

## WRITING SPOTLIGHT

### Reviewing a Web Site

The following review is a good example of a student's response to an assignment asking her to find a Web site that promised to be useful for a research project and to evaluate it by the criteria we have listed.

Cindy Barbera
Dr. Michael Johnston
English 102
March 2003

Evaluating Gangresearch.net

The GangResearch site at **http://www.gangresearch.net**, authored by John M. Hagedorn, is devoted to the academic study of gangs. Its purpose is stated in the "About Us" link, to be "a website dedicated to providing quality research on gangs to students, academics, public officials, the media, and the general public." The site author also explains his intention to avoid bias very clearly:

> While most "gang" websites either present the views of law enforcement or give unverified or questionable information, Gangresearch.net seeks to dispel stereotypes and present research, original documents, and helpful links.

Hagedorn says he alone is responsible for its content, and that no organization or institution is associated with it, other than the fact that he uses the University of Illinois–Chicago (UIC) server. It is the repository for documents of the Chicago Gang History Project that he has worked on for many years.

There is a tremendous amount of information available on the site. The Archive section has links to other sources of information on gangs from UIC library, online seminars on gangs, syllabi for his courses, and a whole section of links just on definitions of gangs. The site also included many other links, such as to the National Gang Youth Center, legislation

Barbera 2

on gangs, a slide show with charts showing statistics on gangs, a section on media images of gangs, FBI Crime Reports, and a lot more.

The site is also well designed. It invites a reader to learn more. A click on the link to "Resources" opens a flashing text that says "Research not Stereotypes." One of the headings on the home page says "people and folks," which I learned later is the title of one of Hagedorn's books. This suggests to me that he doesn't automatically take an anti-gang, a "gang members are bad," point of view. Even a gang member would feel welcome to read more on this site. Basic information is on the home page without clicking on links, but the author doesn't clutter it up with too many words. It is easy to read, and the colors, mostly black print on a white background with many colored graphics and links, are not distracting.

Barbera 3

After seeing only this much, I was convinced that this is a reliable site for use in academic study. However, I thought I'd better check out the author, John C. Hagedorn. If he had good credentials, I knew this site would help me with research on why people join gangs. When I found Hagedorn's resume linked to the site, I read that he is an Associate Professor of Criminal Justice at UIC. He has won many honors for his work and has a list of five books and dozens of articles and grants to his credit, adding up to $1.5 million. One great thing was that the full texts of several of his articles in journals are linked to the site.

This is an awesome site with tons of information on it that I can use for research. Hagedorn puts his lifetime of research out where students can use it. I wish all professors would make it this easy for students to find and read the research they have done. I would give him an A+.

## your turn

Choose a Web site on your topic and write a 500-word review of it. Would you recommend this site as a reliable source for research? If so, how might it be used? Support your statements with examples from the site. Place the Author's name, Title, and URL at the top of the page. Send your review to your classmates via e-mail (preferably a discussion list) so that they can click on the URL in the citation and read your review while looking at the site. As a class, discuss the conclusions of the reviews. Do you agree with them?

## Conducting Field Research

**Field research**—gathering information you gather yourself as opposed to reading and recording it from a source—can add an interesting and personal touch to your research efforts. Here we'll consider two types of field research: interviews and polls or surveys.

*Interviews*: What could be a more powerful introduction to an essay on the problem of skyrocketing prescription drug costs than the testimony of someone who has had to stop buying drugs needed to control a life-threatening condition such as high blood pressure or heart disease? If you can locate one or more experts on your topic, an eyewitness to events you are writing about or someone with firsthand experience of a social problem, consider including an interview or two among your research sources. A face-to-face interview with someone on your campus, such as a professor, should not be difficult to arrange. Interviews with people distant from you may be done by phone or e-mail, making it fairly simple to get their own words exactly as they say them or want them to be recorded. Don't overlook the retiree next door, who might give you insights on the history of your area. Remember—the generations are still around that remember the Great Depression, World War II, the Kennedy assassination, and life before television, computers, routine commercial air flight, or the conquest of space.

When using an interview, keep these guidelines in mind. Make an appointment with your subject at a time convenient to him or her. Introduce yourself, explain the purpose of your research, and let the subject know what you hope to learn from the interview. Choose a public location or place of employment such as a coffee shop or an office; do not go to the person's home or invite him or her to yours unless you already know each other well. Indicate how much time you expect the interview to take. Arrive on time with a written list of prioritized questions and a means of recording answers, such as a notebook and pen or small tape recorder. A laptop would also work well, as you can type up comments and have your interviewee review them. Ask permission to use the tape recorder and, if this is granted, place it unobtrusively where it will pick up the sound. Be on time, and take your leave when your time is up.

After briefly establishing rapport with the subject, begin asking your questions. Ask the most important questions early in the interview in case the conversation gets sidetracked or your time runs out. Record the date and time of the interview for use in your Works Cited or bibliographic list (that is, your list of sources used in your project). Follow up the interview with a thank-you letter or note.

### your turn

Use a class discussion list to get ideas for people to interview, places to look for sources, and comments on your project as it develops. If you join a national or international list, you may find excellent sources of information, but remember to behave professionally on such lists. With classmates, an ongoing discussion of the challenges and discoveries made by other class members can help you test ideas, find additional sources, and get a sense of what your audience knows and thinks about your subject before you write your paper.

*Polls and surveys*: Although creating and administering a poll or survey may be beyond the scope of your current work or abilities (unless you are doing guided work in the social sciences), there are ways to use informal polls to collect some basic information. For instance, MisterPoll at **http://www.misterpoll.com/** allows you to construct an online survey, to which you can invite participants to answer questions, offer feedback, and share ideas. Of course, any "results" you might take from such a poll will not be definitive; only a trained researcher in statistics can construct a poll carefully enough to claim that results from it are reliable. However, using such short polls can give you information on what people think about your research topic—information that you might not otherwise have thought about. For instance, a survey of students in your class (or in your composition instructor's other classes) can help you get an idea of whether there is a need for a child-care facility on campus, gauge students' attitudes on issues, or establish that more effort should be made to address a common problem.

## Stage 4. Finding Information, Part Two: Recording Information

After you have found material to use, keeping track of it is crucial. Otherwise, you might quickly confuse yourself about where you found what. Here are some strategies for recording information about the sources you find.

### Constructing Annotated Bibliographies

An **annotated bibliography** is an alphabetized list of sources you might use with a notation, or brief note, about what kind of information is contained in each source. Though largely considered a very "traditional" format, annotated bibliographies offer an excellent way to keep track of sources in an orderly, organized fashion. Working with a computer makes compiling them even easier. Let's look at each item—the bibliography and the annotation—in a bit more detail.

A **bibliography** is simply a list of sources. In the past, even the relatively recent past, it referred largely to print sources (books and articles read on paper), but now it will include materials you can locate and save digitally. (Some people call a list of digital sources a "Webliography," but we generally include electronic as well as print materials in a "bibliography.") To prepare the format properly, alphabetize the entries and write them according to MLA style for print sources and Columbia Online Style for electronic sources (or ask your instructor if he or she has another preference for the citation style you should use). See the appendix to this book for the correct formats. Double-space throughout; do not put any extra space between entries.

An **annotation** is a note, usually a brief summary, placed under the citation for a source. For most assignments, a two- or three-sentence summary will probably suffice. When you are taking notes for research purposes, however, you may want to develop more extensive annotations. Regardless, include enough information so that you know, and can intelligently communicate to others, exactly what is available in the source.

Here are some hints for preparing individual entries for your annotated bibliography.

- Read the article, encyclopedia entry, or enough of the book (such as the introduction) to understand the author's main point. With scholarly articles, pay attention to the **abstract**, the summary sometimes printed at the beginning of the article. Or look for a subheading such as "Conclusions" or "Results."
- Summarize the text, using action verbs as much as you can. Using action verbs generally makes your writing more assertive and authoritative than relying on passive constructions. For instance, consider how this sounds: "C. Arden Pope *presents* evidence that the number of deaths from heart disease increases proportionately to increases of particulate pollution levels in the air." The sentence sounds weaker if it begins this way: "The evidence *provided by* C. Arden Pope . . ."
- Remember to alphabetize your list according to MLA style guidelines or the citation style preferred by your instructor.

• Staple or clip copies of your paper sources to the back of your assignment. You do not need to print out sources accessed electronically because the information you provide in your bibliography will allow anyone else to find those sources online.

## WRITING SPOTLIGHT

### A Student's Annotated Bibliography

As Hershield began collecting potential sources for his project, both primary and secondary, he constructed an annotated bibliography to help him keep track of the materials he might want to use. Here is a sample of his annotated bibliography.

PRIMARY SOURCES

Timberlake, Henry. *A True and Strange Discourse of the Travailes of Two English Pilgrimes.* London, 1603.

Henry Timberlake's book, a firsthand account of an early-seventeenth-century pilgrimage to Jerusalem, includes details of Holy Land sites and references to their situation based on landmarks in London.

Wheeler, John. *A Treatise of Commerce reproduced from the London edition of 1601, with a bibliographical note by George Burton Hotchkiss.* New York: Columbia UP, 1931.

This economics paper delivered in 1601 to the British Parliament by John Wheeler, a member of the Merchant Adventurers of England, was to gather support for the expansion of sea trade. It expresses, in some detail, the ideology of the organization.

SECONDARY SOURCES

Lingelbach, William E. *The International Organization of the Merchant Adventurers of England.* Philadelphia: U of Pennsylvania 1903.

This short book detailing the subject of the Merchant Adventurers includes the purpose of the organization and the individuals who made significant contributions.

Peters, F. E. *Jerusalem.* Princeton, NJ: Princeton UP, 1985.

This analysis of pilgrimage to Jerusalem examines the purpose of pilgrimage and how it has evolved over time.

## your turn

For this exercise, you will need to visit your college library in person and via the Web and explore its online databases to find sources for an annotated bibliography. Choose a topic, or if your instructor assigns you one, find information on that subject. You may, for example, look for information on issues of health, the environment, gender, or a historical period or event (e.g., "the Irish Potato Famine"). If you want to get off to a quick start on a future assignment, choose a topic you may want to explore further in a research paper.

Then develop a bibliography containing entries from each of these sources:

1. A newspaper, book, or magazine article published before 1865 (if applicable).
2. An encyclopedia volume physically in your library. Photocopy the entry and attach it to your final bibliography.
3. An online encyclopedia.
4. A scholarly journal that is on paper in your library (photocopy all or part).

5. A government document (e.g., use Marcive or GPO Access; ask a librarian if you need assistance).
6. An article found in a business index.
7. *The Reader's Guide to Periodical Literature.*
8. A book from your school's library (photocopy the parts you use).
9. A book listed in WorldCat or another database of books (accessed from the Library Electronic Resources Web page). Develop your bibliographic note from the database entry.
10. An electronic book (sign up for netLibrary or another e-book service if available).
11. An article in a scholarly journal not found in your library. Try databases such as Academic Search Premier, Ebsco Online, or FastDoc. Look on the library's Electronic Resources page, or use a search engine such as Google (**http://www.google.com**). Develop your bibliographic note from the article's abstract, if provided.
12. A Web site sponsored by an *academic* institution.

If you need assistance at any point, ask a librarian. Most librarians will be delighted to help you find information and acquaint you with information-retrieval sources.

## Taking Notes

While you are reading source material for a research project, or even while conducting an interview, you need to create your own record of everything you find that supports your investigation. For a short paper in which you use only a few sources, it may be possible to do what too many students are tempted to do for longer papers as well: print out or copy the sources, highlight the potentially useful passages, and draft the paper from the highlighted copies. Although it may seem more efficient at the time to skip taking your own notes for a *longer* essay, this isn't a good idea. When it is time to draft your document, you are likely to have to deal with a hodgepodge of raw material that you have no record of having mentally processed and which you still must take time to put into your own language. The result is usually unnecessary stress and an inferior project.

The process of taking notes from your sources gives you a chance to select what you think is important, think about how you might use it, and reflect on where it might fit into the organizational scheme that should be taking shape in your head. Above all, it will allow you to summarize important points or arguments and to devise language of your own, language you can actually use in your essay, long before you are ready to begin writing your first draft. Ideally, you should write your paper from the notes you made while reflecting on your sources, not from piles of printouts of your sources. If you have copies of your sources, then you should keep them nearby as you write and consult them if you need to, but you should have notes in which you have recorded the information and ideas you find.

In high school or perhaps even in college, you may have learned to take notes for a research paper or project on 3" × 5" or 4" × 6" note cards. You would then organize the cards according to an outline and write your paper from the cards. The basic principle that made this process useful is one that remains valuable—namely, the importance of creating your own collection of ideas, noting reactions to your reading, recording thoughts about your subject, and, most of all, crafting your ideas in your own language.

Today, computers offer options for note-taking that allow you to accomplish the same ends without writing by hand on note cards if you prefer not to. You can, for example, record your notes from one source digitally in one document. You can then rearrange your notes, space them for printing out on separate pages for each subtopic, and cut and paste them into other documents as needed (always transferring the author's name and the page number with each one). You can still key them to sections of your outline and print them to spread out before you, one section at a time, when you are ready to draft that section. For instance, you may develop a detailed outline early in the process, then key each item in your notes to a section or subsection of the outline. That is, if a note contains information in section II. B. of your outline, write "II B" by it and then cut and paste the relevant notes into each section. That way, you can print out the outline with the notes collected under each topic and read them over before you begin to write. Such a strategy should work for any organizational scheme you are using, even if you are not constructing a formal outline.

*Above all, remember to gather key publication information about each source,* including the author's (or authors') name(s), the exact title, the date of publication, the publisher, and, for text sources, the place the piece was published. If you are using a digital source, you may copy and paste the author's name, the title, and URL into the page. If you quote material from a Web site, you need to record the *exact* Web site address, usually found on your browser in a box called "address."

You might also *truncate* a URL to find out more information about the organization that put the material on the Web. Here's an example of **truncating.** If you're quoting a source on teen pregnancy, your URL might look like this:

**http://www.plannedparenthood.org/teens/index.html**

To find out more about the source and what organization sponsors the Web site, you can truncate—or "lop off"—what follows the URL's first slash (/), like this:

**http://www.plannedparenthood.org/**

Truncating lets you know, in this case, that Planned Parenthood is the sponsoring organization for the information you are using. To help keep track of this information, you might also take time at this point to create a citation identical to what you will need for a Works Cited list, using the style or combination of styles you have been assigned to use (e.g., MLA for print sources, COS for online ones). This practice will save you much time in the long run because you will have a citation you can cut and paste into any page where you place information from that source. When the time comes to make a list of Works Cited, all you have to do is collect your citations and arrange them alphabetically on the Works Cited page.

After creating a citation or transferring one to the top of a fresh document, you are ready to begin taking notes from that source. Your notes may take several forms. Don't be afraid to combine or vary them according to your needs. Remember, your notes are ultimately for your own use, although you may be asked to turn them in with your project. If you use a note-taking program for collecting and organizing notes, the principles don't change. You still need to start by recording author or title and page number (or URL), and then make sure that this information travels with the note to any spot where you incorporate it, or information from it, into your draft.

The notes you take will be of several kinds: *evaluation, quotation, summary*, or *paraphrase*. You will have to determine what kind of note suits your purpose.

EVALUATION NOTES As you locate new sources, evaluate them for your purposes. The articles you find in scholarly journals will have been screened for accuracy and reliability by a process of extensive peer review, as will some of the more scholarly sites you find on the Web. In addition, your reactions to the content and ideas found in the articles or on Web sites will be important to record as you think of them. With your notes, include evaluative comments both on the article or document as a whole and on specific ideas or uses of evidence in them. Record your own thoughts, reactions, and questions in your notes as you proceed. You should also read "against the grain" and look for false information or evidence of bias. If you find it, consider this question: Is the source useful for academic research? Well, yes and no, depending on your purpose. If your project is about bias on Web sites, or if you want to represent a point of view in the words of its advocates, then yes. If you are looking for an impartial evaluation of an issue, then no. These sources may become immensely valuable to you in comparing and evaluating arguments as you use the notes in writing your paper. As you go along, evaluate each source as critically as you can.

RECORDING QUOTATIONS As you collect information, you may decide to record exact quotations for use in your writing. When is it appropriate to collect and use quotations?

If your source is an authority on the subject you are writing about, someone whose words carry weight because of his or her reputation, including them may lend weight to your argument. Quote the words of a spokesperson who can represent the position of a group, and remember that it's not really fair to let an opponent characterize those who hold an opposing position. For example, one would not credibly quote Rush Limbaugh to represent the position of the National Organization for Women (NOW) on an issue, especially after he has publicly revealed his bias by characterizing feminists as "feminazis." A quotation from NOW President Kim Gandy would be more appropriate, even if you are arguing *against* a position that NOW holds. In general, the views of individuals or groups holding controversial positions should be stated in their own words, using quotation marks to indicate that they are the ones speaking. Also, if a writer uses uniquely expressive language or articulately captures an idea, you might want to consider quoting his or her words. If the wording is ordinary, summarize or paraphrase instead.

Let's look at an example. If you are quoting from Planned Parenthood's Web site about good parenting, you might be tempted to use a quotation in the following way:

> According to Planned Parenthood, "There are all kinds of families in the world today, and there are all kinds of parents" ("How to Be a Good Parent"). (http://www.plannedparenthood.org/guidesparents/SEXGUIDESHOW.HTML)

This, however, is a *weak* quotation. The "information" is pretty obvious and is worth putting in your own words, as opposed to wasting a quotation on it. The following is a more effective use of quoted material:

> According to Jon Knowles, Director of Sexual Health Information for Planned Parenthood, there are "seven levels of basic needs" that children have, and we need to acknowledge those needs if we are to raise our children to be healthy. The first need is "meeting our children's bodily needs" ("How to Be a Good Parent"). (http://www.plannedparenthood.org/guidesparents/SEXGUIDESHOW.HTML)

What's more effective about this use of quoted material? First, the writer is providing more information about who is speaking in the quotation. Second, the quotation refers not to general, common knowledge but to very *specific* information that is contained within the Planned Parenthood Web site. Finally, the writer does not hesitate to use *parts* of quotations, weaving them into her own text. This is an effective strategy that shows you are really working closely with a source.

Remember, quotation notes are just that: *exact* quotations of the wording used in your source. Avoid overusing quotations. It is easy to cut and paste, or simply to copy, quotations from a source that looks informative. One potential drawback of overusing this strategy is that when it is time to draft the paper, you must still exert the mental energy to put the quotation into your own language. A research paper should not consist of a string of quotations you have drawn from other sources. As a rule of thumb, you should limit your use of quotations to no more than about 10 percent of the essay. You can save yourself time later by using quotation notes judiciously while doing your research.

**MAKING SUMMARY NOTES** Summary notes are useful when you are working with a large number of sources and need to record the gist of an article or a source. A summary contains the main points, including the conclusion and reasons for the main argument(s), but it leaves out *specific* details. Summaries may range in length from roughly one-tenth to about one-third of the length of the original article, and sometimes you may choose to summarize just a couple of paragraphs from an article. Summary notes are especially helpful when the material does not require concentrated effort to understand. Save those passages for ***paraphrasing***.

**TIPS ON SUMMARIZING**

- Capture the main idea, without your own commentary or opinion.
- Use *small* quotations, perhaps a phrase or a very short sentence, if you need to record a particularly important phrase or comment.
- Include the author(s) and title in your summary; this will help you create an in-text citation.

Let's look at the Introduction to sociologist Will Wright's book *Social Logic of Health* to demonstrate summary writing:

> [I]f the "health" that physicians understand as the goal of their profession is in some way conceptually different from the "health" that insurance companies finance or the "health" that environmentalists feel is threatened or that holistic practitioners feel is achievable, then the arguments and evidence that each group advances or that social scientists advance in support of different positions will be essentially incommensurable and thus useless as the basis for intelligent institutional decisions. (Wright 2–3)

One way of summarizing the passage might be as follows:

> This means that if insurance companies, the medical community, environmentalists, and social scientists each mean something different when they refer to "health," it will be impossible for them to work together to make decisions on behalf of the whole community.

Do you think this summary captures the meaning of the original? Can you improve on it?

PARAPHRASING NOTES A **paraphrase** is a kind of translation, not into a foreign language but (assuming you are working in English) from someone else's English in to *your* English. It involves putting the language of the source into your own words. Making notes by paraphrasing is valuable for two reasons.

First, paraphrasing requires you to figure out what a passage means so that you can reword it. Doing so can enhance your understanding of the material. In fact, it's a good idea to use this technique regularly with the most difficult material you read, even when you are studying for purposes other than research. To develop a paraphrase, you must grapple with the text, come to an understanding of it, and word it in a way that makes sense to you. Second, by paraphrasing you devise language that you can use in your paper to avoid excessive quoting. Of course, you will include an **in-text citation**, or information such as the author's name, a title, and a page number (if present), with every paraphrased passage to indicate your source, but you should not use quotation marks unless your paraphrase includes three or more words in a row copied verbatim from the source. If it does, place quotation marks around those words. (See the appendix for more information on creating in-text citations.)

Paraphrasing requires some time and effort to learn to do properly, but with practice you will get the hang of it and be able to do it with relative ease. Because paraphrasing requires more time than writing summaries or recording quotations, you will want to use it selectively.

To paraphrase a passage, follow the steps listed here. You will create three complete versions of the text in addition to the original one.

*Step 1:* Choose the passage you will paraphrase and rewrite it, changing the vocabulary, using synonyms wherever possible, but being careful to keep the original meaning. Put it into completely different words. *Keep no more than two words in a row from the original version.*

*Step 2:* Working with the version you made in step 1, look at each sentence to see how you might rearrange the clauses and phrases so that structurally it does not duplicate the sentences in the original. Then look at the arrangement of ideas in the passage as a whole. Reorganize the order of ideas so that it is different from that of the original, but be careful not to confuse or alter the meaning.

*Step 3:* Read through the version you created in step 2, looking for ways to improve the style, to make it sound more natural. Incorporate those changes. When you have finished, this version will be your paraphrase. You should have devised language that you can use in your essay, if you wish.

Follow these steps the first time you create a paraphrase. After that, if you keep in mind all that you need to change (language, syntax, arrangement, style), with a little practice, you will soon be able to do it all in one step.

## your turn

Choose a 300-word section from an article or book you find to be somewhat difficult to understand. Paraphrase it, creating a new version for each step of the process. When you have finished, post your final paraphrases online for your classmates and read one another's. Which ones do you think are the most readable? Which ones manage to keep the original meaning of the text? Were the paraphrases, as a rule, longer or shorter than the original passage?

### Managing Your Time

It takes time to do research carefully, to assimilate the material, develop your own ideas, and to write about what you have found. In a composition class, your teacher may require you to turn in evidence of your work at each stage by a certain date (e.g., research proposal, annotated bibliography or notes, outline, rough draft, and other steps). In other classes, you may be assigned a research project at the beginning of the term that is not due until the final week of the course. What may seem like a long time will go fast, so it's important to start early and use the time well. Create your own schedule, allowing adequate time for finding sources and taking notes, for collecting data, and for planning, drafting, revising, and finishing your project. The research and composition process for a major essay or project should not be packed into two weeks at the end. How much time should you allow? After completing a variety of projects for this course, you should have an idea of how long it will take you to do others.

## Stage 5: Analyzing Your Information

Ideally, you should be analyzing information as you need it. A researcher must make an initial decision about what to record, and what is worth remembering, at the time of taking notes. You should take more notes than you will need, but you cannot write everything down. Some judgment about the reliability of the source, the authority or qualifications of the writer on that subject, and any possible biases will need to be made early.

After you have collected all your data, analyze the arguments presented, considering whether factual information provided by other authors has contradicted or discredited information you might initially have thought reliable, or raised questions that must be answered before you can answer your own research question. Sometimes researchers merely end up with new questions—but this is a valuable result that can launch further research.

Here are some general tips to help you sift through the information you collect as part of a research project. Analysis primarily involves dividing up your material so that you can discuss it in a coherent and organized fashion. If, for instance, you are looking at different theories about the possibility of life on Mars, you might initially divide up your sources into (1) those who think there is a possibility of life on Mars and (2) those who do *not* think so. Within each category, you could arrange the sources (and your summaries, paraphrases, etc.) for discussion on the basis of which theories seem the most convincing, from the weakest to the strongest. If two theories directly contradict one another, you might consider discussing them at the same time. You can also, after summarizing the material you've discovered, make your own interpretation, stating why—specifically—you were convinced by one set of theories (or one particular theory) and not others.

Another strategy is to pose a "critical question" and then use your sources to answer it. For instance, Hershield Keaton collected all of his sources, summarized them using an annotated bibliography, and began arranging them in the following categories:

> Background, information about Henry Timberlake
>
> Summary of the travel writings
>
> **Critical question**: Why has this book remained popular over such a long period? Offer different theories to explain continued popularity:
>
> - It allowed the reader to visualize movement from one place to another. (Use Source A.)
> - It was useful as a travel guide for potential voyagers. (Use Source B.)

- It provides a guide for those seeking to do "trade" and conduct business in the East. (Use Source C.)
- It offered a fascinating account of a rudimentary incubation process—among the first! (Use Sources D, E, and F.)

As you can see, the *analysis* comes in brainstorming answers to the "critical question" that Hershield poses to himself. He uses his sources to help him answer that question; in fact, each one of his answers comes from a different source. Also, the brainstorming suggested to him a rudimentary organizational strategy for his project. Read on to see how his essay turned out.

**HYPERtext**

To see the hypertext version of Keaton's project, go to **http://chass.colostate-pueblo.edu/history/seminar/timberlake.htm**. What do you think about this presentation? Is the Web an effective medium for publishing original research work? Why or why not?

## A Student Research Writer in Action: A Research Project

In designing his research procedure, Hershield Keaton used resources available to anyone, but he also relied on the knowledge and expertise of specialists in the field he was investigating—a good idea in any research endeavor. With the help of his professor he obtained Timberlake's Diary, and thinking creatively about all the resources he might draw upon, he held phone and e-mail interviews with a librarian at the British Library, where Timberlake's Diary is kept. He then posted his primary source material, no longer under copyright, and his essay on the Web for anyone to read. At the end he included a list of works consulted during his research in which he found useful background information that he did not refer to directly in his essay, as well as the required list of Works Cited in the paper. As you read through Hershield's paper, note how he has used the research process to create a thoughtfully developed essay that generously uses sources, some of which took some resourcefulness to find, to explore the answers to his questions.

Keaton 1

Hershield Keaton

Dr. Bea Spade

World History

April 2002

The Travel of Henry Timberlake to Jerusalem:
A Pilgrimage That Hatched an Idea

**Introduction**

On January 1601, a native Englishman, Henry Timberlake, set sail from London, England, on an adventure of faith, fame, and fortune. During the first year of his approximately two-year-long trip, as recorded in his diary, he made a pilgrimage to Jerusalem from the port city of Alexandria, Egypt. In order to visit Jerusalem, he traveled by booking his own way with a caravan headed to Damascus. During this journey, John Burrell, also from England, accompanied him. The round trip from Alexandria to Jerusalem took just over fifty days, with Henry spending less than a full week in the Holy Land—a whirlwind tour by any standards, contemporary or ancient (Timberlake, Henry 1–26).

Timberlake's travel account, *A True and Strange Discourse of the Travailes of two English Pilgrimes*, begins and ends suddenly. There is no preface or introduction to the book he wrote. The entire narrative was written upon his return to Alexandria as a letter to a friend, and I felt as if he were writing a personal letter directly to me; there is just that personal feeling to the text. In reality, the published account was written to the man responsible for its publication in 1603, a Mr. Thomas Archer. According to historian Douglas Bisson, Archer was an associate of Timberlake, like him a member of the Company of Merchants of London, which became the English East India Company around 1603 (22–46).

Timberlake's book was so popular that it was reprinted eight times before the end of 1631 (DNB 881). Adventurous travel accounts about faraway locations had become very popular in England during the mid-sixteenth century. Much of the desire for information concerning exotic places can be attributed to Francis Drake's return from his voyage around the world. After Drake's return to England, there was a literary hunger for stories of drama, and danger (Keay 272). In 1580, several published accounts of his sold numerous copies. Timberlake's account helped fulfill that hunger, and it left us with much more to think about as well.

**Timberlake's Travel Account**

*A True and Strange Discourse* has also been included in Robert Burton's *Two Journeys to Jerusalem*, published six times between 1635 and 1796, and in the first volume of *Harleian Miscellany* (1808). The book has been reprinted in its original form over the course of time, with the original copy remaining in the British Library.

Timberlake's style of writing apparently targeted a growing middle class merchant society which might be tempted to make a pilgrimage to the "Holy Land." I believe the book could also have appealed to the lower classes, based on its entertainment value, and as a brief work that could easily be read in a single sitting. The book itself is organized around a pilgrimage in which there is constant movement as the author takes the reader on a round trip to and from the Holy Land.

*A True and Strange Discourse* was probably written to promote the trade of arranging travel for pilgrims to Jerusalem. In fact, Timberlake's book provided a step-by-step guide on how to get to the Holy Land. However, for those unable to make the physical journey, the book allowed the reader to close his or her eyes and form a mental picture of the trip. It would therefore be possible for the reader to imagine making a pilgrimage. The book's description of locations referenced to London landmarks would make it much easier for someone to concoct a mental picture of the sites in the Holy Land. Surprisingly, in spite of the popularity of this account, Timberlake did not publish any other literary works after this single book, nor had he published anything prior to this.

**The Life of Henry Timberlake: ????–1626**

Henry Timberlake was reared in the southern town of Gloucester, England as the son of a well-to-do seafaring merchant. His father, Alexander Timberlake, was a member of the Merchant Adventurers of England, an organization Henry joined later in his life. Though I was unable to determine whether he had any brothers or sisters, the published genealogy of the Timberlake family does include a grand-nephew, also named Henry Timberlake, who was born in the colonial province of Virginia about 1730 (Timberlake, Alexander 22–26).

Keaton 4

What little information I was able to uncover on the life of Timberlake relates to his business activities. The British Museum and the St. John's College research libraries both contain personal letters to and from Timberlake, donated by The East India Company in the early 1700s. Typically access to this information is only through personal visit; however, I was able to make phone calls to both institutions and receive answers to key questions.

Based on several sources where I have found mention of Timberlake, he appears to have been well respected and a good friend. One example can be found in John Sanderson's account of his travel to Jerusalem in 1601. In his account Sanderson talks of seeing Henry and expresses some empathy for the troubles he had upon arrival in the city. Throughout all of the materials I have read, I have found no harsh statements about Henry as a person, but these materials are mostly business-related. To say anything more about his life would be irresponsible without viewing other materials.

Indeed, after hard searching, I conclude that some lesser figures of history will remain an enigma to the researcher. I do not feel that there is information available that could provide a more complete view of this individual as something more than a man of trade. To represent a full story on Henry Timberlake would require a considerable amount of time and access to material in British archives; only then might we know his true significance from a historical standpoint.

But we do have his book, and it tells its own magnificent story.

Keaton 5

**The Travels, The Book**

*A True and Strange Discourse of the Travailes of two English Pilgrimes: what admirable accidents befell them in their journey to Jerusalem, Gaza, Grand Cayro, Alexandria, and other places: Also what rare Antiquities, Monuments and notable memories (concording with the ancient remembrances in the holy scriptures) they saw in Terra Sancta, with a perfect description of the Countries about them. A discourse of no less admiration then well worth the regarding: written by one of them, on behalf of himselfe, and his fellowe Pilgrime.* This short book with a very long title has provoked more questions for me (mostly due to its compact size) than a lengthier book might have. There is no introduction, no preface, no information concerning the author; nor are the motives for writing this account given. Despite this lack of information, the book has been reprinted quite regularly over the past four hundred years. Why? What is the appeal of this particular book that should cause it to be read and re-read over such a long period of time? What kinds of unique information might it contain that would make it attractive to generations of readers? To provide context to my questions I would like to provide a brief summary of the book itself.

Henry Timberlake was the captain of the English merchant ship *Troyane* (Timberlake, Henry 3). Over a period of several years he ferried both Christians and Muslim pilgrims to Alexandria, Egypt (Bisson 25). He was a member of the Merchant Adventurers of England and a joint stock holder of the East India Company. On this particular trip he had brought trade goods to Egypt (Timberlake, Henry 8). The primary export from England during this time was raw wool, so this was probably the main cargo. He also brought back spice from these voyages. The spice came over the Arabian Desert in caravans from port cities in the Indian Ocean, Arabian Gulf, and the Red Sea (Geber 67–75). However, on this particular trip Timberlake had also brought three hundred pilgrims to Egypt. The combination of sea travel and overland caravans brought the goods to market and the people to their destination faster than sailing around the African Continent.

Either of these two routes was dangerous and much of the merchandise was lost in the process. All travel at this time of history was dangerous with opportunists around every bend and lurking in every cove, just waiting to liberate any and every item of value. Henry was an opportunistic individual who saw that by transporting pilgrims to Alexandria he could maximize the profitability of his time and resources.

Timberlake begins his account in "grand Cayro" with his companion, John Burrel. The two men travel on their own to a city named Canko (a small village east of Cairo), where they join a caravan headed to Damascus. The next several days are spent in the nearby city of Philbits where he goes into great detail concerning the artificial incubation of chicken eggs. After a thorough description of this phenomenon the journey heads into the Arabian Desert.

During the trip there are four stops where the Turks charge taxes. One of the reasons given for the taxes is to pay for protection from the "wild Arabs" while crossing the desert. The trip has its only exciting moment when a band of Arabs attack on the fourth day. Timberlake reports one casualty, several wounded, and the loss of a single camel carrying

Keaton 7

calicoes. He mentions that the only reason they do not go after the raiders is that it is dark. The time of the attack is uncertain since all travel was at night, with the days spent resting. I have yet to understand the reasoning for this since at this time of year the desert is not hot. The remainder of the journey was conducted, however, without incident.

Once the two men arrive at Jerusalem, a new difficulty arises. Pilgrims were not allowed into the city without a sponsor, and the Turks did not acknowledge the Queen of England, since she paid no tribute to them. Burrel, who spoke Greek, is admitted with the Greek Orthodox Church sponsoring him. Timberlake refuses to deny his religion or his country and is imprisoned. His deliverance from prison comes with the help of their guide. When the two were in grand Cayro, a Muslim pilgrim from Algiers who was on the ship agreed to go with them to Jerusalem and then back to Alexandria. The guide goes to the city authorities and negotiates Henry's release.

Henry spends very little time in the city visiting sites, but the two do spend several days going to various sites outside of the city. Towards the end of their stay, Henry ventures out to the surrounding areas and describes in detail the location of many of the religious sites. The details are given with reference to distances between landmarks in London. This allows anyone familiar with London to imagine the position of one place in respect to another. At this point, Henry decides to leave Jerusalem with his Muslim guide. It is evident from the text that his prior companion does not leave with him. Perhaps he joins with the five Englishmen who have recently arrived. One of these individuals is John Sanderson, who in his pilgrimage account, *The Travels of John Sanderson in the*

Keaton 8

*Levant*, mentions meeting Timberlake and Burrel, but does not mention the latter returning with him.

Henry and his guide make an agreement with two "wild Arabs" to carry them back to Grand Cayro. On the return trip, there is no mention of paying any taxes. He also mentions that the two guides they have hired were two of the band that attacked his previous caravan. There is little time spent describing the return to Grand Cayro, and the return trip takes only four days total. The Muslim guide goes on his way at this point, with Henry retiring to his ship by himself.

**Continuing Popularity of the Travel Account . . . and Chickens?**

Why has this book remained popular over such a long period? I believe that in an era when the average person did not travel long distances, it allowed the reader to visualize movement from one place to another. In this way, readers with a vivid imagination could conduct their own metaphysical pilgrimages. Many people could not afford to go on a pilgrimage, and it is possible that a savvy businessman saw a way to provide a story of pilgrimage that offers the reader escape from ordinary surroundings to an adventurous journey to the Holy Land.

Besides supplying a fantasy pilgrimage for the reader, the book is useful as a travel guide for potential voyagers. It provides a handbook to sites in and around Jerusalem. The book is compact and could easily be carried along with the future pilgrim. Henry was methodical in relating the exact locations of the majority of holy sites, thus allowing the visitor to conveniently find all of the popular sites. Potential travelers

Keaton 9

also have an idea of what taxes they could expect to pay on their overland journey and the process for admittance into the city of Jerusalem itself. It would have been important to make the trip seem achievable to the potential pilgrim. Of course, Timberlake would directly and indirectly have benefited from the increase of travel to the Holy Land.

As a member of the East India Company it was becoming important to create and open new areas of trade. Membership in the company guaranteed the two hundred and eighteen members a share in any new ventures (Kinney 87–93). It became essential to aid all other members in establishing new trade, and trade was essential to England also. Queen Elizabeth presented her last address to Parliament in December 1600. In her address, she focused on the need to open trade routes and increase markets for English products, while bringing in rare commodities to the country. At the same time she chartered the Merchant Adventurers of England as the East India Company. Their charter addressed the concept of free trade with everyone. A portion of the profits from the company would go directly to the government, but it would remain a private endeavor (Wheeler 112–33). At this time, the Dutch East India Company was making a huge profit. It was the hope of the English that they would be as financially successful as the Dutch were. An essential difference existed between the two, however; the Dutch tried to enforce exclusive trading privileges with their partners, while the English were seeking *free* trade.

The English East India Company was a merger between the two largest trade companies in England, the Levant and the Muscovite trading companies. These two powerhouses represented the bulk of England's merchant fleet with approximately sixty ships. One of the ships was the Troyane, owned by Henry Timberlake (John Sanderson was on the Levant), who through his multiple associations became one of the two hundred and eighteen original members of the Honorable Company (East India Company 151–67). One of the goals at this time was to find if a north-west passage existed from the Mediterranean to the Indian Ocean. The discovery of a north-west route to India was a goal of both the Levant Trade Company and Henry Timberlake, according to the expert on voyages of sixteenth century exploration, Thomas Rundall (57, 61–63). What he found instead, of all things, was the chicken incubator.

In the early part of his journey, Timberlake provides details concerning how the Egyptians had perfected the artificial process of hatching chickens. Out of a twenty-six-page book, three pages are specifically dedicated to this single event. I believe this becomes even more significant when it is remembered that the entire account was not written down until his return to Alexandria. He mildly encouraged his friend to see what might be done with this idea in England, since at this point in history only the Chinese and the Egyptians had perfected the science of egg incubation, according to Jonathan Harper's *Short History of the Egg in English Society* (5–6). Visitors had been infatuated with this process for some time but had not been allowed access to study the entire procedure. Indeed, as early as 1490, Father Felix Fabri had mentioned seeing how the Egyptians incubated eggs ("A Word").

One of the important ingredients for incubating eggs in Egypt was camel dung. Henry realized that acquiring this would be a problem in England, but through trial and error he eventually developed an alternative bed for the eggs to lie on. The bed he devised was actually a large rubber bladder filled with warm water (Harper 72). The details of how the water was maintained at a steady temperature are a mystery to me, but the discussion of the device says that the bladder did allow for universal temperature regulation. Rubber was another development introduced by the Honorable Company, referred to as India Rubber. The proof of Henry's involvement with the development of the Western incubator came by contacting the British Library, which maintains the original copy of Henry's will. In his will one of the items left to his executor was a paper relating to the manufacture of the egg incubator (Knight Interview).

Abraham Jacob was the executor of Henry's estate in 1626. The rights to Timberlake's book were sold for one thousand English pounds on September 27, 1626. The legal rights to the incubator were given to the East India Company shortly thereafter. It was early in the 1700s before any effort was made to fully develop the marketing of this device. The initial production name of the device was the Amazing Western Egg Incubator. The development of this idea coincided with the Industrial Revolution in England, when labor and raw material were cheap.

Through the use of cheap labor the incubation units could be produced inexpensively, while promising economic benefits to the potential buyer. With the growth of cities throughout Europe there was a growing problem of feeding everyone. England has a fairly short growing season, with little tillable land to feed a hungry urban population. Produce has remained popular over the years and, by using the incubator, greater

Keaton 12

numbers of poultry can be produced year round. To this day most chicks in Europe and the Americas are hatched from commercial incubators (Andre). Over time the technology has changed very little, although it has spread beyond the hatching of eggs. It is easy to see how the use of incubators in hospitals for newborns has affected the entire world. Additionally, the idea of an indoor heating system could be considered an offshoot of the idea of regulating an enclosed environment.

So in answer to the question of what kind of unique information Timberlake's book might contain to explain its long-lasting interest for readers, I would suggest that at least one of his discoveries is the lowly chicken incubator. I see an adventurer who went on a pilgrimage to the Holy Land and hatched an idea in the process. The idea eventually was to appeal to a wide portion of the world of consumption. Timberlake wrote his book for those without means of travel as an adventure, and as a guidebook for those with the economic resources to book passage on ships. While traveling thousands of miles to acquire expensive spices for the wealthy, he also saw a potential to develop a product that would feed the masses. Henry's actions are a turning point in pilgrimage. He became the first person to go on a "working pilgrimage," or what we might call a "working vacation."

I must believe his religious sincerity for traveling to Jerusalem, but I also suspect he was not about to miss an opportunity to make a profit. Henry was of the Protestant faith, and he believed that it was good to make money. In his book, Timberlake proves to be a resourceful man. An example of this is his trip to and from Jerusalem. When he went to Jerusalem, he

Keaton 13

traveled with a thousand-member caravan and paid taxes for protection from what he believed to be "wild Arabs." In order to return to his ship quickly he hired two of them. He actually identified the duo as members of the marauding attackers who attacked his caravan when he was headed to Jerusalem only a couple of weeks earlier. Besides the fact that the return trip takes only one-third of the time of the original, he obviously paid no taxes at the four toll locations. Is it possible he wanted to take something back without anyone asking him any questions?

As you can see, there are many questions remaining concerning his pilgrimage. Was he a religiously focused traveler headed to the Holy Land, or was his trip for profit? It is possible that Henry was a new breed of pilgrim who saw pilgrimage as a way to combine business with pleasure.

Keaton 14

WORKS CITED

Andre, Pamela. "History of the Chicken Incubator." Personal e-mail (18 Feb. 1999).

Bisson, Douglas R. *The Merchant Adventurers of England.* Newark: U of Delaware P, 1993.

East India Company. *Charters granted to the East India Company, from 1602; also the treaties and grants, made with, or obtained from, the princes and powers in India to 1772.* London, 1773.

East India Company. *First Voyage of the English East India Company, in 1601, Under the Command of Captain James Lancaster.* Edinburgh, 1824.

Keaton 15

Fabri, Felix. *The Book of the Wanderings of Felix Fabri (Circa 1480–1483 A.D.).* Trans. Aubrey Stewart. London, 1896.

Geber, Jill Louise. *The East India Company and Southern Africa: A Guide to the Archives of the East India Company and the Board of Control, 1600–1858.* London: Hakluyt Society, 1998.

Harper, Jonathan. *A Short History of the Egg in English Society.* London: Sampson Low, Marston, n.d.

Keay, John. *The Honorable Company: A History of the East India Company.* New York: HarperCollins, 1993.

Kinney, Arthur F. *Elizabethan Backgrounds; Historical Documents of the Age of Elizabeth I.* Hamden, CT: Archon Books, 1975.

Knight, Jennifer. "Henry Timberlake ????–1626." Personal e-mail (20 Feb. 1999).

Knight, Jennifer. Phone Interview. (26 Mar. 1999; 30 Mar. 1999).

Rundell, Thomas. *Narratives of Voyages Towards the North-West in Search of Passage to Cathay and India, 1496–1631.* London, 1849.

Sanderson, John. *The Travels of John Sanderson in the Levant.* Ed. W. Forster. London: Hakluyt Society, 1931 [1601].

Timberlake, Alexander. *Genealogy of Henry Timberlake.* Alexandria, VA, 1887.

"Timberlake, Henry." *Dictionary of National Biography.* New York: Macmillan, Smith, Elder, 1908.

Timberlake, Henry. *A True and Strange Discourse of the Travailes of two English Pilgrimes.* London, 1603.

Wheeler, John. *A Treatise of Commerce Reproduced from the London Edition of 1601, with a Bibliographical note by George Burton Hotchkiss.* New York: Columbia UP, 1931.

"A Word about Felix Fabri." http://www.asan.com/users/beaks/felix.htm (20 Feb. 1999).

## questions for discussion

1. Does the introductory section capture your interest? Does it give you enough background information to make you wonder about Timberlake's diary?
2. Where is the thesis stated in the essay? Do you think it is stated as clearly or effectively as it might be? If you were offering peer review, would you suggest any revisions in the way the thesis is handled?
3. The author divides his essay into sections with headings in bold print. Do these headings serve the reader in any way? Would you have omitted them? Could you have improved on them? If so, how?
4. Look at Hershield's Works Cited and Works Consulted lists. Although he started by searching electronic databases and using search engines, Hershield ended up using mainly print-based sources for his project, including some that would have been difficult to locate without electronic research tools. How do you explain his heavy reliance on print sources? What difference does the topic of the essay make in the kinds of sources (electronic or print) that ultimately prove useful?
5. Hershield's paper seems to be geared more to providing information than making an argument. If he had wanted to emphasize his argument in his paper, how might he have done it?
6. Hershield published his essay on the Web, along with a map of Timberlake's itinerary and a photographic image of the original text for readers to examine. Think about a research project you have done or are doing. What kinds of supplementary materials or links might you want to provide with an essay if you were to publish it on the Web? How would these assist your reader?
7. If you were to annotate Hershield's essay, providing marginal notes on specific features that demonstrate strengths or weaknesses in research, documentation, organization, and verbal communication, what would you point out?

## *Useful Links*

In this chapter we have provided you with many of our favorite links about research writing. You will find them with a careful Web search. Here are some others to consider.

- The Humanities Department and the Arthur C. Banks Jr. Library of Capital Community College in Hartford, Connecticut, have prepared a useful and substantive "Guide for Writing Research Papers Based on Modern Language Association (MLA) Documentation" at **http://Webster.commnet.edu/mla/index.shtml.** Information about taking notes, using outlines, and incorporating quotations is particularly useful.
- Sarah Hamid's guide, "Writing a Research Paper," at Purdue's OWL site (**http://owl.english.purdue.edu/workshops/hypertext/ResearchW/**), has good questions to ask yourself about *revising* your research essay.
- George Mason University's New Century College provides good tips on "Research Writing Strategies:" **http://classWeb.gmu.edu/nccwg/write-strategy.htm**.

Books on research writing are available through your local bookstore. Moira Anderson Allen's *Writing.com: Creative Internet Strategies to Advance Your Writing Career*, though intended for those seeking to earn a living by writing offers great advice about a variety of strategies for doing research online and joining electronic writing groups to get feedback on your work.

## Additional Writing Activities

1. "What's in a Name"? Write a documented paper on your name based on research in genealogical resources on the Web, an interview with someone who knows how you got your first name, or research on famous people who share your name (and may give it a certain connotation). What language is it derived from? Use your first, middle, or last name, or all three. How do the meanings of them combined add up? What associations would you like your name to have after you have developed a reputation of your own?
2. Visit the "Traveling to Jerusalem" home page at **http://chass.colostate-pueblo.edu/history/seminar/seminar97.html** and choose a diary to read from a time period and country you are interested in. Develop a research proposal and an annotated bibliography of sources for a research project on a question suggested by what you read in the diary, or on one of the societies the traveler encounters on the trip.

3. Design a research project that you can do on a source of environmental contamination in your area, either of air, water, or land. Do preliminary research by keying your zip code into the Environmental Scorecard at **http://www.scorecard.org/**, a database of statistics reported by companies to the state and compiled in the Toxics Release Inventory (TRI). After checking your local area to locate possible sources of pollution, look at individual sources in the ranked lists on the Scorecard. Choose one of them to investigate further. If there are none in your locale, choose another area you are curious about (your hometown, where your grandparents live, where you might like to live). Do research in the site and elsewhere, including the Web; look for medical information to identify diseases that are associated with exposure to particular pollutants. Write an essay profiling your community, presenting your information, documenting each source, and explaining why you think there is or is not too much air, water, or land pollution in your area.

# PART three

# Writing Destinations


CHAPTER 7

Putting It All Together: Combining Research and Argument

CHAPTER 8

Putting It All Online: Research and Argument on the World Wide Web

CHAPTER 7

# Putting It All Together: Combining Research and Argument

Now that you have developed some facility with reading, understanding, and writing arguments, it's time to practice structuring arguments that incorporate research and outside sources. Our hope is that you will find the careful crafting of an argument to be an intellectually challenging, playful, and ultimately invigorating experience—as many students have found it to be. Developing a claim, using appropriate support and outside sources, considering potential counterarguments and rebuttals—all of this is part of the "play" of argument. Contributing to the development of ideas, issues, and debates through argument can be exhilarating, prompting the writer to enter important conversations and make useful contributions. Using research to write arguments can also help you clarify your own ideas and positions on a variety of topics. In the process, you should discover that argumentative skills are useful in everyday personal, business, community, and general academic life.

The goal of this chapter is to provide you with some strategies and examples for composing argumentative texts and projects based on research. *You can use everything you've been learning about academic writing, argument, and research to assist you in writing arguments in academic contexts.* Think about what you've learned so far as you read this chapter.

## Crafting Print-Based Researched Arguments: Some Basic Guidelines

In any argumentative writing you undertake, particularly *academic* writing, you will want to make your **claim** (or conclusion) clear by locating it prominently in the introduction and reiterating it (though not simply restating it) in the conclusion. You will need to provide **grounds** for your claim(s), and you will want to acknowledge **warrants**, or supporting principles and assumptions, that your audience will be likely to accept. Revisit the material on Toulmin's and Rogers's strategies of argument in Chapter 4 if you need to. You can also use your knowledge of the writing process to think about your own writing at all stages, from the initial outlining to the revision stages, to assist you in composing an argument. Above all, as we've stated on numerous occasions about a variety of writing situations and contexts, understanding the needs and position of your **audience** will make a world of difference in how you approach the design of any argument you want to make.

---

**REVIEWING TOULMIN'S TERMS**

**Claim:** The conclusion or main point of an argument.

**Warrant:** The general principle or assumption that links the support to the claim.

**Backing:** Support for the warrant of an argument; may be stated or unstated.

**Grounds or data:** Evidence or assertion advanced in support of the claim.

**Rebuttal:** Answers to anticipated counterarguments or objections to any part of an argument.

**Qualifier:** Words that indicate the extent to which a statement is true (e.g., *mostly, almost always*).

---

## Introducing an Argument: Considering Audience

Before composing an argumentative piece, think carefully about who will be reading it—even if your instructor is your primary audience. Will the audience be limited to four or five people in a peer response group? Will all your classmates receive it as an attachment to a posting on a discussion list? Is it for a more general public, such as the readers of your local newspaper? Are you planning to post it to the Web for everyone who visits your site? Whatever the case, keep your readers in mind as you try to answer the following questions:

1. What can I expect my readers to know about my subject?
2. What are they likely to think about my issue?
3. How can I express to them that I respect them and their thoughtful attention to this issue?
4. Will they disagree strongly with me even before they hear my arguments? (If so, I need to win their sympathy somehow . . . but how?)
5. Will they be likely to agree with me?
6. If not, what would it take to get them to listen, and what would it take to convince them that I have a point?
7. Is there any point on which we might agree, a point that I might advance to win their respect?
8. Will we have common ground, or a starting point from which to discuss issues of mutual concern, even if we ultimately disagree?
9. What kind of evidence do I need to show them in order to substantiate my claim(s)?

Finally, consider this: the more controversial or politicized the issue, then the more entrenched the positions of those who disagree with each other will seem to be. Some audiences will not be won over, even by the most carefully considered argument. Can you think of any debates whose participants are not likely to see eye to eye at any stage of the process of thinking through and arguing about an issue? Knowing ahead of time what topics will be such "hot" ones with your audience is vital. Such knowledge will help you develop your own position carefully, with both your audience's views and reservations in mind.

Let's look at an example of how one student writer attempted to consider his audience carefully when crafting his argumentative essay about a potentially controversial topic. In writing "Global Warming: America's Eager Contribution to Ecology," Joel Tucker knew that he would have to convince his audience, in the opening paragraphs, that his subject was significant and that his readers needed to pay attention to his topic. He faced the challenge of writing about a subject that many people have heard about (pollution of the environment in general and global warming in particular) but that some might think is passé or uninteresting. Moreover, Joel's goal was not just to raise awareness about global warming; he wanted to argue that the United States contributes to such global warming—and that with a concerted effort we can put a stop to it. Joel wanted to forward a debatable argumentative claim, and he knew that his ideas would not necessarily be well received by all of his readers.

To address his readers' potential hesitancy, Joel described a scene from a science fiction novel, set in an ecologically devastated future, both to grab the reader's attention and to make a point about the importance of his topic.

Tucker 1

Joel Tucker

Global Warming: America's Eager Contribution to Ecology

Mankind is becoming increasingly aware of the fact that our planet is being polluted, degraded, and ecologically destroyed. People debate the seriousness and relevance of issues such as deforestation and global warming, but no one can dispute the legitimate fact that we have damaged our

Tucker 2

home in irresponsible and terrible ways, ways that will have long term effects on our planet. Quite often, if there is any debate over the matter of our environment, it involves how society should address the issue of pollution and conservation. Valuable time is lost debating over which action should be taken, and we are finding new ways to poison ourselves every day. Will we wake up one day and find that society, as we know it, has disintegrated? How would society react if current lifestyles were one day permanently disabled? Do we honestly believe that we can keep on flourishing through our wasteful and selfish habits without paying the consequences for our lack of foresight? It is obvious that if we destroy the earth's ecology by continuing to pollute and degrade it, we will also destroy society as we know it.

Interestingly, Octavia Butler addresses this issue in her novel, *Parable of the Sower*. In this novel, the year is 2024, and poverty abounds, crime is rampant, disease is uncontrolled, and the economy has collapsed. There are many contributing factors to society's demise in the novel. But it is interesting that the author decided to include global warming as one of the catalysts. Notice this statement made early in the book by Lauren, the novel's main character: "People have changed the climate of the world. Now they are waiting for the old days to come back" (50). Of course, this was not a positive change or even a desired one, yet it played a crucial role in the shaping of their present society. On an even worse note, it was a rather permanent change. Notice Lauren's next statement: "We can't make the climate change back, no matter why it changed in the first place. We can't do anything" (50). Of course, the author is not making the claim here that global warming was

Tucker 3

entirely responsible for the downfall of society. She does make it clear, though, that it did have a serious impact on society in this novel. I agree with Butler on this issue, and I believe that if left unchecked at its current rate, pollution and the destruction of our environment will have devastating consequences on society now and in the future. . . .

Note Joel's strategies. The first paragraph introduces the topic of the paper and concludes with a series of questions designed to prompt the reader to consider the topic more carefully and to suggest the kinds of issues Joel will be addressing in his piece. But Joel knew that this would not be enough to compel the reader to stay with him; he could not assume that the reader would necessarily care about his subject. Therefore, in the next paragraph, he described a scene from Octavia Butler's novel *Parable of the Sower*, which offers a striking portrait of a world devastated, in part, by pollution and global warming. More significantly for Joel's argument, the novel describes how the actions of humans have harmed the planet.

Viewed according to Toulmin's scheme, we can identify here both a warrant and a backing for that warrant. The *warrant*, or primary assumption that Joel makes in these paragraphs, is that we *should* care about what happens to our environment—and that most people do, in fact, care. The *backing* comes perhaps in the use of the science fiction novel, which is concerned in part with the future devastation of the planet as a result of human indiscretion. Granted, it's fiction, but it establishes that there are indeed people who are worried about the future impact of pollution on the planet.

Another potential warrant made in these paragraphs is the assumption that changing our behaviors now can help mitigate the dire future consequences of pollution. This warrant, though, will quickly become part of Joel's main *claim*, which we can see in his **thesis statement**, placed pivotally at the conclusion of the second paragraph, at the end of his introduction:

> I agree with Butler on this issue, and I believe that if left unchecked at their current rate, pollution and the destruction of our environment will have devastating consequences on our society now and in the future.

Of course, to demonstrate this—to prove that there is a causal connection between pollution and the "destruction of our environment," as well as the resulting "devastating consequences"—Joel knew that he would have to *show* us some research to help him make his point—and to convince us that he has a good insight into this issue. In Toulmin's terms, he knew he had to provide sufficient grounds to help him support his claim. Let's turn our attention now to strategies for conducting research, using Joel's work as an example.

## Considering Research and Drafting an Outline or Project Plan

After you have collected information about your topic, begin thinking about how to use any information collected. Consider carefully whether your sources help you support a particular claim you are making, or whether they provide potential rebuttals and counterarguments that you will want to discuss. You may want to separate your sources into different categories, depending on the specific issues or information they cover. As you sift through your notes, ideas for organizing them will probably come to you, and a structure or plan for your project will emerge.

When Joel consulted a number of sources, including information on the Web and in print journals and magazines, he found numerous potential sources that he could use in constructing his argument. In fact, there were far too many to consider thoroughly, since many scholars and laypersons have written about pollution and global warming. So, while researching, he began to narrow his topic. He knew that he'd first want to convince his readers of an urgent need to address his topic, but then he

**INTERtext**

For more on research strategies, see Chapter 6.

would want to address particular kinds of pollution that contribute to the destruction of the environment. While searching through his information, he found some fascinating information from the federal government about global warming that he could use, but he also decided that *water pollution* would be a striking subtopic on which to focus. After all, water pollution is a specific kind of pollution that he could talk about and that his readers might find compelling and worthy of comment. With this in mind, he settled on three articles from *U.S. News & World Report* and one document from the Environmental Protection Agency (EPA), whose reports he could access online:

WORKS CITED

Loeb, Penny. "Advances, Setbacks in Clean-Water Quest." *U.S. News & World Report* 21 Sept. 1998.

"Very Troubled Waters." *U.S. News & World Report* 28 Sept. 1998.

Satchell, Michael. "Pollution Count." *U.S. News & World Report* 30 Sept. 1996.

United States. *Environmental Protection Agency Report*. 17 Nov. 1999 <http://www.epa.gov/global warming/climate/index.html>.

---

Joel knew that for a relatively short researched argument of five or six typed pages, these would probably be sufficient, although using a few more sources might be desirable.

As we've suggested, Joel's research actually helped him develop a sense of how he could focus his paper. Indeed, as *you* collect information and think about your sources and your research question, you might make a rough outline to refine steadily as your ideas develop. Some outlines are fairly simple, more like plan sheets than anything else. Keep in mind that the purpose of an outline or plan sheet is to help you lay out your thinking and sources so that you can see what you're doing, where you're going, and how you're using the materials you have found. Joel—already knowing that he wanted to use the science fiction novel in his introduction—came up with this rough outline.

*Introduction*: Use Butler's *Parable of the Sower*.

*First section:* Provide information about global warming. Use information to convince audience that pollution *is* a problem.

**INTER**text

For more on outlining, see Chapter 1.

*Second section:* Talk specifically about *water* pollution as a particularly devastating kind of pollution.

*Third section:* Talk about what *we* can do about pollution.

*Conclusion:* ???

A more formal version of this plan might look like this:

I. Introduction
   A. Opening questions to "hook" the reader.
   B. Use of *Parable of the Sower* to provide a "dramatic" picture of pollution.
II. Global Warming—information from EPA
III. Water Pollution
   A. Importance of water: use Loeb & Satchell sources.
   B. Failing attempts to keep water supply clean: use "Very Troubled Waters" source.
IV. Addressing Pollution: what can we do about it?
V. Conclusion—???

You probably noticed that Joel, in the second outline, keyed his sources to particular places in his project where he felt they would most help him make his points clearly. Initially, he was also a little unsure about what he wanted to do in the conclusion, but that was acceptable at this point. He expected that, as he wrote, ideas for creating a conclusion would probably come to him. Now let's consider strategies for drafting and for thinking about how you can use sources effectively.

## Drafting and Incorporating Sources

Once you are ready to start drafting, it's a good idea to take your notes and sources for the first section of your outline or project plan and read through them. Then draft that section. Do the same with section two, continuing through the outline or project plan. As you draft, you may find yourself reconsidering how you use your sources, or even the order of items in your outline—but that's fine. Don't hesitate to redraft your outline or project plan when better ideas come along. Incorporate any reference to sources or direct quotations smoothly into your text by introducing the source or quotation in your own words. Citations for each source should already be with your notes. As you use an idea or information from each source, make an **in-text citation** for the source—*whether you are using a quotation or not.* Be sure to include the page number for any print sources.

Let's look at how Joel incorporated quotations and sources into his own text. In the first section of his project, after the introduction, he knew that he wanted to talk about global warming and provide some reliable information that climate change is an environmental trend caused by air pollution. His most reliable sources on the topic, he felt, came from the EPA, a government agency charged with helping us protect the environment and our natural resources. Observe what Joel does in the following paragraph:

> But where do we start discussing a topic as large as our environment? Let's consider a few areas of legitimate concern. The topic of global warming is something that has been argued over for years now, and scientists still cannot find common ground. A few scientists even claim that there is no such thing as a global warming trend. But consider these well established facts published by the Environmental Protection Agency (EPA): "Since the beginning of the industrial revolution, atmospheric concentrations of carbon dioxide have increased nearly 30%, methane concentrations have more than doubled, and nitrous oxide concentrations have risen by about 15%" (EPA). No doubt we can blame a lot of these increases on "Big Business" and the Industrial Age. However, the average consumer plays a role here, too, and we'll look at that later. The EPA's report continues: "These increases have enhanced the heat-trapping capability of the earth's atmosphere. Global temperatures are rising" (EPA).

The paragraph opens with a good question, inviting the readers to consider a specific issue within the larger topic of pollution. But Joel had to note that not everyone agrees that global warming actually exists; he was aware, as Toulmin would point out, that **rebuttals** to the argument for global warming must at least be acknowledged and considered if the argument is to be compelling to a variety of readers, some of whom might be skeptical about the initial claim.

To address potential rebuttals, Joel offered evidence or *grounds* that we need to pay attention to global warming by introducing some statistics from the EPA report:

> Since the beginning of the industrial revolution, atmospheric concentrations of carbon dioxide have increased nearly 30%, methane concentrations have more than doubled, and nitrous oxide concentrations have risen by about 15%. (EPA)

This first quotation describes increases in certain gases, and Joel realized that this statement, though important, might not be sufficient to convince his readers that they are connected to global warming. To make that causal connection clearer, he followed up with another quotation from the EPA:

> These increases have enhanced the heat-trapping capability of the earth's atmosphere. Global temperatures are rising. (EPA)

At this point, the reader may be thinking the following: "Well, OK, so the temperature is rising. What's the big deal?" Joel anticipated such a question, which led him to his next paragraph, in which he provided further information from the EPA, dramatically connecting rising temperatures and environmental corrosion:

> What has been the result of this increase in global temperature? There has definitely been a lot of research on global warming, especially in the last decade or so. Often studies contradict each other and make the issue seem more confusing than it really is. The EPA has reviewed these studies and has come to the following conclusions:
>
> > Observations collected over the last century suggest that the average land surface temperature has risen 0.45–0.6° C (0.8–1.0° F) in the last century. Precipitation has increased by about 1 percent over the world's continents in the last century. High latitude areas are tending to see more significant increases in rainfall, while precipitation has actually declined in many tropical areas. Sea level has risen worldwide approximately 15–20 cm (6–8 inches) in the

last century. Approximately 2–5 cm (1–2 inches) of the rise has resulted from the melting of mountain glaciers. Another 2–7 cm has resulted from the expansion of ocean water that resulted from warmer ocean temperatures. (EPA)

By themselves these figures hardly seem substantial, yet what is their true impact? While it is true that we can only speculate on this matter, the majority of opinions agree that these increases are undesirable. The Environmental Protection Agency once again states: "The continued addition of greenhouse gases to the atmosphere is likely to raise the earth's average temperature by several degrees in the next century, which will, in turn, raise the level of the sea. There is likely to be an overall trend toward increased precipitation and evaporation, more intense rainstorms, and drier soils" (EPA). Yes, when one stands back and looks at the whole picture the outcome looks quite frightening. Scientists for some time now have pointed to the damaging effects of global warming on human health, agriculture, various ecosystems, and weather patterns. If you're still asking yourself how this all affects you personally, consider this question. What society can prosper or even survive without adequate health, food, and other vital resources?

---

Note the opening question, anticipating readers' questions about the effects of global warming: "What has been the result of this increase in global temperature?" To answer, Joel decided to use a longer quotation from the EPA, one that would better address the complexity of the issue. But note that he didn't just "plop down" the quotation and leave the reader to decide how to interpret it. He followed up with his own commentary. In fact, he used another question to form a transition from the quotation to his own discussion: "By themselves these figures hardly seem substantial, yet what is their true impact?" He then answered that question, using a mix of his own commentary and one other, shorter quotation from the EPA.

In the following section on water pollution, Joel used information from several sources. It's interesting to see how he combined this material. The opening sentence of the following paragraph moves us from the global warming section of his paper to the new section on water pollution. Note how Joel used his sources in the rest of the paragraph:

To continue our conversation on the environment, let's next consider the state of our most important natural resource—water. The majority of us who live in First World countries take our easy access to clean water for granted. All we have to do is walk several feet to the faucet or the shower and we have instant access to clean, filtered water. However, any health official will quickly point out to you the devastating effects that lack of fresh, clean water has on Third World countries and their societies. In Butler's novel, lack of fresh, clean drinking water is one of the major problems society faces. The main character Lauren draws it to our attention that in her world, "water now costs several times as much as gasoline" (16). Could this be a problem for us someday soon? Will bottled water someday be a necessity rather than the luxury that is today? Considering the fact that we irresponsibly continue to find new ways to destroy our waterways, it is certainly a possibility. Journalist Penny Loeb shares these eye-opening statistics with us: "The U.S. Public Interest Research Group reported that nearly 1 billion pounds of toxic chemicals were discharged into America's waters between 1992 and 1996" ("Advances"). A similar report by writer Michael Satchell states:

> From 1990 to 1994, about 1.5 billion pounds of chemicals—many dangerous to children—were released into lakes and streams and along coasts. The discharges included heavy metals such as arsenic and lead and others that cause cancer or damage to the nervous and reproductive systems. The massive legal dumping represents only a fraction of the overall toxic problem; many polluting operations—sewage plants, utilities, mines and municipal incinerators—are not required to report their discharges.

Of course, this was a report considering the effects of legal dumping on our waterways. When one considers that this is dwarfed by the illegal dumping activities that occur every day worldwide, it truly is amazing that we haven't poisoned ourselves on a larger scale already.

---

Were you surprised to see Joel return to Butler's novel and mention it again? Incorporating a short quotation into his own sentence, Joel made a startling point about the potential long-term consequences of not caring for our water supplies:

> In Butler's novel, lack of fresh, clean drinking water is one of the major problems society faces. The main character Lauren draws it to our attention that in her world, "water now costs several times as much as gasoline" (16).

An attentive reader will observe that it is just fiction—not fact. Joel knew he needed to address this distinction, so, immediately following his quotation from Butler's novel, he posed questions that lead us to startling quotations—from Penny Loeb and Michael Satchell—which provide concrete information about unfortunate trends in increasing water pollution. Joel was careful to include in-text citations when he quoted or used information. Using authors' names, giving titles, and providing page numbers wherever available allows readers to locate additional information about sources in the bibliography or Works Cited list. The combination of commentary and carefully documented sources helped Joel compose some compelling text in support of his claim—that pollution is a serious problem, and one that demands our attention.

## Composing Concluding Arguments

At some point, at least after you have drafted your text, you will want to consider your conclusion. Ideally, a concluding paragraph (or two) should reflect on what you have attempted to demonstrate in your paper. You may reiterate your claim, but you should not simply restate it as it stands in the introductory paragraphs. You might also consider offering advice on what kinds of questions your readers can ask to further the discussion you raise in your paper. Or you might point them in the direction of additional resources to research and consider. In some ways, the conclusion requires a great deal of creativity; after all, you are wrapping up your arguments, and you want your reader to remember what you have said. Don't hesitate to draft several versions and solicit feedback from peers and your instructor.

You may be wondering how Joel decided to conclude his paper. Has an interesting idea occurred to you as you've read through the paragraphs we've discussed? Check out Joel's conclusion and think about its merits.

I find it particularly unsettling that a statement made at the conclusion of *Parable of the Sower* fits so well today with our society's present situation. At the conclusion of this novel this statement is made:

> As bad as things are, we haven't even hit bottom yet. Starvation, disease, and drug damage have only begun. Federal, state, and local governments still exist and sometimes they manage to do

> something more than collect taxes and send in the military. That may be a hopeful sign—or perhaps it's only more evidence of what I just said: We haven't hit bottom yet. (294)

Will some of us one day mutter similar words? How far are we today from the bottom? As we go about our daily lives, the environment of our precious home is under serious attack. One day soon our earth will lash out and fight back. If it goes down, it will be sure to take everything else down with it.

Joel reiterates his claim, but he also returns us to the beginning of the essay, reminding us about Butler's novel, *Parable of the Sower*, which he used to introduce his topic. This is an effective strategy: Joel has referred to the novel at a few key points throughout his essay to give us a striking picture of the consequences of unchecked pollution. Returning to the novel in the conclusion gives the essay a sense of closure, of having returned us to our initial point of departure, but it also leaves us with powerful imagery to consider further.

*Remember: Writing is recursive.* As with any writing project, peer review and revision are essential steps. You may need to revise again after the instructor sees your paper or after peer review. Also, keep everything, including notes, copies of sources, Web addresses, brainstorming exercises, drafts, and all supplemental materials, until you have a grade for the course in hand. All teachers have heard horror stories of source material that disappeared prematurely. We know of one student who had to visit a smelly city dump searching for note cards to check one page reference after her oral examiners had found it missing in her master's thesis—not an ideal way to spend a weekend.

## WRITING SPOTLIGHT

### Research and Rogerian Argument

In the preceding pages, we've used Joel's essay on pollution to model strategies for incorporating research into your own writing, applying Toulmin's scheme for understanding the key parts of an argument. To provide you an example of Rogerian argument that relies on research and outside sources, we include below both an original assignment asking for a Rogerian argument and a student's work in response to that assignment. The assignment itself models how a Rogerian strategy can be used to craft an argument, and the student's essay is a good (though not perfect) model of how to incorporate sources into a Rogerian argument. Read and see what you think, considering the questions for discussion that follow.

## The Assignment

Raise a question on some controversial issue (i.e., a question about which reasonable people may disagree) concerning health issues, gender issues, an ethical issue, the environment, or any other topic agreed on with your instructor. Explain in detail two or more positions that people have taken when attempting to answer this question. Then, analyze the arguments on each side, considering the factual accuracy, reasoning, and ethical assumptions (principles) contained in each. Identify any logical fallacies, factual errors, or weaknesses such as hasty generalization in each argument. Show also where the facts presented are supported by reliable authority and research and where the reasoning is logical. In other words, show the strengths and weaknesses, soundness or unsoundness of each argument.

Try to identify any points on which the opponents agree. If the issue is highly contentious, you might find only one, and it may be very general, such as, "Both sides agree that the decision made should be one that will provide energy (or clean air/or economic growth/or access to health care, etc.) over the long term for the greatest number of people." If you can find more than one point of mutual agreement, point them out and discuss the possibility of both sides' coming together on several more critical points.

Then develop a position of your own using the common ground you identified as its foundation. Use the analysis of the arguments, facts, reasoning, and principles you did earlier to help you choose which facts, reasons, principles, and so on to employ, and which ones to ignore. If, for example, you found factual errors, you would not use those as evidence to support your position.

With an attitude of respect, and considering the values your readers may hold dear, adjust your position as much as possible without compromising your values to reflect any points on which you can agree with each other. Assume your reader is an ethical, intelligent person who thinks issues through carefully and attempts to make decisions based on reason and worthy principles (unless she or he indicates otherwise!). Use any kind of appeal you think will be effective, and remember to consider *logos, ethos*, and *pathos*.

Use at least ten sources of a variety of types, including one interview of a person who has knowledge of some aspect of this issue or who is willing to articulate his or her position on it. Cite the interview in the Works Cited list at the end of the paper. Quote your opponent's own words where possible when representing his or her view, or paraphrase (and cite them, of course).

After completing a research proposal and having it initialed or examined by the instructor, begin your research, taking notes carefully from your sources. Post your topic and the arguments you have identified on both sides to the class e-mail discussion list or other online forum. Invite your classmates to identify any problems they can find with all the arguments. Read what your classmates have posted and respond with comments on the strengths and weaknesses of their arguments, and with suggestions for further research.

(Ultimately, the length of the paper is up to your instructor, but 2,000 words might be an appropriate length for this assignment.)

## A Student's Essay

Scott Pedram wrote the following essay in response to the preceding prompt. Read it carefully, and consider the questions after it to help you evaluate how successful Scott was in completing the assignment and in using a Rogerian argumentative strategy.

Pedram 1

Scott Pedram

Dr. Margaret Barber

English 102

May 2003

Should the Boy Scouts of America Rescind Its Policy of Discrimination Against Homosexuals?

The Declaration of Independence famously says that "We hold these truths to be self-evident, that all men are created equal." This phrase invokes thoughts of other words and ideas commonly associated with the United States of America such as "freedom," "equality," "acceptance," and "tolerance." However, the Boy Scouts of America must have a different definition of the word "all." On February 6, 2002, the Boy Scouts of America (BSA) released an official resolution excluding homosexuals from serving in its organization (BSA, "Resolution"). The BSA supports their argument by claiming that homosexuals are not positive role models for youth. There are, however, many people who disagree with this stance; thus there is a new question to be answered: Should the Boy Scouts of America rescind its policy of discrimination against homosexuals?

All advocates of Scouting, regardless of their position on this most controversial topic, would agree that they only want what is best for the youth. To understand both sides of the issue fully, it is essential that the basic goals of Scouting are known so that we can have an appreciation of the Scout Oath and Law. The primary purpose of the Scouting program is to help promote the development of character in young individuals in the hopes it will lead them to be better citizens.

One of the major means of achieving this is by encouraging Scouts to follow the Scout Oath: On my honor I will do my best; To do my duty to God and my country and to obey the Scout Law; To help other people at all times; To keep myself physically strong, mentally awake, and morally straight (Birkby 5). Further, every member of BSA is expected to abide by and uphold the following definition of a Scout: "A Scout is trustworthy, loyal, helpful, courteous, kind, obedient, cheerful, thrifty, brave, clean and reverent" (Birkby 7–8). Within these two statements lies the essence of Scouting.

Having reviewed these basic concepts, let us now examine both sides of the issue at hand.

There have been two major court cases in recent history supporting the position of keeping the anti-gay policy. In 1981, Eagle Scout Tim Curran sued the Mt. Diablo Council of the Boy Scouts of America after being denied an Assistant Scoutmaster position exclusively on the basis of his sexual orientation. On March 23, 1998, the California Supreme Court unanimously ruled in favor of the Boy Scouts saying "the organization is not a business and therefore not subject to the state's anti-discrimination law" (Chiang). The case of Boy Scouts of America vs. Dale began when the Boy Scouts discovered a newspaper article in which Dale was revealed as the co-president of the Gay, Lesbian, Bi-Sexual, Transgender (GLBT) organization at Rutgers University. He was fired from his position as an Assistant Scoutmaster at the age of 20 in 1990 as a result of the publication (Bierbauer).

In 1992, "Dale sued under New Jersey's anti-discrimination act, which bars discrimination based on race, national origin or sexual orientation, among others, in places of 'public accommodation'" (Beirbauer). Before the case made it to the United States Supreme Court, it was held in the New Jersey Supreme Court that the Boy Scouts had wrongfully and illegally fired Dale and that BSA was in violation of the "public accommodation" provision within the anti-discrimination act (Beirbauer). The United States Supreme Court accepted the case after the BSA had appealed and on June 28, 2000, ruled in favor of the Boy Scouts of America on the presumption that they were "a private group and therefore the anti-discrimination law does not apply in the case" (Beirbauer). According to Gregg Shields, the Boy Scouts' spokesman, "A homosexual is not a role model for traditional family values," and "homosexuality does not fit into the group's Oath, in which Scouts pledge to 'keep myself physically strong, mentally awake and morally straight'" (HateCrime).

The high courts of America have given the Boy Scouts the legal right to discriminate, but this does not mean that they *should* discriminate. The following statements will demonstrate that the BSA's discrimination policy is completely unjust and not in line with BSA's stated ideals and values.

First, the current BSA policy may be harmful to gay youth. Under the current policy, "no homosexual conduct is required for the BSA to expel a Scout or adult leader. Only the admission that a youth or adult is, or might be, homosexual, is sufficient for immediate expulsion from the BSA under its discrimination policy" (BSA Discrimination). The reasoning is that "[w]hile an adult will probably be aware of his/her sexual orientation, a Scout who is coming out of puberty and entering adolescence may not" (BSA Discrimination). Admittedly, adolescence can be an extremely confusing period for youth. But I wonder what might happen if a young person thinks he might be gay. What kind of support would such a boy receive if he were to confide in his fellow scouts or scoutmaster? Unfortunately, with BSA's current policy, when he needs support the most, it will not be available to him from the Boy Scouts. In fact, even more pressure is placed upon the youth with the possibility of his being expelled from an organization due to his sexual orientation (BSA Discrimination).

Regarding the subject of role models, according to the New Jersey appellate court, "There is absolutely no evidence before us, empirical or otherwise, supporting a conclusion that a gay scoutmaster, solely because he is a homosexual, does not possess the strength and character necessary to properly care for, or to impart BSA humanitarian ideals to, the young boys in his charge" (Davidson). The court goes on to state that there is also insufficient evidence to prove that any "male, simply because he is gay, will somehow undermine BSA's fundamental beliefs and teachings" (Davidson). These findings are in accord with the policy of the American Psychiatric Association (APA) policy on homosexuality: "In December 1973, the American Psychiatric Association's Board of Trustees deleted homosexuality from its official nomenclature of mental disorders in the *Diagnostic and Statistical Manual of Mental Disorders*, Second Edition (DSM-I)" (APA). With this deletion, the APA verified that homosexuality is not any sort of mental disorder and thus should not be treated as such. The rulings from both the New Jersey appellate court and the APA completely neutralize the BSA's beliefs that a gay man cannot be a suitable role model for the youth.

What of the BSA's position? How does the BSA support its views? One might find support for its discriminatory policy in the *Boy Scout Handbook*, which instructs Scouts to be a person of strong character, guide your life with honesty, purity, and justice. Respect and defend the rights of all people. Your relationships with others should be honest and open. Be clean in your speech and actions, and faithful in your religious beliefs. The values you follow as a Scout will help you become virtuous and self-reliant (Birkby 551).

Avowed homosexuals are commonly referred to those who have "come out" of the closet and therefore are being honest and open with others. Therefore, the preceding statement suggests how an avowed homosexual is actually living up to the "morally straight" value of the Scout Oath. Also, while the term "straight" is frequently used today to imply heterosexuality, the term first appeared in a book on "sex deviants" in 1941, long after the Oath was written, and did not reach mainstream culture until the 1970's. Therefore, for one to declare that the original writers of the Scout Oath used the term "morally straight" as an implication of heterosexuality is erroneous (BSA Discrimination). Furthermore, "it is easy to find in the huge *Oxford English Dictionary* that in the early years of this century when the Scout oath was written 'straight' meant 'honest, upright, candid'" (Varnell). An openly gay person *is* being "honest, upright, [and] candid" about his identity. In a pamphlet published by the World Organization of the Scout

Movement (WOSM), of which the Boy Scouts of America are a member, "Scouting is open to all, regardless of race or creed, in accordance with the purpose, principles and method conceived by its founder Robert Baden-Powell (WOSM, "Scouting Is"). Why, then, should an open, honest gay person be banned from Scouting? This sort of contradiction has no place in such an organization that prides itself on truth and honesty. Moreover, as a federally chartered organization, the BSA is obligated to serve all boys (Religious Tolerance).

Another example of this contradiction is a position statement released by the Boy Scouts of America. The main point in this position statement is as follows: "On June 28, 2000, the United States Supreme Court reaffirmed the Boy Scouts of America's standing as a private organization with the right to set its own membership and leadership standards" (BSA, "Position Statements"). This refers to the BSA's "right" to discriminate, which could also be seen as an effort to condemn or suppress diversity, even though the very title of the Position Statement is "In Support of Diversity." This is undoubtedly and unambiguously a contradiction within the organization. Such contradictions make the arguments presented by the BSA less credible.

The BSA apparently enacted this policy after yielding to pressure from church groups, such as The Church of Jesus Christ of Latter-day Saints, which requires its youngsters to be Scouts. However, not all churches agree. Some religious groups have expressed their dissatisfaction with the BSA: "[R]eform Jewish leaders are recommending that parents withdraw their children from membership in the Boy Scouts of America and that synagogues end their sponsorship of Scout troops"

Pedram 7

(HateCrime). In one suit, "the Orchard Ridge United Church of Christ in Madison has withdrawn its sponsorship of a Boy Scout troop because of the national organization's policy excluding gay Scouts and leaders" and "the [Episcopal] Rev. Robert Bryant . . . pointed out that the BSA's policy affects not only gay scouts and scoutmasters but their heterosexual relatives, and, in some cases, the clergy in parishes sponsoring scout troops" (HateCrime). As Dr. John Beuhrens so eloquently stated, "concern is not for the children. The concern is the religious politics they're playing" (Beuhrens), referring to the Boy Scouts' stance on the issue.

Furthermore, numerous other groups oppose the BSA's position. In a Gay Issues Poll conducted by Zogby International on the campus of Hamilton College and co-released by Hamilton College and MTV, 70.5% of those 932 people polled were in favor of an openly gay man being permitted to serve as a Boy Scout Leader if he is otherwise qualified (Hamilton College). In response to the BSA's position, many agencies, including some branches of the United Way, have already withdrawn support or funding of the Boy Scouts of America. Many government entities have also withdrawn support as illustrated when the Los Angeles City Council unanimously voted to free all associations with the Boy Scouts of America. A Manhattan, New York, school district has revoked its support of the Scouts, and, in 2000, Connecticut state employees can no longer make donations to the Boy Scouts via payroll deduction. Most public schools in California will no longer sponsor local Scout troops, and local Scout troops are no longer allowed to use parks, schools, and other municipal sites in Chicago, San Francisco and San Jose, Calif. In addition, judges in San Francisco severed all ties with the Boy Scouts, and, in December 2000, the Los Angeles Unified School District began limiting Boy Scout activity, such as recruiting, on campuses. Also, in a unanimous decision the Minneapolis school board has ended its sponsorship of Boy Scout troops and forbids the Scouts from recruiting new youth in schools (HateCrime).

In addition to government entities, there have also been numerous private businesses that have ceased support, including Chase Manhattan Bank, Levi-Strauss & Co., and Textron, Inc. In a recent $400,000 donation to the United Way by Wells Fargo, it was asked that the donation be steered away from the Boy Scouts. In addition, Novell, Inc., has ceased matching contributions from their employees to the Boy Scouts of America, and, in September 2001, the CVS pharmacy chain ended their financial support to the Boy Scouts. Both the Carrier Corporation and HSBC bank have stopped supporting the Boy Scouts, and in a similar venture as Wells Fargo, Scripps Networks has requested that their corporate gift to the United Way *not* make its way to the Boy Scouts (HateCrime). By no means could this be considered a full listing of all entities that have withdrawn support. It is only a sampling.

Ultimately, the arguments presented by the Boy Scouts of America are unsound, and its policy, which amounts to discrimination against homosexuals, should be abolished. This policy has the potential to harm everyone involved, including the youth the BSA maintains they are trying to protect. Once again, gay men are fully capable of serving as excellent role models and leaders in the Boy Scouts of America, as well as being fully able to live up to the Scout Oath and Law. By

Pedram 9

excluding and expelling all homosexuals, there is an enormous risk of emotional damage to young gay scouts who are just beginning to discover their sexuality. In fact, if avowed homosexuals were allowed to serve in the Boy Scouts, all Scouts, both heterosexual and homosexual, would be able to see a successful gay man in a positive manner. This would expand minds and our ability to accept those different from us, resulting in a better society. As Sir Robert Baden-Powell, Founder of Scouting and Chief Scout of the World, said in a farewell message to his Scouts, "Try and leave this world a little better than you found it and when your turn comes to die, you can die happy in feeling that at any rate you have not wasted your time but have done your best" (WOSM B-P).

Pedram 10

WORKS CITED

American Psychiatric Association. "Gay and Lesbian Issues." *American Psychiatric Association.* 9 Jan. 1996. http://www.psych.org/public_info/homose~1.cfm (18 Nov. 2002).

Beuhrens, John. "Homosexuality and the Boy Scouts: What is a Proper Role Model?" *Mars Hill Forum.* 23 Oct. 2000. http://www.mars-hill-forum.com/forumdoc/m056opgu.html (17 Nov. 2002).

Bierbauer, Charles and Reuters. "Supreme Court says Boy Scouts can Bar Gay Troop Leaders." *CNN.com.* 28 June 2000. http://www.cnn.com/2000/LAW/06/28/scotus.gay.boyscouts/ (18 Nov. 2002).

Birkby, Robert C. *The Boy Scout Handbook.* Tenth Edn. Irving, Tex.: Boy Scouts of America, 1990.

Boy Scouts of America. "Position Statements: In Support of Diversity." *The Boy Scouts of America.* http://www.scouting.org/media/positions/diversity.html (18 Nov. 2002).

Boy Scouts of America. "Resolution." *Boy Scouts of America.* 6 Feb. 2002. http://www.scouting.org/media/press/020206/resolution.html (17 Nov. 2002).

BSA Discrimination. "A Review of BSA's Gay Policy." *BSA Discrimination.* http://www.bsa-discrimination.org/Gays-Top/Review_BSA_Gay_Policy/review_bsa_gay_policy.html (18 Nov. 2002).

Chiang, Harriet. "State Top Court Says Boy Scouts Can Ban Gays." *SFGate.com.* 24 March 1998. http://www.sfgate.com/cgi-bin/article.cgi?file=/chronicle/archive/1998–03–24-MN6939.DTL (20 Nov. 2002).

Davidson, Jon W. "Gay Scouts Make Good Scouts." *Lambda Legal.* 2 July 1998. http://www.lambdalegal.org/cgi-bin/iowa.documents/record?record=257 (18 Nov. 2002).

"Declaration of Independence." *U.S. National Archives & Records Administration.* 4 July 1776. http://www.archives.gov/exhibit_hall/charters_of_freedom/declaration/declaration_transcription.html (19 Nov. 2002).

Hamilton College. "Hamilton College Gay Issues Poll." *Hamilton College.* 27 Aug. 2001. http://www.hamilton.edu/news/gayissuespoll/default.html (17 Nov. 2002).

HateCrime.org. "Background on the Boy Scouts' Discrimination Against Gay Troop Leaders and Gay Scouts." *HateCrime.org.* http://www.hatecrime.org/subpages/boyscouts.html (19 Nov. 2002).

Religious Tolerance. "Boy Scouts of America Recent Court Cases." *Religious Tolerance.* http://www.religioustolerance.org/bsa_1.htm (17 Nov. 2002).

Pedram 12

Varnell, Paul. "Scouting the Gay Ban." *Independent Gay Forum.* 20 Oct. 1999. http://www.indegayforum.org/articles/varnell6.html (17 Nov. 2002).

World Organization of the Scout Movement. "'B-P'—Chief Scout of the World." *World Organization of the Scout Movement.* http://www.scout.org/wso/facts/bp.html (17 Nov. 2002).

World Organization of the Scout Movement. "Scouting Is . . ." *World Organization of the Scout Movement.* http://www.scout.org/wso/scoutis.html (17 Nov. 2002).

**HYPER**text

For more information on the Boy Scouts of America, see the BSA National Council Website at **http://www.scouting.org/**.

## questions for discussion

1. Do you think Scott's argument qualifies as a Rogerian argument? Why or why not? How does he attempt, early in the essay, to establish common ground with those who might disagree with him? Is this attempt successful? How might you have improved on it?
2. Do you think Scott makes good use of his sources both in supporting his own position *and* in representing those who would disagree with him? Are the kinds of sources he uses diverse enough? Are there any sources you might not have used if this were your paper?
3. Toward the end of the essay, Scott lists numerous agencies that have ceased funding the BSA. What is he trying to accomplish with this listing? Is his strategy successful, or would you have approached this material in a different way? How?

4. Late in his essay, Scott argues that reversing the BSA's ban on openly gay Scouts and Scoutmasters "would expand minds and our ability to accept those different from us, resulting in a better society." Do you agree? Is Scott perhaps making too general a claim here? Why or why not?
5. Scott's is a well-organized, if short, paper that combines argument and research. What suggestions would you make to Scott in a peer-review session? Write a peer-review message e-mail for Scott and e-mail it to others who have read this essay. Confer on how you would advise Scott to revise.

## *Useful Links*

As usual, numerous online resources can assist you in the careful crafting of your arguments. Consider some of the following and share some of your favorites with your classmates.

- The University of Maryland University College has a helpful site on "Writing Arguments" at **http://www.umuc.edu/prog/ugp/ewp_writingcenter/writinggde/chapter8/chapter8-04.shtml.** Check out their sound advice and augment what you've learned about writing arguments in this chapter.
- The strategies about argument and persuasive writing strategies at **http://www.stark.kent.edu/writing/argument.htm,** hosted by Kent State University's Stark Campus, are particularly useful for thinking about using research and outside sources strategically.

- Go to the Companion Website to find a complete online chapter on writing multi-genre projects.
- Finally, the Paradigm Online Writing Assistant has an excellent site on writing arguments at **http://www.powa.org/argument/index.html.**

## A Writer in Action: Alfie Kohn and the Issue of Competition

In his controversial book *No Contest: The Case Against Competition*, Alfie Kohn makes a case for getting rid of grades in schools and allowing students to learn without having to worry about competing for, or being judged by, the scores they make on tests. In his chapter, "Is Competition

More Enjoyable? On Sports, Play, and Fun," he discusses the question of whether competition makes certain activities, including sports, more enjoyable. As you read his piece below, identify one or more of Kohn's arguments and claims, study his citations and explanations, and consider how you might write a brief piece responding to Kohn's ideas. You may need to do some research on your own to see if other commentators draw different conclusions from the research he cites.

---

## Is Competition More Enjoyable?*

### ON SPORTS, PLAY, AND FUN

*That ain't no way to have fun, son.*
—*Randy Newman*

Alfie Kohn

. . . Competitive games obviously are different from the competition we find in most other realms of our lives. "To live with the hope of immediate success and fear of immediate failure in an enterprise which has no significance beyond itself is a totally different thing from living permanently on the brink of that abyss into which competitive industry throws its failures," as John Harvey put it. Still, the fact that competition is so unpleasant—often the source of considerable anxiety—in other contexts is worth keeping in mind as we ponder the question posed by this chapter's title. The pressure to be a winner on the playing field is not totally different from its counterpart in the office, so we are entitled to a measure of skepticism as we consider the prospect of competing for enjoyment. In any case, there is no denying that this country's most popular recreational activities are structured so that one individual or team must triumph over the other. Sports, in particular, are competitive by definition,** while, in practice, the extent of their competitiveness

---

*Excerpts from "Is Competition More Enjoyable? On Sports, Play, and Fun" (pages 79–87, and 91–95) in *No Contest: The Case Against Competition* (Revised Edition) by Alfie Kohn

**I take *sports* to refer to certain competitive games that require vigorous physical activity. It follows, then, that *noncompetitive sports* is a contradiction in terms, but the extent of competition in a given sporting event is not fixed.

is such that George Leonard referred to our "overblown, institutionalized, codified worship of winning."

Just as competition is the salient characteristic of sport, so is sport, in turn, a prominent feature of American life. The vernacular of football and baseball has leached into the language. We take for granted the astonishing fact that results of various competitive games automatically qualify as "news"; indeed, every daily newspaper and local television news program in the country reserves space or time to report on the results of these pastimes. Certain sporting events are among our most popular forms of entertainment, with the Super Bowl being watched in some forty million households each year. Sociologist Harry Edwards once set out, rather playfully, to determine "the relative impact of sports as opposed to politics." At the height of a hotly contested mayoral election in New York City, he stopped 150 passers-by and asked them, "Who is going to win?" Thirty-four people named one of the candidates and most of the rest said, "The Mets." Even if the story is apocryphal, finally, it may be worth thinking seriously about the college administrator who once said he wanted a university that the football team could be proud of.

## The Question of Play

Except for the people who depend on them for their livelihood, sports, like all other forms of recreation, presumably exist for no other reason than to provide enjoyment. Thus we are led to ask whether competition truly represents the most enjoyable arrangement we can imagine in a recreational setting. Let us narrow the question by first considering the phenomenon of play, which might be thought of as enjoyment in its purest form. (The next section will address the larger question of whether we need to compete to have fun.) As I noted in chapter 2, one of the classic works on the subject, Johan Huizinga's *Homo Ludens*, goes so far as to suggest that play and competition are virtually synonymous. Other students of play, such as Roger Caillois and Jean Piaget, have treated competition as a kind of play, if not its prototype. I want to challenge not only Huizinga's extreme position but even the weaker claim that competition and play are compatible. To do so, it makes sense to begin by defining play.

A review of the literature discloses considerable overlap—which is not to say consensus—among previous efforts. Huizinga, who goes on to argue that play is the touchstone of civilization itself, offers a rather broad definition. He proposes that play is "a free activity standing quite consciously outside 'ordinary' life as being 'not serious,' but at the same time absorbing the player intensely and utterly . . . occurring within certain limits of space, time, and meaning, according to fixed rules." The critical part of this definition, I think, is the reference to freedom. Play must be chosen voluntarily, and it is chosen because it is pleasing. Other activities are commended to us because of their utility, their instrumental worth. Play, by contrast, is intrinsically gratifying; it is an end in itself. We do not play in order to master a particular skill or to perform well, although these may be adventitious results. The master aphorist G. K. Chesterton perfectly captured the spirit of play when he said, "If a thing is worth doing at all, it is worth doing badly." Results will not matter, in other words, if we love what we are doing for its own sake. (That this idea seems peculiar, if not unnerving, to us is evidence of how little room our worldview makes for play.) Play represents a "process orientation," a concern for what one is doing in itself, as opposed to a "product orientation," in which one's activity is justified by what it contributes to some other goal. Play, quite justifiably conceived as the opposite of work, has no goal other than itself.

This is not to say that play cannot turn out to be useful or cannot be encouraged for heuristic purposes. Adults, who are typically less process-oriented than children, often read serious business into children's play. It is seen as (1) an opportunity for the player to experiment with roles and cultural norms, develop the ego, and enhance a sense of personal competence; (2) an opportunity for the player to work through unconscious fears; (3) a diagnostic tool by which the psychotherapist can gain access to the child's inner life; and (4) a way to instill certain values in a child. The player, though, does not engage in play for these purposes—or for any purpose except to have fun. As soon as play becomes product-oriented or otherwise extrinsically motivated, it ceases to be play.

Two final points need to be made about the nature of play. First, while we sometimes speak of play as relaxing, it tends not to be homeostatic (that is, motivated by a need to produce a state of rest or balance). On the contrary, the person at play delights in seeking out challenges and overcoming them. Second, while all human behavior is in some sense rule-governed, and while we can and do play within specific structures, the tendency of play to be free suggests that it is also more or less spontaneous. Thus, rules, while not precisely inimical to play, may frustrate its purest expression. An activity might be said to approximate play in inverse proportion to the extent to which it is rule-bound.

Huizinga was probably not the first and certainly not the last to complain that "with the increasing systematization and regimentation of sport, something of the pure play-quality is inevitably lost. . . . The real play-spirit is threatened with extinction." He wrote that in 1944, and books lamenting sport's fall from grace, as it were, are still being published regularly. The diminution of playfulness is often high on the list of grievances. It is said that our leisure activities no longer give us a break from the alienating qualities of the work we do; instead, they have come to resemble that work.

The chief reason our recreation is like our work is that it has become more competitive. But sports, by definition, have always been competitive. By virtue of this fact, sports never really qualified as play in the first place. Although it is not generally acknowledged, most definitions of play do seem to exclude competitive activities. First, competition is always highly rule-governed. "If the participants do not mutually define themselves as opponents, rules are mostly irrelevant," writes Frank Winer. (To be precise, they are not *always* irrelevant in the absence of competition. We will see shortly that noncompetitive games, too, can have rules. Still, rules tend to be more numerous and more rigid in competitive activities.) Second, competition often is motivated by a search for approval, which is an extrinsic motivator and thus irrelevant to play. Third, and most important, competition is goal-oriented striving *par excellence.* Novak is quite right to insist that "play is to be played exactly because it *isn't* serious; it frees us from seriousness." Competition, though, is very serious indeed—unavoidably so. Consider the following passage from Joseph Heller's novel *Something Happened,* in which a school gym teacher is complaining to the narrator about the behavior of the latter's son:

> "I try to give him a will to win. He don't have one. . . . He passes the basketball deliberately—he does it deliberately, Mr. Slocum, I swear he does. Like a joke. He throws it away—to some kid on the other team just to give him a chance to make some points or to surprise the kids on his own team. For a joke. That's some joke, isn't it? . . . When he's ahead in one of the relay races, do you know what he does? He starts laughing. He does that. And then slows down and waits for the other guys to catch up. Can you imagine? The other kids on his team don't like that. That's no way to run a race, Mr. Slocum. Would you say that's a way to run a race?"
>
> "No." I shake my head and try to bury a smile. Good for you kid, I want to cheer out loud . . . for I can visualize my boy clearly far out in front in one of his relay races, laughing that deep, reverberating, unrestrained laugh that sometimes erupts from him,

> staggering with merriment as he toils to keep going and motioning liberally for the other kids in the race to catch up so they can all laugh together and run alongside each other as they continue their game (after all, it is only a game).

Contrast the whimsical, mischievous, other-affirming, spur-of-the-moment delight depicted here with the grim, determined athletes who memorize plays and practice to the point of exhaustion in order to beat an opposing team. Clearly competition and play tug in two different directions. If you are trying to win, you are not engaged in true play. Several investigators have come to just this conclusion. M. J. Ellis, in his study of play, writes that "feelings of power, trophies, or money for the winners . . . are extrinsic to the process. To the degree that competition is sustained by extrinsic pressures, it is not play. . . . In this sense, competition and play are antithetical." Similarly, Günther Lüschen remarks that the more sport is extrinsically rewarded, "the more it tends to be work; the less it tends to be play." But we do not even need to point to the trophies and the money: The very experience of having beaten someone else is extrinsic to the process itself. The presence of this reward structure in competition disqualifies it as play.

Here, too, is sociologist Harry Edwards:

> The bracketing off of play from the activities of daily life predisposes it to restriction within nonutilitarian bounds. Thus, none of the following actors could be considered as engaging in play: the office worker or executive who takes part in a badminton match [substitute "squash" or "handball"] in order to relax and take a break from the rigors of work; the professional participant in football; the high school and college football participants who see themselves as preparing for a college athletic grant-in-aid or for a professional career; persons who engage in such activities as card games with the goal of winning or gaining financially; or participants in checkers or chess.

Edwards inexplicably stops short of making his generalization explicit: the point is that *any* activity whose goal is victory cannot be play. Another perspective is provided by psychologist Mihaly Csikszentmihalyi's study of the "flow" experience—a sensation of total, unself-conscious involvement that is associated with play. Csikszentmihalyi comments that if basketball "is not as flow-producing as composing music, for instance, that is at least partly because its competitive structure fails to isolate the activity from everyday life, making concentration and the loss of ego relatively more difficult."

William A. Sadler, finally, notes that sports not only are not isolated from daily life (as play must be), but they actively train participants for that life as it is lived in our society.

> Athletes often are well aware that what they do is not play [he writes]. Their practice sessions are workouts; and to win the game they have to work harder. Sports are not experienced as activities outside the institutional pattern of the American way of life; they are integrally a part of it. . . . In other words, the old cliché is true: "Sports prepare one for life." The question which must be raised is: "what kind of life?" The answer in an American context is that they prepare us for a life of competition.

Competitive recreation is anything but a time-out from goal-oriented activities. It has an internal goal, which is to win. And it has an external goal, which is to train its participants. Train them to do what? To accept a goal-oriented model. Sports is thus many steps removed from play.

The argument here is not merely academic. Even when they do not talk explicitly about play, apologists for sport like to argue that it offers a "time out" from the rest of life. No matter how brutal or authoritarian sports might be, we are supposed to see them as taking place in a social vacuum. This claim has the effect of excusing whatever takes place on a playing field. (While governor of California, Ronald Reagan reportedly advised a college football team that they could "feel a clean hatred for [their] opponent. It is a clean hatred since it's only symbolic in a jersey.") It also has the effect of obscuring the close relationship between competitive recreation and the society that endorses it.

That relationship, as Sadler saw, is reciprocal. Sports not only reflect the prevailing mores of our society but perpetuate them. They function as socializing agents, teaching us the values of hierarchical power arrangements and encouraging us to accept the status quo. In a 1981 study of children's competitive soccer and hockey programs in New York and Connecticut, Gai Ingham Berlage was even more specific: "The structural organization of [these] programs resembles the structural organization of American corporations. . . . The values stressed in children's competitive sports are also similar to corporate values." It is hardly a coincidence, then, that the most vigorous supporters of competitive sports—those who not only enjoy but explicitly defend them—are political conservatives (Michael Novak, Spiro Agnew, and William J. Bennett are among those quoted in these pages) or that interest in sports is highest in the more politically conservative regions of the country.

Writing in the *Journal of Physical Education and Recreation*, George Sage observed that

> organized sport—from youth programs to the pros—has nothing at all to do with playfulness—fun, joy, self-satisfaction—but is, instead, a social agent for the deliberate socialization of people into the acceptance of . . . the prevailing social structure and their fate as workers within bureaucratic organizations. Contrary to the myths propounded by promoters, sports are instruments not for human expression, but of social stasis.

Sport does not simply build character, in other words; it builds exactly the kind of character that is most useful for the social system. From the perspective of *our* social (and economic) system—which is to say, from the perspective of those who benefit from and direct it—it is useful to have people regard each other as rivals. Sports serve the purpose nicely, and athletes are quite deliberately led to accept the value and naturalness of an adversarial relationship in place of solidarity and collective effort. If he is in a team sport, the athlete comes to see cooperation only as a means to victory, to see hostility and even aggression as legitimate, to accept conformity and authoritarianism. Participation in sports amounts to a kind of apprenticeship for life in contemporary America, or, as David Riesman put it, "The road to the board room leads through the locker room."

One of the least frequently noticed features of competition—and, specifically, of its product-orientation—is the emphasis on quantification. In one sense, competition is obviously a process of ranking: who is best, second-best, and so forth. But the information necessary to this process is itself numerical. There are exceptions—one can usually determine who crosses the finish line first just by watching, for example—but competition usually is wedded to specific measures of how much weight, how many baskets, how much money, and so on. Competition not only depends on attention to numbers—it shapes and reinforces that attention. By competing, we become increasingly reliant on quantification, adopting what one thinker calls a "prosaic mentality" in the course of reducing things to what can be counted and measured—a phenomenon that obviously extends well beyond the playing field. Play, by contrast, is not concerned with quantifying because there is no performance to *be* quantified. Like the seven-year-old athlete who was asked how fast he had run and replied, "As fast as I could," the process-oriented individual gladly gives up precision—particularly precision in the service of determining who is best—in exchange for pure enjoyment. He who plays does not ask the score. In fact, there is no score to be kept.

Within the confines of a competitive game, finally, there exists a phenomenon that could be called "process competition." This is the in-the-moment experience of struggling for superiority that is sometimes seen as an end in itself rather than simply a step toward the final victory. Thus, college football coach Joe Paterno: "We strive to be Number One. . . . But win or lose, it is the competition which gives us pleasure." For enjoyment to derive wholly from the process of besting another person is more than a little disturbing, but it does more nearly qualify as play since it is a process. What we need to ask is whether it really is the essence of competitive recreation. After waxing rhapsodic over process competition. Stuart Walker writes: "The philosophy [athletes] hear announced is that the game's the thing, participation is what matters. But the questions they hear asked are, Who beat whom? Who got the medals? . . . The modern competitor feels that to be approved, admired, respected, he must win." In fact, there is nothing especially modern about this phenomenon. The concern with who beat whom—the "product" of the event—is hardly an accidental feature of competition; it is not an afterthought that just receives too much attention these days. To structure an event as a competition is often to cause participants to struggle against each other in-the-moment, but it is first and foremost to designate a goal: victory. Process competition may exist as a pocket of play (though a rather ugly version thereof), but the overall effort is unavoidably product-oriented. It should come as no surprise, moreover, to find that this pocket will shrink: the last chapter considered the corrosive effect of extrinsic motivation upon intrinsic motivation. Any gratification from the game itself can be expected to diminish when an external reward (victory with its trappings) is introduced. And there is no competition without such reward. Overall, then, we must conclude that the pure pleasure of play excludes sports and all other competitive activities. . . .

The constituents of enjoyment that are used to argue for recreational competition actually do not, for the most part, require competition at all. We do not need to try to beat other people in order to have a good time. Why, then, are competitive games so popular? The first response is that the extent of their popularity may not be so great as we imagine, at least if participation is our standard of measure. Some people, of course, avoid or drop out of sports because of disabilities, other interests, an aversion to exercise, and so forth. But a huge proportion dislike such activities precisely because they are competitive. "For many children competitive sports operate as a failure factory which not only effectively eliminates the 'bad ones' but also turns off many of the 'good ones,'" writes sports psychologist Terry Orlick. "In North America it is not uncommon to lose from 80 to 90 percent of our registered organized sports participants by 15 years of age." Research in nonrecreational settings clearly shows that those who are not successful in initial competitions continue to perform poorly, thereby setting up a vicious cycle. Other research suggests that these individuals drop out when given the chance.

Many people who defend competition actually encourage this, invoking a "survival of the fittest" ethic. School athletic programs implicitly do likewise, concentrating resources where the very best athletes are. Expressions of indifference or even satisfaction when many participants drop out of a given activity are disturbing under any circumstances, but they seem particularly outrageous when it comes to recreation. What, after all, is the point of games if not to encourage widespread participation and enjoyment? This sort of attitude has become self-defeating, moreover, since many accomplished (or potentially excellent) athletes find the competitive pressure distasteful and onerous enough to bail out.

The situation has reached the point that dozens of magazine articles and popular books are published every year decrying the excessive competitiveness of children's athletic programs, such as Little League baseball. The spectacle of frantic, frothing parents humiliating their children in their quest for vicarious triumph is, of course, appalling, and the cheating and violence that result will be explored in a later chapter. For now, consider the simple fact that these experiences with competition are so unpleasant as to lead uncounted children to leave sports permanently.

Is this mass exodus a bad thing? Unlike most critics, I am not at all sure that it is. In order to regret the fact that children are turned off to sports, you must assume that competition *itself* is unobjectionable if not delightful—and that potential athletes are alienated only because they receive too large a dose. I propose instead that while ill effects increase in direct proportion to the extent of competitiveness in an activity, it is competition itself that is to blame (although its effect will depend on an individual's temperament and specific experiences). There is no threshold of competitiveness below which we could expect all children to enjoy sports. From this position, it follows that disaffection with sports should not occasion regret on our part—unless children generalize their reaction to all physical activity.

My point in showing that the competitive dimension of sports is creating millions of future ex-jocks is not to argue that this is a tragedy but only to show that the link between competition and fun is largely spurious. Some people quit sports outright, while others may continue participating from force of habit, out of an unrelenting need to demonstrate their competence, or for any one of a number of other reasons that have little to do with genuine enjoyment. For all the emphasis on competitive recreation in our culture, then, its popularity is not what it first appears.

But what of those who *do* enjoy such activities? A cross-cultural perspective is helpful here, reminding us that the members of some societies not only cooperate in their work but also enjoy noncompetitive pastimes. The unavoidable implication is that we are socialized to regard competition as an indispensable part of having a good time. We have been raised to associate recreation with the win/lose model that pervades our society, to assume that having fun means someone has to wind up a loser. We enjoy what we have been brought up to enjoy. A child in our culture knows without thinking how he is supposed to have fun with his friends: play a game whose structure requires that not everyone can be successful. When he does not play, he goes to watch other people play such games. This socialization is so thorough that alternatives to competitive recreation are almost inconceivable to many of us. "How can it be a game if no one wins?" we ask, with genuine puzzlement—the same puzzlement occasioned by talk of cooperative education.

In resisting competitive recreation, most liberal-minded writers have implicitly or explicitly suggested that we should place less emphasis on winning. We can stop keeping score, for example, and try to shift our focus from winning to having fun. "Every young athlete should be judged *only on his own or her own*," sports psychologists Thomas Tutko and William Bruns urge. "They should not be measured in terms of how they do as compared to others." This amounts to suggesting that we be less intentionally competitive even within a structurally competitive environment. Like most reformist approaches to systemic problems, this recommendation is likely to be limited in its effectiveness. Where we are unable or unwilling to abandon competitive games, minimizing the importance of who wins and who loses does indeed make sense. But the usefulness of this approach depends on the kind of game involved.

It is relatively easy to stop keeping score in golf, which consists of two or more people taking turns at independent pursuits and then comparing their success at the end. A more interdependent competitive activity, however, makes this far more difficult, if not impossible: "One simply cannot expect two tennis players to place their shots in such a position, provided they did possess the necessary skill, as to assist in the increased development of the opponent. This is simply not the *reason* for the sport as we know it today. The name of the game *is* win." It is not merely that tennis is structured so that only one player can win in the end, but that in each instant of play success consists in hitting the ball so that one's opponent is unable to return it. All team sports, as well as most competitive indoor games (e.g., chess, poker), are more like tennis than like golf. In such cases, well-meaning exhortations to be less competitive seem naive at best.

To say we find competition enjoyable because we are socialized to do so is not merely to say that we teach our children to *want* to win, but that we offer them games where the whole point is to win. The only real alternative is noncompetitive games, and children, as we saw earlier, generally prefer these games once they are exposed to them—an extraordinarily suggestive finding.

But how are such games played? All games involve achieving a goal despite the presence of an obstacle; in football, for example, the goal is to move a ball from one point to another, and the obstacle is the other team. In noncompetitive games, the obstacle is something intrinsic to the task itself rather than another person or persons. If coordinated effort is required to achieve the goal, then the game becomes not merely noncompetitive but positively cooperative. Such coordination invariably involves the presence of rules. While competitive activities are particularly dependent on rules—and inflexible rules, at that—it is not the case that the only alternative to competition is the "Caucus-race" described in *Alice in Wonderland*, in which participants "began running when they liked, and left off when they liked." While such an activity more closely approximates pure play, noncompetitive games are generally rule-governed. Thus, the presence of rules does not imply the presence of competition.

Partly because they do have rules, noncompetitive games can be at least as challenging as their competitive counterparts. They are also a good deal of fun, and, like the Caucus-race, can have the happy result that "'*Everybody* has won and *all* must have prizes.'" Consider musical chairs, an American classic for small children. In this game, a prototype of artificial scarcity, $x$ players scramble for $x - 1$ chairs when the music stops. Each round eliminates one player and one chair until finally one triumphant winner emerges. All of the other players have lost—and have been sitting on the sidelines for varying lengths of time, excluded from play. Terry Orlick proposes instead that when a chair is removed after each round, the players should try to find room on the chairs that remain—a task that becomes more difficult and more fun as the game progresses. The final result is a group of giggling children crowded onto a single chair.

This is only one of hundreds of noncompetitive games that Orlick has invented or discovered, and they have been collected in *The Cooperative Sports and Games Book* (1978) and *The Second Cooperative Sports and Games Book* (1982). Another good collection is Jeffrey Sobel's *Everybody Wins: Noncompetitive Games for Young Children* (1983). As early as 1950, Theodore F. Lentz and Ruth Cornelius published their own manual of cooperative games. Among them are Cooperative Chinese Checkers, the object of which is not to move one's marbles faster than the other player but to coordinate the two players' movements so that they reach their respective home sections simultaneously. In Cooperative Bowling, similarly, the purpose is to "knock down the ten pins in as many rounds as there are players"—a very challenging task indeed. Other cooperative games require that each player make a specified contribution to the goal, that all the players attempt to reach a certain score (as in Cooperative Shuffleboard, which requires a modified court), or that all players work together against a time limit. Orlick also has defused the competitive element in more traditional games by manipulating the scoring procedures or constitution of teams. In "Bump and Scoot" volleyball, for example, a player who hits the ball over the net immediately moves to the other side. "The common objective [is] to make a complete change in teams with as few drops of the ball as possible." A small family business in Ontario, Canada, called Family Pastimes manufactures about fifty indoor games for adults and children, including cooperative versions of chess, backgammon, go, Scrabble, and Monopoly. There may well be other such publications and products, but with a little ingenuity anyone can invent or reinvent many such games. Change the rules of Scrabble, for example, so that the two players try to obtain the highest possible combined score. Allow each to see the other's letters. The game is at least as challenging with this adaptation, given that one must be thinking about saving certain spaces on the board for one's partner and anticipating later developments from a joint perspective.

Note the significance of an "opponent" becoming a "partner." This is far more than a semantic transformation: the entire dynamic of the game shifts, and one's attitude toward the other player(s) changes with it. Even the friendliest game of tennis cannot help but be affected by the game's inherent structure, as described earlier. The two players are engaged in an activity that demands that each try to make the other fail. The good feeling that attends a cooperative game—the delight one is naturally led to take in another player's success—may cast in sharper relief the posture one routinely adopts toward other players in competitive games—perhaps without even being aware of it. Cooperative recreation can, in other words, allow us to experience retrospectively just why competition is less enjoyable—and less innocuous—than we may have otherwise assumed.

## questions for discussion

1. Kohn argues that, "Just as competition is the salient characteristic of sport, so is sport, in turn, a prominent feature of American life." Do you agree? Is competition one of the key characteristics or one of the most important *defining* aspects of sport? Can you envision "sport" *without* competition?
2. Identify a counterargument in Kohn's analysis. Does the writer successfully address potential counterarguments to his claims about sport, competition, and play?
3. Much of Kohn's argument rests on his definition of *play*. What is that definition, and do you agree with it? How might Kohn's understanding of sport and competition change if he assumed a different definition of play?
4. Kohn asserts that "Sport does not simply build character . . . ; it builds exactly the kind of character that is most useful for the social system." Do you agree? What specific aspects of sport are "most useful for the social system"? Which might not be?
5. Which argumentative mode would you use to describe Kohn's approach: Aristotelian logic, Toulmin's model, or Rogerian argument? Explain.
6. Can you find grounds to construct a different argument, using as much reliance on educational research as Kohn does? Can you find experts who refute Kohn's position directly or offer convincing evidence to the contrary?
7. Discuss the statement made by Vince Lombardi, a legendary former coach of the University of Notre Dame's football team: "Winning isn't everything: it's the only thing." What do you think he meant? Develop arguments that either support his claim or argue against it. Is he correct about some arenas of life and not others? Which ones? Why or why not? On the basis of what you know and have read,

how would Kohn respond? (If you would like to know more about Vince Lombardi and his philosophy, do a quick Web search. You'll find lots of information—and many fan sites.)

## *Additional Writing Activities*

1. After reading and thinking carefully about Kohn's essay, consider composing your own argument in which you support a claim that competition is good. What evidence would you draw on to support this claim? How might you use a Rogerian strategy to reach a compromise with Kohn and his views? You might try using Toulmin's scheme to outline both Kohn's argument and your own. Then examine the arguments to consider a Rogerian negotiation.
2. Experiment with an argument in self-defense—an "apology." The apology is at least as old as Socrates, whose self-defense is the subject of Plato's dialog, *The Apology*. More recently, Dr. Martin Luther King Jr. composed his now classic apology, an eloquent statement in his own defense, his "Letter from Birmingham Jail." Such apologies are designed to defend one's beliefs and values, particularly as such form the basis of moral codes and ethical choices. Find and read King's "Letter" with your classmates online, and discuss the ways that it does or does not conform with a Rogerian approach to argument. Write an essay defending or critiquing King's "Letter" from a Rogerian stance.
3. Joel's and Scott's writing, which was discussed at length, offers some models for practicing argument using research. Compose a letter to us, the authors of this textbook, in which you argue that one of your own essays or writing projects could serve as a model combining research and argument, and suggest that we consider publishing your work in a future edition of this textbook. You'll want to present your argument carefully, highlighting the characteristics of your work that make it a "model" piece of writing. You might also research some sources of information about good writing, using your research to help you support your claim that your writing should be published in this textbook.

CHAPTER 8

# Putting It All Online: Research and Argument on the World Wide Web

Increasingly, writers are using Web sites to compose arguments and present their research. In fact, one of the initial purposes of the Internet was to provide a way for academics and scholars to share and discuss research findings with one another—quickly and easily. Since then, many writers have put forward their arguments via the Web. This chapter examines several ways in which the Web has become a venue for presenting arguments, debates, and research.

Before we begin, we have to address two important issues. First, as you can imagine, an essential element of writing with and for the Web is learning to integrate visual and other kinds of nontextual materials into your composition. We will focus our attention in this chapter on general issues of writing and publishing via the Web, such as composing in hypertext and using Web sites to craft compelling arguments. Second, we are assuming that you have some access to and familiarity with either a Web editor (such as FrontPage or Dreamweaver) or facility with simple coding in HTML, as well as knowledge of how to upload HTML files to a server. There are many books and guides to help you learn to create simple Web pages, and numerous online guides exist as well. We'll mention these later in the chapter, and your instructor might actually offer you some basic tutorials in composing and uploading Web pages. (You may be surprised by how easy it is to publish Web pages.)

Even if you are not going to learn to compose in HTML or experiment with a Web editor, this chapter can still be useful for you—for two reasons. First, at the end of the chapter, we'll show you how to compose articles for submission to e-zines, or "electronic magazines," many of which accept articles that have been written with a word processor and are not coded in HTML. Second, in an increasingly digital world, learning to appreciate and navigate the new rhetorics of the World Wide Web is a useful and necessary skill, even if you're not yet writing directly for Web publication. This chapter is designed to help you consider some of the ways in which writing *on* and *for* the Web invites us to reflect on new rhetorical considerations and possibilities. Go to the Companion Website to find a complete online chapter on desktop publishing.

## Strategies for Crafting Researched Web Texts

### Writing with Hypertext: Some Initial Considerations

Many different kinds of Web pages and sites are published and updated, frequently on a daily basis. Almost all of them have one significant component in common—the use of **hypertext,** one of the primary features of Web writing. According to Constance Hale and Jessie Scanlon's *Wired Style: Principles of English Usage in the Digital Age*, hypertext is a "system of linking electronic documents" (97). Eastgate, a famous online publisher of hypertext documents, defines hypertext similarly: "Hypertext is a kind of writing. While most writing is typically presented in a sequence

**HYPERtext**

Hypertext as a *concept* is not really new. Do a quick Web search on the name Vannevar Bush (search "Vannevar Bush" with Google for best results), and see if you can trace the history of hypertext from early visions of linked texts to its contemporary manifestation on the World Wide Web.

(e.g., in a book, the second page always comes directly after the first), hypertext uses links to create multiple paths through a document" (**http://www.eastgate.com/**).

In many ways, it is the *reader*'s ability to navigate a hypertextual document that opens up the most interesting possibilities—and challenges—of composing and reading with hypertext. For instance, whereas we usually read a print document from "beginning to end," a hypertextual document can be experienced differently each time by clicking on different links, and readers may engage the document in very divergent ways depending on which links they explore. For that reason, you'll want to compose a hypertextual document so that readers can clearly follow your thinking in the Web text but also feel free to move about it at will.

## your turn

We can begin "thinking hypertextually" by asking a deceptively simple question: How is composing for the Web different from composing for print? As you've worked through this textbook, you've probably already thought about this question on a few different occasions. If so, what similarities and differences have you come up with? Use a discussion board, chat room, or face-to-face discussion to consider this question. Compare and contrast Theory.org at **http://www.theory.org.uk/**, an innovative site about studying popular culture, with more "static" sites about popular culture such as Popcultures.com at **http://www.popcultures.com/**.

Let's turn our attention now to a few key ways in which hypertext can help us organize our writing, particularly if we are moving from print-based texts to the Web.

## Using Hypertext to Organize a Document, Part One: Source Linking

One way to use hypertext in a *research* project is to link your readers directly to the sources of information you are drawing on or alluding to—if these sources exist on the Web. Hale and Scanlon say that hypertext "is reminiscent of the links between a footnote and the main body of your high school theme papers, except that connections rely on computer code rather than superscript numbers" (97). As you examine the following Web page, think about the number of ways in which the page's author is using hypertext.

Notice how the writer offers links, often called **embedded links,** to *Star Wars,* Jim Carrey, and Quentin Tarantino, so you can find out more information about them. This is fairly simple source linking, and many

who use hypertext will offer hyperlinks directly to the material they are quoting from or referring to, if such information is readily available on the Web.

One of the simplest ways to play with hypertext in your own writing is to provide links to online sources that you use or quote from in your work. After you have composed some text using a word processor, check to see if the program you are working with allows you to insert hyperlinks. Many word processors will allow you to do this. For instance, Microsoft Word offers a function for including hyperlinks, generally found under the *Insert* tab.

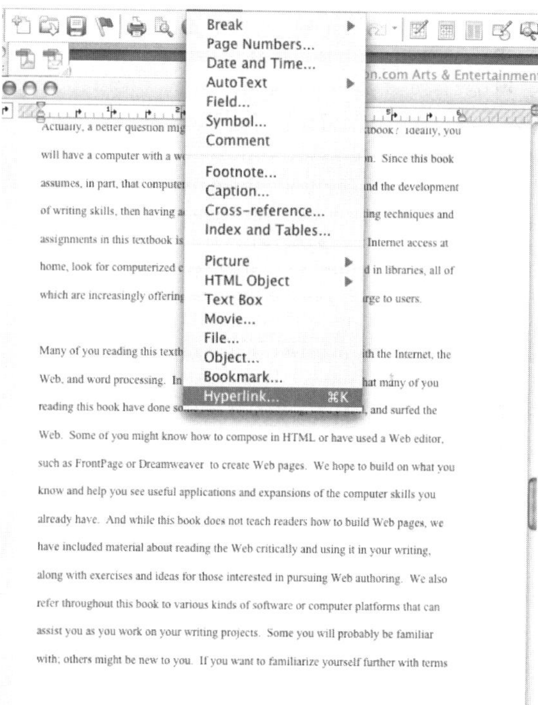


Let's look at an example of such source linking, moving from a word-processed document to a Web text. Jonathan gave a presentation—from a linear, written-out text—entitled "Ravers and Skaterpunks on the Web: Writing (about) Youth Cultures in the Computerized Composition Course." The essay/presentation primarily dealt with how he uses Web-based writing by ravers and other subcultural groups for discussion in his writing courses. He had the opportunity to recraft his original word-processed text into a Web-based format for publication in the journal *Kairos.* The idea of publishing the piece on the Web excited him primarily because he would have the opportunity to link his readers directly to the Web sites that he talks about in his essay. For instance, a static page went from this—

> When I began incorporating examinations of youth cultures into my writing classroom, I puzzled over providing a framework within which students could critically examine youth cultures—both as youth represent themselves and their cultures *and* as others represent youth cultures, for whatever purposes. A central question helped me organize my pedagogical approach: "How are youth represented, either by themselves, by various subcultures, or by the culture at large?" Imbedded in this question are *two* important literacy concerns: (1) the politics of representation and (2) the increasing multi-dimensionality (or multi-mediascape) through which representations are constructed, disseminated, consumed, and resisted. I encountered this confluence when teaching, in a first-year writing class, Douglas Rushkoff's *Playing the Future: What We Can Learn from Digital Kids*, which provides an excellent starting-off point for discussions of youth cultures and their representation.

—to this:

> A central question helped me organize my pedagogical approach: "How are youth represented, either by themselves, by various subcultures, or by the culture at large?" Imbedded in this question are *two* important literacy concerns: (1) the politics of representation and (2) the increasing multi-dimensionality (or multi-mediascape) through which representations are constructed, disseminated, con-

> sumed, and resisted. I encountered this confluence when teaching, in a first-year writing class, Douglas Rushkoff's *Playing the Future: What We Can Learn from Digital Kids*, which provides an excellent starting-off point for discussions of youth cultures and their representation.

The inclusion of the simple source link allows the reader to pursue more information about one of the primary sources the author cites and discusses in his text.

## your turn

Play with such source linking in one of your own word-processed texts, using your word processor's tools to create simple hyperlinks to the Web sites you refer to, or to sites that your readers can use to find additional information about your topic. Keep in mind that you may want to link readers to sources that you do not necessarily quote from or directly use but that may nonetheless be of use to readers wanting further information—or another viewpoint. What information will you want to give to "clue" your reader as to what is connected via the hyperlink?

## Using Hypertext to Organize a Document, Part Two: Text Chunking

Many Web documents, especially those found in online magazines or e-zines, use hypertext to link readers to sources of additional information and to "cut up" larger chunks of text into more reader-friendly pieces. For instance, Salon.com frequently features rather "long" pieces—"long," that is, if they were printed on paper—that would be difficult to read online, primarily because the reader would have to keep scrolling down to get to the end of the article. To counter this, *Salon*'s editors and Web authors have cleverly divided up many of these features into smaller sections, providing a hyperlink with a leading question or attention-getting tag at the bottom of the page. Of course, the tags are designed to get you to "click" to the next section.

For example, check out this article, entitled "Betting on Uncle Sam" (**http://www.salon.com/tech/feature/2002/10/05/gambling/index.html**). The article begins with this short blurb:

> Online gamblers are waiting for legislators to make their Wild West world a safer place to wager—but the government keeps waffling.

Once you get to the bottom of the first page, you see the following:

> **Next page** | Are online casinos a hotbed of al-Qaida money laundering?
> 1, 2, 3

The hyperlinked question serves a rhetorical purpose, designed to lure you into the next panel. Does it work? Look through a variety of articles at Salon.com, and examine the many ways this strategy works. How might you improve on this strategy if *you* were to write an article for Web publication?

Let's look at another example, returning to Jonathan's attempt to turn his written-out presentation into a Web text. After linking readers to other sources on the Web, his next major rhetorical decision revolved around dividing the essay into sections that would move the reader through it in such a way that each successive page would build on the preceding one, thus furthering the argument he wanted to make about how students enjoyed analyzing youth subcultures in writing courses. He took a cue from the various sections that were already present in his piece—an introduction, a review of previous writing about the subject, a discussion of what he did with raver sites in his classroom, his own critique of his work and consideration of potential rebuttals and counterarguments, and a conclusion.

As you can see, the sections—each now an individual node in the Web text—pretty much follow the movement of an essay from beginning to end. But also consider the "Note on Navigation" that Jonathan includes. With such a note, he invites his readers to experience the Web text in a variety of ways, either following his argument from "beginning"

**INTERtext**

Salon.com is an e-zine, or "electronic magazine," a genre particular to the Web. Later in this chapter you'll find more information on e-zines and their use of hypertext.

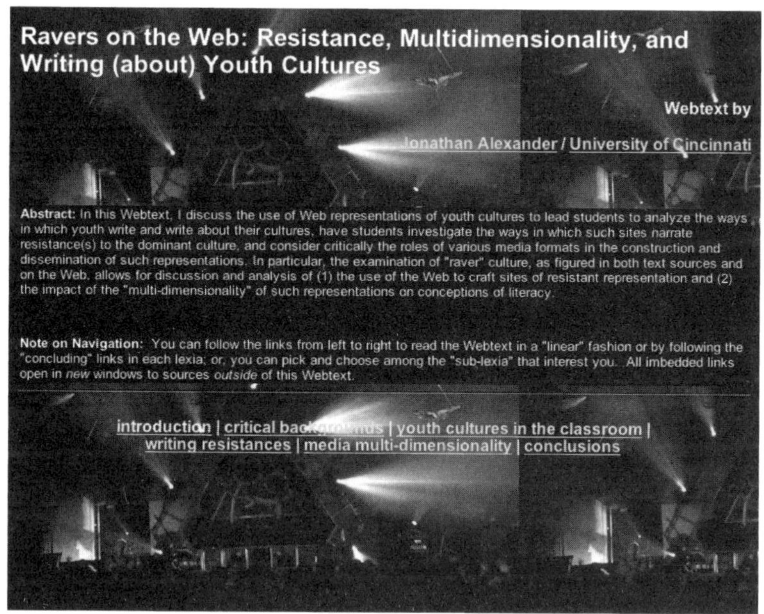


to "end" or picking and choosing their own path on the basis of their own interests. What would you do? What is the advantage of including both options? What might be some of the *disadvantages*?

"I don't like scrolling"

Some writers also play with **delaying the thesis** in their Web texts. For instance, you might chose not to announce your primary point or goal in the Web text on the welcome or opening page. And, as with delaying a thesis in a print essay, delaying your thesis in a Web text can create a sense of expectation in your reader. You'll be inviting him or her to consider a number of possibilities about your topic *before* revealing your particular stance. Such a strategy, if handled effectively, can be engaging, giving readers a sense of the process of reading your work as an adventure that you are embarking on together. If you decide to experiment with this, though, think about the following questions: Is the reader sure to get to your point *eventually*? How can you keep the reader's interest throughout all of your pages, until he or she comes to your main point?

*Remember:* Web surfers tend to be impatient, so you don't want to leave them guessing where your Web text is going in terms of the primary point (or points) you are trying to make. Be sure to include clear directions and indicate what lies where in your site. For instance, look again at the menu bar that Jonathan composed for his piece:

introduction | critical backgrounds | youth cultures in the classroom | writing resistances | media multi-dimensionality | conclusions

Such a menu bar can provide a guide for readers of your site. It helps them navigate your writing and understand your intentions in composing the site.

Of course, these are only a few possible ways to move from print-based to hypertextually enhanced writing. Can you think of other possibilities? How might the author's choices have been different if he had composed initially in hypertext or had conceived his piece first as a Web text, not as a print-based document? As you compose, it's a good idea to keep a running journal of the choices you made in the process of thinking hypertextually. Frequently, writing instructors have their students craft meta-writing essays detailing what rhetorical decisions they had to make. Questions to consider include the following: How did you decide to craft your piece? What was your rationale? How have peers responded? How might you reshape your piece as you revise and consider additional feedback?

## your turn

Take one of your completed pieces or essays and think of how you could create hyperlinks within it to link your readers to relevant sources on the Web or on other Internet platforms. Then, plan to completely revise the essay as a Web text or page, dividing the different parts of the essay into separate screens so as to *move* the reader through your text in a coherent and meaningful way? You can also do this as a group activity, discussing the choices you make at each step.

## your turn again

Even if you lack the time or skills to make a Web page right now, you can still benefit from thinking hypertextually. Think of an issue on which you have an informed opinion that you would like to present to others. Describe a Web page you would like to design that effectively makes your argument for you. How might you use links to present your claim, support your argument, and accomplish your purpose? When finished, meta-write, answering the following questions. Why did you choose the links you did? Why did you design the site as you did? What kinds of images, graphics, or other multimedia could you use to help you make your points more clearly and effectively? Once you have worked through these questions, see if you have come up with any ideas for revising your more "traditional" piece, based on the insights you gleaned from *thinking* hypertextually. For more on composing arguments as Web texts, read the next section.

# Hypertext, the Web, and Argument

Some writers have attempted to use hypertext not just to link readers to sources and to "chunk" their texts into different sections, but as a tool to explore ways of presenting complex arguments. In "Argument in Hypertext," Locke Carter maintains that "[f]or a hypertextual argument to succeed, it should clearly employ the fundamentals of giving good reasons and ample evidence" (**http://english.ttu.edu/carter/5368/Resources/ArgumentInHypertext.pdf**). This much, then, about crafting good arguments remains constant across the many forms and media you might choose to present your ideas, points, and claims. At the same time, hypertext and Web texts offer us new possibilities in presenting arguments. What might some of those possibilities be? And what are some of the *challenges* of writing and presenting arguments with hypertext?

Clearly, one thing to keep in mind is that the Web offers quantities of information about numerous subjects—including some that may be contrary to the claims and arguments you are making. Should you link your readers to information that might serve as a rebuttal or counterargument to your claims? Would failing to do so make you seem biased or manipulative to your readers, as though you are willing to provide them only information that supports your own views and claims?

Some writers' use of the Web to craft and present arguments is complex and compelling. Take a look at Tom Formaro's "Argumentation on the Web: Challenging Traditional Notions of Communication" at **http://users.rcn.com/mackey/thesis/thesis.html.** Formaro's basic thesis is summed up nicely as follows:

> *This work examines* how *argumentation* in hypertext alters *author, reader,* and *text.* Because the dynamic of author/reader/text changes in hypertext, making an argument in this medium also changes. The idea that the author is solely responsible for making the argument in hypertext does not take into account readers' ability to easily access multiple texts by multiple authors. Readers take on increased responsibility for making sense of what they read.

Formaro appropriately uses a hypertextually rich document to discuss how crafting arguments with hypertext is very different from composing arguments for linear, print-based formats. His primary point is that *readers* of Web-based arguments have much more freedom—and responsibility—in making meaning out of Web texts. Unlike print-based documents such as a magazine article or a book, hypertexted documents allow readers to navigate at will, and surfers can easily piece together information in ways that the author might not have intended. In a print-based document, which is typically read from beginning to end, the reader follows the train of thought traced by the writer; as we discussed in the preceding chapter, it is as though the writer takes the reader on a journey through his or her thinking to see how the writer has arrived at particular conclusions, insights, or claims. With a hypertext document, however, the writer can lay out his or her thinking, but the *reader* can choose where to go, what to read, and what connections to make between the various ideas and bits of information presented. Therefore, the reader of hypertext seems much more likely to come to his or her own conclusions—not necessarily those of the author. This is why Formaro says that readers of hypertext have "increased responsibility for making sense of what they read."

How does Formaro use hypertext to demonstrate this? He lays out his ideas as clearly as he can and his text begins with a note on navigation:

## How to Use This Hypertext

**A Caveat**

I've chosen to use frames because of the effect frames have on the boundaries of a work. What you'll notice throughout this piece is that when you jump to other sites from links I've provided, you haven't really left this work at all. The Links sidebar and the title remain visible. The boundary between my work and the work of others becomes difficult to discern.

Blurring the boundaries between works is the reason for the frames and illustrates an important point about hypertext on the World Wide Web. I'll discuss this idea formally throughout the work, especially when considering the World Wide Web and texts. If you are not using a frames compatible browser, you will still be able to view the work, but the boundary between this piece and others to which it is linked will be more distinct.

**Navigation Tips**

I do provide suggestions, in the way of arrows, on the way I would navigate through this piece. They are only suggestions, however, and I encourage you to jump about in the piece as you see fit. Take chances. Follow links that look interesting to you and don't worry about making sure you've read everything. The point of this piece is to let *you* decide what you want to read and in what order to do so.

However, should you choose to follow my line, here are some tips:

- The right arrow icon, , takes you to the node I would put next in the progression of the discussion at hand.
- The left arrow icon, , takes you to the node I would put before the current node.
- The up arrow, , returns to either a gathering node for a the subject (say, postmodernism or introductions).

In many nodes I do provide other links that go in multiple directions. And, of course, you can always use the links in the sidebar or at the bottom to go to areas that interest you.

So to get started use the links in the sidebar or click the arrow to go to the node I think is a good place to start.

| Sections | General Index | Authors Index | Topics Index |
| Bibliography | Navigation Tips |

Tom Formaro's Home Page

Clicking on "Places to Start" at the bottom of the page gives you a further sense of how you can navigate the major **nodes** or sections of the site:

**Places to Start**

This node lists suggestions on possible places to start reading this work. The thing to remember is that these are merely suggestions as to where I might begin and aren't necessarily the beginning of the work (you, as the reader, define the beginning of the work).

- The Sections node is at the top of my hierarchy for this work. From this node, you can go directly to six threads in the work: Background, Argument, Author, Reader, Text, and Implications.
- An Introduction?—Something of an introduction (as much as there can be in a hypertext).
- Beginnings—Why beginnings are problematic in hypertext.
- Topics Index—If you're interested in certain topics, this is a good place to see what concepts appear in the work. Also, if you'd like to see bits and pieces of hypertext theory, the Topic Index contains a list of excerpts from hypertext theorists.
- General Index—An alphabetical index of each node in the work. Pick a node at random and see where you go from there.
- Authors Index—A list of authors cited throughout the work.

The node entitled Sections presents the basic argument in detail, and you can link to each node within Sections to follow Formaro's argument from beginning to end, as it were.

**Sections in this Work**

Throughout this work, I try to give control (especially in terms of navigation) to you, the reader, as much as possible. The sidebar contains links to the various indexes that allow you select nodes of interest without my imposing a great deal of my own structure. (If you like, you could simply go through each node in the General Index in the alphabetic order in which they appear--producing quite an interesting reading--and there would be very little structure imposed by me.)

But I have conceived of structure for this work, a structure you can see by following the arrow buttons. This node is also one in which my structure is evident. The links below are to the six major divisions of this work, the privileged elements, if you will. This node is at the highest level in *my* hierarchy. Whereas the indexes are simply listings of nodes (by topics, by authors' names, or in alphabetical order) the links provided here take you to conceptual threads in the work.

| Sections | General Index | Authors Index | Topics Index |
| Bibliography | Navigation Tips |

As you can see, this node provides all the major pieces of the argument Formaro is presenting:

You can read about the "background" to his argument and then discover how he thinks the "author," the "reader," and the "text," as well as "argument" itself, change when perceived or understood hypertextually. Finally, Formaro offers us some of his ideas about the "implications" of hypertext when writers compose for the Web. Namely, writers need to be sensitive to the greater freedom readers have when navigating hypertext.

Of course, this is a fairly cogently laid out presentation, which you can follow from a beginning (Background) to an end (Implications)—a format that seems to mimic the basic structure of an argument, with a claim introduced, a body of text exploring and defending it, and a conclusion summing up the work and sending the reader off to ponder the matter further.

So, what about that claim—that *readers* assume more responsibility for making meaning out of hypertextually presented arguments? Formaro uses hypertext to present the reader with numerous options for reading his text. Note, for instance, that you can navigate the site by looking through the various Topics covered, checking out the General Index ("an alphabetical index of each node in the work"), and surfing the site by browsing through the Authors mentioned throughout the piece. The links or menu bar to the left keeps such options open throughout your reading of this Web text, and numerous embedded hyperlinks on each page allow you to pursue thoughts, ideas, and interests at will.

This openness truly *does* make you, the reader, at least partially responsible for navigating and making sense of the site. Formaro has produced an intriguing argument about hypertext *in* hypertext—noting that although he can lay out the information as succinctly as possible, it is still our responsibility as readers to construct our own opinions and responses to the site. The many hypertextual options throughout the site underscore that responsibility.

## Topics Index

This node contains links to topics or concepts that appear throughout the piece. Some nodes are listed under more than one topic when that node either contains multiple topics or it doesn't quite fit under one of the topics I've designated (see Burke's notion of "container and thing contained"). As with the rest of the work, these topic designations are simply how *I* would categorize them, and should be seen as suggestions. The topics are listed alphabetically as are the titles of the nodes listed beneath each topic.

| Argumentation | Authors | Beginnings/Introductions | Freedom |
|---|---|---|---|
| Hypertext Theory (Literature) | Linearity | Print vs. Hypertext | Privileging |
| Professional Communication | Postmodernism | Readers/Reading | Text/Textuality |

**Argumentation**

- Author/Reader Relationship
- Argument or Database?
- Argument or Research?
- Argumentation on the World Wide Web
- Constructing an Argument
- Freedom and the Argument
- Is This Argumentation?
- Linearity and Print
- Privileging and Argumentation
- Reading and Writing on the Computer Screen
- Re-evaluating the Elements
- Rhetorical Argumentation
- Rhetorical Moves
- The Shifting Center
- Temporary Arguments
- What the Argument Says

Top

### your turn

Explore Mark Bernstein's "Hypertext Gardens: Delightful Vistas," at **http://www.eastgate.com/garden/Enter.html**, as a hypertext argument. In this piece, Bernstein asks a question that many authors of hypertext ponder frequently: "How can the craft of hypertext invite readers to stay, to explore, and to reflect?" Note how Bernstein attempts to answer this question, paying particular attention to his use of hypertext. How is it similar to—and different from—Formaro's? Who do you think argues more effectively using the Web?

## Considering Rebuttals or Counterarguments with Hypertext

To get a taste of how arguments about complex issues can be presented on the Web, as well as how *rebuttals* and *counterarguments* can be treated hypertextually, check out Hot Guns, at **http://www.pbs.org/wgbh/pages/frontline/shows/guns/**, which was originally broadcast as a *Frontline* documentary that aired on public television. The Web site captures the complexity of the various views—both pro and con—that continue to be hashed out and developed in the debate over the regulation of guns in a society that offers a constitutional right to "bear arms." Take a look at the opening page:

You can tell, just by looking at this page, that an argument is being represented. The section "pro/con" signals the presence of a debate, and you can click on the link to that section to read various articles about the control of handguns. Some argue vigorously that handguns should be controlled and assert that their control would reduce the threat of violent crime across the country. Others maintain that there is no causal connection between the availability of handguns and violent crime and that the freedom to bear arms should be guarded and protected. The site also provides "interviews" with various experts and interested parties, giving you additional information—both pro and con—on the issue.

In terms of audience sensitivity, the site is designed to engage the reader, to draw you in so that you will be willing to read the various positions stated throughout the site. You probably noticed the "quiz," for instance; quizzes are a frequently used device on Web sites to entice you to find out what you know about a particular subject—and to stay to find out more. And while the Hot Guns site emphasizes the current "sides" in the debate surrounding gun control, it also uses some of the Web's features to *further* the debate. The "discussion" section presents reader comments and invites you to participate in the discussion, sending in your own thoughts and ideas via e-mail. Note how the site designers frame the discussion with an argumentative question:

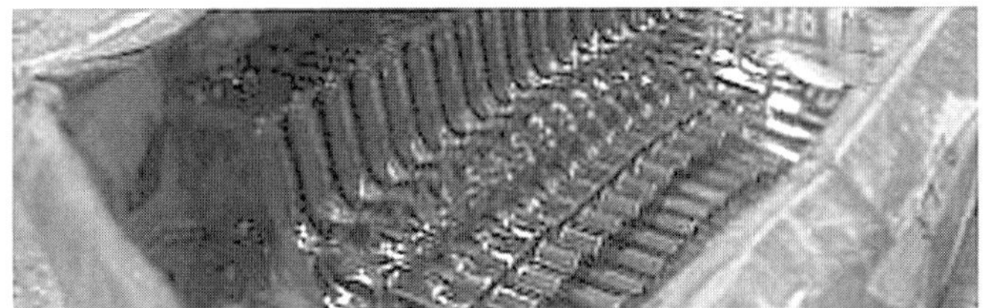

**do our gun laws make it easy to put guns in the hands of criminals? tell us what you think?**

As you know, arguments tend to favor one position over another; or, as Toulmin might say, arguments forward claims, with grounds and consideration of potential rebuttals. As you go through the site, do you sense a "favored" position? Is the site designed to influence you to favor gun control? Or does there seem to be another purpose behind it? Ultimately, the main argument of this site might be to convince us that the issue of gun control is far more complex and difficult than we imagined, as opposed to simply determining if guns should be controlled or not. In general, you might find that arguments presented thus on a Web invite us—with a number of reader-engaging formats, venues, and creative uses of hypertext—to consider multiple points of view. In the process, seeing the important issues in black-or-white or either/or terms might become difficult.

Look again at how *Hot Guns* approaches the issue of gun control: presenting the reader with a variety of views and letting him or her decide which side of the debate—if either—is more convincing. Doing this—

linking readers to a variety of views, even ones you might not hold—could foster more creative compromises or negotiations in crafting solutions to thorny issues or debates. Regardless of your initial views about gun control upon entering the site, you may find yourself thinking about the issue in a more complex way after reading the multiple views presented. In fact, you might attempt to negotiate a view between the two extremes: banning all guns, on one hand, and not placing any restrictions on guns at all, on the other. In this case, you would, of course, be practicing a Rogerian strategy.

**ELECTRONIC**issues

### HYPERTEXT AND READING

While hypertext obviously allows Web readers to "go where they will," affording greater flexibility and freedom in reading, some have argued that this is a detriment to reading and writing, specifically in that such freedom potentially contributes to creating shorter attention spans or reduced powers of concentration in readers. After all, the moment you are bored, you can click away. What do you think? Consider composing an argument—perhaps even as a Web page—that argues for a particular side in this debate.

## your turn

For even more challenging online arguments, check out two controversial sites: The Westboro Baptist Church Homepage at **http://www.godhatesfags.com/** and Stormfront White Pride World Wide at **http://www.stormfront.org/**. What arguments are presented here? How is the Web used as a tool to communicate each group's beliefs? What special Web or hypertextual features are deployed? What assumptions and potential argumentative fallacies can you find in each? What biases are apparent in each? How far did you need to read into the site before its bias became apparent to you? Discuss such questions either face-to-face with your classmates or in an electronic forum, such as a discussion board.

## Blogs and Argument

Blogs and **blogging** are a fairly recent development on the World Wide Web. According to Debbie Weil, the term *blog* is "a contraction of 'Web log' and can be used as a verb or a noun. There is no standard definition of a blog, but it usually means a Web page that is updated daily by one person who posts a continuing stream of personal commentary and links, writing in an informal, conversational style" (**http://www.clickz.com/em_mkt/b2b_em_mkt/print.php/870481**).

Weil offers Jason Kottke's blog, at **http://www.kottke.org/index.html**, as an example of a well-designed, effective blog—which makes sense, since Kottke is a professional Web designer. Kottke offers his own amusing definition of a blog: "A weblog is a frequently updated, chronologically ordered collection of hypertext fragments. Is that clear? (OK, it's a journal with the newest stuff at the top.)" (**http://www.kottke.org/about/index.html**). Rhetorically, blogs provide a space for the dissemination of alternative views on a variety of subjects. Steven McLaughlin notes blogs' new potential for publishing people's personal thoughts. "And unlike the diaries of historical figures and ordinary people of the past," he observes, "these are real-time conversations that a multitude of readers are privy to on a global scale" (**http://saltire.weblogger.com/articles/writingren**). Similarly, Charles Cooper maintains that, "to the degree that they complement, supplement and otherwise advance understanding of our human condition, bloggers far and wide merit serious praise. Because they help tell the story" (**http://news.com.com/2010–1074–281560.html?legacy=cnet**). Some businesses are using them now for employees to communicate—necessarily behind internal firewalls. The Google sales team, for example, uses a blog for thinking collaboratively.

In terms of developing arguments, blogs allow you to add comments about a particular subject continually, responding to issues raised or critiques offered by people who e-mail you or to additional information you come across, day by day. For instance, see Allan Karl's weblog at **http://radio.weblogs.com/0108247/**, which offers his musings—sometimes sequential, sometimes not—on a variety of subjects, frequently politics. Karl posts nearly daily with his views on a variety of contemporary situations and issues, and he often quotes those with whom he agrees and those with whom he disagrees; of course, we get to read all about *why* he disagrees!

**for the sake of clarity - The Digital Tavern**

*Allan Karl's Blog -There are no strangers here. Only friends you haven't met.*

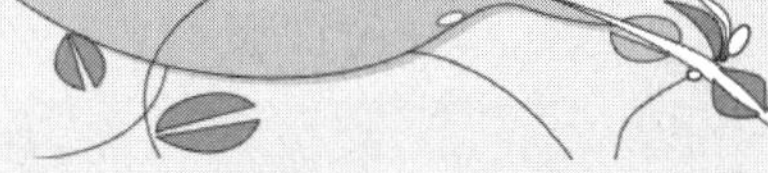

 **Monday, August 23, 2004**

**Bloglet Subscription Issues**

Received a bunch of emails over the weekend from subscribers who haven't been receiving the Bloglet subscription email notices. I know they went out last week regarding the motorcycle accident post but it seems that many didn't receive it. I'm trying to debug this but it may be an issue with Bloglet. Or, perhaps it's the wrath of karma haunting me for being so absent from updating -- for the sake of clarity -- but this has passed.

Let me know if you receive a notice on this post. We'll call it our little test.

Thanks for your patience.

10:06:33 PM permalink | Comment (0) | trackback (0)

**Saturday, August 21, 2004**

**Symbian Pet Peeve.**

I really love my Symbian-based Sony Ericsson P900 SmartPhone. Like a TREO or a Palm-based device, I used a stylus pen to enter text for messages, calendar, contact or simple navigation using the Symbian UIQ v2.1 interface.

But unlike the original Graffiti that I used to use with my last SmartPhone that was Palm-based to make a "T" you simply draw it on the screen as you would printing on paper: a quick vertical line then lift the stylus and cross that line making your "t". But that vertical line without the crossed "t" is an "L".

So follow me here. To make a space between words you simply draw a simply quick horizontal line. Voila! A space and then you can begin entering your next word. Here's where it gets tricky and basically pisses me off. If I write a word that ends in two "L's" and then I draw that quick horizontal line to denote a space before the next word, the system turns that second "L" into a "T"; it mistakenly thinks I'm trying to cross that "L" and make it a "T".

Think of how many words end in two "L's":

- well
- still
- will
- bill
- fill
- tell
- chill
- till

Well, you get the idea. Anyone using Symbian, the Sony Ericsson P900 (or P800 for that matter) and have any idea if there is a work around? This is really annoying.

7:43:10 PM permalink | Comment (0) | trackback (0)

**Friday, August 20, 2004**

**Leave My Foot Alone!**

So I decided to take a walk along the beach the other day. Trying to be careful not to give my ankle to much flex and being careful not to fall to test the titanium plate and scres in my writst even as I precariously teetered on the rocks above the tide pools, I was committed to not letting the detriment of a broken bone nor taxed ligaments interfere with my active lifestyle.

**August 2004**

| Sun | Mon | Tue | Wed | Thu | Fri | Sat |
|---|---|---|---|---|---|---|
| 1 | 2 | 3 | 4 | 5 | 6 | 7 |
| 8 | 9 | 10 | 11 | 12 | 13 | 14 |
| 15 | 16 | 17 | 18 | 19 | 20 | 21 |
| 22 | 23 | 24 | 25 | 26 | 27 | 28 |
| 29 | 30 | 31 | | | | |

Jul Sep

Enter your email address to subscribe to **The Digital Tavern**

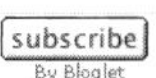

By Bloglet

- Contact Me

**Monthly Archives**

May 2002
June 2002
July 2002
August 2002
September 2002
October 2002
November 2002
December 2002
January 2003
February 2003
March 2003
April 2003
May 2003
June 2003
July 2003
August 2003
September 2003
October 2003
November 2003
December 2003
January 2004
February 2004
March 2004
April 2004
May 2004
June 2004
July 2004
August 2004

Listed BLOGSHARES

- Contact Me

A screenshot from The Digital Tavern, a blog by Allan Karl.

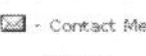

10:44:05 PM permalink | Comment (0) | trackback (0)

**More Airport Express**

If you haven't read my Airport Express experience jump over there now and get up to speed. I've had a number of comments and emails regarding the sporadic "skipping" or cutting in and out of the audio that I experienced. As noted earlier, since I took the Airport Express off WDS and configured a profile to simply just "join an existing Airport network" I've had few problems.

That's not to say that it hasn't skipped out on me on one or two occasions. But I simply attribute this to either background tasks involving network operations, the fact that the G4 Cube running iTunes is a tired old 450 Mhz machine or that background operations on the Cube such as syncing my iDisk might cause a glitch now and then.

Most exciting is my latest addition. I finally purchased the Airport Express Stereo Connection Kit. This kit at $39.95 offers three accessories. First, is a standard "Y" type cable that enables you to connect the Airport Express' stereo-mini jack to analog stereo-in RCA jacks on a stereo or A/V receiver. Additionally, you get an extension cord that allows you to bypass the built in power plug that comes with the Airport Express and move the unit away from the wall or more importantly from a clogged power strip. Finally, it gives you an optical digital audio cable.

The Airport Express' mini jack is a multi-purpose analog/digital output jack. With this cable (available at the time of writing only from Apple in this kit) you can connect the Airport Express to the optical digital input of any receiver or A/V receiver offering an optical input jack. Now I'm streaming pure digital signal from my G4 Cube to my Sony ES A/V receiver in my great/living room.

I've now buried my Airport Express into the depths of the spaghetti farm formed by too many cables connecting too much equipment to my A/V receiver. But it's a pleasure to simply send iTunes audio to my home stereo. Now I can find any of the 14,000 songs in seconds and play it on demand. Now this is starting to feel like a Digital Hub.

10:35:30 PM permalink | Comment (0) | trackback (0)

A screenshot from The Digital Tavern.

What are some of the advantages—and disadvantages—of arguing in this way? Certainly, a blogger can respond immediately to comments received via e-mail and can thus address potential counterarguments and rebuttals to ideas or thoughts presented. The writing thus gains in sophistication as various, sometimes contrary ideas are encountered and discussed. At the same time, if you have not been following a particular blog for a while, you might get lost in the discussion and have to backtrack through quite a bit of screen text to find out what's going on. Or, more frequently, the blogger will simply "sound off" on a particular topic and never return to it, thus sacrificing depth of discussion for a quick sound "byte."

## your turn

Some blogs are fairly academic in nature, such as Adrian Miles's blog at **http://hypertext.rmit.edu.au/vog/vlog/.** Spend some time at Adrian's blog and note how he processes his research and academic interests via a blog. In particular, check out the link to "akademic werds," which takes you to some of Adrian's hypertext essays about various subjects, many dealing with film and cinema studies. Do you always follow the language and terms he uses? Note how even a seemingly open and democratic forum, such as the blog, uses "insider" language to mark a particular academic community.

**HYPERtext**

To sift through a variety of blogs, many offering sustained discussions and arguments about particular topics, check out Eatonweb Portal at **http://portal.eatonweb.com/**, which lists numerous blogs alphabetically. For assistance in setting up your own blog, try Blogger at **http://www.blogger.com/** and Weblogger at **http://www.weblogger.com.** Finally, Virginia Montecino has a great online resource site on weblogging: **http://mason.gmu.edu/~montecin/blog.html**.

## WRITING SPOTLIGHT

### Writing and Blogging

In the following article, "Blogarithms: With the Internet, Everyone Becomes a Writer," Maria Rogers offers a nice overview of blogging and how it gives many amateur writers the opportunity to express views, debate ideas, and connect with other readers. As you read through this informative piece, consider the merits—and drawbacks—of blogging. How might this form of communication, as snazzy as it is, appeal to only certain kinds of writers, as opposed to making "everyone" on the Internet a writer?

---

### Blogarithms

With the Internet, Everyone Becomes a Writer

By Maria Rogers

If you have pent-up aggression or a political peeve, a pet bunny that's really cute—or a fetish for dressing like one—you can now write about it on the Internet for the whole world to read.

The latest Internet trend is the blog, short for "Web log." Blog spots are Web sites resembling journals. Words, rather than graphics and sound, are what make a blog. Owners and visitors post their thoughts and responses, making blogs interactive diaries.

"A blog is a Web page made up of usually short, frequently updated posts that are arranged chronologically— like a 'what's new' page or a journal, according to **Blogger.com**. "The context and purposes of blogs varies greatly—from links and commentary about other Web sites, to news about a company/person/idea, to diaries, photos, poetry, mini-essays, project updates, even fiction. Blog posts are like instant messages to the Web."

Brian Griffin operates the Cincinnati Blog (**www.cincinnati.blogspot.com**), which he touts as the "Blog of Record for the Cincy Area."

"I'm a news junkie," Griffin says.

He started his blog, focusing mostly on analysis of the media and politics, in May 2002. Searching local and national media mentions of Cincinnati, he tries to keep his readers informed about what's happening around town, but also takes a critical look at how it's reported.

"To me, the advantage of a blog over a Web page comes in the ease and simplicity of updating the blog," Griffin says. "A normal Web page requires more knowledge of HTML programming and the process to update the page requires far greater time lining up the text and editing the code. . . . The blog page is all in a general template that can be customized. But once the form is set, you can update it as fast as your PC and Internet connection allows."

The Sept. 11, 2001 terrorist attacks on the United States fueled the creation of blogs, especially about politics, according to Griffin. A new generation—known as the "war bloggers"—was born.

"I'd seen a few (blogs) at the end of 2001 here and there, but I really didn't know much about it," Griffin says.

Chris Anderson of Norwood, who started a blog called "Queen City Soapbox" (**www.queencity.blogspot.com**) in August 2002, says bloggers are divided into "linkers" and "thinkers." Thinkers tend to write longer messages about their thoughts and opinions, while linkers write shorter commentaries linking to Web sites for readers to study on their own.

### Stop me before I blog again

Blogging—writing and reading blog spots—can consume a whole evening, Anderson says.

The key for him is keeping a balance between social time, work and blogging. He originally planned to blog for three months and then decide whether to continue. Now, he says, he can't give it up.

"If I go more than a couple of days without doing it, I start to feel bad," Anderson says. "I don't want it to consume my life, but I find it enjoyable."

Blog spots tend to build on one another. Posting messages on other people's blogs with links back to his own blog lets Griffin share his opinions on a broader scale and steer more traffic to his site. Griffin says he enjoys writing and getting feedback.

"It can get to be fun or nasty once in a while," he says.

Bloggers tend to be nitpickers, according to Griffin, and scrutinizing a news column line by line is one of their pastimes.

On Jan. 28, his blog addressed a news report on Cincinnati Vice Mayor Alicia Reece.

"Vice Mayor Alicia Reece deserves kudos for getting the attention of the *Washington Times*," Griffin wrote. "The 'Moonie Times', as it is called, is a conservative newspaper with a small yet influential conservative audience. The article is fair, accurate and generally unbiased. It could have had a quote from a boycott supporter, but they did not return the reporter's phone calls."

The blog world takes this kind of analysis to another level, through an activity called "fisking." The term arose when bloggers began breaking down the writing of Robert Fisk, a British journalist, and posting a retort to each of his comments.

"He would make a certain claim about terrorism or the Palestinian issue and that same day they would write a whole thing about it," Griffin says.

The world of blogs is known as the blogosphere and is open to constant updates and changes.

"Most people who do them do them up to date," Griffin says. "There's blogs about every little topic under the sun. Some people call it an addiction, and it can be."

Most blogs aren't politically oriented, according to Anderson.

"The vast majority of blogs are more like personal journals," he says. "I think to do it the way that we're doing it probably takes a little bit of ego in thinking that people want to read your opinion."

Bloggers aren't just criticizing the media but influencing it as well. Griffin points to the scandal over racist remarks last year by U.S. Sen. Trent Lott (R-Miss). The tumult started on blogs, he says.

Tracking the visitors to his site helps Griffin understand who his audience is. Some of the traffic comes from City Hall and downtown corporations.

"I've been getting a lot from colleges," he says. "Somebody from Harvard is reading my blog, and I have no idea why."

Architect, radio talk show host and former city council candidate John Schlagetter has added " blogger" to his list of titles. His mind works like a spreadsheet, seeing patterns and analyzing data naturally.

"I thought it was just a great way to do self-publishing," Schlagetter says. "I just needed an outlet because I was calling (WDBZ) too much."

Schlagetter recently launched a new branch to his blog (**www.foregenitor.com/weblog/blogger**), documenting his correspondence with political leaders.

"I thought it would also be good to post all my e-mail correspondence with council and the mayor," Schlagetter says. "It's a medium for self-expression. It's a medium for retorts. For anyone who's ever suffered the ignominy of writing a Pulitzer Prize–winning letter to the editor and never seeing it published, blogging is for you."

### questions for discussion

1. After reading the article above and browsing through a few different blogs, do you agree with the contention that "with the Internet, everyone becomes a writer"? Why or why not?
2. Is there a particular kind of writing, or a particular kind of subject, that you feel works well in the blog format? What kinds of subjects or analyses would *not* work on a blog? Why?
3. If you were to work on your own blog, what subjects would you discuss? What subjects would you *avoid* discussing, and why? Do you think that bloggers should have to describe the content of their blogs, noting potentially "touchy" subjects or "adult" issues, *before* readers browse through their postings?

## Some Questions and Issues to Consider about Web Authoring

If you are experimenting with creating Web texts, particularly those involving research-based arguments, you'll want to consider a number of questions as you begin working on a Web-based project. For instance, ask yourself: What is my purpose in using such a visual form as the Web? What can I accomplish *visually* with this site that I cannot accomplish without it? What specific features of Web writing, such as the ability to mix texts and graphics, allow me to do something I cannot do any other way? What are some of the advantages to writing on the Web as opposed to composing print-based text? Obviously, the ability to link readers to sources easily and quickly is a bonus. What might be some other advantages?

Indeed, there are a number of rhetorical issues you'll want to consider before you use hypertext, and you may want to consult a guide—either in print or online—as you consider working with hypertext. We mention a few guides in Useful Links below. See also the following pointers from the Web Design Group at **http://www.htmlhelp.com/design/style/**. In particular, two points are worth focusing on:

- Make it usable out of context, so a reader isn't lost when he [or she?] comes in through the back door.
- Use images and icons in a responsible way.

Note that clarity—in terms of what links to what and why—is definitely a priority value in thinking and writing hypertextually.

Here are some other tips for writing for the Web and for thinking specifically about the *visual* impact of your pages.

- In many ways, the opening or "welcome" pages for your Web site—the first pages your Web readers will see—serve as your "introduction," and they are just as important as in print, perhaps more so. If your welcome pages do not capture interest with the first screen, a reader can, and will, easily go elsewhere. Also, keep in mind that you cannot expect anyone to scroll down several screens or follow too many links to get to the point. As in print-based writing, clarity and conciseness are highly prized values—perhaps even more so in writing for the Web, where the ever-present option to click instantly into another site tends to make readers impatient.
- Links should be clearly marked so that readers know how you are using hypertext, or links, and—ideally—have a rough sense of where the various links will take them.
- In general, flashing or blinking graphics are annoying. Use them judiciously.

Finally, here are some questions to ask about a completed set of Web pages.

- Do all the elements—visuals, texts, links, etc.—work together and complement one another?
- Do any of the visuals (or the text, for that matter) potentially distract readers from your *intention* in communicating with the Web site?
- Would the composition as a whole gain by either deleting or adding specific visuals or graphics? Specific bits of text?

*Don't forget*: You can solicit feedback from your audience by including a guest book and asking visitors to comment on the design or your site. Then, use this feedback in *re*designing your Web work.

**ELECTRONICissues**

### OTHER CONSIDERATIONS ABOUT HYPERTEXT AND WEB DESIGN

There is nearly endless debate, or so it seems, about what constitutes good Web design. You can find numerous online forums discussing the issue, and you've probably overhead classmates talking about Web pages they like and ones they do *not* like. Debating the topic is not only playful but useful as we try to work out what is "good" and effective Web design. Of course, we can really only measure "good" and "effective" in terms of the rhetorical context or situation being addressed in the site. But that doesn't mean that some rules—or at least conventions—aren't already being established about what passes as good Web design.

For instance, "Web Pages That Suck," at **http://www.webpagesthatsuck.com/**, is a neat site that attempts to clarify for us what constitutes good—and, more important, *bad*—Web design. The site features a "daily sucker," a page exemplifying what the site authors think of as particularly poor Web design. You can also take a tour of poorly designed pages, each of which is glossed with commentary, in frames, about what is "wrong" with the page.

Take the tour and, based on the examples and commentary given, construct a list of criteria with which the site designers evaluate Web pages. Do you agree with their criteria? Which ones would you add or delete? Are there any pages that the site authors identify as "bad" that you liked? Which ones, and why?

## Writing for E-Zines

Many people think that "writing for the Web" means creating a Web page, either with HTML, XTML, or a Web editor such as Dreamweaver or FrontPage. However, posting your own Web site is not the only way you can publish your work on the Web. Many writers and editors have set up electronic magazines called Web zines or e-zines, which regularly request submissions. Most of the time all you need is a word processor and an e-mail account to submit. The remainder of this chapter will explore how e-zines offer you the possibility to publish your writing on the Web—with little or no technical expertise.

Let's start with some simple definitions. E-zines are Web-based collections of writing and artwork that are published on a regular basis. They contain a variety of writing, from short news items to in-depth features, opinion pieces, and editorials. In a way, e-zines are the Web's equivalent of print newspapers and magazines, but in many other ways, e-zines are more than just electronic magazines. They may have more in common with (and often draw their inspiration from) the "zines" of sub- and countercultures. These "zines," written and produced by youth, generally consist of photocopied articles and artwork stapled together and distributed in coffeeshops and bookstores. The content of the zines varies widely, but many zine authors and editors have been interested in publishing material that questions conventions and expectations for "normalcy." For this reason, their content can often be provocative and startling—as well as ceaselessly inventive and original.

Many e-zine writers and Web publishers share in this tradition, capitalizing on the relative ease of putting up a Web site to showcase contributors' thoughts and art. The Web has been a welcome and useful medium for e-zines because an author, artist, or editor can reach many more people through the Web than through photocopied flyers and chapbooks. Taking advantage of the interactive nature of the Web as a communications medium, many e-zines also have message boards or chatrooms in which readers can respond directly to authors and artists. In this way, information and opinion can be shared and virtual communities of like-minded people can be formed.

Much writing in e-zines uses the same kinds of strategies discussed throughout this book: awareness of audience and potential readers; use of clear theses, claims, or focus points; development of ideas through writing; use of backing and grounds to support claims and theses; and even consideration of alternative points of view, rebuttals, or counterarguments. Because the writing is published on the Web, much of it also takes advantage of some of the special features of Web writing, such as the use of hypertext and multimedia communication, including sound and video clips.

An example, Salon.com, will help us see these features in action. *Salon* is one of the most widely read e-zines on the Web, and you can tell why from its list of menu items. Articles in *Salon* are diverse, covering a variety of topics. Most of the writing is crisp, fun, and engaging, dealing with popular subjects in a knowledgeable yet often humorous way.

By mixing news reports "from the wires" (containing mostly factual information about world and national events) with opinion and thought-provoking pieces, *Salon* caters to a readership that wants to be informed *and* entertained. Many of the featured pieces are "thought-provokers," so you can imagine that the majority of them are argumentative in nature. Spend some time at Salon.com examining the contents and the individual writing styles of the contributors. You will notice that the writers, though not academics, adhere to many of the principles of argumentative writing discussed earlier in this book: most respond to specific ideas, offer critiques, and consider counterarguments and potential rebuttals.

Furthermore, since the articles are published on the Web, writers can hyperlink to information or articles that they might mention or refer to in their own pieces. For instance, when science fiction writer David Brin talks about why he prefers *Star Trek* to *Star Wars*, he can link you directly to a review of *Episode I: The Phantom Menace* to help make his point.

Note that Brin also uses hyperlinks to refer you to explanations of some of his references, with which you may or may not be familiar. Such online referencing complements Brin's argument, allowing you to link directly to material he is describing and (sometimes!) critiquing. You can compare Brin's ideas with those on other sites, coming to your own conclusions in the process, perhaps even critiquing Brin's assertions on the basis of what you find when you follow his hyperlinks!

## your turn

Obviously, you could find content similar to Brin's article in a print magazine such as *Time* or *People*. What is the advantage of publishing such pieces on the Web? Discuss this with your classmates making a list of pros and cons for Web versus print publication. Which do *you* prefer? Why? Is there some content you'd rather see online? In print? Why?

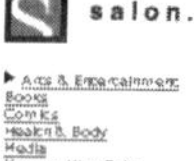

salon.com

**Arts & Entertainment**

E-mail this story
Print this story

>> MOVIES

- Arts & Entertainment
- Books
- Comics
- Health & Body
- Media
- Mothers Who Think
- News
- People
- Politics 2000
- Technology
- - Free Software Project
- Travel & Food

Columnists

"The WELL's the **smartest person in the world.** Oh, sure, its brain is in many different heads, but that's just a **technicality.**

Being online at The WELL has given me a stable and consistent **social base.** If, say, something comes up where **it makes sense** for me to move to Duluth or somewhere, I wouldn't be worried about moving to a strange place. Because there's at least one **familiar thing** and it's **not McDonalds.**

I've lived in Philadelphia and upstate New York and South Korea and rural Pennsylvania. No matter where I go, I'm **still here.**"

## "Star Wars" despots vs. "Star Trek" populists

Why is George Lucas peddling an elitist, anti-democratic agenda under the guise of escapist fun?

BY DAVID BRIN

June 15, 1999

"But there's probably no better form of government than a good despot."
– George Lucas (New York Times interview, March 1999)

Well, I boycotted "Episode I: The Phantom Menace" -- for an entire week.

Why? What's to boycott? Isn't "Star Wars" good old fashioned sci-fi? Harmless fun? Some people call it "eye candy" -- a chance to drop back into childhood and punt your adult cares away for two hours, dwelling in a lavish universe where good and evil are vividly drawn, without all the inconvenient counterpoint distinctions that clutter daily life.

Got a problem? Cleave it with a light saber! Wouldn't you love -- just once in your life -- to dive a fast little ship into your worst enemy's stronghold and set off a chain reaction, blowing up the whole megillah from within its rotten core while you streak away to safety at the speed of light? (It's such a nifty notion that it happens in three out of four "Star Wars" flicks.)

Anyway, I make a good living writing science-fiction novels and movies. So "Star Wars" ought

Besides publishing articles in a nifty and engaging Web format, e-zines usually serve the needs and interests of specific communities or particular readerships, and thus they are generally very attuned to issues of audience. This can easily be seen by comparing two very different e-zines: *Salon* (**http://www.salon.com**) and *Get Underground* (**http://www.getunderground.com/**). Just looking at the main entrance pages for each e-zine, what do you notice as significant differences?

On one hand, both e-zines seem to have a similar layout: some articles are featured in the center of the page, while links to other sections of the e-zine take you to additional reading material. Graphics and pictures are judiciously placed for visual appeal, and both e-zines even have a "headlines" or "from the wires" section, reporting on breaking news. On the other hand, once you begin examining the content of the articles, you will see that *Salon* and *Get Underground* are catering to two different audiences. Let's see how.

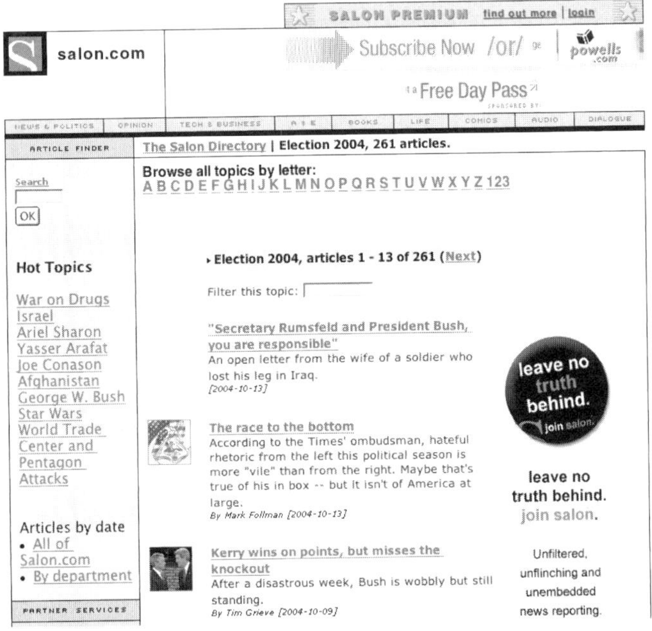

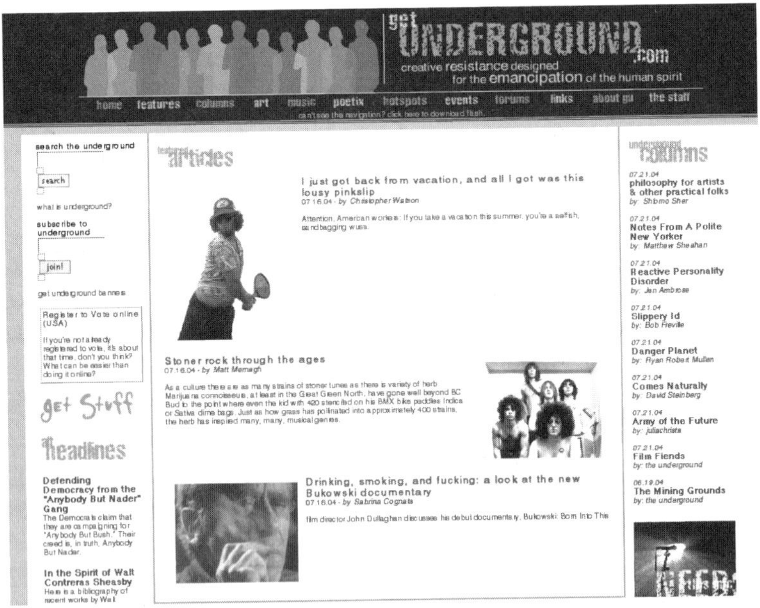

get UNDERGROUND .com
creative resistance designed for the emancipation of the human spirit
home features columns art music poetix hotspots events forums links about gu the staff
search the underground
search
what is underground?
subscribe to underground
join!
Register to Vote online (USA)
featured articles
I just got back from vacation, and all I got was this lousy pinkslip
07.16.04 - by Christopher Watson
Stoner rock through the ages
07.16.04 - by Matt Memagh
Drinking, smoking, and fucking: a look at the new Bukowski documentary
07.16.04 - by Sabrina Cognata
get Stuff
headlines
Defending Democracy from the "Anybody But Nader" Gang
In the Spirit of Walt Contreras Sheasby
underground columns
07.21.04 philosophy for artists & other practical folks by: Shlomo Sher
07.21.04 Notes From A Polite New Yorker by: Matthew Sheahan
07.21.04 Reactive Personality Disorder by: Jan Ambrose
07.21.04 Slippery Id by: Bob Freville
07.21.04 Danger Planet by: Ryan Robert Mullan
07.21.04 Comes Naturally by: David Steinberg
07.21.04 Army of the Future by: juliachrista
07.21.04 Film Fiends by: the underground
06.19.04 The Mining Grounds by: the underground

Screen Clips from Salon.com copyright © 2004, reprinted by permission of Salon.com.

For many, *Salon* seems like a digitized variety magazine with something for everyone. Topics, unspecified in the submissions guidelines, are often wide-ranging, covering many different interest categories, such as books, business, comics, health, news, people, politics, sex, and tech. However, the attempt to appeal to the widest variety of individuals cruising the Web results in prose that sometimes limits eccentricities of voice or idiosyncrasies of style. Certainly, most articles begin with the standard engaging narrative, but the majority of the prose attempts to be readily accessible—and the result is generally well-organized reports and perfunctory investigations that move the reader with leading questions through screen after screen of clearly marked subsections of the essays. The emphasis throughout is on clarity, coupled with just enough leading questions to get you to click through to the next screen.

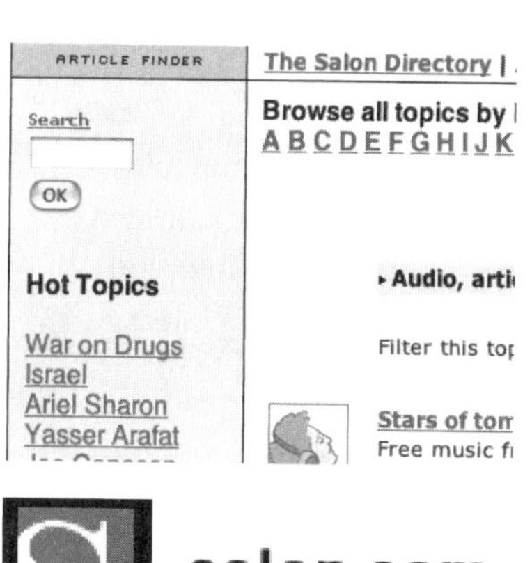

Given the length of some of the featured articles, *Salon* assumes that you have time to read, scroll, and click through an article. Perhaps this is why the e-zine is called “Salon”—which seems reminiscent of a parlor in which you can sit back and enjoy a piece of writing at leisure. Our guess is that the title—Salon—is supposed to evoke the intellectual salons of the eighteenth and nineteenth centuries, often presided over by ladies of the nobility or the so-called bluestockings, women with artistic and literary interests or pretensions. At such salons, gentlemen gathered with their female counterparts to discuss the topics of the day. *Salon*'s contents are a lot like the conversations in the old salons as we have them recorded in novels, plays, diaries of past centuries.

In contrast, *Get Underground* features writing and artwork mostly by young people and "underground" or alternative writers and artists. If *Salon*'s focus is on mainstream news and popular culture (e.g., *Star Trek* vs. *Star Wars*), then *Get Underground*'s is on alternative, largely noncommercial, fringe art, including performance poetry, avant-garde art, and writing that is radical in its social and political critiques. The About section gives us a glimpse of this focus:

> Underground culture is the visionary vanguard that propels us towards creative possibilities. It is a fusion of art, music, dance, writing, photography, and poetry in perpetual renaissance. Strip away the marketed gloss of the mainstream and it is there—the substance underneath—simple, yet progressive, drawing bold strokes of creative resistance designed for the emancipation of the human spirit.

Contributors to *Get Underground* write on a variety of topics, but many come from a liberal, even leftist political perspective. They question the status quo, not simply report on it. For instance, antiwar and pro-peace writing is common on the site, and graphic artists use their work to depict suffering in other nations caused by war, corporate greed, and racial prejudice. Satire is in abundance as well. One columnist, Matthew Sheahan, in his article "Extreme Sports New York Style: How to Cope with Subway Surfing," writes humorously of the trials and tribulations of using mass transit in the United State's largest city; in his view, taking the subway is akin to a full-body contact sport.

You can see how *Salon* and *Get Underground* are aimed at two different audiences—one revolving around what it thinks a general, educated, leisurely readership would (or *should*) want to know, the other focusing on more radical, alternative perspectives; one seeking to explain and appeal, the other promoting a questioning of the dominant culture. In

**INTERtext**

Like almost any publication for the Web, e-zine writing allows you to use **hyperlinks** and **visual rhetoric** to craft your writing. Refer to Chapter 5 on visual rhetoric and literacy and Chapter 8 on hypertext for more information on what you might want to consider when writing for the Web, regardless of whether you are composing directly in HTML or with a Web editor or are working on a piece to submit for Web publication.

some ways, one could argue that e-zines seek to *create* certain readerships, certain audiences. For instance, *Salon* and *Get Underground* seem as though they are edited for two different cultures: a more general culture of people who have time to browse through articles about items of popular interest and a very specific, alternative subculture of youthful questioners and radical thinkers.

## Preparing to Submit an Article to an E-Zine

Now that you have had a chance to read through a few e-zines, it's time to consider how *you* might submit an article for potential publication on an e-zine. Keep this in mind: writing for e-zines offers you the opportunity to see your writing as *engaged* with particular audiences and *contextualized* within a larger forum of interests and ideas. Put simply, e-zines allow us not only to publish our writing but to meet and talk with writers, editors, and others interested in making good writing accessible to a wide variety of people. In an e-zine, your writing and thinking enter a conversation—often a rambunctious one—facilitated by Web and Internet technologies.

What should you be looking for, then, if you want to publish on an e-zine? Consider the following carefully.

First, examine a number of different e-zines. Then choose one that you find interesting, and write a piece that you think would appeal to its editors. To be successful, you should be able to demonstrate how your piece meets the stated criteria of the e-zine. You can even state your reasoning in a cover letter or "cover e-mail" when you submit your piece. You might also want to spend some time prewriting about the e-zine to help you begin thinking critically about how choice of subject and consideration of audience—the basic writing situation—are *key* factors in successfully writing for e-zines. Make sure you have thoroughly researched and become familiar with both the content and the style of articles published in the e-zine.

Second, since e-zine articles usually contain hyperlinks to other articles, either as references or for further reading possibilities, you will want to consider what kinds of *hyperlinks* you could include, and where they should go, in your piece. Basically, having a couple of links handy is not a bad idea, even if they only link to additional information on the Web that you refer to in your piece.

Third, once you have thought carefully about the e-zine to which you want to submit some writing, look carefully for submission guidelines, which will tell you how to send the editor(s) your piece. Usually, editors accept material electronically, as a document attached to an e-mail message. Follow their guidelines carefully—this will make a good impression. In the body of the e-mail (to which your document is attached), write a short note introducing yourself and your piece, and commenting on its appropriateness for the e-zine to which you're sending it. Don't rattle on about yourself; get to the point. Remember, editors often have a lot of submissions to read, so they appreciate conciseness.

Fourth, after you've sent your piece, you might have to wait a couple of weeks for a response, but that's normal. Don't bombard the editor with weekly (or daily) messages about the status of your submission. That's annoying, and will likely get your submission rejected pretty quickly. If the piece is accepted, you may be asked to *revise*. Do so—it's good for you. If the piece is *not* accepted, don't give up hope. Work on it (especially if the editor makes some suggestions), and submit it somewhere else. It's not uncommon for an editor (or two or three) to reject a piece but for another editor to love it. Remember: editors are looking for writing that

**HYPERtext**

The Web hosts hundreds, possibly thousands of e-zines. For a sampling, check out the E-Zine Webring (**http://nav.webring.org/cgi-bin/navcgi?ring=ezines;list**) or the Zines Online Webring (**http://www.webring.org/cgi-bin/webring?ring=mags;list**).

fits their e-zines; if your piece doesn't fit, that doesn't mean it's bad—it's just a bad match for the specific aims and goals of that particular e-zine.

While having a piece rejected isn't fun, we must acknowledge that one of the major benefits of writing for possible e-zine publication is the opportunity to work with an *editor*. If an editor rejects a piece (and this *does* happen, so be warned), he or she will usually send some comments about why, as well as what the writer could do to improve the piece. Generally, writing is rejected because it doesn't fit in with the goals of the e-zine; that is, it doesn't really address the interests and concerns of the e-zine's regular audience. So writers have to check out carefully the kind of writing (including topics, style, attitude, tone) that an e-zine usually publishes *before* flooding them with writing.

If your piece is accepted, an editor will probably ask for some revisions. This is not uncommon, even for seasoned and professional writers. In fact, *most* writers have to revise at least somewhat. The chance to work with an editor, who is usually a seasoned writer herself, gives an author the opportunity to learn from a pro, as well as the chance to see a piece with a different set of reading eyes.

## your turn

There are a number of reflection activities you can try to get you started thinking about how writing a piece for an e-zine can strengthen your work as a writer. Consider some of the following.

1. Write a review of your favorite e-zine, commenting on the kind and quality of articles present. You should consider comparing and contrasting the e-zine under review with others that you have encountered, particularly with one that you think is *not* as successful. You might also compare the language used in e-zines with that of other kinds of writing, such as academic writing and research papers. What are e-zine writers allowed to get away with that other writers cannot? Do e-zine writers sacrifice credibility (or gain it) by using less formal, less conventional writing styles and strategies?
2. Participate actively in a message board associated with an e-zine and keep a journal of your experiences. Summarize them in a short report for your classmates or friends. You can even use your thoughts about an e-zine's message board as part of a review of an e-zine.

3. Examine the kinds of hyperlinks that articles in e-zines use, keeping in mind that use of links can vary widely from one e-zine to another. Do you see any commonalities of usage? Are they distracting or do they complement what the authors are writing about? How would you use links in pieces you might write for possible e-zine publication? You might also examine the way in which visuals, such as pictures, fonts, and other graphics, are used in conjunction with text.

## *Useful Links*

There are many helpful guides, both online and available through your local bookstore, for learning how to build Web pages. You've probably seen some with titles like *Building a Web Site for Dummies*. Different books offer a variety of approaches, including some that attempt to teach software "visually," as a series of explanatory pictures, while others provide more technical information. Use what you think is best for you and will accommodate your preferred learning style.

Of course, much of this information can be found online. Virginia Montecino has a great list of "how-to" online resources at **http://mason.gmu.edu/~montecin/how-to.htm**. In addition to learning more about PowerPoint, Internet Etiquette, and MOOs, check out her links under "Web Publishing." Alan Richmond's "Web Developer's Virtual Library" at **http://wdvl.internet.com/Authoring/Style/** is also very useful. And *CIO Magazine* hosts a list of Web Writing Style Resources—good for a start—at **http://www.cio.com/central/style.html**. As you surf around, you'll inevitably find more sites you can use; keep a list for yourself and others.

## A Writer in Action: Mark Bernstein on Hypertext

To read more about hypertext and its impact on how writers compose for the Web, check out "Cutting Edge," some of Eastgate's essays on hypertext writing and theory, at **http://www.eastgate.com/Edge.html**. In particular, spend some time with Mark Bernstein's "Patterns of Hypertext" at **http://www.eastgate.com/patterns/Patterns.html**, which attempts to argue that we need to develop more sophisticated ways of talking about the experience of hypertext and the Web. Think about the following questions.

## questions for discussion

1. Is "Patterns of Hypertext" a hypertext document? Why or why not?
2. Bernstein says, "The reader's experience of many complex hypertexts is not one of chaotic disorder, even though we cannot yet describe that structure concisely; the problem is not that the hypertexts lack structure but rather that we lack words to describe it." Do you agree or disagree? Why? How might Bernstein's relatively straightforward, even linear approach to hypertext—with simple links at the bottom of the page, advancing you to the next page—support his assertion? How might his own use of links, compared to other more complex uses of hypertext, actually *weaken* his argument?
3. Which of Bernstein's patterns would best describe his document? Can you think of any additional patterns that he has overlooked? What are some examples on the Web?
4. Using Bernstein's list and discussion of hypertext patterns in this essay, argue that a particular hypertext—either one you find on the Web or one of your own devising—both conforms to and attempts to break out of a particular pattern that Bernstein has identified.

## *Additional Writing Activities*

1. As a class, create a Web site on which you post reviews of local restaurants. Ask the restaurants for menus to scan into the site. Decide as a class how to organize the site. Develop a response form for students to use when visiting restaurants, including questions on prices, family-friendly atmosphere, quantity and quality of food, and so on. Then decide how to advertise your site to the whole campus. Consider, in a piece of meta-writing, how you are using various argumentative strategies to compose this site. If you cannot actually construct a Web site, then write an essay about what you would include in such a site.
2. Develop a sales presentation, using PowerPoint if desired, designed to get potential investors to put up money for development of your new (hypothetical) invention. What argumentative strategies are most effective? How does using PowerPoint aid your presentation of your claims? How might it hamper you?

3. Take an argumentative paper that you have been working on and consider how it could be "translated" to the Web. What would you have to change to make the piece "work" as a Web page or Web site? What would be some of the benefits of posting or rewriting your argument for Web publication? What might be some of the drawbacks? Consider drafting a short paper about such a project, reflecting on your own intuitive understanding of how arguments might work as Web texts.
4. Trade printed essays with a classmate and write a report in which you describe how you would change your colleague's essay into a hypertextually rich document or a Web text. Then share with one another your thoughts about what you would do, and discuss the choices you would make for one another's work in a chat or via a discussion board. Consider how someone else would prepare your writing for Web publication. Did that person make the choices *you* would have made? Are there any you would really disagree with? Did some of your classmate's choices surprise you or potentially alter the focus or goal of your print essay?
5. Rewrite the essay on sex education that appeared earlier as a Web text, using source linking and also linking readers to arguments *against* your position. Or, if you disagree with the writer, compose a similar print-based or Web-based text arguing for your position, using the essay printed here as one of the pieces you'll need to consider when thinking about possible rebuttals or counterarguments. If you rewrite the essay as a Web text, consider the following: What do you have to change in the original to incorporate linkages to views directly counter to your own? How else might you prepare the piece for possible Web publication?
6. Work with a colleague on an issue (such as sex education, gun control, or another topic of your choice), and compose two separate texts—one advocating a particular view of the subject (such as pro–comprehensive sex education) and the other advocating a different view (such as pro–abstinence-only education). Then rewrite *both* pieces as *one* project for a hypertextually rich Web publication. If you are drawn to one side over the other, how might you try to emphasize your leaning toward that side, even though you are including information, references, sources, and

links to multiple sides of the debate? You can also rewrite both pieces to present both sides of the debate in an attempt to foster a creative compromise or third approach to the issues raised. Think Rogerian! Then, think of how you might use a blog to track and develop a variety of views, such as your own evolving views about sex education. What could be some of the benefits—and complications—of using such a strategy? Finally, create an entry for Wikipedia or another online encyclopedia about "sex education." Use Wikipedia's guides for writing a "great article," considering the merits and limitations of the guidelines: **http://www.wikipedia.org/wiki/Wikipedia:How_to_write_a_great_article.**

7. Locate an e-zine that accepts reviews—perhaps of movies, television shows, or restaurants. Examine the content and style of the published pieces and submit a review to the e-zine.
8. You probably have written several pieces various courses that, with a bit of tweaking, could be revised for online publication. Consider doing so, thinking first about the e-zine(s) to which you would submit your piece. Keep track of the changes you make in "transforming" or "translating" your piece for e-zine publication. You might even concoct a narrative that offers a series of guidelines for others thinking about doing such "translation."
9. While many pieces published in e-zines are relatively short, some e-zines, such as Salon.com, publish longer pieces that incorporate a variety of outside sources. If you have written a research paper, perhaps as part of an assignment using this book, think about how it might be "translated" or revisioned for submission to an e-zine. Again, keep track of the changes you make; you will learn much about yourself as a writer and about the writing process by being attentive to such changes.
10. If you are interested in e-zines and have tried submitting to one or two, perhaps with some success, consider the following writing challenge. Write a brief guide to "submitting to e-zines," detailing your experience in reading e-zines and corresponding with e-zine editors. How would you supplement (or even challenge) advice we have offered in this chapter? Your work could be helpful to others thinking about submitting a piece to an e-zine.

# Appendix: Documenting Sources

## Part 1: MLA Style

A list of examples of citations for a Works Cited list using the Modern Language Association's documentation style appears here, with each example followed by the parenthetical citation to be used in the text. Alphabetize entries in the Works Cited list, and double-space throughout. Use a hanging indent to achieve the correct left margin. The basic format used with MLA style is as follows:

> Author's last name, first name. "Title of the chapter, article, or essay." Title of Complete Work. Ed., Trans., Comp. Version or edition. Volume and number(s) used; Name of series. City where published: Name of publisher, year published.

Use as many elements as apply in each case, in the order given, omitting any that do not apply. If the city of publication is not widely recognized for publishing, indicate the state's name with the post office abbreviation (e.g., Urbana, IL). Formats for citing one or more authors are the same for books, articles, and other kinds of sources.

To create a parenthetical citation, use the first item in the citation in the Works Cited list, which will usually be the author's last name or the title. Abbreviate long titles to avoid distracting the reader from the content of the text itself. The typical format for the in-text citation is: (author page). If you have worked the author's name into the text, there is no need to repeat it in the parenthetical citation; the page number will suffice. Place the parenthetical citation at the end of the passage cited, outside the quotation marks but inside other punctuation (usually a period). With indented passages, however, place the parenthetical citation *after* the final punctuation.

For the many variations on these basic formats, see your handbook or the *MLA Handbook for Writers of Research Papers*, 6th edition, by Joseph Gibaldi (New York: MLA, 2003).

## *Sample Formats*

### 1.1 Book with one author.

First we show you an example of a citation as it should appear in the list of Works Cited; then we show you an example of the in-text citation.

Sontag, Susan. <u>Regarding the Pain of Others.</u> New York: Farrar, 2003.

(Sontag 23)

### 1.2 Book with two or three authors.

See 1.6 for more than three authors.

Hale, Constance, and Jessie Scanlon. <u>Wired Style: Principles of English Usage in the Digital Age.</u> New York: Broadway, 1999.

(Hale and Scanlon 42)

### 1.3 More than one book by the same author(s).

Alphabetize by title.

Hawisher, Gail E., and Cynthia L. Selfe, eds. <u>Literacy, Technology and Society: Confronting the Issues.</u> Englewood Cliffs, NJ: Prentice, 1997.

———, eds. <u>Literate Lives in the Information Age: Narratives on Literacy from the United States.</u> Mahwah, NJ: Erlbaum, 2004.

(Selfe and Hawisher, <u>Literacy</u> 51)

(Selfe and Hawisher, <u>Literate Lives</u> 64)

### 1.4 Article, essay, chapter, poem, in an edited book.

Wysocki, Anne, and Johndan Johnson-Eilola. "Blinded by the Letter: Why Are We Using Literacy as a Metaphor for Everything Else?" <u>Passions, Pedagogies, and 21st Century Technologies.</u> Ed. Gail E. Hawisher and Cynthia L. Selfe. Logan: Utah State UP, 2000. 349-68.

(Wysocki and Johnson-Eilola 367)

### 1.5 Translated work.

Omit publisher if published before 1900.

Fabri, Felix. <u>The Book of the Wanderings of Felix Fabri (Circa 1480-1483 A.D).</u> Trans. Aubrey Stewart. London, 1896.

(Fabri 15)

### 1.6 Article in a periodical.

Pope, C. Arden III, Richard T. Burnett, Michael J. Thun, Eugenia E. Calle, Daniel Krewski, Kazuhiko Ito, George D. Thurston. "Lung Cancer, Cardiopulmonary Mortality, and Long-Term Exposure to Fine Particulate Air Pollution." JAMA, 287 (2002), 1132-41.

(Pope *et al.* 1132-35)

### 1.7 Article in an encyclopedia or dictionary.

Use the topic of the entry as the title, omitting page numbers if entries are listed alphabetically.

"Academy." The Concise Oxford English Dictionary. Ed. Judith Pearsall. 10th ed. Oxford: Oxford UP, 2002.

("Academy")

### 1.8 Newspaper article.

La Ferla, Ruth. "Store for Designer Clothing Displays Political Leanings." New York Times. 4 June 2004: A26.

(La Ferla)

### 1.9 Multivolume work.

Omit publisher's name for works published before 1900.

Crockett, David. "Raccoon in a Bag." Speech to House of Representatives, Mar. 1830. A Library of the World's Best Orations. Ed. David J. Brewer. Vol. 4. St. Louis, 1899.

(Crockett 1482)

### 1.10 Interview.

Knight, Jennifer. Telephone interview. 26 Mar. 1999.

Lazar, Anna. E-mail interview. 7 June 2004.

(Knight)

(Lazar)

### 1.11 Film.

Jurassic Park. Dir. Steven Spielberg. Perf. Sam Neill, Laura Dern. Umvd, 1993.

(Jurassic Park)

### 1.12 World Wide Web site with individual authorship.

Ball, Cheryl E. Home page. 20-21 Aug. 2003. 7 June 2004. <http://www.hu.mtu.edu/|ceball/>.

(Ball)

### 1.13 World Wide Web site with corporate, organizational, or institutional authorship.

Purdue University. Online Writing Lab. 1995-2003. Maint. Erin Karper and David Neyhart. 8 June 2004. <http://owl.english.purdue.edu/>.

(Purdue)

### 1.14 Article in an online periodical.

King, Kathleen P. "Exploring Feminist Research and Pedagogy in a Crucible of Tragedy: International Perspectives Creating Meaning and Response."

Radical Pedagogy 5.2 (2003). <http://radicalpedagogy.icaap.org/>.

(King)

### 1.15 Electronic book.

If previously printed, give the original source.

MacAvoy, Paul, and Ira Millstein. The Recurrent Crisis in Corporate Governance. New York: Palgrave Macmillan, 2003. NetLibrary. 7 June 2004. <http://www.netlibrary.com/Reader>.

(MacAvoy and Millstein)

### 1.16 Article in an online newspaper.

"Thousands Wait Hours to Pay Respects at Ronald Reagan Library." 8 June 2004. <http://www.usatoday.com/news/washington/2004-06-08-reagan-tuesday_x.htm>.

("Thousands Wait")

### 1.17 Article from an online database.

Rathjen, Friedhelm. "James Joyce as a Cyclist." Joyce Studies Annual 14 (Summer 2003): 175-82. Academic Search Premier. Colorado State University-Pueblo Library. 7 June 2004. <http://www.epnet.com/>.

(Rathjen)

### 1.18 E-mail.

Message to an individual:

McAdow, Lewis H. "NCAA/Academic Penalties." E-mail to the author. 6 June 2004.

(McAdow)

Message to an electronic discussion list:

Hochman, Will. "Argument by Collage." Online posting. 28 Apr. 2004. TechRhet. 7 June 2004. <TechRhet@interversity.org>.

(Hochman)

### 1.19 Computer software.

ArcView. Vers. 9.0. San Diego, CA: ESRI, 2004.

## Part 2: APA Style

The basic format for a list of sources using the documentation style recommended by the American Psychological Association (APA) is as follows:

Author's surname, initial(s) of given name(s). (Date of publication). Title of the chapter, article, essay, or other part of the book used. *Title of complete work* (Name of Trans.). City where published: Publisher.

Use as many elements as apply in each case, in the order given, omitting any that do not apply. The format for citing one or more authors is the same for books, articles, and other kinds of sources. Title the list "References," and alphabetize entries according to the first word in each citation. Use a hanging indent to achieve the correct left margin.

The typical form for an in-text citation is: (Author, year). If the citation refers to a direct quotation, include a page number (Author, year, p. xxx).

A list of examples of citations using APA style appears next, followed by the in-text citation that would be used with each. For a more comprehensive treatment of possible variations, see your handbook or the *Publication Manual of the American Psychological Association,* 5th edition (Washington, DC: APA, 2001).

### *Sample Formats*

First we show you an example of a citation as it should appear in the References list; then we show you the in-text citation.

#### 2.1 Book with one author.

Sontag, S. (2003). *Regarding the pain of others*. New York: Farrar.

(Sontag, 2003)

#### 2.2 Book with two or three authors.

See 2.6 for more than three authors.

Hale, C., & Scanlon, J. (1999). *Wired style: Principles of English usage in the Digital Age*. New York: Broadway Books.

(Hale & Scanlon, 1999)

#### 2.3 More than one book by the same author(s) or editor(s).

List works with earliest dates first.

Hawisher, G. E., & Selfe, C. L. (Eds.). (1997). *Literacy, technology and society: Confronting the issues*. Englewood Cliffs, NJ: Prentice Hall.

—— (Eds.). (2004). *Literate lives in the Information Age: Narratives on literacy from the United States*. Mahwah, NJ: Erlbaum.

(Hawisher & Selfe, 1997)

(Hawisher & Selfe, 2004)

### 2.4 Article, essay, chapter, poem in an edited book.

Wysocki, A., & Johnson-Eilola, J. (2000). Blinded by the letter: Why are we using literacy as a metaphor for everything else? In G. E. Hawisher & C. L. Selfe (Eds.), *Passions, pedagogies, and 21st century technologies* (pp. 349–368). Logan: Utah State UP.

(Wysocki & Johnson-Eilola, 2000)

### 2.5 Translated work.

Fabri, F. (1896). *The book of the wanderings of Felix Fabri (circa 1480–1483 A.D.)* (A. Stewart, trans.). London: Palestine Pilgrims' Text Society. (Original work published 1483)

(Fabri, 1483/1896)

### 2.6 Article in a periodical.

With more than three authors, name the first six and use "et al." for the others.

Pope, C. A. III, Burnett, R. T., Thun, M. J., Calle, E. E., Krewski, D., Ito, K., et al. (2002). Lung cancer, cardiopulmonary mortality, and long-term exposure to fine particulate air pollution. *Journal of the American Medical Association 287*, 1132–1141.

First in-text citation:

(Pope, Burnett, Thun, Calle, Krewski, Ito, et al., 2002)

Subsequent citations:

(Pope et al., 2002)

### 2.7 Article in an encyclopedia or dictionary.

Omit page numbers if entries are listed alphabetically.

Academy. (2002). In J. Pearsall (Ed.), *Concise Oxford English dictionary* (10th ed., p. 6). Oxford: Oxford UP.

(Academy)

### 2.8 Newspaper article.

La Ferla, R. (2004, June 4). Store for designer clothing displays political leanings. *New York Times*, p. A26.

(La Ferla, 2004, June 4)

### 2.9 Multivolume work.

Crockett, D. (1830, March) Raccoon in a bag [speech]. In D. J. Brewer (Ed.) (1899), *A library of the world's best orations* (Vol. 4, pp. 1482–1483). St. Louis, MO: Ferd. P. Kaiser.

(Crockett, 1830)

### 2.10 Interview.

APA style omits interviews carried out by telephone or face-to-face from the Reference list, but it does require citation within your text. The parenthetical citation would read:

(Knight, J., personal communication, March 26, 1999)

### 2.11 Film.

Kennedy, K. (Producer), & Spielberg, S. (Director). (1993). *Jurassic Park* [Motion picture]. United States: Umvd.

(Kennedy, 1993)

**2.12 World Wide Web site with one author.**

Ball, C. E. (20–21 Aug. 2003). Home page. http://www.hu.mtu.edu/|ceball/.

(Ball, 20–21 Aug. 2003)

**2.13 World Wide Web site with corporate, organizational, or institutional author.**

Purdue University. (1995–2003). *Online writing lab.* http://owl.english.purdue.edu/.

(Purdue, 1995–2003)

**2.14 Article in an online periodical.**

King, K. P. (2003). Exploring feminist research and pedagogy in a crucible of tragedy: International perspectives creating meaning and response. *Radical Pedagogy 5* (2). Retrieved June 6, 2004, from http://radical pedagogy.icaap.org/.

(King, 2003)

**2.15 Electronic book.**

If previously printed, give the original source.

MacAvoy, P., & Millstein, I. (2003). *The recurrent crisis in corporate governance*. New York: Palgrave Macmillan. Retrieved June 7, 2004, from http://www.netlibrary.com/Reader.

(MacAvoy & Millstein, 2003)

**2.16 Article in an online newspaper.**

Thousands wait hours to pay respects at Ronald Reagan Library. (2004, June 8). *USA Today*. Retrieved

from http://www.usatoday.com/news/washington/
2004-06-08-reagan-tuesday_x.htm.

(Thousands wait, June 8, 2004)

### 2.17 Article from an online database.

Rathjen, F. (2003, Summer). James Joyce as a cyclist. *Joyce studies annual*, 14, 175-182. Retrieved June 7, 2004, from the *Academic Search Premier* database.

(Rathjen, F., Summer 2003)

### 2.18 E-mail.

Omit citations of personal e-mail and messages from nonarchived discussion lists from the Reference list. In-text citations should use this format:

(McAdow, L. H., personal communication, June 6, 2004)

### 2.19 Computer software.

ArcView (Version 9.0) [Computer software]. San Diego, CA: ESRI.

## Part 3: Columbia Online Style (COS)

Columbia Online Style (COS) offers an "umbrella" style for documenting electronic sources that can be used when other styles such as MLA, APA, and CMS (*Chicago Manual of Style,* also known as "Turabian") are used for the printed sources in a document.

COS uses two basic formats. The "Humanities" version is employed for documenting electronic sources when you cite print sources with MLA or CMS. Use the "Scientific" version when you are using APA or another scientific style (e.g., CBE) for print sources. Both versions are given here, with examples of the format for parenthetical citations used in the text with each.

The basic format for a citation in the Humanities version of COS is as follows:

```
Author's last name, first name [or name of corporate or
     institutional author]. "Title of document." Title
     of Complete Work or Site. File or version number.
     Date of publication or last revision. Electronic
     address (date of access).
```

The basic format for a citation in the Scientific version of COS is as follows:

```
Author's last name, Initial(s) [or name of corporate
     or institutional author]. Date of publication.
     Title of document. Title of complete work or site.
     Edition or revision. Electronic address or name
     of database and its publisher. (Access path or
     file number) (date of access).
```

Omit any of the elements included above that are not found in your source. Use italics rather than underlining for titles of complete works (including Web sites) with COS, even when using MLA as your basic style for printed sources. MLA style's underlining does not mix well with some word-processing programs' automatic underlining of URLs. Allow the word processor to make line breaks in long URLs. Do not add them yourself.

For a list of sample formats in Columbia Online Style, go to the Companion Website for this book at **www.ablongman.com/alexander**.

# CREDITS

Abel, Jessica, *As I Live and Breathe,* page 10. Copyright © Jessica Abel. All Rights Reserved. Reprinted by permission.

advertisement: "My adrenaline fix isn't what it used to be. Double the dose. AMD me," copyright © 2003 Advanced Micro Devices, Inc. All rights reserved. Reprinted with permission.

Amazon.com screen shot, copyright © 2004 Amazon.com, Inc. Reprinted by permission. All Rights Reserved.

Blake, William, "The Tyger," (plate 50 of Blake's *Songs of Innocence and Experience,* copy C). Lessing J. Rosenwald Collection, Library of Congress. Copyright © 2004 the William Blake Archive. Used with permission.

Brin, David. Excerpt from "*Star Wars" Despots vs. "Star Trek" Populists* by David Brin, which appeared on the 6/15/99 in the Arts & Entertainment Section of Salon.com, copyright © 1999, reprinted by permission of Salon.com. The full article can be viewed in the archives of the Salon.com Web site at http://archive.salon.com/ent/movies/features/1999/06/15/brin_main/index2.html.

Broglio, Ronald S. and Ruegg, F. William. An excerpt from "Transformation: What Immortal Hand or Eye?", reprinted by permission of Ronald S. Broglio and F. William Ruegg.

Carraher, Lee. "64 bits, It's More Than 2 x 32 bit" by Lee Carraher. Reprinted with permission.

Copeland, John, image of Captain Picard vs. Darth Vader in "*Star Wars" Despots vs. "Star Trek" Populists.* Copyright © John Copeland. All rights reserved. Reprinted by permission.

Crockett, David. "A Raccoon in a Bag" by David Crockett. Delivered in March 1830 before a Committee of the House of Representatives.

Cummings, e.e. "r-p-o-p-h-e-s-s-a-g-r". Copyright 1935, © 1963, 1991 by the Trustees for the e.e. cummings Trust. Copyright © 1978 by George Firmage from *Complete Poems: 1904-1962* by e.e. cummings, edited by George J. Firmage. Used by permission of Liveright Publishing Corporation.

Fabrikant, Sara Irina, "Cartographic Variations on the Presidential Election 2000 Theme." Reprinted with permission.

Gangresearch.net screen shot, reprinted by permission John Hagedorn, webmaster.

Geer, Galen L. "The Path of Words" by Galen L. Geer. Reprinted with permission.

Getunderground.com screen shot. All Rights Reserved.

"Global Temperature Changes" from U.S. National Climatic Data Center, 2001, as appeared on the Wildlife Foundation of Florida, Inc., Magazine. Reprinted with permission.

Gould, Stephen Jay. Excerpt from "Jurassic Park" by Stephen Jay Gould in *Past Imperfect, History According to the Movies* by Mark C. Carnes. Copyright © 1995, 1996 Agincourt Press. Reprinted by permission of Henry Holt and Company, LLC.

Hawisher, Gail E. and Selfe, Cynthia L. Excerpted from "Fleeting Images" in *Passions, Pedagogies, and 21st Century Technologies* by Gail E. Hawisher and Cynthia L. Selfe, copyright © 1999 Utah State University Press, reprinted by permission of Utah State University Press.

Hostiuck, Katherine E. "Join the US Navy Today" by Maureen. Reprinted with permission.

"Hot Guns" screen shot. http://www.pbs.org/wgbh/pages/frontline/shows/guns/ from FRONTLINE at www.pbs.org/wgbh/pages/frontline/shows/guns Copyright © 1998 WGBH-Boston, Media Library and Archives.

"How to use this hypertext" screen shot from http://users.rcn.com/mackey/thesis/explain.html. All Rights Reserved.

Isabella Rossellini photo from David Lynch's *Blue Velvet.* Copyright © PhotoFest. Used with permission.

"Joe Chemo" spoof ad courtesy of Adbusters, http://www.adbusters.org. All rights reserved. Reprinted with permission.

Kannenberg, Jr., Gene. Excerpt from chapter three in *Form, Function, Fiction: Text and Image in the Comics Narratives of Winsor McCay, Art Spiegelman, and Chris Ware* by Gene Kannenberg, Jr., copyright © 1996, 2003 by Gene Kannenberg, Jr.

Kingsolver, Barbara. "A Fist in the Eye of God" from *Small Wonder: Essays* by Barbara Kingsolver, copyright © 2002 by Barbara Kingsolver. Reprinted by permission of HarperCollins Publishers, Inc.

Kohn, Alfie. Excerpts from "Is Competition More Enjoyable? On Sports, Play, and Fun" (pages 79–87, and 91–95 in *No Contest: The Case*

*Against Competition* (Revised Edition) by Alfie Kohn. Copyright © 1992 by Alfie Kohn. Reprinted by permission of Houghton Mifflin Company. All rights reserved.

Leston, Robert. "Towards Reconciliation: Common Ground in the Education Curriculum," copyright © by Robert Leston, reprinted by permission of the author.

Title page of "Liber Generationis," *The Lindisfarne Gospels*. Collection of the British Library; reprinted with permission.

Map of US for 2000 Presidential Election. Reprinted with permission.

Moonwatcher the ape in Stanley Kubrick's 2001: A Space Odyssey. Copyright © by Warner Bros. Studios. All rights reserved. Reprinted with permission.

Net Chick screen shot. http://www.flank.com/sites/netchick/index.html

"Obsession" spoof ad, courtesy of Adbusters, http://www.adbusters.org. All rights reserved. Reprinted with permission.

Oliver, Antonio S. Excerpt from "The Unusual Structure of MAUS" written by Antonio S. Oliver. Reprinted with permission.

Pedram, Scott. "Should the Boy Scouts of America Rescind its Policy of Discrimination Against Homosexuals?" by Scott Pedram. Reprinted with permission.

PETA. Screen shot from the PETA home page, reprinted by permission of People for the Ethical Treatment of Animals.

PETA. Screen shot of PETA action alerts from the PETA home page, reprinted by permission of People for the Ethical Treatment of Animals.

"Pieces of the argument from Formaro's article" screen shot from http://users.rcn.com/mackey/thesis/explain.html. All Rights Reserved.

"Ravers on the Web." Material from YOUth and AIDS Web Project Web site, reprinted by permission of Professor Jonathan F. Alexander.

Rogers, Maria. "Blogarithms" by Maria Rogers from *City Beat,* Vol. 9, Issue 13, Feb 5– Feb 11, 2003, Copyright © 2003, reprinted by permission of Cincinnati City Beat.

Rushkoff, Douglas. "Introduction: The Children of Chaos" from *Playing the Future: What we Learn From Digital Kids* by Douglas Rushkoff, copyright © 1996 by Douglas Rushkoff. Reprinted by permission of HarperCollins Publishers, Inc.

Sagan, Carl. "Can We Know the Universe? Reflections on a Grain of Salt" from *Broca's Brain: Reflections on the Romance of Science* by Carl Sagan, copyright © 1979 by Carl Sagan. Reprinted with permission from the Estate of Carl Sagan.

Screen Beans clip art images © A Bit Better Corporation. www.bitbetter.com.

Screen Shot of the October 30, 2002 home page of Salon.com, copyright © 2002, reprinted by permission of Salon.com.

"Sections in this work" screen shot from http://users.rcn.com/mackey/thesis/explain.html. All Rights Reserved.

Spiegelman, Art, from *Maus I: A Survivor's Tale/My Father Bleeds History* by Art Spiegelman, copyright © 1973, 1980, 1981, 1982, 1984, 1985, 1986 by Art Spiegelman. Used by permission of Pantheon Books, a division of Random House, Inc.

Spiegelman, Art, from *Maus II: And Here My Troubles Began* by Art Spiegelman, copyright © 1986, 1989, 1990, 1991 by Art Spiegelman. Used by permission of Pantheon Books, a division of Random House, Inc.

Sturhann, Chris, cartoon: "I don't like scrolling." Copyright © Chris Surhann. All rights reserved. Reprinted with permission.

Thorn, Isaac. "A New Take on the Columbine Tragedy" by Isaac Thorn. Reprinted with permission.

"Topics Index" screen shot from http://users.rcn.com/mackey/thesis/explain.html. All Rights Reserved.

Tucker, Joel. "Global Warming: America's Eager Contribution to Ecology" by Joel Tucker. Reprinted with permission.

University of Cincinnati Library homepage screen shots, copyright © 2004 by The University of Cincinnati.

Weblog screen shot from http://radio.weblogs.com/0108147. Reprinted by permission of UserLand Software.

Whittle, Robin, Elongated Slinky sculpture. Copyright © Robin Whittle, www.firstpr.com.au/slinky. Reprinted by permission.

YOUth and AIDS web project flash entrance. Material from YOUth and AIDS Web Project Web site, reprinted by permission of Professor Jonathan F. Alexander.

YOUth and AIDS web project counter. Material from YOUth and AIDS Web Project Web site, reprinted by permission of Professor Jonathan F. Alexander.

YOUth and AIDS web project opening page webtext. Material from YOUth and AIDS Web Project Web site, reprinted by permission of Professor Jonathan F. Alexander.

YOUth and AIDS web project Toolbar. Material from YOUth and AIDS Web Project Web site, reprinted by permission of Professor Jonathan F. Alexander.

# INDEX


Abel, Jessica, 189–190
Abstracts, and academic writing, 70
Academic community, academic writing for, 53–54
Academic readers
  and the argument, 69–71
  and conventions and expectations, 61–72
  and online (electronic) journal, 64
  and reading critically, 62–64
  and reading log, 64
  and research, 225
  and skeptical attitude, 63–64
Academic research, 226–227
  and collaborative research, 227
  reasons for, 225–226
  vs. popular reporting, 226–227
Academic Search Premier (bibliographical database), 231
Academic writing, 3, 52
  and abbreviated style, 71, 89
  and abstract, 70
  analysis, 79–87
  and the argument, 69–71
  audience, 53–54
  characteristics of, 54, 59–61
  and citations, 65–66
  and citing sources, 65
  and comparison and contrast, 73–76
  and conclusion, 70
  and definition of terms, 76–79
  and documentation, 64–68
  and electronic communications forms, 87–91
  and electronic discussion lists, 87–91
  and e-mail, 87–91
  example of, 55–59
  and familiar genres, 68
  mechanically correct, 72
  and organization, 68, 69, 70
  and outside sources, 64–68
  peer review, 64
  popular, 54, 55, 59–61
  purpose of, 53

Academic writing (*cont.*)
strategies, 61, 69, 73–87
and style, 71–72
and thesis, 70
and vocabulary building, 73
Active reading, 62
Advertisements
analysis of, 85–87, 96–97
and ethos, 100–101, 101–102
and pathos, 100–101, 101–102
and visual argument, 204–205
and visual rhetoric, 204
on the Web, 204–205
American Psychological Association (APA) style, 65
example of, 376–381
Analogies, and argument, 120–121
and false analogy, 164
and logical fallacies, 164
Analysis
of academic writing, 79–87
of advertisements, 85–86, 96–97
and persuasion, 96–98
Analytical definition, 76
Annotated bibliography, 254–256
definition of, 254–255
example of, 256–257
hints for preparing, 255–256
Annotation, definition of, 255
APA style. *See* American Psychological Association style
Arguing ad hominem, 167
Argument
and academic reading and writing, 69–71
and analogies, 120–121
and assumptions, 122–124, 124–126
basic form of, 107–109
and blogs, 348–351
and cause and effect, 118–119
and combining multiple strategies, 130, 138
components of, and Toulmin's model, 146–151
and critical reading, 95–98
deductive argument, 113, 114–117
definitional argument, 121–122
definition of, 94–95
elements of, 98–107
evaluation of, 158–161
in hypertext, 339–354
inductive argument, 113–114
kinds of, 113–122
and logical fallacies, 161–167
and research, 286–287, 329
thinking through using the computer, 151–152
Argumentative writing, 3, 8
Argument from ignorance, 167
Aristotelian argument, 98–105
claim with stated reasons, 107–109
and confrontation, 152
deductive argument, 113, 114–117
and ethos, 100–104
example of, 114–117
inductive argument, 113–114
limits to, 143–146
and logos, 105, 107
and pathos, 99–100
Artbabe.com (Web site), 189–190
Article, 20
as academic writing genre, 68
submission to e-zines, 363–366
Assumption, 122–126
definition of, 122
example argument using, 124–126
Audience
for academic writing, 53–54
for e-zines, 359
and hypertext, 345–346
for researched argument, 287, 288–289

for visual argument, 215–216
for writing project, 7, 9–11
Author
of Web site, and reliability as research source, 248
of Web site, and researched Web text, 354–356
Autobiographical writing, 3

Background
of research proposal, 238
Backing
and argument, evaluation of, 159
as component of argument, 147, 149–150
Begging the question, 165
Bibliographical databases, 230–231
Bibliographic entries, 65–66
works cited list, 66
Bibliography
definition of, 255
style of, 255
Blind writing, 14
Blogging, 348
overview, 351–354
Blogs
and argument, 348–351
and computer technologies, 3
definition of, 348
Web sites, 348–351
Book reviews, 20
as academic writing genre, 68
Books, as academic writing genre, 68
Boolean search, 230, 247
Brochures, and visual literacy, 199
Broglio, Ronald S., 189

"Can We Know the Universe? Reflections on a Grain of Salt" (Sagan), 55–59, 63
Capital Community College (Web site)
"Guide for Writing Research Papers Based on Modern Language Association Documentation," 283
Carter, Locke
"Argument in Hypertext," 339
Causal fallacy, 163
Cause-and-effect argument, 118–119
and logical fallacies, 162–164
CBE. *See* Council of Biology Editors
Chapter, book, as academic writing genre, 68
Charts, and visual literacy, 183–184, 194–196
Chat rooms
and computer technologies, 3
and electronic discussion lists, 90
rules for, 11
Cheat sites, 67
Chicago Manual of Style (CMS), 65
Chronological order, 69
Circular argument, 166
Citational styles, 65
Citations 65–66
Citing sources
and academic writing, 65
Claim
and argument, evaluation of, 158
as component of argument, 146, 149
and researched argument, 287
with stated reasons, and Aristotelian argument, 107–109
Classical argument, 97, 142
Clear expression, in academic writing, 72
Climactic order, 27
CMS. *See* Chicago Manual of Style
Coherence
rewriting and revising for, 35, 36–37
and transitions, 36

Collaborative research
  and academic research, 227
Columbia Online Style (COS), 65, 255
  example of, 381–382
Comics, and visual imagery, 189–193
  example of, 190
Common ground, and Rogerian argument, 153
Communication skills, 3
Comparison and contrast
  and academic writing, 73–76
Compromise, and Rogerian argument, 153
Computer technology
  and writing skills, 3–4
Concentration, and first draft, 23–24
Conclusion
  and academic writing, 70
  and deductive argument, 114, 115
  and first draft, 27–29
  and researched argument, 299–300
Conference papers, 20
Confrontation, and Aristotelian argument, 152
Consensus, and Rogerian argument, 153
Contemporary argument, 142
  example of, 169–180
  Rogerian argument, 152–154
  Toulmin's model, 146–152
Context, and visual action, 186
Contractions, in academic writing, 71
Contrast and compare
  and academic writing, 73–76
Conventions, and academic readers, 61–72
Copyright, 242
Correlation, 163
COS. *See* Columbia Online Style
Council of Biology Editors (CBE), 65
Counterargument, 126–127
  and hypertexts, 344–347
Countercultures, and e-zines, 357
Courseware, 39
Creativity, in writing, 3
Critical reading, and argument, 95–98
Critical surfing, and research sources, 247–249
Crockett, David
  "Raccoon in a Bag," 109, 110–113
cummings, e. e., 197–198

Databases
  library, 244
  *See also* Bibliographical databases
Data collection
  analyzing, 265–267
  and annotated bibliography, 254–256
  and literature review, 243–244
  and note-taking, 258–265
  and research process, 243–254, 254–265, 265–267
Deductive argument, 113, 114–117
  and conclusion, 114, 115
  and enthymeme, 115
  and inductive argument, distinguishing between, 146
  and invalid argument, 116
  and premises, 114–115
  and probability, 114
  and sound argument, 115–116
  and syllogism, 113, 114
  and unsound argument, 116
  and valid argument, 116
Deductive reasoning
  example of, 114–117
Definitional argument, 121–122
  and begging the question, 165
  and logical fallacies, 164–165
Definition of terms
  and academic writing, 76–79
  analytical definition, 76

complexity of, example of, 77, 78
descriptive definition, 76–77
etymological definition, 76
expanded definition, 77
functional definition, 76
historical definition, 76
and negation, 77
operational definition, 76
and stipulation, 77
Delaying the thesis, and hypertext, 338
Description, of research proposal, 238–239
Descriptive definition, 76–77
Descriptive examples, 69
Dialogic process, 157
Digest form, and electronic discussion lists, 90
The Digital Tavern (Weblog), 349–350
Documentation, and academic writing, 64–68
Documentational style, 65
of bibliography, 255
Document organization
and hypertext, 332–335, 335–339

Eastgate (online publisher), 330–331
Editing, 42–45
Education Resources Information Center, 231
Electronic communication forms, 61
and academic writing, 87–91
and list "hog," 89
and "lurk," 89, 90
Electronic discussion groups
and computer technologies, 3
and e-mail, 87
Electronic discussion lists, 87–91
and chat rooms, 90
and conferencing software, 90
and digest form, 90
guidelines for participation, 90
hints for joining, 90
and "listserv," 90
and message board, 90
and synchronous conversation, 90, 91
Electronic genres, 20
Electronic journals, and academic reading, 64
*The Elements of Style* (Strunk and White), 38
E-mail, 3
and electronic discussion groups, 87
and peer review, 39
Embedded link, 332
Emoticons, in academic writing, 71, 90
Enthymeme, 115
Essay, 20
as academic writing genre, 68
and researched argument, example of, 302–312
Essay examination, as academic writing genre, 68
Ethos, 100–104
and advertisements, 100–101, 101–102
and political campaigns, 103–104
and Rogerian argument, 153
Etiquette, for peer reviewer, 39
Etymological definition, 76
Evaluation notes, and note-taking, 260–261
Evidence
quality of, and argument, evaluation of, 159–160
and research sources, 243–244
Examples, and inductive argument, 113
Expanded definition, 77
Expectations, of academic readers, 61–72
Exploration, and academic writing, 54
Expository writing, 8

E-zines (electronic magazines), 68
- article submission, 363–366
- audience, 359
- definition of, 357
- and hyperlink, 358
- and hypertext, 335–336
- and sub- and countercultures, 357
- Web host, 364
- writing for, 357–366
- writing strategies, 357–358

Fallacies of avoidance
- and arguing ad hominem, 167
- and arguing ad populem, 167
- and argument from ignorance, 167
- and circular argument, 166
- and ignoring the question, 165
- and logical fallacies, 165–167
- and non sequitur, 166
- and red herring, 166
- and straw man, 166–167

False analogy, 164

Feedback, peer review, 38–39

Field research
- interviews, 253
- polls and surveys, 254
- and research sources, 252–254
- *See also* Research

First draft
- advice for writing, 28
- concentration, 23–24
- conclusions, effective, 27–29
- effective introductions, 25–26
- hints for writing, 23–29
- physical comfort, 24
- and researched argument, 294–299
- starting to write, 25
- and theses, effective, 26–27
- writing under pressure, 24–25

Flash design, 212–213

Foreign words, in academic writing, 72

Formaro, Tom
- "Argumentation on the Web: Challenging Traditional Notions of Communication," 340–344

Forms or genres, and writing project, 20–21

Frame of reference, 84

Fransecky, R., 185

Freewriting
- and blind writing, 14
- and prewriting, 13–15
- and time management, 14

Freire, Paulo, 154, 157

Functional definition, 76

Genres
- and academic writing, 68
- and writing project, 20–21

Google (search engine), 129, 230

Gould, Stephen Jay, 80–84
- *The Structure of Evolutionary Theory,* 54

Grammar checkers, 43–45

Graphics
- and visual argument, 211–213
- and visual literacy, 184

Graphs
- and text manipulation, 196–199
- and visual literacy, 194–196, 196–199

Grounds
- and argument, evaluation of, 160–161
- as component of argument, 147, 150
- and researched argument, 287

Hale, Constance, 38, 330

Hamid, Sarah
- "Writing a Research Paper," 283

Hasty generalization, 162, 163
  and slippery slope, 164
Hawisher, Gail E., 218
Hirsch, E. D., 154, 157
Historical definition, 76
HTML, 203
  coding in, 330
Hyperlink
  and e-zines, 358
  and word processor, 332
Hypertext
  argument in, 339–354
  audience, 345–346
  counterargument, 344–347
  definition of, 330–331
  and delaying the thesis, 338
  document organization, 332–335, 335–339
  and e-zines, 335–336
  and hyperlink, 332
  and nodes, 342
  and reading, 347
  rebuttals, 344–347
  source linking, 332–335
  and Web design, 355–356
  and Web writing, 330–331
Hypertextual documents, navigation of, 331
Hypertextual writing, 3

Ignoring the question, 165
Illuminated manuscripts, 187
Images
  in text, and poetry, 188–189
  and visual literacy, 183, 184
  and visual text, 186–189
  and Web design, 202–203
Inductive argument, 113–114
  and deductive argument, distinguishing between, 146
Inquiry, and academic writing, 54
Insufficient data
  and hasty generalization, 162, 163
  and logical fallacies, 162
  and overgeneralization, 162
  and stereotyping, 162
Intellectual property, 66
Interactive reading, 62
Internet
  and research, 329
Internet abbreviations, 71, 89, 90
Interviews, and field research, 253
In-text citations, 65
In-text references, 65
Introductions, effective
  and first draft, 25–26
Invalid argument, 116
ISPs. *See* Internet service providers

Janik, Richard, 146
Java applets, 202–203
Journal writing, and prewriting, 13
"Jurassic Park" (Gould), 80–84

Kannenberg, Gene, 192
Karl, Allan
  Weblog, 348, 349–350
Key publication information
  and note-taking, 259
  and prewriting, 12
King, Stephen
  *On Writing,* 21
Kingsolver, Barbara
  "A Fist in the Eye of God," 169–180

Leston, Robert, 154, 157
  "Towards Reconciliation: Common Ground in the Education Curriculum," 154–157
LexisNexis Academic (bibliographical database), 230, 231

Librarians, and prescreened Web sites, 249
Librarians' Index to the Internet (Web site), 249
Library
  bibliographical database, 231
  databases, 244
  online tools, 244
  research sources, 243–244
*Library of Congress,* 245
List "hog," 89
Listing
  and prewriting, 16–18
  and word processors, 16
Literature review, and data collection, 243–244
Literature survey, as academic writing genre, 68
Logical argument. *See* Logos
Logical fallacies, 161–167
  and analogies, 164
  and cause-and-effect argument, 162–164
  and definitional argument, 164–165
  and fallacies of avoidance, 165–167
  and insufficient data, 162
Logos, 105, 107
Lovett, John, 218
"Lurk," 89, 90

McLaughlin, Steve
  Weblog, 348–351
Message board, and electronic discussion lists, 90
Microsoft Word
  and hyperlinks, 332
Miles, Adrian
  Weblog, 350–351
Modern Language Association (MLA) style, 65, 66, 255
Mok, Clement, 217
Multimedia reports, 199–200
Multiuser Object-Oriented Systems (MOOs), 90

Narrative illustrations, 69
*National Libraries of the World Web*
  Web site, 246
Navigation
  of hypertextual documents, 331
  of Web text, 340–341
Negation, and definition of terms, 77
Negotiation, and Rogerian argument, 153
Networked computer, 39
Newsletters, and visual literacy, 199
Nodes, and hypertext, 342
Nonconfrontational argumentation, 152–153
Non sequitur, 166
Note-taking, 258–265
  on computers, 259
  evaluation notes, 260–261
  and key publication information, 259
  and laptop computers, 13
  paraphrasing, 263–265
  and prewriting, 12–13
  recording quotations, 261–262
  summary notes, 262–263
  and truncating a URL, 260

Online assistance Web sites, 38
Online encyclopedia
  Wikipedia, 129
Online glossary, 103
Online journal, 64
Online library catalogs, 245–246
Online magazines, 233
  *See also* E-zines
Online newspapers, 233
Online publishing, 330–331
Online Writing Lab, Purdue (Web site), 38, 201

Operational definition, 76
Organization
  and academic writing, 68, 69, 70
  of writing project, 20–23
Outline
  development, 21–23
  and researched argument, 292–294
Outside sources, and academic writing, 64–68
Overgeneralization, 162

Paraphrasing
  and note-taking, 263–265
  steps to, 264–265
Parenthetical citation, 66
Pathos, 99–100
  and advertisements, 100–101, 101–102
  example of, 101–102, 103–104, 109–113
  and political campaigns, 103–104
Peer review, 38–42
Peer reviewer
  etiquette for, 39
  and what to look for, 40
  Web site, 101–102, 105–107
Persuasion, and analysis, 96–98
Persuasive writing, 3, 8
  and argumentation, 97–98
Pictures, and visual literacy, 184, 194
Plagiarism, how to avoid, 67–68
Playfulness, in writing, 2–3
*Playing the Future* (Rushkoff), 130–138
Poetry
  and text manipulation, example of, 197–198
  and visuals and images in text, 188–189
Political campaign
  and ethos and pathos, 103–104
Polls and surveys
  and field research, 254
Popular academic writing, 54, 55, 59–61
  example of, 55, 59–61
Popular reporting, vs. academic research, 226–227
*Post hoc, ergo propter hoc* ("after the fact, therefore because of the fact"), 163
PowerPoint, 22–23, 199–200
Premises
  and deductive argument, 114–115
  major premises, 115
  minor premises, 115
Prescreening
  of Web site, and librarians, 249
Presentation software, 199–200
Prewriting
  about reading, 12–13
  finding a focus, 18–19
  and freewriting, 13–15
  goals, 12
  and journal writing, 13
  and key publication information, 12
  and listing, 16–18
  and note-taking, 12–13
  questions to consider, 18–19
  strategies, 11–19
Primary sources, 243
Print-based text, vs. researched Web texts, 355
Probability, and deductive argument, 114
Project plan, and researched argument, 292–294
Proofreading, 35, 42–45
Purpose
  of academic writing, 53
  of Web site, and reliability as research source, 247–248
  of writing project, 7–8, 10

Qualifier, as component of argument, 147, 150–151

"Raccoon in a Bag" (Crockett), 109, 110–113
Random sample
  and argument, evaluation of, 161
Reading
  and hypertext, 347
  prewriting about, 12–13
Reading critically, and academic readers, 62–64
Reading log, and academic reading, 64
Rebuttals
  and argument, evaluation of, 161
  and hypertexts, 344–347
Recording information, and research process, 254–265
Recording quotations, and note-taking, 261–262
Recursiveness, of research process, 227–228
Red herring, 166
Research, 224–226
  and academic readers, 225
  and argument, 286–287, 329
  hands-on, 225
  and Internet, 329
  in writing, 3
Researched argument
  audience, 287, 288–289
  claim, 287
  conclusion, 299–300
  and essay, example of, 302–312
  and first draft, 294–299
  grounds, 287
  guidelines, 287–302
  outline or project plan, 292–294
  and research sources, 294–299
  and Rogerian argument, 287
  and Toulmin's model, 287
  warrants, 287
Researched Web text
  and hypertext, 330–339
  and source linking, 332–335
  strategies for crafting, 330–339
  and text chunking, 335–339
  vs. print-based text, 355
  and Web author, 354–356
Research process, 227–267
  creating a proposal, 237–240
  data collection, 243–254, 254–265, 265–267
  identifying a research question, 233–237
  identifying research question, 233–237
  preliminary research, 229–233
  recording information, 254–265
  as recursive, 227–228
  and research topic, 232–233, 235–236
  stages of, 229
Research project
  example of, 268–281
  and Web site, review of, 249
Research proposal, 237–240
  basic parts, 238–239
  copyright rules, 242
  example of, 240–242
  feedback, 238
  goals, 238
Research question, identifying, 233–237
Research reports, 20
  as academic writing genre, 68
Research sources
  and Boolean search, 230, 247
  critical surfing, 247–249
  and evidence, 243–244
  and field research, 252–254
  library, 243–244
  library catalogs, 245–246
  primary sources, 243
  and relevance to topic, 243
  and researched argument, 294–299

secondary sources, 243
on the Web, 246–249
Web site, reliability of, 247–249
Research topic
development, 235–236
narrowing a topic, 230
questions to ask, 236–237
and research sources, relevance of, 243
tips for finding, 232–233
Reservations
and argument, evaluation of, 161
as component of argument, 147, 151
Revised draft, sample of, 45–49
Rewriting and revising
for coherence, 35, 36–37
e-zine article submission, 364–365
online assistance Web sites, 38
radical, 35–36
for style, 35, 37–38
for unity, 35, 36
and word processors, 34–38
and writing process, 34–38
Rhetorical situation, 7, 37
"Rhetoric and Composition" (Web site), 129
*Rhetoric* (Aristotle), 98
Rieke, Stephen, 146
Rogerian argument, 152–154
and common ground, 153
and compromise or negotiation, 153
and consensus, 153
dialogic process, 157
and ethos, 153
example of, 154–157
nonconfrontational argumentation, 152–153
and researched argument, 287
Rogers, Carl, 142, 152
Rogers, Maria
"Blogarithms: With the Internet, Everyone Becomes a Writer," 351–354
Ruegg, F. William, 189
Rushkoff, Douglas, 130
*Playing the Future,* 130–138
Web site, 139, 140

Sagan, Carl, 54, 62–63
"Can We Know the Universe? Reflections on a Grain of Salt," 55–59, 63
and popular academic writing, 55, 59–61
Salon.com (Web site), 335–336, 358
*Salon* (e-zine), 75, 335–336, 358, 359–363
Scanlon, Jessie, 38, 330
Search directory, 230
Search engine(s), 213, 230, 234
and Boolean search, 230, 247
and loading images, 202
and narrowing a topic, 230
Search for knowledge
and academic writing, 54
Secondary sources, 243
Sheidley, Bill, 28
Sight-challenged, and Web design, 202
Significance, of research proposal, 239
Sinclair, Carla, 218, 219–221
Situation, and visual action, 186
Slinky, as image for research process, 227–228
Slippery slope, 164
Sound argument, 116
Sound effects, and visual argument, 216
Source linking
example of, 333–335
and hypertext, 332–335
Sources
of research proposal, 239

Spade, Beatrice, 239
Spell-checkers, 43–45
Spiegelman, Art, 191–192
Spoof ads, 204–205
Stafford, Barbara Maria, 186–187
"'Star Wars' Despots vs. 'Star Trek' Populists" (Brin), 74–75, 358
Steinem, Gloria, 153
Stereotyping, 162
Stipulation, and definition of terms, 77
Stoll, Carolyn, 200
Straw man, 166–167
*The Structure of Evolutionary Theory* (Gould), 54
Strunk, William, 38
Style
  and academic writing, 71–72
  rewriting and revising for, 35, 37–38
Subcultures, and e-zines, 357
Sullivan, Patricia A., 218
Summary notes, and note-taking, 262–263
Syllogism, and deductive argument, 113, 114
Symbols, and visual literacy, 183, 185, 186
Synchronous conversation
  and electronic discussion lists, 90, 91
  Multiuser Object-Oriented Systems, 90

Text manipulation
  and graphs, 196–199
  and poetry, example of, 197–198
  on the Web, 197
  and word processors, 197, 198
Thesis
  and academic writing, 70
  climactic order, 27
  and first draft, 26–27
Thesis clarification, 21
Thesis sentence, 108
Thomas, Lewis, 54
Time management
  and data collection, 265
  and freewriting, 14
Title, of research proposal, 238
Topic. *See* Research topic
Toronto University
  Visual Literacy homepage, 217
Toronto University Writing Centre
  Web site, 91
Toulmin, Stephen, 142, 146
Toulmin's model, 146–152
  and backing, 147, 149–150
  and claim, 146, 149
  components of, 146–151
  and the computer, 151–152
  and grounds or data, 147, 150
  and qualifier, 147, 150–151
  and researched argument, 287–288
  and reservations, 147, 151
  and warrant, 147, 149
"Towards Reconciliation: Common Ground in the Education Curriculum" (Leston), 154–157
Tracking changes, and peer review, 41
Transitions, and coherence, 36

Unity, rewriting and revising for, 35, 36
Unsound argument, 116
U.S. Copyright Office
  Web site, 242
*The Uses of Argument* (Toulmin, Rieke, and Janik), 146

Valid argument, 116
Verbal text, vs. visual text, 186
Visual actions
  context and situation, 186
  and visual literacy, 185–186
Visual argument, 183–184
  and advertisements, 204–205
  audience, 215–216

effectiveness of, 206–209
and graphics, 211–213
and pop-up ads, 213
in print, 204–205
and sound effects, 216
on the Web, 204–217
Visual cues, and visual literacy, 183
Visual literacy, 183–184
and brochures, 199
and charts, 183–184, 194–196
and comics, 189–193
definition of, 185
and graphic manipulation of text, 196–199
and graphics, 184
and graphs, 194–196, 196–199
and images, 183, 184
and newsletters, 199
and pictures, 194
study of, 186–187
and symbols, 183, 185, 186
and visual actions, 185–186
and visual cues, 183
and visual presentations, 199–201
and visual text, 186–189
on the Web, 184, 202–204
and Web design, 202–203
and women on the Web, 218–221
*Visual Literacy: A Way to Learn—to Teach* (Fransecky and Debes), 185
Visual presentations, 199–201
guidelines, 201
Visual rhetoric, 184–201
and advertisements, 204
definition of, 184
study of, 186–187
Visual text
and images, 186–189
and poetry, 188–189
and visual literacy, 186–189
vs. verbal text, 186
Vocabulary building, and academic writing, 73

Warrant
and argument, evaluation of, 158–159
as component of argument, 147, 149
and researched argument, 287
the Web
advertisement on, 204–205
and graphic manipulation of text, 197
hypertextual writing on, 3
research sources on, 246–249
visual argument on, 204–217
visual literacy on, 184, 202–204
women on, and visual literacy, 218–221
writing on, 330
Web author
of site, and reliability as research source, 248
of site, and Researched Web text, 354–356
Web browsers, and image loader, 202
Web design
guidelines, 355–356
and hypertext, 355–356
and images, 202–203
and reliability as research source, 248
and sight-challenged, 202
and visual literacy, 202–203
Web Design Group (Web site), 355
Web editor, 330
Webliography, 255
Weblogger (Weblog), 351
Web pages, 20
Web sites, 3
prescreened, and librarians, 249
reliability of, as research source, 247–249

Web text
  navigation of, 340–341
Web writing
  and hypertext, 330–331
  tips for, 355
Welty, Eudora, 34–38
Westboro Baptist Church Homepage (Web site), 347
White, E. B., 38
Wikipedia (online encyclopedia), 129
*Wired Style: Principles of English Usage in the Digital Age* (Hale and Scanlon), 38, 330
Women on the Web, and visual literacy, 218–221
Word processor
  and backing up your work, 18
  and grammar checkers, 43–45
  and graphic manipulation of text, 197, 198
  and hyperlinks, 332
  and listing, 16
  and rewriting and revising, 34
  and spell-checkers, 43–45
  and Track Changes function, 41
  and writing skills, 3
Works cited list, 66
Wright, Will
  *Social Logic of Health,* 263
Writing
  creativity in, 3
  for e-zines, 357–366
  kinds of, 3
  persuasion in, 3, 8, 97–98
  playfulness in, 2–3
  under pressure, and first draft, 24–25
  research in, 3
  values, 61
  on the Web, 330. See also Researched Web text
"Writing a Research Paper" (Hamid), 283
Writing process, 6–7
  academic writing strategies, 61
  editing, 42–45
  first draft, 23–29
  and first draft
  peer review, 38–42
  prewriting strategies, 11–19
  proofreading, 42–45
  revised draft, 45–49
  rewriting and revising, 34–38
  and writing project
Writing project
  approach to, 7–10
  audience, 7, 9–11
  forms or genres, 20–21
  organization of, 20–23
  outline development, 21–23
  purpose of, 7–8, 10
  thesis clarification, 21
Writing skills
  and computer technologies, 3–4
  and word processors, 3

Zauderer, Vic, 217